Learn Selenium

Build data-driven test frameworks for mobile and web applications with Selenium Web Driver 3

Unmesh Gundecha
Carl Cocchiaro

BIRMINGHAM - MUMBAI

Learn Selenium

Copyright © 2019 Packt Publishing

First published: July 2019

Production reference: 1120719

Published by Packt Publishing Ltd.
Livery Place
35 Livery Street
Birmingham
B3 2PB, UK.

ISBN 978-1-83898-304-8

www.packtpub.com

Contributors

About the authors

Unmesh Gundecha has an experience of over 16 years in Agile software development, test automation, and DevOps methodologies. He is an Agile, open source, and DevOps evangelist with extensive experience in a diverse set of tools and technologies. He has extensive hands-on experience in building sustainable and repeatable test automation solutions for web and mobile platforms, APIs, and CLI apps with continuous integration and delivery pipelines, using best-of-breed open source and commercial tools. He is the author of Selenium Testing Tools Cookbook and Learning Selenium Testing Tools with Python, both by Packt Publishing.

Carl Cocchiaro has a bachelor's degree in business and over 30 years of experience in the software engineering field, designing and building test frameworks for desktop, browser, and mobile applications. He is an expert in the Selenium WebDriver/TestNG Java-based technologies. He is a certified SilkTest engineer and has architected UI and RESTful API automation frameworks for 25 major corporations. Carl is currently a software architect, quality engineering at RSA/Dell technologies, Boston, MA, USA.

Packt is searching for authors like you

If you're interested in becoming an author for Packt, please visit `authors.packtpub.com` and apply today. We have worked with thousands of developers and tech professionals, just like you, to help them share their insight with the global tech community. You can make a general application, apply for a specific hot topic that we are recruiting an author for, or submit your own idea.

`mapt.io`

Mapt is an online digital library that gives you full access to over 5,000 books and videos, as well as industry leading tools to help you plan your personal development and advance your career. For more information, please visit our website.

Why subscribe?

- Spend less time learning and more time coding with practical eBooks and Videos from over 4,000 industry professionals

- Improve your learning with Skill Plans built especially for you

- Get a free eBook or video every month

- Mapt is fully searchable

- Copy and paste, print, and bookmark content

Packt.com

Did you know that Packt offers eBook versions of every book published, with PDF and ePub files available? You can upgrade to the eBook version at `www.packt.com` and as a print book customer, you are entitled to a discount on the eBook copy. Get in touch with us at `customercare@packtpub.com` for more details.

At `www.packt.com`, you can also read a collection of free technical articles, sign up for a range of free newsletters, and receive exclusive discounts and offers on Packt books and eBooks.

Table of Contents

Preface

The Selenium WebDriver 3.x is an open source API to test both browser and mobile applications. With a solid foundation, you can easily perform end-to-end testing on web and mobile browsers.

You'll begin by being introduced to the Selenium page object design patterns in software development. You'll architect your own framework with a scalable driver class, Java utility classes, and support for third-party tools and plugins. You'll design and build a Selenium grid from scratch to enable the framework to scale and support different browsers, mobile devices, and platforms. You'll strategize and handle rich web UI using the advanced WebDriver API and learn techniques to handle real-time challenges in WebDriver. You'll perform different types of testing, such as cross-browser testing, load testing, and mobile testing. Finally, you will also be introduced to data-driven testing using TestNG to create your own automation framework.

By the end of this Learning Path, you'll be able to design your own automation testing framework and perform data-driven testing with Selenium WebDriver.

This Learning Path includes content from the following Packt products:

- Selenium WebDriver 3 Practical Guide - Second Edition by Unmesh Gundecha
- Selenium Framework Design in Data-Driven Testing by Carl Cocchiaro

Who this book is for

This Learning Path is ideal for software quality assurance/testing professionals, software project managers, or software developers interested in using Selenium for testing their applications. Professionals responsible for designing and building enterprise-based testing frameworks will also find this Learning Path useful. Prior programming experience in Java and TestNG is necessary.

What this book covers

Chapter 1, *Introducing WebDriver and WebElements*, will start off with an overview of Selenium and it's features. Then, we quickly jump into WebDriver by describing how it perceives a web page. We will also look at what a WebDriver's WebElement is. Then, we talk about locating WebElements on a web page and performing some basic actions on them.

Chapter 2, *Using Java 8 Features with Selenium*, will talk about prominent Java 8 features such as Streams API and Lambda expressions for processing the list of WebElements. The Stream API and Lambda expression help in applying functional programming style to create readable and fluent tests.

Chapter 3, *Exploring the Features of WebDriver*, will talk about some advanced features of WebDriver, such as taking screenshots of web pages, executing JavaScript, handling cookies, and handling Windows and Frames.

Chapter 4, *Exploring Advanced Interactions of WebDriver*, will dive deeply into more advanced actions that WebDriver can perform on the WebElements of a web page, such as the dragging and dropping of elements from one frame of a page to another and right/context-clicking on WebElements. We're sure you will find this chapter interesting to read.

Chapter 5, *Understanding WebDriver Events*, will deal with the event-handling aspect of WebDriver. To state a few, events can be a value change on a WebElement, a browser backnavigation invocation, script execution completion, and so on. We will use these events to run accessibility and performance checks.

Chapter 6, *Exploring RemoteWebDriver*, will talk about using RemoteWebDriver and Selenium Standalone Server for executing tests on remote machines from your machine.You can use the RemoteWebDriver class to communicate with the Selenium Standalone Server on a remote machine to run commands on the desired browser installed on the remote machine. One of its popular use cases is browser compatibility testing.

Chapter 7, *Setting up Selenium Grid*, will talk about one important and interesting feature of Selenium named Selenium Grid. Using this, you can execute automated tests on a distributed computer network using Selenium Grid. We will configure a Hub and Nodes for cross-browser testing. This also enables running tests in parallel and in a distributed architecture.

Chapter 8, *Data-Driven Testing with TestNG*, will talk about using the data-driven testing technique with TestNG. Using the data-driven testing approach, we can reuse a test with multiple sets of test data to gain additional coverage.

Chapter 9, *Building a Scalable Selenium Test Driver Class for Web and Mobile Applications*, shows users how to get started with designing and building the Selenium Framework driver class. This class is the engine that drives the browser and mobile applications. With Selenium WebDriver technology, users can test all the popular browsers and mobile devices using the same driver class and programming language. The Selenium WebDriver technology is platform independent and has various language bindings to support cross-browser and device testing in a single code base.

Chapter 10, *Selenium Framework Utility Classes*, describes how to design Java utility classes to support the framework components that are non-specific to any of the applications under test. Users will learn how to build classes to perform file I/O operations, data extraction, logging, synchronization, result processing, reporting, global variables, and many more.

Chapter 11, *Best Practices for Building Selenium Page Object Classes*, introduces users to designing and building application-specific classes following the Selenium Page Object Model. Users will be guided through designing abstract base classes, deriving sub-classes, and structuring classes to use common inheritance methods to ensure that page elements and methods are stored in central locations. In following these design principles, users will create an abstract separation layer between the page object and test classes in the framework.

Chapter 12, *Defining WebDriver and AppiumDriver Page Object Elements*, presents users with design techniques to ensure that elements are defined using best practices for locators, minimum number of elements defined in page object classes, how to build locators on the fly, and when to use static verses dynamic locators to test page object elements.

Chapter 13, *Building a JSON Data Provider*, explains how to design and build a TestNG DataProvider class using the JSON protocol to store data. The concept of data-driven test frameworks is introduced, and how to use a DataProvider to extract data on the fly to ensure that standards for data encapsulation and DRY approaches are being followed is covered.

Chapter 14, *Developing Data-Driven Test Classes*, explores how to design data-driven test classes using the TestNG technologies. This includes TestNG features such as annotations, parameters, attributes, use of DataProviders in test classes, data extraction, exception handling, and setup/teardown techniques.

Chapter 15, *Encapsulating Data in Data-Driven Testing*, describes the use of encapsulation in data-driven testing. This will include JSON data manipulation, use of property files, processing JVM arguments, casting JSON data to Java objects, supporting multiple drivers, and parallel testing.

Chapter 16, *Designing a Selenium Grid*, presents the Selenium Grid Architecture, including designing a virtual grid in the Cloud, how to build the grid hub, browser nodes, and Appium mobile nodes, using the grid console, how to cast tests to the RemoteWebDriver, and supporting third-party grids.

Chapter 17, *Third-Party Tools and Plugins*, details methodologies in using third-party tools and plugins in the Selenium Framework design. This will include the IntelliJ IDEA Selenium plugin, TestNG for results processing, the HTML Publisher Plugin, BrowserMob, ExtentReports, and Sauce Labs.

Chapter 18, *Working Selenium WebDriver Framework Samples*, provides users with a real working sample framework including Selenium driver and utility classes, page object base and subclasses, DataProvider class, data-driven test class, JSON data file, TestNG test IListener class, and ExtentReports IReporter classes. Users will be able to install the files in their own project, use the supplied Maven pom.xml file to pull down the required JAR files, and run the sample data-driven tests against a real practice website across multiple browser types.

To get the most out of this book

The reader is expected to have a basic idea of programming, preferably using Java because we take the reader through several features of WebDriver using code examples. The following software is required for the book:

1. Java JDK 1.8
2. IntelliJ IDEA 2017.3+
3. Selenium WebDriver 3.7.1+ JAR
4. Selenium Stand-alone Server 3.7.1+ JAR
5. Appium Java Client 5.0.4+ JAR
6. Appium Server 1.7.1 JAR for iOS or Linux

7. TestNG 6.11 JAR
8. ExtentReports 3.1.0 JAR
9. Browsers: Google Chrome 62.0, Mozilla Firefox 57.0, Microsoft Internet Explorer 11.0
10. Drivers: chromedriver.exe 2.33, geckodriver.exe 0.19.1, IEDriverServer.exe 3.7.1+
11. Apple Xcode and iPhone Simulators for iOS
12. Google Android SDK and Samsung Galaxy emulators for Linux
13. VMware virtual machines

Installing Java

In this book, all the code examples that we show covering various features of WebDriver will be in Java. To follow these examples and write your own code, you need the Java Development Kit installed on your computer. The latest version of JDK can be downloaded from the following link:

```
http://www.oracle.com/technetwork/java/javase/downloads/jdk8-downloads-2133151.html
```

Installing Eclipse

This book is a practical guide that expects the user to write and execute WebDriver examples. For this, it would be handy to install a Java IDE. The Eclipse IDE is a popular choice in Java user community. The Eclipse IDE can be downloaded from `https://www.eclipse.org/downloads/`.

Download the example code files

You can download the example code files for this book from your account at `www.packtpub.com`. If you purchased this book elsewhere, you can visit `www.packtpub.com/support` and register to have the files emailed directly to you.

You can download the code files by following these steps:

1. Log in or register at `www.packtpub.com`.
2. Select the **SUPPORT** tab.
3. Click on **Code Downloads & Errata**.
4. Enter the name of the book in the **Search** box and follow the onscreen instructions.

Once the file is downloaded, please make sure that you unzip or extract the folder using the latest version of:

- WinRAR/7-Zip for Windows
- Zipeg/iZip/UnRarX for Mac
- 7-Zip/PeaZip for Linux

The code bundle for the book is also hosted on GitHub at `https://github.com/PacktPublishing/Learn-Selenium`. In case there's an update to the code, it will be updated on the existing GitHub repository.

We also have other code bundles from our rich catalog of books and videos available at `https://github.com/PacktPublishing/`. Check them out!

Conventions used

There are a number of text conventions used throughout this book.

`CodeInText`: Indicates code words in text, database table names, folder names, filenames, file extensions, pathnames, dummy URLs, user input, and Twitter handles. Here is an example: "`beforeMethod()`, which is annotated with the `@BeforeMethod` TestNG annotation."

A block of code is set as follows:

```
<input id="search" type="search" name="q" value="" class="input-text
required-entry" maxlength="128" placeholder="Search entire store here..."
autocomplete="off">
```

When we wish to draw your attention to a particular part of a code block, the relevant lines or items are set in bold:

```
WebElement searchBox = driver.findElement(By.id("q"));
```

Bold: Indicates a new term, an important word, or words that you see onscreen. For example, words in menus or dialog boxes appear in the text like this. Here is an example: "To run the tests, right-click in the code editor and select **Run As | TestNG Test**, as shown in the following screenshot."

Get in touch

Feedback from our readers is always welcome.

General feedback: If you have questions about any aspect of this book, mention the book title in the subject of your message and email us at customercare@packtpub.com.

Errata: Although we have taken every care to ensure the accuracy of our content, mistakes do happen. If you have found a mistake in this book, we would be grateful if you would report this to us. Please visit www.packt.com/submit-errata, selecting your book, clicking on the Errata Submission Form link, and entering the details.

Piracy: If you come across any illegal copies of our works in any form on the Internet, we would be grateful if you would provide us with the location address or website name. Please contact us at copyright@packt.com with a link to the material.

If you are interested in becoming an author: If there is a topic that you have expertise in and you are interested in either writing or contributing to a book, please visit authors.packtpub.com.

Reviews

Please leave a review. Once you have read and used this book, why not leave a review on the site that you purchased it from? Potential readers can then see and use your unbiased opinion to make purchase decisions, we at Packt can understand what you think about our products, and our authors can see your feedback on their book. Thank you!

For more information about Packt, please visit packt.com.

1
Introducing WebDriver and WebElements

In this chapter, we will look briefly into Selenium, its various components, such as Appium, and proceed to the basic components of a web page, including the various types of WebElements. We will learn different ways to locate WebElements on a web page and execute various user actions on them. We will cover the following topics in this chapter:

- Various components of Selenium Testing Tools
- Setting up a project in Eclipse with Maven and TestNG
- Locating WebElements on a Web Page
- Actions that can be taken on the WebElements

Selenium is a set of widely popular tools used to automate browsers. It is largely used to test applications, but its usages are not limited to testing. It can also be used to perform screen scraping and automate repetitive tasks in a browser window. Selenium supports automation on all the major browsers, including Google Chrome, Mozilla Firefox, Microsoft Internet Explorer and Edge, Apple Safari, and Opera. Selenium 3.0 is now a part of W3C standards and is supported by major browser vendors.

Selenium Testing Tools

Selenium 3.0 offers three important tools, Selenium WebDriver, Selenium Server, and Selenium IDE. Each of these tools provides features to create, debug, and run tests on supported browsers and operating systems. Let's explore each of them in detail.

Selenium WebDriver

Selenium WebDriver is the successor of Selenium RC (Remote Control), which has been officially deprecated. Selenium WebDriver accepts commands using the JSON-Wire protocol (also called Client API) and sends them to a browser launched by the specific driver class (such as ChromeDriver, FirefoxDriver, or IEDriver). This is implemented through a browser-specific browser driver. It works with the following sequence:

1. The driver listens to the commands from Selenium
2. It converts these commands into the browser's native API
3. The driver takes the result of native commands and sends the result back to Selenium:

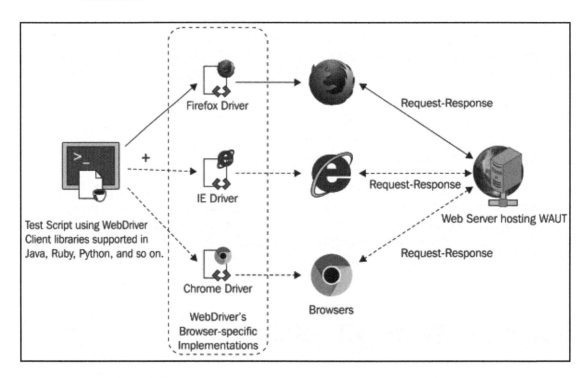

We can use Selenium WebDriver to do the following:

- Create robust, browser-based regression automation
- Scale and distribute scripts across many browsers and platforms
- Create scripts in your favourite programming language

Selenium WebDriver offers a collection of language-specific bindings (client libraries) to drive a browser. WebDriver comes with a better set of APIs that meet the expectations of most developers by being similar to object-oriented programming in its implementation. WebDriver is being actively developed over a period of time, and you can see many advanced interactions with the web as well as mobile applications.

The Selenium Client API is a language-specific Selenium library that provides a consistent Selenium API in programming languages such as Java, C#, Python, Ruby, and JavaScript. These languages bindings let tests to launch a WebDriver session and communicate with the browser or Selenium Server.

Selenium Server

Selenium Server allows us to run tests on browser instances running on remote machines and in parallel, thus spreading a load of testing across several machines. We can create a Selenium Grid, where one server runs as the Hub, managing a pool of Nodes. We can configure our tests to connect to the Hub, which then obtains a node that is free and matches the browser we need to run the tests. The hub has a list of nodes that provide access to browser instances, and lets tests use these instances similarly to a load balancer. Selenium Grid enables us to execute tests in parallel on multiple machines by managing different types of browsers, their versions, and operating system configurations centrally.

Selenium IDE

Selenium IDE is a Firefox add-on that allows users to record, edit, debug, and play back tests captured in the *Selenese* format, which was introduced in the Selenium Core version. It also provides us with the ability to convert these tests into the Selenium RC or Selenium WebDriver format. We can use Selenium IDE to do the following:

- Create quick and simple scripts using record and replay, or use them in exploratory testing
- Create scripts to aid in automation-aided exploratory testing
- Create macros to perform repetitive tasks on Web pages

The Selenium IDE for Firefox stopped working after the Firefox 55 moved to the WebExtension format from XPI format and it is currently no longer maintained.

Differences between Selenium 2 and Selenium 3

Before we dive further into Selenium 3, let's understand the differences between Selenium 2 and Selenium.

Handling the browser

As the Selenium WebDriver has been as the W3C Standard, Selenium 3 brings a number of changes to the browser implementations. All of the major browser vendors now support WebDriver specification and provide the necessary features along with the browser. For example, Microsoft came with EdgeDriver, and Apple supports the SafariDriver implementation. We will see some of these changes later in this book.

Having better APIs

As W3C-standard WebDriver comes with a better set of APIs, which meet the expectations of most developers by being similar to the implementation of object-oriented programming.

Having developer support and advanced functionalities

WebDriver is being actively developed and is now supported by Browser vendors per W3C specification; you can see many advanced interactions with the web as well as mobile applications, such as File-Handling and Touch APIs.

Testing Mobile Apps with Appium

One of the major differences introduced in Selenium 3 was the introduction of the `Appium` project. The mobile-testing features that were part of Selenium 2 are now moved into a separate project named Appium.

`Appium` is an open source mobile-automation framework for testing native, hybrid, and web mobile apps on iOS and Android platforms using the JSON-Wire protocol with Selenium WebDriver. `Appium` replaces the iPhoneDriver and AndroidDriver APIs in Selenium 2 that were used to test mobile web applications.

`Appium` enables the use and extension of the existing Selenium WebDriver framework to build mobile tests. As it uses Selenium WebDriver to drive the tests, we can use any programming language to create tests for a Selenium client library.

Setting up a project in Eclipse with Maven and TestNG using Java

Selenium WebDriver is a library that helps you automate browsers. However, much more is needed when using it for testing and building a test framework or automating browsers for non-testing purposes. You will need an Integrated Development Environment (**IDE**) or a code editor to create a new Java project and add Selenium WebDriver and other dependencies in order to build a testing framework.

In the Java development community, Eclipse is a widely-used IDE, as well as IntelliJ IDEA and NetBeans. Eclipse provides a feature-rich environment for Selenium WebDriver test-development.

Along with Eclipse, Apache Maven provides support for managing the life cycle of a test project. Maven is used to define the project structure, dependencies, build, and test-management.

We can use Eclipse and Maven to build our Selenium WebDriver test framework from a single window. Another important benefit of using Maven is that we can get all the Selenium library files and their dependencies by configuring the pom.xml file. Maven automatically downloads the necessary files from the repository while building the project.

In this section, we will learn how to configure Eclipse and Maven for the Selenium WebDriver test development. Most of the code in this book has been developed in Eclipse and Maven.

You will need Eclipse and Maven to set up the test-development environment. Download and set up Maven from `http://maven.apache.org/download.html`. Follow the instructions on the Maven download page (see the Installation Instructions section of the page).

Download and set up Eclipse IDE for Java Developers from `https://eclipse.org/downloads/`

Along with Eclipse and Maven, we will also use TestNG as a testing framework for our project. The TestNG library will help us define test cases, test fixtures, and assertions. We need to install the TestNG plugin for Eclipse via Eclipse Marketplace.

Let's configure Eclipse with Maven to develop Selenium WebDriver tests using the following steps:

1. Launch the **Eclipse IDE**.
2. Create a new project by selecting **File | New | Other** from the Eclipse **Main Menu**.
3. On the **New** dialog, select **Maven | Maven Project**, as shown in the following screenshot, and click **Next**:

4. The **New Maven Project** dialog will be displayed. Select the **Create a simple project (skip archetype selection) checkbox** and click on the **Next** button, as shown in the following screenshot:

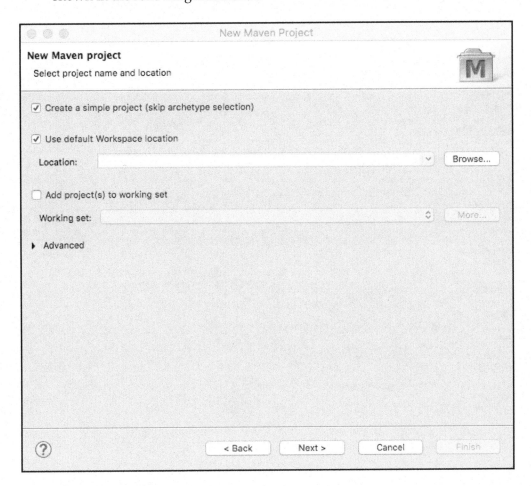

5. On the **New Maven Project** dialog box, enter *com.example* in the **Group Id:** textbox and *chapter1* in the **Artifact Id:** textbox. You can also add a name and description. Click on the **Finish** button, as shown in the following screenshot:

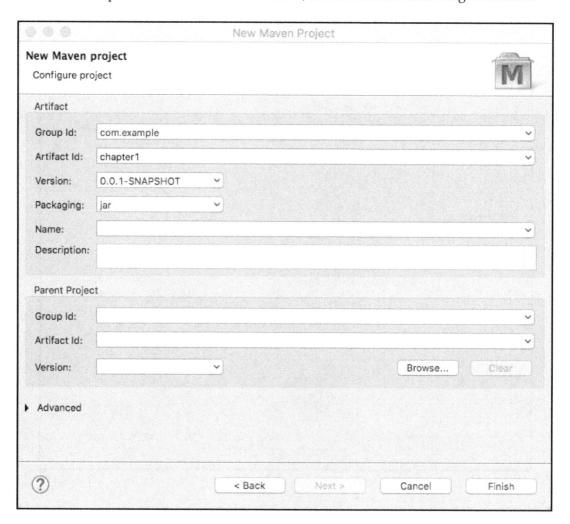

6. Eclipse will create the *chapter1* project with a structure (in **Package Explorer**) similar to the one shown in the following screenshot:

7. Select **pom.xml** from **Package Explorer**. This will open the **pom.xml** file in the editor area with the **Overview** tab open. Select the **pom.xml** tab next to the **Overview** tab, as shown in the following screenshot:

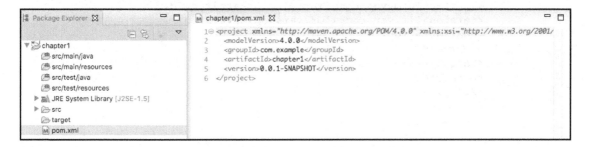

8. Add the Selenium WebDriver and TestNG dependencies highlighted in the following code snippet to **pom.xml** in the between `project` node:

```
<properties>
 <java.version>1.8</java.version>
 <selenium.version>3.13.0</selenium.version>
 <testng.version>6.13.1</testng.version>
 <maven.compiler.version>3.7.0</maven.compiler.version>
</properties>

<dependencies>
 <dependency>
 <groupId>org.seleniumhq.selenium</groupId>
 <artifactId>selenium-java</artifactId>
 <version>${selenium.version}</version>
 </dependency>
 <dependency>
 <groupId>org.testng</groupId>
 <artifactId>testng</artifactId>
 <version>${testng.version}</version>
 </dependency>
</dependencies>

<build>
 <plugins>
 <plugin>
 <groupId>org.apache.maven.plugins</groupId>
 <artifactId>maven-compiler-plugin</artifactId>
 <version>${maven.compiler.version}</version>
 <configuration>
 <source>${java.version}</source>
 <target>${java.version}</target>
 </configuration>
 </plugin>
 </plugins>
</build>
```

9. Select **src/test/java** in **Package Explorer** and right-click on it to show the menu. Select **New | Other**, as shown in the following screenshot:

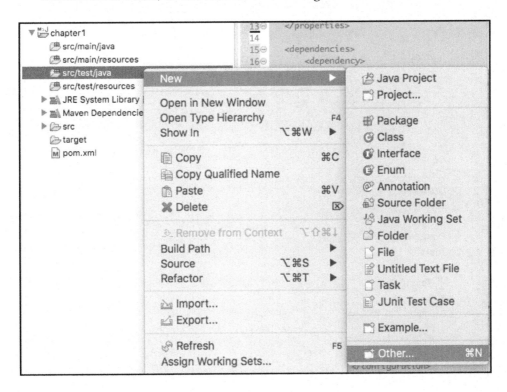

10. Select the **TestNG** | **TestNG** class from the **Select a wizard** dialog, as shown in the following screenshot:

11. On the **New TestNG class** dialog box, enter */chapter1/src/test/java* in the **Source folder:** field. Enter **com.example** in the **Package name:** field. Enter **NavigationTest** in the **Class name:** field. Select the **@BeforeMethod** and **@AfterMethod** checkboxes and add `src/test/resources/suites/testng.xml` in the **XML suite file:** field. Click on the **Finish** button:

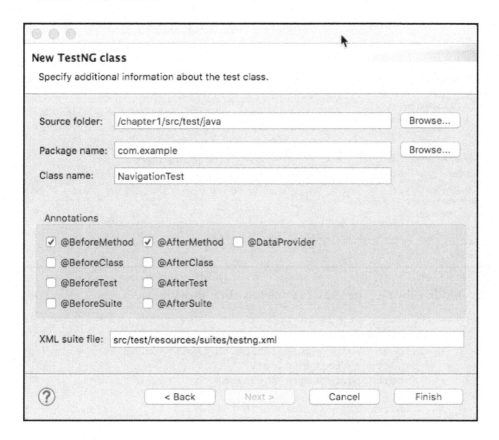

12. This will create the **NavigationTest.java** class in the **com.example** package with TestNG annotations such as @Test, @BeforeMethod, and @AfterMethod, and the beforeMethod and afterMethod methods:

13. Modify the NavigationTest class with following code:

```
package com.example;
import org.openqa.selenium.WebDriver;
import org.openqa.selenium.chrome.ChromeDriver;
import org.testng.Assert;
import org.testng.annotations.*;

public class NavigationTest {

    WebDriver driver;

    @BeforeMethod
    public void beforeMethod() {

        // set path of Chromedriver executable
        System.setProperty("webdriver.chrome.driver",
                "./src/test/resources/drivers/chromedriver");

        // initialize new WebDriver session
        driver = new ChromeDriver();
```

```
        }

        @Test
        public void navigateToAUrl() {
            // navigate to the web site
            driver.get("http://demo-store.seleniumacademy.com/");
            // Validate page title
            Assert.assertEquals(driver.getTitle(), "Madison
Island");
        }
        @AfterMethod
        public void afterMethod() {

            // close and quit the browser
            driver.quit();
        }
    }
```

In the preceding code, three methods are added as part of the NavigationTest class. We also declared a WebDriver driver; instance variable, which we will use later in the test to launch a browser and navigate to the site.

beforeMethod(), which is annotated with the @BeforeMethod TestNG annotation, will execute before the test method. It will set the path of the *chromedriver* executable required by Google Chrome. It will then instantiate the driver variable using the ChromeDriver() class. This will launch a new Google Chrome window on the screen.

The next method, navigateToAUrl(), annotated with the @Test annotation is the test method. We will call the get() method of the WebDriver interface passing the URL of the application. This will navigate to the site in the browser. We will check the title of the page by calling TestNG's Assert.assertEquals method and the getTitle() method of the WebDriver interface.

Lastly, afterMethod() is annotated with the @AfterMethod TestNG annotation will close the browser window.

We need to download and copy the chromedriver executable from https://sites.google.com/a/chromium.org/chromedriver/downloads. Download the appropriate version based on the Google Chrome browser version installed on your computer as well as the operating system. Copy the executable file in the /src/test/resources/ drivers folder.

To run the tests, right-click in the code editor and select **Run As | TestNG Test,** as shown in the following screenshot:

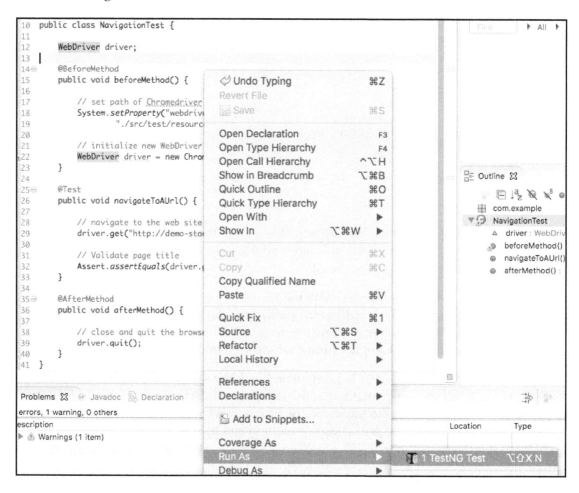

This will launch a new Google Chrome browser window and navigate to the site. The test will validate the page title and the browser window will be closed at the end of the test. The TestNG Plugin will display results in Eclipse:

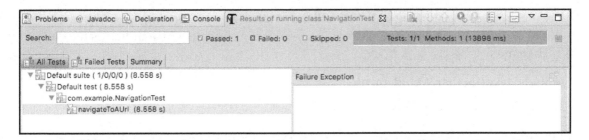

You can download the example code files for all the Packt books you have purchased from your account at `http://www.packtpub.com`. If you have purchased this book elsewhere, you can visit http://www.packtpub. com/support and register to have the files emailed directly to you. The example code is also hosted at `https://github.com/PacktPublishing/Selenium-WebDriver-3-Practical-Guide-Second-Edition`

WebElements

A web page is composed of many different types of HTML elements, such as links, textboxes, dropdown buttons, a body, labels, and forms. These are called WebElements in the context of WebDriver. Together, these elements on a web page will achieve the user functionality. For example, let's look at the HTML code of the login page of a website:

```html
<html>
<body>
    <form id="loginForm">
        <label>Enter Username: </label>
        <input type="text" name="Username"/>
        <label>Enter Password: </label>
        <input type="password" name="Password"/>
        <input type="submit"/>
    </form>
    <a href="forgotPassword.html">Forgot Password ?</a>
</body>
</html>
```

In the preceding HTML code, there are different types of WebElements, such as `<html>`, `<body>`, `<form>`, `<label>`, `<input>`, and `<a>`, which together make a web page provide the Login feature for the user. Let's analyze the following WebElement:

```html
<label>Enter Username: </label>
```

Here, `<label>` is the start tag of the WebElement label. `Enter Username:` is the text present on the `label` element. Finally, `</label>` is the end tag, which indicates the end of a WebElement.

Similarly, take another WebElement:

```
<input type="text" name="Username"/>
```

In the preceding code, `type` and `name` are the attributes of the WebElement `input` with the `text` and `Username` values, respectively.

UI-automation using Selenium is mostly about locating these WebElements on a web page and executing user actions on them. In the rest of the chapter, we will use various methods to locate WebElements and execute relevant user actions on them.

Locating WebElements using WebDriver

Let's start this section by automating the Search feature from the Homepage of the demo application, `http://demo-store.seleniumacademy.com/`, which involves navigating to the homepage, typing the search text in the textbox, and executing the search. The code is as follows:

```java
import org.openqa.selenium.By;
import org.openqa.selenium.WebDriver;
import org.openqa.selenium.WebElement;
import org.openqa.selenium.chrome.ChromeDriver;
import org.testng.annotations.AfterMethod;
import org.testng.annotations.BeforeMethod;
import org.testng.annotations.Test;

import static org.assertj.core.api.AssertionsForClassTypes.assertThat;

public class SearchTest {

    WebDriver driver;

    @BeforeMethod
    public void setup() {
        System.setProperty("webdriver.chrome.driver",
                "./src/test/resources/drivers/chromedriver");
        driver = new ChromeDriver();
        driver.get("http://demo-store.seleniumacademy.com/");
    }
```

```
@Test
public void searchProduct() {
    // find search box and enter search string
    WebElement searchBox = driver.findElement(By.name("q"));
    searchBox.sendKeys("Phones");
    WebElement searchButton =
            driver.findElement(By.className("search-button"));
    searchButton.click();
    assertThat(driver.getTitle())
            .isEqualTo("Search results for: 'Phones'");
}

@AfterMethod
public void tearDown() {
    driver.quit();
}
}
```

As you can see, there are three new things that are highlighted, as follows:

```
WebElement searchBox = driver.findElement(By.name("q"));
```

They are the findElement() method, the By.name() method, and the WebElement interface. The findElement() and By() methods instruct WebDriver to locate a WebElement on a web page, and once found, the findElement() method returns the WebElement instance of that element. Actions, such as click and type, are performed on a returned WebElement using the methods declared in the WebElement interface, which will be discussed in detail in the next section.

The findElement method

In UI automation, locating an element is the first step before executing any user actions on it. WebDriver's findElement() method is a convenient way to locate an element on the web page. According to WebDriver's Javadoc (http://selenium.googlecode.com/git/docs/api/java/index.html), the method declaration is as follows:

```
WebElement findElement(By by)
```

So, the input parameter for the findElement() method is the By instance. The By instance is a WebElement-locating mechanism. There are eight different ways to locate a WebElement on a web page. We will see each of these eight methods later in the chapter.

The return type of the `findElement()` method is the WebElement instance that represents the actual HTML element or component of the web page. The method returns the first WebElement that the driver comes across that satisfies the locating-mechanism condition. This WebElement instance will act as a handle to that component from then on. Appropriate actions can be taken on that component by the test-script developer using this returned WebElement instance.

If WebDriver doesn't find the element, it throws a runtime exception named `NoSuchElementException`, which the invoking class or method should handle.

The findElements method

For finding multiple elements matching the same locator criteria on a web page, the `findElements()` method can be used. It returns a list of WebElements found for a given locating mechanism. The method declaration of the `findElements()` method is as follows:

```
java.util.List findElements(By by)
```

The input parameter is the same as the `findElement()` method, which is an instance of the `By` class. The difference lies in the return type. Here, if no element is found, an empty list is returned and if there are multiple WebElements present that satisfy the locating mechanism, all of them are returned to the caller in a list.

Inspecting Elements with Developer Tools

Before we start exploring how to find elements on a page and what locator mechanism to use, we need to look at the HTML code of the page to understand the Document Object Model (**DOM**) tree, what properties or attributes are defined for the elements displayed on the page, and how JavaScript or AJAX calls are made from the application. browsers use the HTML code written for the page to render visual elements in the browser window. It uses other resources, including JavaScript, CSS, and images, to decide on the look, feel, and behavior of these elements.

Here is an example of a login page of the demo application and the HTML code written to render this page in a browser, as displayed in the following screenshot:

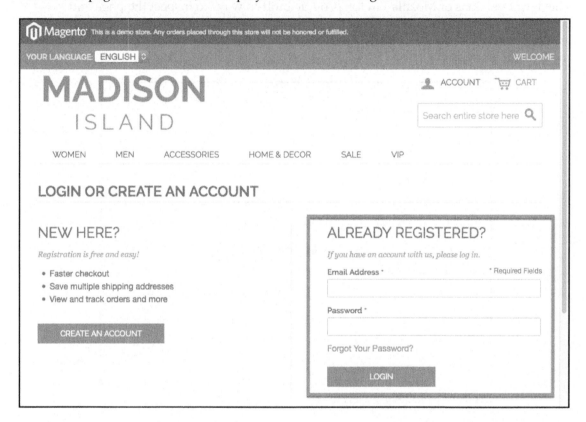

We need tools that can display the HTML code of the page in a structured and easy-to-understand format. Almost all browsers now offer Developer tools to inspect the structure of the page and associated resources.

Inspecting pages and elements with Mozilla Firefox

The newer versions of Mozilla Firefox provide built-in ways to inspect the page and elements. To inspect an element from the page, move the mouse over the desired element and right-click to open the pop-up menu. Select the **Inspect Element** option, as shown in the following screenshot:

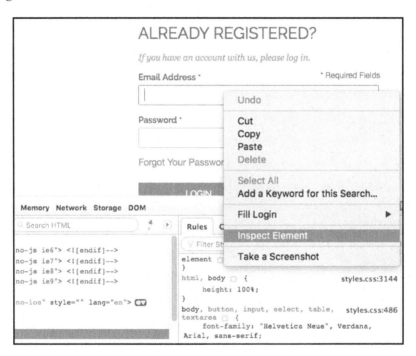

This will display the **Inspector** tab with the HTML code in a tree format with the selected element highlighted, as shown in the following screenshot:

Using **Inspector**, we can also validate the XPath or CSS Selectors using the search box shown in the **Inspector** section. Just enter the XPath or CSS Selector and **Inspector** will highlight the elements that match the expression, as shown in the following screenshot:

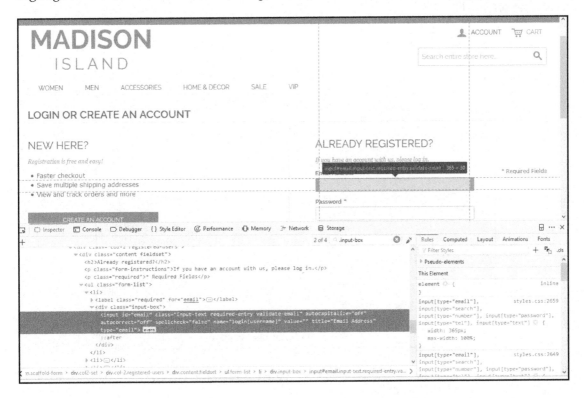

The Developer tools provide various other debugging features. It also generates XPath and CSS selectors for elements. For this, select the desired element in the tree, right-click, and select the **Copy > XPath** or **Copy > CSS Path** option from the pop-up menu, as shown in the following screenshot:

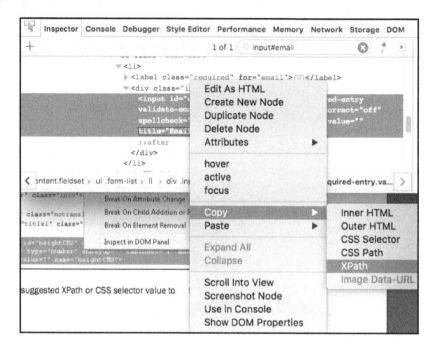

This will paste the suggested XPath or CSS selector value to the clipboard to be used later with the findElement() method.

Inspecting pages and elements in Google Chrome with Developer Tools

Similar to Mozilla Firefox, Google Chrome also provides a built-in feature to inspect pages and elements. We can move the mouse over a desired element on the page, right-click to open the pop-up menu, and then select the **Inspect element** option. This will open Developer tools in the browser, which displays information similar to that of Firefox, as shown in the following screenshot:

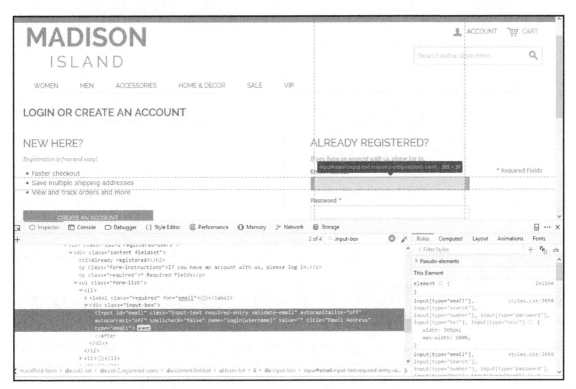

Similar to Firefox, we can also test XPath and CSS Selectors in Google Chrome Developer tools. Press *Ctrl + F* (on Mac, use *Command + F*) in the **Elements** tab. This will display a search box. Just enter *XPath* or *CSS Selector,* and matching elements will be highlighted in the tree, as shown in the following screenshot:

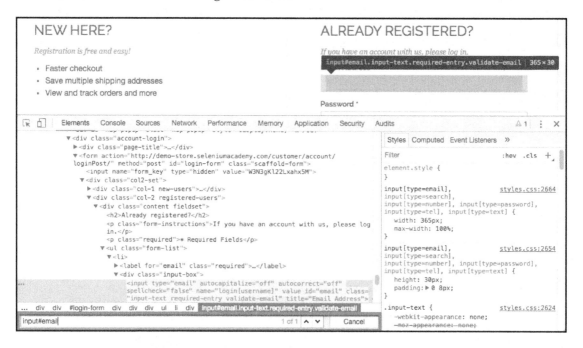

Chrome Developer Tools also provides a feature where you can get the XPath for an element by right-clicking on the desired element in the tree and selecting the **Copy XPath** option from the pop-up menu.

Similar to Mozilla Firefox and Google Chrome, you will find similar Developer tools in any major browser, including Microsoft Internet Explorer and Edge.

Browser developer tools come in really handy during the test-script development. These tools will help you to find the locator details for the elements with which you need to interact as part of the test. These tools parse the code for a page and display the information in a hierarchal tree.

WebElements on a web page may not have all the attributes declared. It is up to the developer of the test script to select the attribute that uniquely identifies the WebElement on the web page for the automation.

Using the By locating mechanism

By is the locating mechanism passed to the `findElement()` method or the `findElements()` method to fetch the respective WebElement(s) on a web page. There are eight different locating mechanisms; that is, eight different ways to identify

an HTML element on a web page. They are located by **ID**, **Name**, **ClassName**, **TagName**, **LinkText**, **PartialLinkText**, **XPath**, and **CSS** Selector.

The By.id() method

On a web page, each element is uniquely identified by an ID attribute, which is optionally provided. An ID can be assigned manually by the developer of the web application or left to be dynamically generated by the application. Dynamically-generated IDs can be changed on every page refresh or over a period of time. Now, consider the HTML code of the Search box:

```
<input id="search" type="search" name="q" value="" class="input-text
required-entry" maxlength="128" placeholder="Search entire store here..."
autocomplete="off">
```

In the preceding code, the `id` attribute value of the search box is `search`.

Let's see how to use the ID attribute as a locating mechanism to find the Search box:

```
@Test
public void byIdLocatorExample() {
    WebElement searchBox = driver.findElement(By.id("search"));
    searchBox.sendKeys("Bags");
    searchBox.submit();
    assertThat(driver.getTitle())
            .isEqualTo("Search results for: 'Bags'");
}
```

In preceding code, we used the `By.id()` method and the search box's `id` attribute value to find the element.

Here, try to use the `By.id` identifier, and use the name value (that is, q) instead of the `id` value (that is, `search`). Modify line three as follows:

```
WebElement searchBox = driver.findElement(By.id("q"));
```

The test script will fail to throw an exception, as follows:

```
Exception in thread "main" org.openqa.selenium.NoSuchElementException:
Unable to locate element: {"method":"id","selector":"q"}
```

WebDriver couldn't find an element by `id` whose value is q. Thus, it throws an exception saying `NoSuchElementException`.

The By.name() method

As seen earlier, every element on a web page has many attributes. Name is one of them. For instance, the HTML code for the Search box is:

```
<input id="search" type="search" name="q" value="" class="input-text
required-entry" maxlength="128" placeholder="Search entire store here..."
autocomplete="off">
```

Here, `name` is one of the many attributes of the search box, and its value is q. If we want to identify this search box and set a value in it in your test script, the code will look as follows:

```
@Test
public void searchProduct() {
    // find search box and enter search string
    WebElement searchBox = driver.findElement(By.name("q"));
    searchBox.sendKeys("Phones");
    searchBox.submit();
    assertThat(driver.getTitle())
            .isEqualTo("Search results for: 'Phones'");
}
```

If you observe line four, the locating mechanism used here is `By.name` and the name is q. So, where did we get this name from? As discussed in the previous section, it is the browser developer tools that helped us get the name of the button. Launch Developer tools and use the inspect elements widget to get the attributes of an element.

The By.className() method

Before we discuss the `className()` method, we have to talk a little about style and CSS. Every HTML element on a web page, generally, is styled by the web page developer or designer. It is not mandatory that each element should be styled, but they generally are to make the page appealing to the end user.

So, in order to apply styles to an element, they can be declared directly in the element tag, or placed in a separate file called the CSS file and can be referenced in the element using the `class` attribute. For instance, a style attribute for a button can be declared in a CSS file as follows:

```
.buttonStyle{
    width: 50px;
    height: 50px;
    border-radius: 50%;
    margin: 0% 2%;
}
```

Now, this style can be applied to the button element in a web page as follows:

```
<button name="sampleBtnName" id="sampleBtnId" class="buttonStyle">I'm
Button</button>
```

So, `buttonStyle` is used as the value for the `class` attribute of the button element, and it inherits all the styles declared in the CSS file. Now, let's try this on our Homepage. We will try to make WebDriver identify the search button using its class name and click on it.

First, in order to get the class name of the search button, as we know, we will use Developers tools to fetch it. After getting it, change the location mechanism to `By.className` and specify the class attribute value in it. The code for that is as follows:

```
@Test
public void byClassNameLocatorExample() {
    WebElement searchBox = driver.findElement(By.id("search"));
    searchBox.sendKeys("Electronics");
    WebElement searchButton =
            driver.findElement(By.className("search-button"));
    searchButton.click();
    assertThat(driver.getTitle())
            .isEqualTo("Search results for: 'Electronics'");
}
```

In the preceding code, we have used the `By.className` locating mechanism by passing the class attribute value to it.

Sometimes, an element might have multiple values given for the `class` attribute. For example, the Search button has *button* and *search-button* values specified in the `class` attribute in the following HTML snippet:

```
<button type="submit" title="Search" class="button search-
button"><span><span>Search</span></span></button>
```

We have to use one of the values of the `class` attribute with the `By.className` method. In this case, we can either use *button* or *search-button*, whichever uniquely identifies the element.

The By.linkText() method

As the name suggests, the `By.linkText` locating mechanism can only be used to identify the HTML links. Before we start discussing how WebDriver can be commanded to identify a link element using link text, let's see what an HTML link element looks like. The HTML link elements are represented on a web page using the `<a>` tag, an abbreviation for the anchor tag. A typical anchor tag looks like this:

```
<a href="http://demo-store.seleniumacademy.com/customer/account/" title="My
Account">My Account</a>
```

Here, `href` is the link to a different page where your web browser will take you when you click on the link. So, the preceding HTML code when rendered by the browser looks like this:

This **MY ACCOUNT** is the link text. So the `By.linkText` locating mechanism uses this text on an anchor tag to identify the WebElement. The code would look like this:

```
@Test
public void byLinkTextLocatorExample() {
    WebElement myAccountLink =
```

```
                  driver.findElement(By.linkText("MY ACCOUNT"));
        myAccountLink.click();
        assertThat(driver.getTitle())
                .isEqualTo("Customer Login");
    }
```

Here, the `By.linkText` locating mechanism is used to identify the **MY ACCOUNT** link.

> The `linkText` and `partialLinkText` methods are case-sensitive.

The By.partialLinkText() method

The `By.partialLinkText` locating mechanism is an extension of the `By.linkText` locator. If you are not sure of the entire link text or want to use only part of the link text, you can use this locator to identify the link element. So, let's modify the previous example to use only partial text on the link; in this case, we will use Privacy from the Privacy Policy link in the site footer:

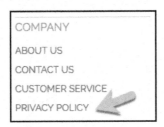

The code would look like this:

```
@Test
public void byPartialLinkTextLocatorExample() {
    WebElement orderAndReturns =
            driver.findElement(By.partialLinkText("PRIVACY"));
    orderAndReturns.click();
    assertThat(driver.getTitle())
            .isEqualTo("Privacy Policy");
}
```

What happens if there are multiple links whose text has *Privacy* in it? That is a question for the findElement() method rather than the locator. Remember when we discussed the findElement() method earlier, it will return only the first WebElement that it comes across. If you want all the WebElements that contain *Privacy* in its link text, use the findElements() method, which will return a list of all those elements.

> Use WebDriver's findElements() method if you think you need all the WebElements that satisfy a locating-mechanism condition.

The By.tagName() method

Locating an element by tag name is slightly different from the locating mechanisms we saw earlier. For example, on a Homepage, if you search for an element with the button tag name, it will result in multiple WebElements because there are nine buttons present on the Homepage. So, it is always advisable to use the findElements() method rather than the findElement() method when trying to locate elements using tag names.

Let's see how the code looks when a search for the number of links present on a Homepage is made:

```
@Test
public void byTagNameLocatorExample() {

    // get all links from the Home page
    List<WebElement> links = driver.findElements(By.tagName("a"));

    System.out.println("Found links:" + links.size());

    // print links which have text using Java 8 Streams API
    links.stream()
            .filter(elem -> elem.getText().length() > 0)
            .forEach(elem -> System.out.println(elem.getText()));
}
```

In the preceding code, we have used the `By.tagName` locating mechanism and the `findElements()` method, which return a list of all the links, that is, the a anchor tags defined on the page. On line five, we printed the size of the list, and then printed text of only links where the text has been provided. We use the Java 8 Stream API to filter the element list and output the text value by calling the `getText()` method. This will generate the following output:

Found links:88
 ACCOUNT
 CART
 WOMEN
 ...

The By.xpath() method

WebDriver uses **XPath** to identify a WebElement on the web page. Before we see how it does that, let's quickly look at the syntax for XPath. XPath is a short name for the XML path, the query language used for searching XML documents. The HTML for our web page is also one form of the XML document. So, in order to identify an element on an HTML page, we need to use a specific XPath syntax:

- The root element is identified as `//`.
- To identify all the div elements, the syntax will be `//div`.
- To identify the link tags that are within the div element, the syntax will be `//div/a`.
- To identify all the elements with a tag, we use *. The syntax will be `//div/*`.
- To identify all the div elements that are at three levels down from the root, we can use `//*/*/div`.
- To identify specific elements, we use attribute values of those elements, such as `//*/div/a[@id='attrValue']`, which will return the anchor element. This element is at the third level from the root within a `div` element and has an `id` value of `attrValue`.

So, we need to pass the XPath expression to the `By.xpath` locating mechanism to make it identify our target element.

Now, let's see the code example and how WebDriver uses this XPath to identify the element:

```
@Test
public void byXPathLocatorExample() {
    WebElement searchBox =
            driver.findElement(By.xpath("//*[@id='search']"));
    searchBox.sendKeys("Bags");
    searchBox.submit();
    assertThat(driver.getTitle())
            .isEqualTo("Search results for: 'Bags'");
}
```

In the preceding code, we are using the By.xpath locating mechanism and passing the XPath of the WebElement to it.

One disadvantage of using XPath is that it is costly in terms of time. For every element to be identified, WebDriver actually scans through the entire page, which is very time consuming, and too much usage of XPath in your test script will actually make it too slow to execute.

The By.cssSelector() method

The By.cssSelector() method is similar to the By.xpath() method in its usage, but the difference is that it is slightly faster than the By.xpath locating mechanism. The following are the commonly used syntaxes to identify elements:

- To identify an element using the div element with the #flrs ID, we use the #flrs syntax
- To identify the child anchor element, we use the #flrs > a syntax, which will return the link element
- To identify the anchor element with its attribute, we use the #flrs > a[a[href="/intl/en/about.html"]] syntax

Let's try to modify the previous code, which uses the XPath locating mechanism to use the cssSelector mechanism:

```
@Test
public void byCssSelectorLocatorExample() {
    WebElement searchBox =
            driver.findElement(By.cssSelector("#search"));
    searchBox.sendKeys("Bags");
    searchBox.submit();
    assertThat(driver.getTitle())
```

```
                .isEqualTo("Search results for: 'Bags'");
    }
```

The preceding code uses the `By.cssSelector` locating mechanism, which uses the css selector `ID` of the Search box.

Let's look at a slightly complex example. We will try to identify the About Us on the Homepage:

```
@Test
public void byCssSelectorLocatorComplexExample() {

    WebElement aboutUs =
            driver.findElement(By
                    .cssSelector("a[href*='/about-magento-demo-store/']"));

    aboutUs.click();

    assertThat(driver.getTitle())
            .isEqualTo("About Us");
}
```

The preceding code uses the `cssSelector()` method to find the anchor element identified by its `href` attribute.

Interacting with WebElements

In the previous section, we saw how to locate WebElements on a web page by using different locator methods. Here, we will see all the different user actions that can be performed on a WebElement. Different WebElements will have different actions that can be taken on them. For example, in a textbox element, we can type in some text or clear the text that is already typed in it. Similarly, for a button, we can click on it, get the dimensions of it, and so on, but we cannot type into a button, and for a link, we cannot type into it. So, though all the actions are listed in one WebElement interface, it is the test script developer's responsibility to use the actions that are supported by the target element. In case we try to execute the wrong action on a WebElement, we don't see any exception or error thrown and we don't see any action get executed; WebDriver ignores such actions silently.

Now, let's get into each of the actions individually by looking at their Javadocs and a code example.

Getting element properties and attributes

In this section, we will learn the various methods to retrieve value and properties from the WebElement interface.

The getAttribute() method

The `getAttribute` method can be executed on all the WebElements. Remember, we have seen attributes of WebElement in the WebElements section. The HTML attributes are modifiers of HTML elements. They are generally key-value pairs that appear in the start tag of an element. For example:

```
<label name="Username" id="uname">Enter Username: </label>
```

In the preceding code, `name` and `id` are the attributes or attribute keys and `Username` and `uname` are the attribute values.

The API syntax of the `getAttribute()` method is as follows:

```
java.lang.String getAttribute(java.lang.String name)
```

In the preceding code, the input parameter is `String`, which is the name of the attribute. The return type is again `String`, which is the value of the attribute.

Now let's see how we can get all the attributes of a WebElement using WebDriver. Here, we will make use of the Search box from the example application. This is what the element looks like:

```
<input id="search" type="search" name="q" value="" class="input-text
required-entry" maxlength="128" placeholder="Search entire store here..."
autocomplete="off">
```

We will list all the attributes of this WebElement using WebDriver. The code for that is as follows:

```
@Test
public void elementGetAttributesExample() {
    WebElement searchBox = driver.findElement(By.name("q"));
    System.out.println("Name of the box is: "
            + searchBox.getAttribute("name"));
    System.out.println("Id of the box is: " +
searchBox.getAttribute("id"));
    System.out.println("Class of the box is: "
            + searchBox.getAttribute("class"));
    System.out.println("Placeholder of the box is: "
```

```
    + searchBox.getAttribute("placeholder"));
}
```

In the preceding code, the last four lines of code use the getAttribute() method to fetch the attribute values of the name, id, class, and placeholder attributes of the WebElement search box. The output of the preceding code will be following:

```
Name of the box is: q
Id of the box is: search
Class of the box is: input-text required-entry
Placeholder of the box is: Search entire store here...
```

Going back to the By.tagName() method of the previous section, if the search by a locating mechanism, By.tagName, results in more than one result, you can use the getAttribute() method to further filter the results and get to your exact intended element.

The getText() method

The getText method can be called from all the WebElements. It will return visible text if the element contains any text on it, otherwise it will return nothing. The API syntax for the getText() method is as follows:

```
java.lang.String getText()
```

There is no input parameter for the preceding method, but it returns the visible innerText string of the WebElement if anything is available, otherwise it will return an empty string.

The following is the code to get the text present on the Site notice element present on the example application Homepage:

```
@Test
public void elementGetTextExample() {
    WebElement siteNotice = driver.findElement(By
            .className("global-site-notice"));
    System.out.println("Complete text is: "
            + siteNotice.getText());
}
```

The preceding code uses the getText() method to fetch the text present on the Site notice element, which returns the following:

```
Complete text is: This is a demo store. Any orders placed through this
store will not be honored or fulfilled.
```

The getCssValue() method

The `getCssValue` method can be called on all the WebElements. This method is used to fetch a CSS property value from a WebElement. CSS properties can be `font-family`, `background-color`, `color`, and so on. This is useful when you want to validate the CSS styles that are applied to your WebElements through your test scripts. The API syntax for the `getCssValue()` method is as follows:

```
java.lang.String getCssValue(java.lang.String propertyName)
```

In the preceding code, the input parameter is the String value of the CSS property name, and the return type is the value assigned to that property name.

The following is the code example to retrieve `font-family` of the text from the Search box:

```
@Test
public void elementGetCssValueExample() {
    WebElement searchBox = driver.findElement(By.name("q"));
    System.out.println("Font of the box is: "
        + searchBox.getCssValue("font-family"));
}
```

The preceding code uses the `getCssValue()` method to find `font-family` of the text visible in the Search box. The output of the method is shown here:

```
Font of the box is: Raleway, "Helvetica Neue", Verdana, Arial, sans-serif
```

The getLocation() method

The `getLocation` method can be executed on all the WebElements. This is used to get the relative position of an element where it is rendered on the web page. This position is calculated relative to the top-left corner of the web page of which the (x, y) coordinates are assumed to be (0, 0). This method will be of use if your test script tries to validate the layout of your web page.

The API syntax of the `getLocation()` method is as follows:

```
Point getLocation()
```

The preceding method obviously doesn't take any input parameters, but the return type is a `Point` class that contains the (x, y) coordinates of the element.

The following is the code to retrieve the location of the Search box:

```
WebElement searchBox = driver.findElement(By.name("q"));
System.out.println("Location of the box is: "
        + searchBox.getLocation());
```

The output for the preceding code is the (x, y) location of the Search box, as shown in the following screenshot:

```
Location of the box is: (873, 136)
```

The getSize() method

The getSize method can also be called on all the visible components of HTML. It will return the width and height of the rendered WebElement. The API syntax of the getSize() method is as follows:

```
Dimension getSize()
```

The preceding method doesn't take any input parameters, and the return type is a class instance named Dimension. This class contains the width and height of the target WebElement. The following is the code to get the width and height of the Search box:

```
WebElement searchBox = driver.findElement(By.name("q"));
System.out.println("Size of the box is: "
        + searchBox.getSize());
```

The output for the preceding code is the width and height of the Search box, as shown in the following screenshot:

```
Size of the box is: (281, 40)
```

The getTagName() method

The getTagName method can be called from all the WebElements. This will return the HTML tag name of the WebElement. For example, in the following HTML code, the button is the tag name of the HTML element:

```
<button id="gbqfba" class="gbqfba" name="btnK" aria-label="Google Search">
```

In the preceding code, the button is the tag name of the HTML element.

The API syntax for the `getTagName()` method is as follows:

```
java.lang.String getTagName()
```

The return type of the preceding method is `String`, and it returns the tag name of the target element.

The following is the code that returns the tag name of the Search button:

```
@Test
public void elementGetTagNameExample() {
    WebElement searchButton = driver.findElement(By.className("search-button"));
    System.out.println("Html tag of the button is: "
            + searchButton.getTagName());
}
```

The preceding code uses the `getTagName()` method to get the tag name of the Search button element. The output of the code is as expected:

```
Html tag of the button is: button
```

Performing actions on WebElements

In the previous section, we saw how to retrieve values or properties of WebElements. In this section, we will see how to perform actions on WebElements, which is the most crucial part of automation. Let's explore the various methods available in the WebElement interface.

The sendKeys() method

The `sendKeys` action is applicable for `textbox` or `textarea` HTML elements. This is used to type text into the textbox. This will simulate the user keyboard and types text into WebElements exactly as a user would. The API syntax for the `sendKeys()` method is as follows:

```
void sendKeys(java.lang.CharSequence...keysToSend)
```

The input parameter for the preceding method is `CharSequence` of text that has to be entered into the element. This method doesn't return anything. Now, let's see a code example of how to type a search text into the Search box using the `sendKeys()` method:

```
@Test
public void elementSendKeysExample() {
    WebElement searchBox = driver.findElement(By.name("q"));
    searchBox.sendKeys("Phones");
    searchBox.submit();
    assertThat(driver.getTitle())
            .isEqualTo("Search results for: 'Phones'");
}
```

In the preceding code, the `sendKeys()` method is used to type the required text in the textbox element of the web page. This is how we deal with normal keys, but if you want to type in some special keys, such as *Backspace, Enter, Tab,* or *Shift*, we need to use a special enum class of WebDriver, named `Keys`. Using the `Keys` enumeration, you can simulate many special keys while typing into a WebElement.

Now let's see some code example, which uses the *Shift* key to type the text in uppercase in the Search Box:

```
@Test
public void elementSendKeysCompositeExample() {
    WebElement searchBox = driver.findElement(By.name("q"));
    searchBox.sendKeys(Keys.chord(Keys.SHIFT, "phones"));
    searchBox.submit();
    assertThat(driver.getTitle())
            .isEqualTo("Search results for: 'PHONES'");
}
```

In the preceding code, the `chord()` method from the `Keys` enum is used to type the key, while the text specified is being given as an input to be the textbox. Try this in your environment to see all the text being typed in uppercase.

The clear() method

The clear action is similar to the `sendKeys()` method, which is applicable for the `textbox` and `textarea` elements. This is used to erase the text entered in a WebElement using the `sendKeys()` method. This can be achieved using the `Keys.BACK_SPACE` enum, but WebDriver has given us an explicit method to clear the text easily. The API syntax for the `clear()` method is as follows:

```
void clear()
```

This method doesn't take any input and doesn't return any output. It is simply executed on the target text-entry element.

Now, let's see how we can clear text that is entered in the Search box. The code example for it is as follows:

```
@Test
public void elementClearExample() {
    WebElement searchBox = driver.findElement(By.name("q"));
    searchBox.sendKeys(Keys.chord(Keys.SHIFT, "phones"));
    searchBox.clear();
}
```

We have used the WebElement's clear() method to clear the text after typing phones into the Search box.

The submit() method

The submit() action can be taken on a Form or on an element, which is inside a Form element. This is used to submit a form of a web page to the server hosting the web application. The API syntax for the submit() method is as follows:

```
void submit()
```

The preceding method doesn't take any input parameters and doesn't return anything. But a NoSuchElementException is thrown when this method is executed on a WebElement that is not present within the form.

Now, let's see a code example to submit the form on a Search page:

```
@Test
public void elementSubmitExample() {
    WebElement searchBox = driver.findElement(By.name("q"));
    searchBox.sendKeys(Keys.chord(Keys.SHIFT, "phones"));
    searchBox.submit();
}
```

In the preceding code, toward the end is where the Search form is submitted to the application servers using the submit() method. Now, try to execute the submit() method on an element, let's say the About link, which is not a part of any form. We should see NoSuchElementException is thrown. So, when you use the submit() method on a WebElement, make sure it is part of the Form element.

Checking the WebElement state

In the previous sections, we saw how to retrieve values and perform actions on WebElements. Now, we will see how to check the state of a WebElement. We will explore methods to check whether the WebElement is displayed in the Browser window, whether it is editable, and if the WebElement is Radio Button of Checkbox, we can determine whether it's selected or unselected. Let's see how we can use the methods available in the WebElement interface.

The isDisplayed() method

The isDisplayed action verifies whether an element is displayed on the web page and can be executed on all the WebElements. The API syntax for the isDisplayed() method is as follows:

```
boolean isDisplayed()
```

The preceding method returns a Boolean value specifying whether the target element is displayed on the web page. The following is the code to verify whether the Search box is displayed, which obviously should return true in this case:

```
@Test
public void elementStateExample() {
    WebElement searchBox = driver.findElement(By.name("q"));
    System.out.println("Search box is displayed: "
            + searchBox.isDisplayed());
}
```

The preceding code uses the isDisplayed() method to determine whether the element is displayed on a web page. The preceding code returns true for the Search box:

```
Search box is displayed: true
```

The isEnabled() method

The isEnabled action verifies whether an element is enabled on the web page and can be executed on all the WebElements. The API syntax for the isEnabled() method is as follows:

```
boolean isEnabled()
```

The preceding method returns a `Boolean` value specifying whether the target element is enabled on the web page. The following is the code to verify whether the Search box is enabled, which obviously should return true in this case:

```
@Test
public void elementStateExample() {
    WebElement searchBox = driver.findElement(By.name("q"));
    System.out.println("Search box is enabled: "
            + searchBox.isEnabled());
}
```

The preceding code uses the `isEnabled()` method to determine whether the element is enabled on a web page. The preceding code returns true for the Search box:

```
Search box is enabled: true
```

The isSelected() method

The `isSelected` method returns a `boolean` value if an element is selected on the web page and can be executed only on a radio button, options in **select**, and checkbox WebElements. When executed on other elements, it will return false. The API syntax for the `isSelected()` method is as follows:

```
boolean isSelected()
```

The preceding method returns a `Boolean` value specifying whether the target element is selected on the web page. The following is the code to verify whether the Search box is selected on a search page:

```
@Test
public void elementStateExample() {
    WebElement searchBox = driver.findElement(By.name("q"));
    System.out.println("Search box is selected: "
            + searchBox.isSelected());
}
```

The preceding code uses the `isSelected()` method. It returns false for the Search box, because this is not a radio button, options in select, or a checkbox. The preceding code returns `false` for the Search box:

```
Search box is selected: false
```

To select a Checkbox or Radio button, we need to call the `WebElement.click()` method, which toggles the state of the element. We can use the `isSelected()` method to see whether it's selected.

Summary

In this chapter, we covered a brief overview of the Selenium testing tools, and the architecture of WebDriver, WebElements. We learned how to set up a test-development environment using Eclipse, Maven, and TestNG. This will provide us with the foundation to build a testing framework using Selenium. Then, we saw how to locate elements, and the actions that can be taken on them. This is the most important aspect when automating Web Applications. In this chapter, we used ChromeDriver to run our tests. In the next chapter, we will learn and implement the Streams API of Java 8 since Selenium 3.0 includes a bunch of features of Java 8.

Questions

1. True or false: Selenium is a browser automation library.
2. What are the different types of locator mechanisms provided by Selenium?
3. True or false: With the `getAttribute()` method, we can read CSS attributes as well?
4. What actions can be performed on a WebElement?
5. How can we determine whether the checkbox is checked or unchecked?

Further information

You can check out the following links for more information on the topics covered in this chapter:

- Read the WebDriver Specification at `https://www.w3.org/TR/webdriver/`
- Read more about using TestNG and Maven in Chapter 1, *Creating a Faster Feedback Loop* from *Mastering Selenium WebDriver* By Mark Collin, Packt Publishing
- Read more about element interaction in *Chapter 2, Finding Elements* and *Chapter 3, Working with Elements* from *Selenium Testing Tools Cookbook*, 2nd Edition, by Unmesh Gundecha, Packt Publishing

Using Java 8 Features with Selenium

2

With Selenium 3.0 moving to Java 8, we can use some of the new features of Java 8, such as Stream API and Lambda or Anonymous functions to create scripts in a functional programming style. We do so by reducing the number of lines of code as well as reaping the benefits of the newer features of the language. In this chapter, we will cover these topics:

- Introducing Java 8 Stream API
- Using Stream API to collect and filter data
- Using Stream API with Selenium WebDriver

Introducing Java 8 Stream API

The Stream API is a new addition to the Collections API in Java 8. The Stream API brings new ways to process collections of objects. A stream represents a sequence of elements and supports different kinds of operations (**filter**, **sort**, **map**, and **collect**) from a collection. We can chain these operations together to form a pipeline to query the data, as shown in this diagram:

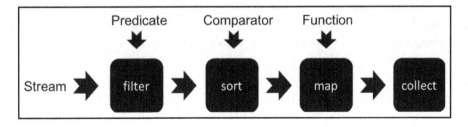

We can obtain a Stream from a collection using the `.stream()` method. For example, we have a dropdown of languages supported by the sample web application displayed in the header section. Let's capture this in an `Array list`, as follows:

```
List<String> languages = new ArrayList<String>();
languages.add("English");
languages.add("German");
languages.add("French");
```

If we have to print the list members, we will use a `for` loop in the following way:

```
for(String language : languages) {
    System.out.println(language);
}
```

Using the streams **API** we can obtain the stream by calling the `.stream()` method on the `languages` array list and print the members in the following way:

```
languages.stream().forEach(System.out::println);
```

After obtaining the stream, we called the `forEach()` method, passing the action we wanted to take on each element, that is, output the member value on the console, using the `System.out.println` method.

Once we have obtained a Stream from a collection, we can use that stream to process the elements or members of the collection.

Stream.filter()

We can filter a stream using the `filter()` method. Let's filter the stream obtained from the `languages` list to filter items starting with **E**, as shown in the following code:

```
stream.filter( item -> item.startsWith("E") );
```

The `filter()` method takes a Predicate as a parameter. The `predicate` interface contains a function called `boolean test(T t)` that takes a single parameter and returns a boolean. In the preceding example, we passed the lambda expression `item -> item.startsWith("E")` to the `test()` function.

When the `filter()` method is called on a Stream, the filter passed as a parameter to the `filter()` function is stored internally. The items are not filtered immediately.

The parameter passed to the `filter()` function determines what items in the stream should be processed and what should be excluded. If the `Predicate.test()` function returns `true` for an item, that means it should be processed. If `false` is returned, the item is not processed. In the preceding example, the `test()` function will return true for all items starting with the character E.

Stream.sort()

We can sort a stream by calling the `sort()` function. Let's use the `sort()` function on the `languages` list, as shown in the following code:

```
languages.stream().sorted();
```

This will sort the elements in alphabetical order. We can provide a lambda expression to sort the elements using custom comparison logic.

Stream.map()

Streams provide a map() method to map the elements of a stream into another form. We can map the elements into a new object. Let's take the previous example and convert the elements of languages list to uppercase, as shown here:

```
languages.stream().map(item -> item.toUpperCase());
```

This will map all elements that are strings in the language collection to their uppercase equivalents. Again, this doesn't actually perform the mapping; it only configures the stream for mapping. Once one of the stream processing methods is invoked, the mapping (and filtering) will be performed.

Stream.collect()

Streams provide the collect() method, among the other methods, for stream processing on the Stream interface. When the collect() method is invoked, filtering and mapping will take place, and the object resulting from those actions will be collected. Let's take the previous example and obtain a new list of languages in uppercase, as shown in the following code:

```
List<String> upperCaseLanguages = languages.stream()
        .map(item -> item.toUpperCase())
        .collect(Collectors.toList());

System.out.println(upperCaseLanguages);
```

This example creates a stream, adds a map to convert the strings to uppercase, and collects all objects in a new list. We can also use the filter or sort method and collect the resulting list based on conditions applied in the filter method.

Stream.min() and Stream.max()

The Streams API provides min() and max() methods—stream processing for finding the minimum or maximum value in the stream respectively.

Let's take an example in the context of the sample application we're testing. We will create a simple Java class called Product that stores the name and price of products returned by the search. We want to find the product that has the minimum price and the one that has the maximum price. Our product class will have two members, as shown in the following code:

```
class Product {
    String name;
    Double price;

    public Product(String name, double price) {
        this.name = name;
        this.price = price;
    }

    public String getName() {
        return name;
    }

    public Double getPrice() {
        return price;
    }
}
```

Let's create a list of products returned by the search result, as shown here:

```
List<Product> searchResult = new ArrayList<>();
searchResult.add(new Product("MADISON OVEREAR HEADPHONES", 125.00));
searchResult.add(new Product("MADISON EARBUDS", 35.00));
searchResult.add(new Product("MP3 PLAYER WITH AUDIO", 185.00));
```

We can call the .min() function by passing the comparison attribute, in this case, price, using the .getPrice() method. The .min() function will use the price attribute and return the element that has the lowest price, as shown in this code:

```
Product product = searchResult.stream()
        .min(Comparator.comparing(item -> item.getPrice()))
        .get();

System.out.println("The product with lowest price is " +
product.getName());
```

The get() method will return the object returned by the min() function. We will store this in an instance of Product. The min() function finds **MADISON EARBUDS** as the lowest-priced product, as shown in the following console output:

The product with lowest price is MADISON EARBUDS

As opposed to the min() function, the max() function will return the product with the highest price, as shown in the following code:

```
product = searchResult.stream()
        .max(Comparator.comparing(item -> item.getPrice()))
        .get();
System.out.println("The product with highest price is " +
product.getName());
```

The max() function finds **MP3 PLAYER WITH AUDIO** as the highest-priced product:

The product with highest price is MP3 PLAYER WITH AUDIO

The min() and max() functions return an optional instance, which has a get() method to obtain the object. The get() method will return null if the stream has no elements.

Both the functions take a comparator as a parameter. The Comparator.comparing() method creates a comparator based on the lambda expression passed to it.

Stream.count()

The streams API provides a count method that returns the number of elements in the stream after filtering has been applied. Let's take the previous example to get a count of Products from the MADISON brand:

```
long count = searchResult.stream()
        .filter(item -> item.getName().startsWith("MADISON"))
        .count();
System.out.println("The number of products from MADISON are: " + count);
```

The count() method returns a long, which is the count of elements matching with the filter criteria. In this example, the following output will be displayed on the console:

```
The number of products from MADISON are: 2
```

Using Stream API with Selenium WebDriver

Now that we have introduced Streams API and its various functions, let's see how we can use them in our tests.

Filtering and counting WebElements

Let's start with a simple test to determine the links displayed on the home page of the sample application. We get all the links from the home page and print their count, followed by the count of links that are visible on the page, as shown in the following code:

```
@Test
public void linksTest() {

    List<WebElement> links = driver.findElements(By.tagName("a"));
    System.out.println("Total Links : " + links.size());

    long count = links.stream().filter(item -> item.isDisplayed()).count();
    System.out.println("Total Link visible " + count);
}
```

In the preceding code, we used the `findElements()` method along with `By.tagName` to get all the links from the home page. However, for finding out the visible links out of them, we used the `filter()` function with a predicate to test whether the links are displayed. This is done by calling the `isDisplayed()` method of the `WebElement` interface. The `isDisplayed` method will return `true` if the link is displayed; otherwise it will return `false`. Finally, we called the `count()` method to get the count of links returned by the `filter()` function. This will show the following output on the console:

```
Total Links : 88
Total Link visible 37
```

Filtering element attributes

In the example code, we will filter a list of images that have an empty `alt` attribute defined. This is useful if you want to check the accessibility of images displayed on the page. As per the accessibility guidelines, all images should have the `alt` attribute defined. This is done by filtering images, by testing the `getAttribute("alt")` method; it returns an empty string, as shown in the following code:

```
@Test
public void imgAltTest() {

    List<WebElement> images = driver.findElements(By.tagName("img"));

    System.out.println("Total Images : " + images.size());

    List<WebElement> imagesWithOutAlt = images.stream()
            .filter(item -> item.getAttribute("alt") == "")
            .collect(Collectors.toList());
    System.out.println("Total images without alt attribute " +
imagesWithOutAlt);
}
```

The `filter()` function will return the list of all image elements that have an empty `alt` attribute defined.

Using the Map function to get the text value from elements

In this example, we will modify the search test we created in earlier chapters to test the results containing the list of expected products, as shown in the following code:

```java
@Test
public void searchProduct() {

    // find search box and enter search string
    WebElement searchBox = driver.findElement(By.name("q"));

    searchBox.sendKeys("Phones");

    WebElement searchButton =
            driver.findElement(By.className("search-button"));

    searchButton.click();

    assertThat(driver.getTitle())
            .isEqualTo("Search results for: 'Phones'");


    List<WebElement> searchItems = driver
            .findElements(By.cssSelector("h2.product-name a"));

    List<String> expectedProductNames =
            Arrays.asList("MADISON EARBUDS",
                    "MADISON OVEREAR HEADPHONES",
                    "MP3 PLAYER WITH AUDIO");

    List<String> productNames = searchItems.stream()
            .map(WebElement::getText)
            .collect(Collectors.toList());

    assertThat(productNames).
            isEqualTo(expectedProductNames);

}
```

In the preceding code, we created a list of all the matching products returned by the findElements() method. We then retrieved the text of each element by calling the map() function and mapped the return values to a list of strings. This is compared with the expectedProductNames list.

Filtering and performing actions on WebElements

Let's further modify the search test and find a product matching with a given name. We will then click on the product to open the product details page, as shown in this code:

```
@Test
 public void searchAndViewProduct() {

        // find search box and enter search string
        WebElement searchBox = driver.findElement(By.name("q"));

        searchBox.sendKeys("Phones");

        WebElement searchButton =
                driver.findElement(By.className("search-button"));

        searchButton.click();

        assertThat(driver.getTitle())
                .isEqualTo("Search results for: 'Phones'");

        List<WebElement> searchItems = driver
                .findElements(By.cssSelector("h2.product-name a"));

        WebElement product = searchItems.stream()
                .filter(item -> item.getText().equalsIgnoreCase("MADISON
EARBUDS"))
                .findFirst()
                .get();

        product.click();

        assertThat(driver.getTitle())
                .isEqualTo("Madison Earbuds");
 }
```

In the preceding code, we used the `filter()` function to find a specific product from the list of WebElements. We retrieved the first matching product, using the `findFirst()` function. This will return a `WebElement` representing the link element. We then clicked on the element to open the product details page in the browser.

Thus, we can use Streams API in a number of ways to create functional, readable code with just a few lines.

Summary

In this short chapter, we learned how to use Selenium 8 Stream API and Lambda functions to simplify the Selenium WebDriver code. This helps you to write code in a functional programming style, which is more fluent and readable. Streams are useful for working with the list of WebElements. We can collect and filter data with a stream easily.

In the next chapter, we will explore the features of WebDriver for taking screenshots, handling Windows and Frames, synchronization, and managing cookies.

Questions

1. Which version of Java Streams API is introduced?
2. Explain the filter function of Streams API.
3. Which method of Streams API will return the number of matching elements from the filter() function?
4. We can use the map() function to filter a list of WebElements by attribute values: True or false?

Further information

You can check out the following links for more information about the topics covered in this chapter:

- Read more about Stream API at `https://www.oracle.com/technetwork/articles/java/ma14-java-se-8-streams-2177646.html` and `https://docs.oracle.com/javase/8/docs/api/java/util/stream/Stream.html`
- Read more about Lambda expressions at `https://docs.oracle.com/javase/tutorial/java/java00/lambdaexpressions.html`

3
Exploring the Features of WebDriver

So far, we have looked at various basic and advanced interactions that a user can perform on a web page using WebDriver. In this chapter, we will discuss the different capabilities and features of WebDriver that enable test script developers to have better control over WebDriver, and consequently of the web application that is being tested. The features that we are going to cover in this chapter are as follows:

- Taking screenshots
- Locating target windows and iFrames
- Exploring Navigate
- Waiting for WebElements to load
- Handling cookies

Let's get started without any further delay.

Taking screenshots

Taking a screenshot of a web page is a very useful capability of WebDriver. This is very handy when your test case fails, and you want to see the state of the application when the test case failed. The TakesScreenShot interface in the WebDriver library is implemented by all of the different variants of WebDriver, such as Firefox Driver, Internet Explorer Driver, Chrome Driver, and so on.

The TakesScreenShot capability is enabled in all of the browsers by default. Because this is a read-only capability, a user cannot toggle it. Before we see a code example that uses this capability, we should look at an important method of the TakesScreenShot interface—getScreenshotAs().

The API syntax for `getScreenshotAs()` is as follows:

```
public X getScreenshotAs(OutputType target)
```

Here, `OutputType` is another interface of the WebDriver library. We can ask WebDriver to output the screenshot in three different formats : `BASE64`, `BYTES` (raw data), and `FILE`. If you choose the `FILE` format, it writes the data into a `.png` file, which will be deleted once the JVM is killed. So, you should always copy that file into a safe location so that it can be used for later reference.

The return type is a specific output that depends on the selected `OutputType`. For example, selecting `OutputType.BYTES` will return a `bytearray`, and selecting `OutputType.FILE` will return a file object.

Depending on the browser used, the output screenshot will be one of the following, in order of preference:

- The entire page
- The current window
- A visible portion of the current frame
- The screenshot of the entire display containing the browser

For example, if you are using Firefox Driver, `getScreenshotAs()` takes a screenshot of the entire page, but Chrome Driver returns only the visible portion of the current frame.

It's time to take a look at the following code example:

```
@BeforeMethod
public void setup() throws IOException {
    System.setProperty("webdriver.chrome.driver",
            "./src/test/resources/drivers/chromedriver");
    driver = new ChromeDriver();
    driver.get("http://demo-store.seleniumacademy.com/");

    File scrFile = ((TakesScreenshot)
driver).getScreenshotAs(OutputType.FILE);
    FileUtils.copyFile(scrFile, new File("./target/screenshot.png"));

}
```

In the preceding code, we used the `getScreenshotAs()` method to take the screenshot of the web page and save it to a file format. We can open the saved image from the target folder and examine it.

Locating target windows and Frames

WebDriver enables the developers to switch between multiple child windows, browser tabs, and frames used in the application. For example, when you click on an internet banking link on a bank web application, it will open the internet banking application in a separate window or Tab. At this point, you may want to switch back to the original window to handle some events. Similarly, you may have to deal with a web application that is divided into two frames on the web page. The frame on the left may contain navigation items, and the frame on the right displays the appropriate web page, based on what is selected in the frame on the left. Using WebDriver, you can develop test cases that can easily handle such complex situations.

The `WebDriver.TargetLocator` interface is used to locate a given frame or window. In this section, we will see how WebDriver handles switching between browser windows and between two frames in the same window.

Switching among windows

First, we will see a code example for handling multiple windows. For this chapter, there is an HTML file provided with this book named `Window.html`. It is a very basic web page that links to Google's search page. When you click on the link, the Google's search page is opened in a different window. Every time you open a web page using WebDriver in a browser window, WebDriver assigns a window handle to that. WebDriver uses the window handle to identify the window. At this point, in WebDriver, there are two window handles registered. Now, on the screen, you can see that the Google's search page is in the front and has the focus. At this point, if you want to switch to the first browser window, you can use WebDriver's `switchTo()` method to do that.

The API syntax for `TargetLocator` is as follows:

```
WebDriver.TargetLocator switchTo()
```

This method returns the `WebDriver.TargetLocator` instance, where you can tell the WebDriver whether to switch between browser windows or frames. Let's see how WebDriver deals with this:

```
public class WindowHandlingTest {

    WebDriver driver;

    @BeforeMethod
    public void setup() throws IOException {
```

```
            System.setProperty("webdriver.chrome.driver",
                    "./src/test/resources/drivers/chromedriver");
            driver = new ChromeDriver();
            driver.get("http://guidebook.seleniumacademy.com/Window.html");
    }

    @Test
    public void handleWindow() {

        String firstWindow = driver.getWindowHandle();
        System.out.println("First Window Handle is: " + firstWindow);

        WebElement link = driver.findElement(By.linkText("Google Search"));
        link.click();

        String secondWindow = driver.getWindowHandle();
        System.out.println("Second Window Handle is: " + secondWindow);
        System.out.println("Number of Window Handles so for: "
                + driver.getWindowHandles().size());

        driver.switchTo().window(firstWindow);
    }

    @AfterMethod
    public void tearDown() {
        driver.quit();
    }
}
```

Observe the following line in the preceding code:

```
String firstWindow = driver.getWindowHandle();
```

Here, the driver returns the assigned identifier for the window. Now, before we move on to a different window, it is better to store this value so that if we want to switch back to this window, we can use this handle or identifier. To retrieve all the window handles that are registered with your driver so far, you can use the following method:

```
driver.getWindowHandles()
```

This will return the set of identifiers of all of the browser window handles opened in the driver session so far. Now, in our example, after we open Google's search page, the window corresponding to it is shown in front with the focus. If you want to go back to the first window, you have to use the following code:

```
driver.switchTo().window(firstWindow);
```

This will bring the first window into focus.

Switching between frames

Let's now see how we can handle switching between the frames of a web page. In the HTML files supplied with this book, you will see a file named Frames.html. If you open that, you will see two HTML files loaded in two different frames. Let's see how we can switch between them and type into the text boxes available in each frame:

```
public class FrameHandlingTest {
    WebDriver driver;

    @BeforeMethod
    public void setup() throws IOException {
        System.setProperty("webdriver.chrome.driver",
                "./src/test/resources/drivers/chromedriver");
        driver = new ChromeDriver();
        driver.get("http://guidebook.seleniumacademy.com/Frames.html");
    }

    @Test
    public void switchBetweenFrames() {

        // First Frame
        driver.switchTo().frame(0);
        WebElement firstField = driver.findElement(By.name("1"));
        firstField.sendKeys("I'm Frame One");
        driver.switchTo().defaultContent();

        // Second Frame
        driver.switchTo().frame(1);
        WebElement secondField = driver.findElement(By.name("2"));
        secondField.sendKeys("I'm Frame Two");
    }

    @AfterMethod
    public void tearDown() {
        driver.quit();
    }
}
```

In the preceding code, we have used switchTo().frame instead of switchTo().window because we are moving across frames.

The API syntax for frame is as follows:

```
WebDriver frame(int index)
```

This method takes the index of the frame that you want to switch to. If your web page has three frames, WebDriver indexes them as 0, 1, and 2, where the zero index is assigned to the first frame encountered in the DOM. Similarly, you can switch between frames using their names by using the previous overloaded method. The API syntax is as follows:

```
WebDriver frame(String frameNameOrframeID)
```

You can pass the name of the frame or its ID. Using this, you can switch to the frame if you are not sure about the index of the target frame. The other overloaded method is as follows:

```
WebDriver frame(WebElement frameElement)
```

The input parameter is the WebElement of the frame. Let's consider our code example: First, we have switched to our first frame and typed into the text field. Then, instead of directly switching to the second frame, we have come to the main or default content and then switched to the second frame. The code for that is as follows:

```
driver.switchTo().defaultContent();
```

This is very important. If you don't do this and try to switch to the second frame while you are still in the first frame, your WebDriver will complain, saying that it couldn't find a frame with index 1. This is because the WebDriver searches for the second frame in the context of the first frame, which is obviously not available. So, you have to first come to the top-level container and switch to the frame you are interested in.

After switching to the default content, you can now switch to the second frame using the following code:

```
driver.switchTo().frame(1);
```

Thus, you can switch between the frames and execute the corresponding WebDriver actions.

Handling alerts

Apart from switching between windows and frames, you may have to handle various modal dialogs in a web application. For this, WebDriver provides an API to handle alert dialogs. The API for that is as follows:

```
Alert alert()
```

The preceding method will switch to the currently active modal dialog on the web page. This returns an Alert instance, where appropriate actions can be taken on that dialog. If there is no dialog currently present, and you invoke this API, it throws back a NoAlertPresentException.

The Alert interface contains a number of APIs to execute different actions. The following list discusses them, one after the other:

- void accept(): This is equivalent to the **OK** button action on the dialog. The corresponding **OK** button actions are invoked when the accept() action is taken on a dialog.
- void dismiss(): This is equivalent to clicking on the **CANCEL** action button.
- java.lang.String getText(): This will return the text that appears on the dialog. This can be used if you want to evaluate the text on the modal dialog.
- void sendKeys(java.lang.String keysToSend): This will allow the developer to type in some text into the alert if the alert has some provision for it.

Exploring Navigate

As we know, WebDriver talks to individual browsers natively. This way it has better control, not just over the web page, but over the browser itself. **Navigate** is one such feature of WebDriver that allows the test script developer to work with the browser's back, forward, and refresh controls. As users of a web application, quite often, we use the browser's back and forward controls to navigate between the pages of a single application, or, sometimes, multiple applications. As a test-script developer, you may want to develop tests that observe the behavior of the application when browser navigation buttons are clicked, especially the **back** button. For example, if you use your navigation button in a banking application, the session should expire and the user should be logged out. So, using the WebDriver's navigation feature, you can emulate those actions.

The method that is used for this purpose is navigate(). The following is its API syntax:

```
WebDriver.Navigation navigate()
```

Obviously, there is no input parameter for this method, but the return type is the WebDriver.Navigation interface, which contains all of the browser navigation options that help you navigate through your browser's history.

Now let's see a code example and then analyze the code:

```
@Test
public void searchProduct() {
    driver.navigate().to("http://demo-store.seleniumacademy.com/");

    // find search box and enter search string
    WebElement searchBox = driver.findElement(By.name("q"));

    searchBox.sendKeys("Phones");

    WebElement searchButton =
            driver.findElement(By.className("search-button"));

    searchButton.click();

    assertThat(driver.getTitle())
            .isEqualTo("Search results for: 'Phones'");

    driver.navigate().back();
    driver.navigate().forward();
    driver.navigate().refresh();
}
```

The preceding code opens the demo application's Homepage, and, at first, searches for `Phone`; then, after the search results are loaded. Now that we have a navigation history created in the browser, it uses WebDriver navigation to go back in the browser history, and then go forward and refresh the page.

Let's analyze the navigation methods used in the preceding code. The line of code that initially loads the demo application's Homepage uses the `to()` method of the `Navigation` class, as follows:

```
driver.navigate().to("http://demo-store.seleniumacademy.com/");
```

Here, the `driver.navigate()` method returns the `WebDriver.Navigation` interface on which the `to()` method is used to navigate to a web URL.

The API syntax is as follows:

```
void to(java.lang.String url)
```

The input parameter for this method is the `url` string that has to be loaded in the browser. This method will load the page in the browser by using the `HTTP GET` operation, and it will block everything else until the page is completely loaded. This method is the same as the `driver.get(String url)` method.

The `WebDriver.Navigation` interface also provides an overloaded method of this `to()` method to make it easy to pass the URL. The API syntax for it is as follows:

```
void to(java.net.URL url)
```

Next, in the code example, we did a search for `Phone`. Then, we tried to use Navigation's `back()` method to emulate our browser's **back** button, using the following line of code:

```
driver.navigate().back();
```

This will take the browser to the home page. The API syntax for this method is pretty straightforward; it's as follows:

```
void back()
```

This method doesn't take any input and doesn't return anything as well, but it takes the browser one level back in its history.

Then, the next method in the navigation is the `forward()` method, which is pretty much similar to the `back()` method, but it takes the browser one level in the opposite direction. In the preceding code example, the following is invoked:

```
driver.navigate().forward();
```

The API syntax for the method is as follows:

```
void forward()
```

This method doesn't take any input, and doesn't return anything either, but it takes the browser one level forward in its history.

The last line of code in the code example uses the `refresh()` method of WebDriver's navigation:

```
driver.navigate().refresh();
```

This method will reload the current URL to emulate the browser's *refresh* (*F5* key) action. The API syntax is as follows:

```
void refresh()
```

As you can see, the syntax is very similar to the `back()` and `forward()` methods, and this method will reload the current URL. Hence, these are the various methods WebDriver provides developers to emulate some browser actions.

Waiting for WebElements to load

If you have a previous UI automation experience, I'm sure you would have come across a situation where your test script couldn't find an element on the web page because the web page was still loading. This could happen due to various reasons. One classic example is when the application server or web server is serving the page too slowly due to resource constraints; the other could be when you are accessing the page on a very slow network. The reason could be that the element on the web page is not loaded by the time your test script tries to find it. This is where you have to calculate and configure the average wait time for your test scripts to wait for WebElements to load on the web page.

WebDriver provides test-script developers with a very handy feature to manage wait time. *Wait time* is the time your driver will wait for the WebElement to load, before it gives up and throws `NoSuchElementException`. Remember, in Chapter 1, *Introducing WebDriver and WebElements*, we discussed the `findElement(By by)` method that throws a `NoSuchElementException` when it cannot find the target WebElement.

There are two ways by which you can make the WebDriver wait for WebElement. They are **Implicit Wait Time** and **Explicit Wait Time**. Implicit timeouts are common to all the WebElements and have a global timeout period associated with them, but the explicit timeouts can be configured to individual WebElements. Let's discuss each of them here.

Implicit wait time

Implicit wait time is used when you want to configure the WebDriver's wait time as a whole for the application under test. Imagine you have hosted a web application on a local server and on a remote server. Obviously, the time to load for a web page hosted on a local server would be less than the time for the same page hosted on a remote server, due to network latency. Now, if you want to execute your test cases against each of them, you may have to configure the wait time accordingly, such that your test case doesn't end up spending more time waiting for the page, or spend nowhere near enough time, and timeout. To handle these kinds of wait-time issues, WebDriver provides an option to set the implicit wait time for all of the operations that the driver does using the `manage()` method.

Let's see a code example of implicit wait time:

```
driver = new ChromeDriver();
driver.navigate().to("http://demo-store.seleniumacademy.com/");
driver.manage().timeouts().implicitlyWait(10, TimeUnit.SECONDS);
```

Let's analyze the following highlighted line of code:

```
driver.manage().timeouts().implicitlyWait(10, TimeUnit.SECONDS);
```

Here, `driver.manage().timeouts()` returns the `WebDriver.Timeouts` interface, which declares a method named `implicitlyWait`, which is where you specify the amount of time the driver should wait when searching for a WebElement on a web page if it is not immediately present. Periodically, the WebDriver will poll for the WebElement on the web page, until the maximum wait time specified to the previous method is over. In the preceding code, 10 seconds is the maximum wait time your driver will wait for any WebElement to load on your browser. If it loads within this time period, WebDriver proceeds with the rest of the code; otherwise, it will throw `NoSuchElementException`.

Use this method when you want to specify a maximum wait time, which is generally common for most of the WebElements on your web application. The various factors that influence the performance of your page are network bandwidth, server configuration, and so on. Based on those conditions, as a developer of your WebDriver test cases, you have to arrive at a value for the maximum implicit wait time, such that your test cases don't take too long to execute, and, at the same time, don't timeout very frequently.

Explicit wait time

Implicit timeout is generic to all the WebElements of a web page. But, if you have one specific WebElement in your application, where you want to wait for a very long time, this approach may not work. Setting the implicit wait time to the value of this very long time period will delay your entire test suite execution. So, you have to make an exception for only a particular case, such as this WebElement. To handle such scenarios, WebDriver has an explicit wait time for a WebElement.

So, let's see how you can wait for a particular WebElement using WebDriver, with the following code:

```
WebElement searchBox = (new WebDriverWait(driver, 20))
        .until((ExpectedCondition<WebElement>) d ->
d.findElement(By.name("q")));
```

The highlighted code is where we have created a conditional wait for a particular WebElement. The `ExpectedCondition` interface can be used to apply the conditional wait to a WebElement. Here, WebDriver will wait for a maximum of 20 seconds for this particular WebElement. The implicit timeout doesn't get applied for this WebElement. If the WebElement doesn't load within the 20 seconds maximum wait time, as we know, the driver throws a `NoSuchElementException`. Thus, you can override the implicit wait time exclusively for the WebElements you think will take more time, by using this handy explicit wait time.

Handling cookies

Let's say you are automating the demo application. There could be many scenarios you want to automate, such as searching for products, adding products to the shopping cart, checkout, returns, and so on. For all these actions, one common thing is to have to log into the demo application in each of the test cases. So, logging into the application in every test case of yours will increase the overall test execution time significantly. To reduce the execution time of your test cases, you can actually skip signing in for every test case. This can be done by signing in once and writing all the cookies of that domain into a file. From the next login onward, you can actually load the cookies from the file and add them to the driver.

To fetch all the cookies that are loaded for a web page, WebDriver provides the following method:

```
driver.manage().getCookies()
```

This will return all the cookies that the web page stores in the current session. Each cookie is associated with a name, value, domain, path, expiry, and the status of whether it is secure or not. The server to validate a client cookie parses all of these values. Now, we will store all of this information for each cookie in a file so that our individual test cases read from this file and load that information into the driver. Hence, you can skip the login, because once your driver session has this information in it, the application server treats your browser session as authenticated and directly takes you to your requested URL. The following is a quick code to store the cookie information:

```
public class StoreCookieInfo {
    WebDriver driver;

    @BeforeMethod
    public void setup() throws IOException {
        System.setProperty("webdriver.chrome.driver",
                "./src/test/resources/drivers/chromedriver");
```

```
            driver = new ChromeDriver();
driver.get("http://demo-
store.seleniumacademy.com/customer/account/login/");
    }

    @Test
    public void storeCookies() {
driver.findElement(By.id("email")).sendKeys("user@seleniumacademy.com");
        driver.findElement(By.id("pass")).sendKeys("tester");
        driver.findElement(By.id("send2")).submit();

        File dataFile = new File("./target/browser.data");
        try {
            dataFile.delete();
            dataFile.createNewFile();
            FileWriter fos = new FileWriter(dataFile);
            BufferedWriter bos = new BufferedWriter(fos);
            for (Cookie ck : driver.manage().getCookies()) {
                bos.write((ck.getName() + ";" + ck.getValue() + ";" + ck.
                    getDomain()
                    + ";" + ck.getPath() + ";" + ck.getExpiry() + ";" +
ck.

                    isSecure()));
                bos.newLine();
            }
            bos.flush();
            bos.close();
            fos.close();
        } catch (Exception ex) {
            ex.printStackTrace();
        }
    }

    @AfterMethod
    public void tearDown() {
        driver.quit();
    }
}
```

From now on, for every test case or a set of test cases, load the cookie information from the browser.data file, and add it to the driver using the following method:

```
driver.manage().addCookie(ck);
```

After you add this information to your browser session and go to the dashboard page, it will automatically redirect you to the home page, without asking for a login, thus avoiding a login every time, for every test case. The code that adds all of the previous cookies to the driver is as follows:

```java
public class LoadCookieInfo {
    WebDriver driver;

    @BeforeMethod
    public void setup() throws IOException {
        System.setProperty("webdriver.chrome.driver",
                "./src/test/resources/drivers/chromedriver");
        driver = new ChromeDriver();
        driver.get("http://demo-store.seleniumacademy.com");
    }

    @Test
    public void loadCookies() {
        try {
            File dataFile = new File("./target/browser.data");
            FileReader fr = new FileReader(dataFile);
            BufferedReader br = new BufferedReader(fr);
            String line;
            while ((line = br.readLine()) != null) {
                StringTokenizer str = new StringTokenizer(line, ";");
                while (str.hasMoreTokens()) {
                    String name = str.nextToken();
                    String value = str.nextToken();
                    String domain = str.nextToken();
                    String path = str.nextToken();
                    Date expiry = null;
                    String dt;
                    if (!(dt = str.nextToken()).equals("null")) {
                        SimpleDateFormat formatter =
                                new SimpleDateFormat("E MMM d HH:mm:ss z
yyyy");
                        expiry = formatter.parse(dt);
                    }

                    boolean isSecure = new Boolean(str.nextToken()).
                            booleanValue();
                    Cookie ck = new Cookie(name, value, domain, path,
expiry, isSecure);
                    driver.manage().addCookie(ck);
                }
            }

    driver.get("http://demo-
```

```
store.seleniumacademy.com/customer/account/index/");
            assertThat(driver.findElement(By.cssSelector("div.page-
title")).getText())
                    .isEqualTo("MY DASHBOARD");

        } catch (Exception ex) {
            ex.printStackTrace();
        }
    }

    @AfterMethod
    public void tearDown() {
        driver.quit();
    }
}
```

Hence, we can be directly taken to the home page without logging in again and again. As you can see, after creating the driver instance, we have the following line:

```
driver.get("http://demo-store.seleniumacademy.com");
```

Ideally, this line should be visible after we have set the cookies to the driver. But the reason it is at the top is that the WebDriver doesn't allow you to set the cookies directly to this session, because it treats those cookies as if they were from a different domain. Try removing the previous line of code and execute it, and you will see the error. So, initially, you will try to visit the home page to set the domain value of the driver to the application server domain and load all the cookies. When you execute this code, initially, you will see the home page of the application.

Hence, you can avoid entering the username and the password on the server, validating them again and again for each test, and thereby save a lot of time, by using the WebDriver's cookies feature.

Summary

In this chapter, we discussed various features of WebDriver, such as capturing screenshots and handling Windows and Frames. We also discussed implicit and explicit wait conditions for synchronization, and we used Navigation and the cookies API. Using these features will help you test your target web application more effectively, by designing more innovative test frameworks and test cases. In the next chapter, we will look at the **Actions** API to perform user interaction using keyboard and mouse events.

Questions

1. Which are the different formats we can use to output a screenshot?
2. How can we switch to another browser tab with Selenium?
3. True or false: The `defaultContent()` method will switch to the previously selected frame.
4. What navigation methods are available with Selenium?
5. How can we add a cookie using Selenium?
6. Explain the difference between an implicit wait and an explicit wait.

Further information

You can check the following links for more information about the topics covered in this chapter:

- You can find out more about how you can use a set of predefined expected conditions while using an explicit wait at `https://seleniumhq.github.io/selenium/docs/api/java/org/openqa/selenium/support/ui/ExpectedConditions.html`
- You can read more about WebDriver's features in Chapter 4, *Working with Selenium API* and Chapter 5 , *Synchronizing Tests*, in *Selenium Testing Tools Cookbook*, 2nd Edition, by Unmesh Gundecha, Packt Publications.

4
Exploring Advanced Interactions of WebDriver

In the previous chapter, we discussed the WebDriver interface and its features, including taking screenshots, working with Windows, frames, alerts, cookies, and synchronizing tests. In this chapter, we will go through some advanced ways of performing actions on WebElements. We will learn how to perform actions, using the actions API of Selenium WebDriver, including the following:

- Complex mouse actions, such as moving the mouse, double-clicking, and dragging and dropping
- Keyboard shortcuts

Understanding the build and perform actions

We know how to perform some basic actions, such as clicking on a button and typing text into a textbox; however, there are many scenarios where we have to perform multiple actions at the same time, for example, keeping the *Shift* button pressed and typing text for uppercase letters, and the dragging and dropping mouse actions.

Let's see a simple scenario here. Open the `http://guidebook.seleniumacademy.com/Selectable.html`. A box of tiles numbered 1 to 12 will appear, as seen in this screenshot:

If you inspect the elements with browser developer tools, you will see an ordered list tag:

```
<ol id="selectable" class="ui-selectable">
    <li class="ui-state-default ui-selectee" name="one">1</li>
    <li class="ui-state-default ui-selectee" name="two">2</li>
    <li class="ui-state-default ui-selectee" name="three">3</li>
    <li class="ui-state-default ui-selectee" name="four">4</li>
    <li class="ui-state-default ui-selectee" name="five">5</li>
    <li class="ui-state-default ui-selectee" name="six">6</li>
    <li class="ui-state-default ui-selectee" name="seven">7</li>
    <li class="ui-state-default ui-selectee" name="eight">8</li>
    <li class="ui-state-default ui-selectee" name="nine">9</li>
    <li class="ui-state-default ui-selectee" name="ten">10</li>
    <li class="ui-state-default ui-selectee" name="eleven">11</li>
    <li class="ui-state-default ui-selectee" name="twelve">12</li>
</ol>
```

If you click a number, its background color changes to orange. Try selecting the tiles 1, 3, and 5. You do that by holding down *Ctrl* + tile 1 + tile 3 + tile 5. This involves performing multiple actions, that is, holding *Ctrl* continuously and clicking on tiles 1, 3, and 5. How do we perform these multiple actions using WebDriver? The following code demonstrates how:

```
@Test
public void shouldPerformCompositeAction() {

    driver.get("http://guidebook.seleniumacademy.com/Selectable.html");
```

```
WebElement one = driver.findElement(By.name("one"));
WebElement three = driver.findElement(By.name("three"));
WebElement five = driver.findElement(By.name("five"));

// Add all the actions into the Actions builder.
Actions actions = new Actions(driver);
actions.keyDown(Keys.CONTROL)
        .click(one)
        .click(three)
        .click(five)
        .keyUp(Keys.CONTROL);

// Generate the composite action.
Action compositeAction = actions.build();

// Perform the composite action.
compositeAction.perform();
}
```

Now, if you refer to the code, we are getting introduced to a new class named `Actions`. This `Actions` class is the one that is used to emulate all the complex user events. Using this, the developer of the test script could combine all the necessary user gestures into one composite action. We have declared all the actions that are to be executed to achieve the functionality of clicking on the numbers 1, 3, and 5. Once all the actions are grouped together, we build that into a composite action. `Action` is an interface that has only the `perform()` method, which executes the composite action. When we execute the test, tiles 1, 3, and 5 will be selected one by one. Finally, tile 5 will be selected, as shown in this screenshot:

1	2	3	4
5	6	7	8
9	10	11	12

So, to make WebDriver perform multiple actions at the same time, you need to follow a three-step process of using the user-facing API of the actions class to group all the actions, then build the composite action, and perform the action. This process can be made into a two-step process, as the `perform()` method internally calls the `build()` method. So the previous code will look as follows:

```
@Test
public void shouldPerformAction() {

    driver.get("http://guidebook.seleniumacademy.com/Selectable.html");

    WebElement one = driver.findElement(By.name("one"));
    WebElement three = driver.findElement(By.name("three"));
    WebElement five = driver.findElement(By.name("five"));

    // Add all the actions into the Actions builder.
    Actions actions = new Actions(driver);
    actions.keyDown(Keys.CONTROL)
            .click(one)
            .click(three)
            .click(five)
            .keyUp(Keys.CONTROL);

    // Perform the action
    actions.perform();
}
```

In the preceding code, we have directly invoked the `perform()` method on the `Actions` instance, which internally calls the `build()` method to create a composite action before executing it. In the subsequent sections of this chapter, we will take a closer look at the `Actions` class. All the actions are basically divided into two categories: mouse-based actions and keyboard-based actions. In the following sections, we will discuss all the actions that are specific to the mouse and keyboard available in the `Actions` class.

Learning mouse based interactions

There are around eight different mouse actions that can be performed using the actions class. We will see each of their syntax and a working example.

The moveByOffset action

The `moveByOffset()` method is used to move the mouse from its current position to another point on the web page. Developers can specify the *x* distance and the *y* distance the mouse has to be moved. When the page is loaded, generally the initial position of the mouse would be (0, 0), unless there is an explicit focus declared by the page.

The API syntax for the `moveByOffset()` method is as follows:

```
public Actions moveByOffset(int xOffSet, int yOffSet)
```

In the preceding code, `xOffSet` is the input parameter providing the WebDriver the amount of offset to be moved along the *x* axis. A positive value is used to move the cursor to the right, and a negative value is used to move the cursor to the left.

`yOffSet` is the input parameter providing the WebDriver the amount of offset to be moved along the *y* axis. A positive value is used to move the cursor down along the *y* axis, and a negative value is used to move the cursor toward the top.

When the `xOffSet` and `yOffSet` values result in moving the cursor out of the document, a `MoveTargetOutOfBounds` exception is raised.

Let's see a working example of it. The objective of the following code is to move the cursor on to tile 3 on the web page:

```
@Test
public void shouldMoveByOffSet() {

    driver.get("http://guidebook.seleniumacademy.com/Selectable.html");

    WebElement three = driver.findElement(By.name("three"));
    System.out.println("X coordinate: " + three.getLocation().getX()
            + ", Y coordinate: " + three.getLocation().getY());
    Actions actions = new Actions(driver);
    actions.moveByOffset(three.getLocation().getX() + 1, three.
            getLocation().getY() + 1);
    actions.perform();
}
```

The output will be as follows:

We have added +1 to the coordinates, because if you observe the element in Firebug, we have a style border of 1 px. The border is a CSS-style attribute, which when applied to an element will add a border of the specified color around the element, with the specified amount of thickness. Though the previous code does move your mouse over tile 3, we don't realize this, because we are not performing any action there. We will see this shortly, when we use the `moveByOffset()` method in combination with the `click()` method.

The click at current location action

The `click()` method is used to simulate the left-click of your mouse at its current point of location. This method doesn't really realize where or on which element it is clicking. It just clicks wherever it is at that point in time. Hence, this method is used in combination with some other action, rather than independently, to create a composite action.

The API syntax for the `click()` method is as follows:

```
public Actions click().
```

The click() method doesn't really have any context about where it is performing its action; hence, it doesn't take any input parameter. Let's see a code example of the click() method:

```
@Test
public void shouldMoveByOffSetAndClick() {

    driver.get("http://guidebook.seleniumacademy.com/Selectable.html");

    WebElement seven = driver.findElement(By.name("seven"));
    System.out.println("X coordinate: " + seven.getLocation().getX() +
            ", Y coordinate: " + seven.getLocation().getY());
    Actions actions = new Actions(driver);
    actions.moveByOffset(seven.getLocation().getX() + 1, seven.
            getLocation().getY() + 1).click();
    actions.perform();
}
```

In the above example we have used a combination of the moveByOffset() and click() methods to move the cursor from point (0, 0) to the point of tile 7. Because the initial position of the mouse is (0, 0), the x, y offset provided for the moveByOffset() method is nothing but the location of the tile 7 element. Now let's try to move the cursor from tile 1 to tile 11, and from there to tile 5, and see how the code looks. Before we get into the code, let's inspect the Selectable.html page using Firebug. The following is the style of each tile:

```
#selectable li {
    float: left;
    font-size: 4em;
    height: 80px;
    text-align: center;
    width: 100px;
}
.ui-state-default, .ui-widget-content .ui-state-default, .ui-widgetheader
.ui-state-default {
    background: url("images/ui-bg_glass_75_e6e6e6_1x400.png") repeat-x
    scroll 50% 50% #E6E6E6;
    border: 1px solid #D3D3D3;
    color: #555555;
    font-weight: normal;
}
```

The three elements with which we are concerned for our offset movement in the preceding style code are: height, width, and the border thickness. Here, the height value is 80px, the width value is 100px, and the border value is 1px. Use these three factors to calculate the offset to navigate from one tile to the other. Note that the border thickness between any two tiles will result in 2 px, that is, 1 px from each tile. The following is the code that uses the moveByOffset and click() methods to navigate from tile 1 to tile 11, and from there to tile 5:

```
@Test
public void shouldMoveByOffSetAndClickMultiple() {

    driver.get("http://guidebook.seleniumacademy.com/Selectable.html");

    WebElement one = driver.findElement(By.name("one"));
    WebElement eleven = driver.findElement(By.name("eleven"));
    WebElement five = driver.findElement(By.name("five"));
    int border = 1;
    int tileWidth = 100;
    int tileHeight = 80;
    Actions actions = new Actions(driver);

    //Click on One
    actions.moveByOffset(one.getLocation().getX() + border,
one.getLocation().getY() + border).click();
    actions.build().perform();

    // Click on Eleven
    actions.moveByOffset(2 * tileWidth + 4 * border, 2 * tileHeight + 4 *
border).click();
    actions.build().perform();

    //Click on Five
    actions.moveByOffset(-2 * tileWidth - 4 * border, -tileHeight - 2 *
border).
            click();
    actions.build().perform();
}
```

The click on a WebElement action

We have seen how to click a WebElement by calculating the offset to it. This process may not be needed every time, especially when the WebElement has its own identifiers, such as a name or an ID. We can use another overloaded version of the click() method to click directly on the WebElement.

The API syntax for clicking on a WebElement is as follows:

```
public Actions click(WebElement onElement)
```

The input parameter for this method is an instance of the WebElement on which the click action should be performed. This method, like all the other methods in the Actions class, will return an Actions instance.

Now let's try to modify the previous code example to use the click(WebElement) method, instead of using the moveByOffset() method, to move to the location of the WebElement and click on it using the click() method:

```
@Test
public void shouldClickOnElement() {

    driver.get("http://guidebook.seleniumacademy.com/Selectable.html");

    WebElement one = driver.findElement(By.name("one"));
    WebElement eleven = driver.findElement(By.name("eleven"));
    WebElement five = driver.findElement(By.name("five"));
    Actions actions = new Actions(driver);

    //Click on One
    actions.click(one);
    actions.build().perform();

    // Click on Eleven
    actions.click(eleven);
    actions.build().perform();

    //Click on Five
    actions.click(five);
    actions.build().perform();
}
```

Now the `moveByOffset()` method has been replaced by the `click(WebElement)` method, and, all of a sudden, the complex coordinate geometry has been removed from the code. If you're a tester, this is one more good reason to push your developers to provide identifiers for the WebElements.

If you observe the previous examples for the `moveByOffset` and `click` methods, all the operations of moving the mouse and clicking on tiles 1, 11, and 5 are built separately and performed separately. This is not how we use our `Actions` class. You can actually build all these actions together and then perform them. So, the preceding code will turn out to be as follows:

```
@Test
public void shouldClickOnElement() {

    driver.get("http://guidebook.seleniumacademy.com/Selectable.html");

    WebElement one = driver.findElement(By.name("one"));
    WebElement eleven = driver.findElement(By.name("eleven"));
    WebElement five = driver.findElement(By.name("five"));
    Actions actions = new Actions(driver);

    actions.click(one)
            .click(eleven)
            .click(five)
            .build().perform();
}
```

The click and hold at current location action

The `clickAndHold()` method is another method of the actions class that left-clicks on an element and holds it without releasing the left button of the mouse. This method will be useful when executing operations such as drag and drop. This method is one of the variants of the `clickAndHold()` method that the actions class provides. We will discuss the other variant in the next section.

Now open the `Sortable.html` file that came with the book. You can see that the tiles can be moved from one position to the other. Now let's try to move tile 3 to the position of tile 2. The sequence of steps that are involved to do this are the following:

1. Move the cursor to the position of tile 3.
2. Click and hold tile 3.
3. Move the cursor in this position to tile 2's location.

Now let's see how this can be accomplished, using the WebDriver's `clickAndHold()` method:

```
@Test
public void shouldClickAndHold() {

    driver.get("http://guidebook.seleniumacademy.com/Sortable.html");

    Actions actions = new Actions(driver);

    //Move tile3 to the position of tile2
    actions.moveByOffset(200, 20)
            .clickAndHold()
            .moveByOffset(120, 0)
            .perform();
}
```

Let's analyze the following line of code:

```
actions.moveByOffset(200, 20)
            .clickAndHold()
            .moveByOffset(120, 0)
            .perform();
```

The tile movement will be similar to the following screenshot:

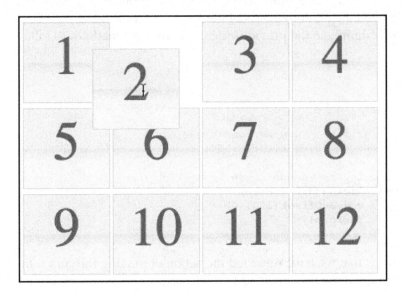

First, we move the cursor to the location of tile 3. Then, we click and hold tile 3. Then, we move the cursor by 120px horizontally to the position of tile 2. The last line performs all the preceding actions. Now execute this in your eclipse and see what happens. If you observe closely, tile 3 doesn't properly go into the position of tile 2. This is because we are yet to release the left button. We just commanded the WebDriver to click and hold, but not to release.

The click and hold a WebElement action

In the previous section, we have seen the clickAndHold() method, which will click and hold a WebElement at the current position of the cursor. It doesn't care about which element it is dealing with. So, if we want to deal with a particular WebElement on the web page, we have to first move the cursor to the appropriate position and then perform the clickAndHold() action. To avoid the hassle of moving the cursor geometrically, WebDriver provides the developers with another variant or overloaded method of the clickAndHold() method that takes the WebElement as input.

The API syntax is this:

```
public Actions clickAndHold(WebElement onElement)
```

The input parameter for this method is the WebElement that has to be clicked and held. The return type, as in all the other methods of the Actions class, is the Actions instance. Now let's refactor the example in the previous section to use this method, as follows:

```
@Test
public void shouldClickAndHoldElement() {

    driver.get("http://guidebook.seleniumacademy.com/Sortable.html");

    Actions actions = new Actions(driver);
    WebElement three = driver.findElement(By.name("three"));

    //Move tile3 to the position of tile2
    actions.clickAndHold(three)
            .moveByOffset(120, 0)
            .perform();
}
```

The only change is that we have removed the action of moving the cursor to the (200, 20) position and provided the WebElement to the clickAndHold() method that will take care of identifying the WebElement.

The release at current location action

Now, in the previous example, we have seen how to click and hold an element. The ultimate action that has to be taken on a held WebElement is to release it so that the element can be dropped or released from the mouse. The `release()` method is the one that can release the left mouse button on a WebElement.

The API syntax for the `release()` method is as follows: `public Actions release()`.

The preceding method doesn't take any input parameter and returns the `Actions` class instance.

Now, let's modify the previous code to include the `release` action in it:

```
@Test
public void shouldClickAndHoldAndRelease() {

    driver.get("http://guidebook.seleniumacademy.com/Sortable.html");

    WebElement three = driver.findElement(By.name("three"));
    Actions actions = new Actions(driver);

    //Move tile3 to the position of tile2
    actions.clickAndHold(three)
            .moveByOffset(120, 0)
            .release()
            .perform();
}
```

The preceding code will make sure that the mouse is released at the specified location.

The release on another WebElement action

This is an overloaded version of the `release()` method. Using this, you can actually release the currently held WebElement in the middle of another WebElement. In this way, we don't have to calculate the offset of the target WebElement from the held WebElement.

The API syntax is as follows:

```
public Actions release(WebElement onElement)
```

The input parameter for the preceding method is obviously the target WebElement, where the held WebElement should be dropped. The return type is the instance of the `Actions` class.

Let's modify the preceding code example to use this method:

```
@Test
public void shouldClickAndHoldAndReleaseOnElement() {

    driver.get("http://guidebook.seleniumacademy.com/Sortable.html");

    WebElement three = driver.findElement(By.name("three"));
    WebElement two = driver.findElement(By.name("two"));
    Actions actions = new Actions(driver);

    //Move tile3 to the position of tile2
    actions.clickAndHold(three)
            .release(two)
            .perform();
}
```

Look at how simple the preceding code is. We have removed all the `moveByOffset` code and added the `release()` method that takes the WebElement with the name `two` as the input parameter.

Invoking the `release()` or `release(WebElement)` methods without calling the `clickAndHold()` method will result in an undefined behavior.

The moveToElement action

The `moveToElement()` method is another method of WebDriver that helps us to move the mouse cursor to a WebElement on the web page.

The API syntax for the `moveToElement()` method is as follows:

```
public Actions moveToElement(WebElement toElement)
```

The input parameter for the preceding method is the target WebElement, where the mouse should be moved. Now go back to the clickAndHold at *current location action* section of this chapter and try to modify the code to use this method. The following is the code we have written in *The click-and-hold-at-current-location action* section:

```
@Test
public void shouldClickAndHold() {

    driver.get("http://guidebook.seleniumacademy.com/Sortable.html");

    Actions actions = new Actions(driver);

    //Move tile3 to the position of tile2
    actions.moveByOffset(200, 20)
            .clickAndHold()
            .moveByOffset(120, 0)
            .perform();
}
```

In the preceding code, we will replace the moveByOffset(x, y) method with the moveToElement(WebElement) method:

```
@Test
public void shouldClickAndHoldAndMove() {

    driver.get("http://guidebook.seleniumacademy.com/Sortable.html");

    WebElement three = driver.findElement(By.name("three"));
    Actions actions = new Actions(driver);

    //Move tile3 to the position of tile2
    actions.moveToElement(three)
            .clickAndHold()
            .moveByOffset(120, 0)
            .perform();
}
```

In the preceding code, we have moved to tile 3, clicked and held it, and then moved to the location of tile 2, by specifying its offset. If you want, you can add the release() method before the perform() method.

There might be a number of ways to achieve the same task. It is up to the user to choose the appropriate ones that best suit the given circumstances.

The dragAndDropBy action

There might be many instances where we may have to drag and drop components or WebElements of a web page. We can accomplish that by using many of the actions seen until now. But WebDriver has given us a convenient out-of-the-box method to use. Let's see its API syntax.

The API syntax for the dragAndDropBy() method is as follows:

```
public Actions dragAndDropBy(WebElement source, int xOffset,int yOffset)
```

The WebElement input parameter is the target WebElement to be dragged, the xOffset parameter is the horizontal offset to be moved, and the yOffset parameter is the vertical offset to be moved.

Let's see a code example for it. Open the HTML file, DragMe.html, provided with this book. It has a square box, as shown in the following screenshot:

You can actually drag that rectangle to any location on the web page. Let's see how we can do that, using WebDriver. The following is the code example for that:

```
@Test
public void shouldDrag() {

    driver.get("http://guidebook.seleniumacademy.com/DragMe.html");

    WebElement dragMe = driver.findElement(By.id("draggable"));
    Actions actions = new Actions(driver);
    actions.dragAndDropBy(dragMe, 300, 200).perform();
}
```

In the preceding code, dragMe is the WebElement that is identified by its id, and that is dragged 300px horizontally and 200px vertically. The following screenshot shows how an element is dragged from this position:

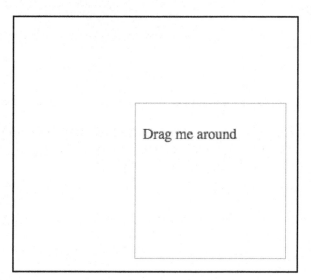

The dragAndDrop action

The dragAndDrop() method is similar to the dragAndDropBy() method. The only difference being that, instead of moving the WebElement by an offset, we move it on to a target element.

The API syntax for the `dragAndDrop()` method is as follows:

```
public Actions dragAndDrop(WebElement source, WebElement target)
```

The input parameters for the preceding method are the WebElement source and the WebElement target, while the return type is the `Actions` class.

Let's see a working code example for it. Open the `DragAndDrop.html` file, which is provided with the book, with two square boxes, as shown in this screenshot:

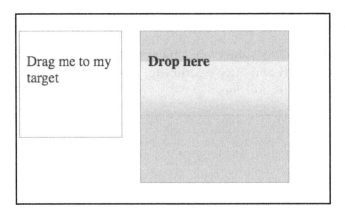

Here, we can actually drag the **Drag me to my target** rectangle to the **Drop here** rectangle. Try that. Let's see how that can be achieved, using WebDriver:

```
@Test
public void shouldDragAndDrop() {

    driver.get("http://guidebook.seleniumacademy.com/DragAndDrop.html");

    WebElement src = driver.findElement(By.id("draggable"));
    WebElement trgt = driver.findElement(By.id("droppable"));
    Actions actions = new Actions(driver);
    actions.dragAndDrop(src, trgt).perform();
}
```

In the preceding code, the source and target WebElements are identified by their IDs, and the `dragAndDrop()` method is used to drag one to the other. Here, out of the script with first square box dropped on the second box shown in the following screenshot:

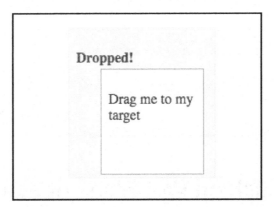

The double click at current location action

Moving on to another action that can be performed using a mouse, `doubleClick()` is another out- of-the-box method that WebDriver provides to emulate the double-clicking of the mouse. This method, like the `click()` method, comes in two flavors. One is double-clicking a WebElement, which we will discuss in next section; the second is clicking at the current location of the cursor, which will be discussed here.

The API syntax is as follows:

```
public Actions doubleClick()
```

Obviously, the preceding method doesn't take any input parameters, as it just clicks on the current cursor location and returns an actions class instance. Let's see how the previous code can be converted to use this method:

```
@Test
public void shouldDoubleClick() {

    driver.get("http://guidebook.seleniumacademy.com/DoubleClick.html");

    WebElement dblClick= driver.findElement(By.name("dblClick"));
    Actions actions = new Actions(driver);
    actions.moveToElement(dblClick).doubleClick().perform();
}
```

In the preceding code, we have used the `moveToElement(WebElement)` method to move the mouse to the location of the button element and just double-clicked at the current location. Here is the output after performing the double-click on the element on the sample page:

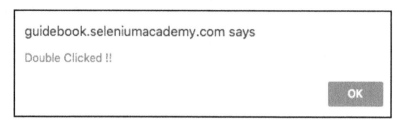

The double click on WebElement action

Now that we have seen a method that double-clicks at the current location, we will discuss another method that WebDriver provides to emulate the double-clicking of a WebElement.

The API syntax for the `doubleClick()` method is as follows:

```
public Actions doubleClick(WebElement onElement)
```

The input parameter for the preceding method is the target WebElement that has to be double-clicked, and the return type is the `Actions` class.

Let's see a code example for this. Open the `DoubleClick.html` file and *single*-click on the **Click Me** button. You shouldn't see anything happening. Now double-click on the button; you should see an alert saying **Double Clicked !!**. Now we will try to do the same thing using WebDriver. The following is the code to do that:

```
@Test
public void shouldDoubleClickElement() {
driver.get("http://guidebook.seleniumacademy.com/DoubleClick.html");

    WebElement dblClick = driver.findElement(By.name("dblClick"));
    Actions actions = new Actions(driver);
    actions.doubleClick(dblClick).perform();
}
```

After executing the preceding code, you should see an alert dialog saying that the button has been double-clicked.

The context click on WebElement action

The `contextClick()` method, also known as *right-click*, is quite common on many web pages these days. It displays a menu similar to this screenshot:

Context / Right click for Menu

    Item 1

    Item 2

    Item 3

    Item 4

    Item 5

    Item 6

This context menu can be accessed by a right-click of the mouse on the WebElement. WebDriver provides the developer with an option of emulating that action, using the `contextClick()` method. Like many other methods, this method has two variants as well. One is clicking on the current location and the other overloaded method is clicking on the WebElement. Let's discuss the context of clicking on WebElement here.

The API syntax for the `contextClick()` method is as follows:

```
public Actions contextClick(WebElement onElement)
```

The input parameter is obviously the WebElement that has to be right-clicked, and the return type is the `Actions` instance. As we do normally, its time to see a code example. If you open the `ContextClick.html` file, you can right-click on the text visible on the page, and it will display the context menu. Now clicking any item pops up an alert dialog stating which item has been clicked. Now let's see how to implement this in WebDriver, using the following code:

```
@Test
public void shouldContextClick() {

    driver.get("http://guidebook.seleniumacademy.com/ContextClick.html");

    WebElement contextMenu = driver.findElement(By.id("div-context"));
    Actions actions = new Actions(driver);
```

```
actions.contextClick(contextMenu)
        .click(driver.findElement(By.name("Item 4")))
        .perform();
}
```

In the preceding code, first we have right-clicked using the `contextClick()` method on the WebElement contextMenu, and then left-clicked on **Item 4** from the context menu. This should pop up an alert dialog saying **Item 4 Clicked**.

The context click at current location action

Now that we have seen context click on a WebElement, it's time to explore the `contextClick()` method at the current mouse location. The API syntax for the `contextClick()` method is as follows:

```
public Actions contextClick()
```

As expected, the preceding method doesn't expect any input parameter and returns the `Actions` instance. Let's see the necessary modifications needed for the previous example to use this method. The following is the code refactored to achieve this:

```
@Test
public void shouldContextClickAtCurrentLocation() {

    driver.get("http://guidebook.seleniumacademy.com/ContextClick.html");

    WebElement contextMenu = driver.findElement(By.id("div-context"));
    Actions actions = new Actions(driver);
    actions.moveToElement(contextMenu)
            .contextClick()
            .click(driver.findElement(By.name("Item 4")))
            .perform();
}
```

The preceding code first moves the cursor to the `div-context` WebElement and then context-clicks it.

Learning keyboard-based interactions

Until now, we have seen all the actions that can be taken using a mouse. Now it's time to look at some of the actions that are specific to the keyboard in the Actions class. Basically, there are three different actions that are available in the Actions class that are specific to the keyboard. They are the keyUp, keyDown, and sendKeys actions, each having two overloaded methods. One method is to execute the action directly on the WebElement, and the other is to just execute the method irrespective of its context.

The keyDown and keyUp actions

The keyDown() method is used to simulate the action of pressing and holding a key. The keys that we are referencing here are the *Shift*, *Ctrl*, and *Alt* keys. The keyUp() method is used to release the key that is already pressed using the keyDown() method. The API syntax for the keyDown() method is as follows:

```
public Actions keyDown(Keys theKey) throws IllegalArgumentException
```

An IllegalArgumentException is thrown when the passed key is not one of the *Shift*, *Ctrl*, and *Alt* keys. The API syntax for the keyUp() method is as follows:

```
public Actions keyUp(Keys theKey)
```

The keyUp action performed on a key, on which a keyDown action is not already being performed, will result in some unexpected results. So, we have to make sure we perform the keyUp action after a keyDown action is performed.

The sendKeys method

This is used to type in alphanumeric and special character keys into WebElements such as textbox, textarea, and so on. This is different than the
WebElement.sendKeys(CharSequence keysToSend) method, as this method expects the WebElements to have the focus before being called. The API syntax for the sendkeys() method is as follows:

```
public Actions sendKeys(CharSequence keysToSend)
```

We expect you to implement a couple of test scripts around these keyboard events using the keyUp, keyDown, and sendKeys() methods.

Summary

In this chapter, we have learned how to use the actions class to create a set of actions, and build them into a composite action to execute it in one pass, using the `perform()` method. In this way, we can aggregate a series of complex user actions into a single functionality, which can be executed in one pass. In the next `chapter`, we will learn WebDriver events and how we can listen and perform advanced actions, using WebDriver.

Questions

1. True or False – the drag and drop action requires the source element and the target element.
2. List the keyboard methods that we can perform using the actions API.
3. Which method of the actions API will help in performing a double-click operation?
4. Using the actions API, how we can perform a save option (that is to say, *Ctrl + S*)?
5. How can we open a context menu using the actions API?

Further information

You can check the following links for more information about the topics we covered in this chapter:

- Read more about Advanced User Interaction
  at `https://github.com/SeleniumHQ/selenium/wiki/Advanced-User-Interactions`
- See Chapter 4 : *Working with Selenium API* in *Selenium Testing Tools* Cookbook, second edition, by Unmesh Gundecha, and Chapter 6, *Utilizing the Advanced User Interactions API* in *Master Selenium WebDriver*, by Mark Collin, for more examples of the actions API

5
Understanding WebDriver Events

Selenium WebDriver provides an API for tracking the various events that happen when test scripts are executed using WebDriver. Many navigation events get fired before and after a WebDriver internal event occurs (such as before and after navigating to a URL, and before and after browser back-navigation) and these can be tracked and captured. To throw an event, WebDriver gives you a class named `EventFiringWebDriver`, and to catch that event, it provides the test-script developer with an interface named `WebDriverEventListener`. The test-script developer should provide its own implementations for the overridden methods from the interface. In this chapter, we will look at the following topics:

- How to listen to and handle various browser-navigation events by using EventFiringWebDriver
- How to listen to and handle web-element action events that get triggered during the execution of test scripts
- Adding additional features to WebDriver to capture performance or accessibility testing

Introducing the eventFiringWebDriver and eventListener classes

The `EventFiringWebDriver` class is a wrapper around the WebDriver that gives the driver the capability to fire events. The `EventListener` class, on the other hand, waits to listen to `EventFiringWebDriver` and handles all of the events that are dispatched. There can be more than one listener waiting to hear from the `EventFiringWebDriver` class for an event to fire. All of the event listeners should be registered with the `EventFiringWebDriver` class to get notified.

The following flow diagram explains what has to be done to capture all of the events raised by `EventFiringWebDriver` during the execution of test cases:

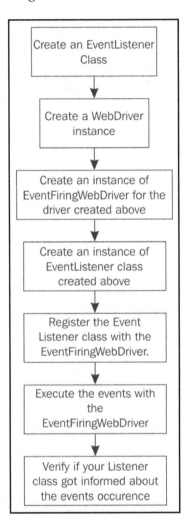

Creating an instance of EventListener

The EventListener class handles all of the events that are dispatched by the EventFiringWebDriver class. There are two ways to create an EventListener class:

- By implementing the WebDriverEventListener interface.
- By extending the AbstractWebDriverEventListener class provided in the WebDriver library.

It is up to you, as a test-script developer, to choose which way to go.

Implementing WebDriverEventListener

The WebDriverEventListener interface has all the event methods declared. The EventFiringWebDriver class, as soon as it realizes an event has occurred, invokes the registered method of WebDriverEventListener. Here, we have created an IAmTheEventListener named class and have implemented WebDriverEventListener. Now we need to provide implementation for all the methods declared in it. Currently, in WebDriverEventListener, there are 15 methods. We will discuss each one of them shortly. Make sure the IDE provides us with the dummy implementation of these methods. The class that we have created with all 15 overridden methods is as follows (we have provided implementations for a couple of methods as an example):

```
public class IAmTheEventListener implements WebDriverEventListener {
    @Override
    public void beforeAlertAccept(WebDriver webDriver) {
    }

    @Override
    public void afterAlertAccept(WebDriver webDriver) {

    }

    @Override
    public void afterAlertDismiss(WebDriver webDriver) {

    }

    @Override
    public void beforeAlertDismiss(WebDriver webDriver) {
    }

    @Override
```

```java
    public void beforeNavigateTo(String url, WebDriver webDriver) {
        System.out.println("Before Navigate To " + url);
    }

    @Override
    public void afterNavigateTo(String s, WebDriver webDriver) {
        System.out.println("Before Navigate Back. Right now I'm at "
                + webDriver.getCurrentUrl());
    }

    @Override
    public void beforeNavigateBack(WebDriver webDriver) {
    }

    @Override
    public void afterNavigateBack(WebDriver webDriver) {
    }

    @Override
    public void beforeNavigateForward(WebDriver webDriver) {
    }

    @Override
    public void afterNavigateForward(WebDriver webDriver) {
    }

    @Override
    public void beforeNavigateRefresh(WebDriver webDriver)      {
    }

    @Override
    public void afterNavigateRefresh(WebDriver webDriver) {
    }

    @Override
    public void beforeFindBy(By by, WebElement webElement, WebDriver
webDriver) {
    }

    @Override
    public void afterFindBy(By by, WebElement webElement, WebDriver
webDriver) {
    }

    @Override
    public void beforeClickOn(WebElement webElement, WebDriver webDriver) {
    }
```

```
    @Override
    public void afterClickOn(WebElement webElement, WebDriver webDriver) {
    }

    @Override
    public void beforeChangeValueOf(WebElement webElement, WebDriver
webDriver, CharSequence[] charSequences) {

    }

    @Override
    public void afterChangeValueOf(WebElement webElement, WebDriver
webDriver, CharSequence[] charSequences) {

    }

    @Override
    public void beforeScript(String s, WebDriver webDriver)        {
    }

    @Override
    public void afterScript(String s, WebDriver webDriver)         {
    }

    @Override
    public void onException(Throwable throwable, WebDriver webDriver) {
    }
}
```

Extending AbstractWebDriverEventListener

The second way to create a listener class is by extending the
AbstractWebDriverEventListene r class. AbstractWebDriverEventListener is an
abstract class that implements WebDriverEventListener. Though it doesn't really
provide any implementation for the methods in the WebDriverEventListener interface,
it creates a dummy implementation such that the listener class that you are creating doesn't
have to contain all the methods, only the ones that you, as a test-script developer, are
interested in. The following is a class we have created that extends
AbstractWebDriverEventListener and provides implementations for a couple of
methods in it. This way, we can override only the methods that we are interested in rather
than all of the methods in our class:

```
package com.example;

import org.openqa.selenium.WebDriver;
```

```
import
org.openqa.selenium.support.events.AbstractWebDriverEventListener;

public class IAmTheEventListener2 extends AbstractWebDriverEventListener {

    @Override
    public void beforeNavigateTo(String url, WebDriver driver) {
        System.out.println("Before Navigate To "+ url);
    }
    @Override
    public void beforeNavigateBack(WebDriver driver) {
        System.out.println("Before Navigate Back. Right now I'm at "
                + driver.getCurrentUrl());
    }
}
}
```

Creating a WebDriver instance

Now that we have created our listener class that listens for all of the events generated, it's time to create our test script class and let it call `IAmTheDriver.java`. After the class is created, we declare a ChromeDriver instance in it:

```
WebDriver driver = new ChromeDriver();
```

The `ChromeDriver` instance will be the underlying driver instance that drives all the driver events. This is nothing new. The step explained in the next section is where we make this driver an instance of `EventFiringWebDriver`.

Creating EventFiringWebDriver and EventListener instances

Now that we have the basic driver instance, pass it as an argument while constructing the `EventFiringWebDriver` instance. We will be using this instance of the driver to execute all of the further user actions.

Now, using the following code, instantiate the `EventListener`,
`IAmTheEventListener.java`, or `IAmTheEventListener2.java` class that we created
previously. This will be the class to which all of the events are dispatched:

```
EventFiringWebDriver eventFiringDriver =
        new EventFiringWebDriver(driver);
IAmTheEventListener eventListener =
        new IAmTheEventListener();
```

Registering EventListener with EventFiringWebDriver

For the event executions to be notified by `EventListener`, we have registered
`EventListener` to the `EventFiringWebDriver` class. Now the `EventFiringWebDriver`
class will know where to send the notifications. This is done by the following line of code:
`eventFiringDriver.register(eventListener);`

Executing and verifying the events

Now it's time for our test script to execute events, such as navigation events. Let's first
navigate to Google and then Facebook. We will use the browser back-navigation to go back
to Google. The full code of the test script is as follows:

```
public class IAmTheDriver {
    public static void main(String... args){

        System.setProperty("webdriver.chrome.driver",
                "./src/test/resources/drivers/chromedriver");

        WebDriver driver = new ChromeDriver();

        try {
            EventFiringWebDriver eventFiringDriver = new
                    EventFiringWebDriver(driver);
            IAmTheEventListener eventListener = new IAmTheEventListener();
            eventFiringDriver.register(eventListener);
            eventFiringDriver.get("http://www.google.com");
            eventFiringDriver.get("http://www.facebook.com");
            eventFiringDriver.navigate().back();
        } finally {
            driver.close();
            driver.quit();
```

```
        }
    }
}
```

In the preceding code, we modify our listener class to record `navigateTo` and `navigateBack` before and after events inherited from the `AbstractWebDriverEventListener` class. The modified methods are as follows:

```
@Override
public void beforeNavigateTo(String url, WebDriver driver) {
    System.out.println("Before Navigate To: " + url
            + " and Current url is: " + driver.getCurrentUrl());
}

@Override
public void afterNavigateTo(String url, WebDriver driver) {
    System.out.println("After Navigate To: " + url
            + " and Current url is: " + driver.getCurrentUrl());
}

@Override
public void beforeNavigateBack(WebDriver driver) {
    System.out.println("Before Navigate Back. Right now I'm at " +
driver.getCurrentUrl());
}

@Override
public void afterNavigateBack(WebDriver driver) {
    System.out.println("After Navigate Back. Right now I'm at " +
driver.getCurrentUrl());
}
```

Now if you execute your test script, the output will be as follows:

```
Before Navigate To: http://www.google.com and Current url is: data:,
 After Navigate To: http://www.google.com and Current url is:
https://www.google.com/?gws_rd=ssl
 Before Navigate To: http://www.facebook.com and Current url is:
https://www.google.com/?gws_rd=ssl
 After Navigate To: http://www.facebook.com and Current url is:
https://www.facebook.com/
 Before Navigate Back. Right now I'm at https://www.facebook.com/
 After Navigate Back. Right now I'm at https://www.google.com/?gws_rd=ssl
```

Registering multiple EventListeners

We can register more than one listener with `EventFiringWebDriver`. Once the event occurs, all of the registered listeners are notified about it. Let's modify our test script to register both our `IAmTheListener.java` and `IAmTheListener2.java` files:

```
public class RegisteringMultipleListeners {
    public static void main(String... args){

        System.setProperty("webdriver.chrome.driver",
                "./src/test/resources/drivers/chromedriver");

        WebDriver driver = new ChromeDriver();

        try {
            EventFiringWebDriver eventFiringDriver = new
                    EventFiringWebDriver(driver);
            IAmTheEventListener eventListener = new IAmTheEventListener();
            IAmTheEventListener2 eventListener2 = new
                    IAmTheEventListener2();
            eventFiringDriver.register(eventListener);
            eventFiringDriver.register(eventListener2);
            eventFiringDriver.get("http://www.google.com");
            eventFiringDriver.get("http://www.facebook.com");
            eventFiringDriver.navigate().back();
        } finally {
            driver.close();
            driver.quit();
        }
    }
}
```

Modify the listeners slightly to differentiate the log statements. Now if you execute the preceding code, you will see the following output:

```
Before Navigate To: http://www.google.com and Current url is: data:,
 Before Navigate To http://www.google.com
 After Navigate To: http://www.google.com and Current url is:
https://www.google.com/?gws_rd=ssl
 Before Navigate To: http://www.facebook.com and Current url is:
https://www.google.com/?gws_rd=ssl
 Before Navigate To http://www.facebook.com
 After Navigate To: http://www.facebook.com and Current url is:
https://www.facebook.com/
 Before Navigate Back. Right now I'm at https://www.facebook.com/
 Before Navigate Back. Right now I'm at https://www.facebook.com/
 After Navigate Back. Right now I'm at https://www.google.com/?gws_rd=ssl
```

Exploring different WebDriver event listeners

We have seen some of the methods in our `EventListeners` that get invoked when their corresponding events are executed, for example, before and after navigation methods are invoked when the `navigateTo` event is triggered. Here, we'll see all the methods that `WebDriverEventListener` provides us.

Listening for WebElement value changes

This event occurs when the value of a WebElement changes when the `sendKeys()` or `clear()` methods are executed on them. There are two methods associated with this event:

```
public void beforeChangeValueOf(WebElement element, WebDriver driver)
```

The preceding method is invoked before the WebDriver attempts to change the value of the WebElement. As a parameter, the WebElement itself is passed to the method so that you can log the value of the element before the change:

```
public void afterChangeValueOf(WebElement element, WebDriver driver)
```

The preceding method is the second method associated with the value-change event that is invoked after the driver changes the value of the WebElement. Again, the WebElement and the WebDriver are sent as parameters to the method. If an exception occurs when changing the value, this method is not invoked.

Listening for the clicked WebElement

This event occurs when a WebElement is clicked, that is, by executing `webElement.click()`. There are two methods to listen for this event in the `WebDriverEventListener` implementation:

```
public void beforeClickOn(WebElement element, WebDriver driver)
```

The preceding method is invoked when the WebDriver is about to click on a particular WebElement. The WebElement that is going to be clicked on and the WebDriver that is clicking on it are sent as parameters to this method so that the test-script developer can interpret which driver performed the click action, and on which element the action was performed:

```
public void afterClickOn(WebElement element, WebDriver driver)
```

The `EventFiringWebDriver` class notifies the preceding method after the click action is taken on a WebElement. Similar to the `beforeClickOn()` method, this method is also sent the WebElement and WebDriver instances. If an exception occurs during a click event, this method is not called.

Listening for a WebElement search event

This event is triggered when the WebDriver searches for a WebElement on the web page using `findElement()` or `findElements()`. There are, again, two methods associated with this event:

```
public void beforeFindBy(By by, WebElement element, WebDriver driver)
```

The preceding method is invoked just before WebDriver begins searching for a particular WebElement on the page. For parameters, it sends the locating mechanism, that is, the WebElement that is searched for, and the WebDriver instance that is performing the search:

```
public void afterFindBy(By by, WebElement element, WebDriver driver)
```

Similarly, the `EventFiringWebDriver` class calls the preceding method after the search for an element is over and the element is found. If there are any exceptions during the search, this method is not called, and an exception is raised.

Listening for browser back-navigation

The browser back-navigation event, as we have already seen, gets invoked when we use the `driver.navigation().back()` method. The browser goes back one level in its history. Just like all the other events, this event is associated with two methods:

```
public void beforeNavigateBack(WebDriver driver)
```

The preceding method is invoked before the browser takes you back in its history. The WebDriver that invoked this event is passed as a parameter to this method:

```
public void afterNavigateBack(WebDriver driver)
```

Just as in all the after <<event>> methods, the preceding method is invoked when the navigate-back action is triggered. The preceding two methods will be invoked irrespective of the navigation of the browser; that is, if the browser doesn't have any history and you invoke this method, the browser doesn't take you to any of its history. But, even in that scenario, as the event is triggered, those two methods are invoked.

Listening for browser forward-navigation

This event is very similar to the browser back-navigation, except that this is browser forward-navigation, so it is using `driver.navigate().forward()`. The two methods associated with this event are:

- `public void afterNavigateForward(WebDriver driver)`
- `public void beforeNavigateForward(WebDriver driver)`

Just as in browser back-navigation, these methods are invoked irrespective of whether or not the browser takes you one level forward.

Listening for browser NavigateTo events

As we've seen earlier, this event occurs whenever the driver executes `driver. get(url)`. The related methods for this event are as follows:

- `public void beforeNavigateTo(java.lang.String url, WebDriver driver)`
- `public void afterNavigateTo(java.lang.String url, WebDriver driver)`

The URL that is used for the driver-navigation is passed as a parameter to the preceding methods, along with the driver that triggered the event.

Listening for script execution

This event is triggered whenever the driver executes a JavaScript. The associated methods for this event are as follows:

- `public void beforeScript(java.lang.String script, WebDriver driver)`
- `public void afterScript(java.lang.String script, WebDriver driver)`

The preceding methods get the JavaScript that was executed as a string, and the WebDriver that executed it as a parameter. If an exception occurs during script execution, the `afterScript()` method will not be invoked.

Listening for an exception

This event occurs when the WebDriver comes across an exception. For instance, if you try to search for a WebElement using `findElement()`, and that element doesn't exist on the page, the driver throws an exception (`NoSuchElementException`). At this point, this event is triggered, and the following method gets notified:

```
public void onException(java.lang.Throwable throwable, WebDriver driver)
```

In all the `after<<event>>` methods, we have seen that they will not be invoked if the driver comes across any exception. In that case, instead of those `after<<event>>` methods, the `onException()` method is invoked and the throwable object and the WebDriver object are sent to it as parameters.

Unregistering EventListener with EventFiringWebDriver

Now, we have seen the different kinds of events that get triggered, and the `EventFiringWebDriver` class that notifies all of the listeners registered to it. If, at any point, you want one of your event listeners to stop listening from `EventFiringWebDriver`, you can do that by unregistering from that driver. The following API unregisters an event listener from a driver:

```
public EventFiringWebDriver unregister(WebDriverEventListener eventListener)
```

The parameter of the method should be the event listener that wants to opt out of getting event notifications.

Performing accessibility testing

We can perform basic accessibility checks by using tools such as Google's Accessibility Developer Tools (https://github.com/GoogleChrome/accessibility-developer-tools). We can inject the Google Accessibility testing library in a web page and perform the Accessibility Audit. This can be done automatically every time afterNavigatTo() is called. In the following code example, we will inject the axe_testing.js file provided by the Google Accessibility Developer Tools and perform the audit, which will print a report on the console:

```java
public class IAmTheEventListener2 extends AbstractWebDriverEventListener {

    @Override
    public void beforeNavigateTo(String url, WebDriver driver) {
        System.out.println("Before Navigate To "+ url);
    }

    @Override
    public void beforeNavigateBack(WebDriver driver) {
        System.out.println("Before Navigate Back. Right now I'm at "
                + driver.getCurrentUrl());
    }

    @Override
    public void afterNavigateTo(String to, WebDriver driver) {
        try {
            JavascriptExecutor jsExecutor = (JavascriptExecutor) driver;
            URL url = new
URL("https://raw.githubusercontent.com/GoogleChrome/" +
                    "accessibility-developer-
tools/stable/dist/js/axs_testing.js");
            String script = IOUtils.toString(url.openStream(),
StandardCharsets.UTF_8);
            jsExecutor.executeScript(script);
            String report = (String) jsExecutor.executeScript("var results
= axs.Audit.run();" +
                    "return axs.Audit.createReport(results);");
            System.out.println("### Accessibility Report for " +
driver.getTitle() + "####");
            System.out.println(report);
            System.out.println("### END ####");
```

```
            } catch (MalformedURLException e) {
                e.printStackTrace();
            } catch (IOException e) {
                e.printStackTrace();
            }
        }
    }
}
```

The report is printed in the console, as shown here:

```
### Accessibility Report for Google####
*** Begin accessibility audit results ***
An accessibility audit found
Warnings:
Warning: AX_FOCUS_01 (These elements are focusable but either invisible or
obscured by another element) failed on the following element:
#hplogo > DIV > .fOwUFe > A
See
https://github.com/GoogleChrome/accessibility-developer-tools/wiki/Audit-Ru
les#-ax_focus_01--these-elements-are-focusable-but-either-invisible-or-
obscured-by-another-element for more information.
Warning: AX_TEXT_02 (Images should have an alt attribute) failed on the
following element:
#hplogo > DIV > .fOwUFe > A > .fJOQGe
See
https://github.com/GoogleChrome/accessibility-developer-tools/wiki/Audit-Ru
les#-ax_text_02--images-should-have-an-alt-attribute-unless-they-have-an-
aria-role-of-presentation for more information.
...
*** End accessibility audit results ***
### END ####
```

This report contains a collection of audit rules that check for common accessibility problems.

Capturing page-performance metrics

Measuring and optimizing the client-side performance is essential for a seamless user experience, and this is critical for Web 2.0 applications using AJAX.

Capturing vital information, such as the time taken for page load, rendering of the elements, and the JavaScript code execution, will help in identifying the areas where performance is slow and optimizes the overall client-side performance.

Navigation Timing is a W3C-Standard JavaScript API to measure performance on the web. The API provides a simple way to get accurate and detailed timing statistics natively for page navigation and load events. It is available on Internet Explorer 9, Google Chrome, Firefox, and WebKit-based browsers.

The API is accessed via the properties of the timing interface of the window.performance object using JavaScript. We will capture the page-load time every time we navigate to a page. This can be done by using JavaScriptExecutor to call winodw.performance in the afterNavigateTo() method in IAmTheEventListener2.java, as shown in the following code snippet:

```
@Override
public void afterNavigateTo(String to, WebDriver driver) {
    try {

        JavascriptExecutor jsExecutor = (JavascriptExecutor) driver;

        // Get the Load Event End
        long loadEventEnd = (Long) jsExecutor.executeScript("return
window.performance.timing.loadEventEnd;");
        // Get the Navigation Event Start
        long navigationStart = (Long) jsExecutor.executeScript("return
window.performance.timing.navigationStart;");
        // Difference between Load Event End and Navigation Event Start is
// Page Load Time
        System.out.println("Page Load Time is " + (loadEventEnd -
navigationStart)/1000 + " seconds.");

    } catch (MalformedURLException e) {
        e.printStackTrace();
    } catch (IOException e) {
        e.printStackTrace();
    }
}
```

As discussed in the previous code, the window.performance object provides us with the performance metric that is available within the Browser Window object. We need to use JavaScript to retrieve this metric. Here, we are collecting the loadEventEnd time and the navigationEventStart time, and calculating the difference between them, which will give us the page-load time.

Summary

In this chapter, you have learned about `EventFiringWebDriver` and `EventListeners`, and how they work together to make a developer's life easier by helping them to debug what is going on at each step while the test cases get executed. You also learned how to use WebDriver events to perform different types of testing on a page, such as accessibility and client-side performance checks. In the next `chapter`, you will learn more about RemoteWebDriver for running tests on remote machines in distributed and parallel mode for Cross-Browser Testing.

Questions

1. You can listen to WebDriver events using `WebDriverEventListener` interface— True or False?
2. How you can automatically clear an input field before calling the `sendKeys` method using `WebDriverEventListener`?
3. Selenium supports accessibility testing— True or False?

Further information

You can check out the following links for more information about the topics covered in this chapter:

- Find out more about the Navigation Timing API at `https://www.w3.org/TR/navigation-timing/`
- Find more details on Google's Accessibility Developer Tools at `https://github.com/GoogleChrome/accessibility-developer-tools`

Exploring RemoteWebDriver

6

So far, we have created our test cases and tried to execute them on various browsers. All of these tests were executed against the browsers that were installed on a local machine where the test cases reside. This may not be possible at all times. There is a high possibility that you may be working on Mac or Linux, but want to execute your tests on IE on a Windows machine. In this chapter, we will learn about the following topics:

- Executing test cases on a remote machine using `RemoteWebDriver`
- A detailed explanation of the JSON wire protocol

Introducing RemoteWebDriver

`RemoteWebDriver` is an implementation class of the `WebDriver` interface that a test-script developer can use to execute their test scripts via the `Selenium Standalone` server on a remote machine. There are two parts to `RemoteWebDriver`: a server and a client. Before we start working with them, let's rewind and see what we've been doing.

The following diagram explains what we've done so far:

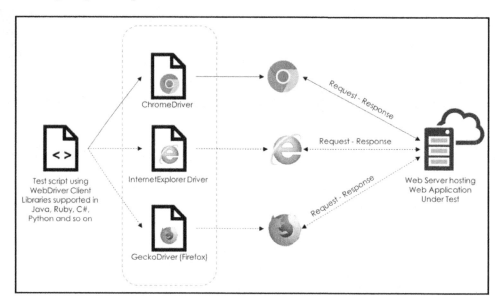

The test script using **WebDriver client** libraries, **Chrome Driver** (or IE Driver or Gecko Driver for Firefox), and Chrome browser (or IE browser or Firefox browser) is sitting on the same machine. The browser is loading the web application, which may or may not be hosted remotely; anyway, this is outside the scope of our discussion. We will discuss different scenarios of test-script execution, as follows:

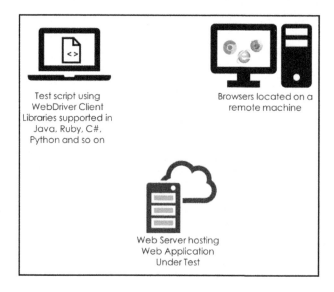

The test script is located on a local machine, while the browsers are installed on a remote machine. In this scenario, RemoteWebDriver comes into the picture. As mentioned earlier, there are two components associated with RemoteWebDriver: the server and the client. Let's start with the Selenium Standalone server.

Understanding Selenium Standalone Server

Selenium Standalone Server is a component that listens on a port for various requests from a RemoteWebDriver client. Once it receives the requests, it forwards them to any of the following: Chrome Driver, IE Driver, or Gecko Driver for Firefox, whichever is requested by the RemoteWebDriver client.

Downloading Selenium Standalone Server

Let's download Selenium Standalone Server and start running it. You can download it from https://www.seleniumhq.org/download/, but, for our purposes, let's download a specific version of it, as we are using WebDriver Version 3.12.0. This server JAR should be downloaded to the remote machine on which the browsers are located. Also, make sure the remote machine has Java Runtime installed on it.

Running the server

Open your command-line tool on the remote machine and navigate to the location where you have downloaded the JAR file. Now, to start Selenium Standalone Server, execute the following command:

```
java -jar selenium-server-standalone-3.12.0.jar
```

The following screenshot shows what you should see in your console:

```
● ● ●                1. java -jar selenium-server-standalone-3.12.0.jar (java)
upgundecha@Unmeshs-iMac  ~/Downloads  java -jar selenium-server-standalone-3.
12.0.jar
16:27:41.623 INFO [GridLauncherV3.launch] - Selenium build info: version: '3.12.
0', revision: '7c6e0b3'
16:27:41.624 INFO [GridLauncherV3$1.launch] - Launching a standalone Selenium Se
rver on port 4444
2018-06-02 16:27:41.742:INFO::main: Logging initialized @443ms to org.seleniumhq
.jetty9.util.log.StdErrLog
16:27:42.044 INFO [SeleniumServer.boot] - Selenium Server is up and running on p
ort 4444
```

Now the server has started and is listening on the `<remote-machine-ip>:4444` address for remote connections from the `RemoteWebDriver` client. The previously seen image (the second image in the *Introducing RemoteWebDriver* section) will appear as follows:

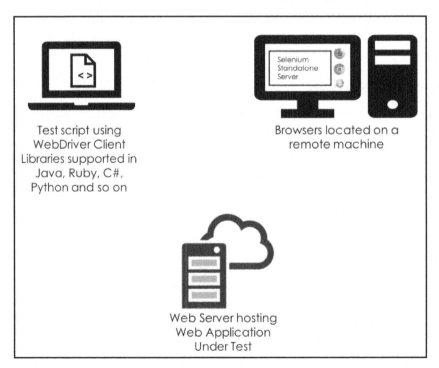

Test script using
WebDriver Client
Libraries supported in
Java, Ruby, C#,
Python and so on

Browsers located on a
remote machine

Web Server hosting
Web Application
Under Test

On the remote machine, Selenium Standalone Server will interface between the test script and the browsers, as shown in the preceding diagram. The test script will first establish a connection with Selenium Standalone Server that will forward the commands to the browser installed on the remote machine.

Understanding the RemoteWebDriver client

Now that we have our Selenium Standalone server up and running, it's time for us to create the RemoteWebDriver client. Fortunately, we don't have to do much to create a RemoteWebDriver client. It's nothing but the language-binding client libraries that serve as a RemoteWebDriver client. RemoteWebDriver will translate the test-script requests or commands to JSON payload and send them across to the RemoteWebDriver server using the JSON wire protocol.

When you execute your tests locally, the WebDriver client libraries talk to the Chrome Driver, IE Driver, or Gecko Driver directly. Now when you try to execute your tests remotely, the WebDriver client libraries talk to Selenium Standalone Server and the server talks to either the Chrome Driver, the IE Driver, or the Gecko Driver for Firefox requested by the test script, using the DesiredCapabilities class. We will explore the DesiredCapabilities class in the next section.

Converting an existing test script to use the RemoteWebDriver server

Let's take a test script that we have executed locally; that is, where the test scripts and the browser were on the same machine:

```
@BeforeClass
public void setup() {

    System.setProperty("webdriver.chrome.driver",
            "./src/test/resources/drivers/chromedriver");
    driver = new ChromeDriver();

}
```

The preceding test script creates an instance of Chrome Driver and launches the Chrome browser. Now, let's try to convert this test script to use `Selenium Standalone Server` that we started earlier. Before we do that, let's see the constructor of `RemoteWebDriver`, which is as follows:

```
RemoteWebDriver(java.net.URL remoteAddress, Capabilities
desiredCapabilities)
```

The input parameters for the constructor include the address (hostname or IP) of `Selenium Standalone Server` running on the remote machine and the desired capabilities required for running the test (for example name of the browser and/or operating system). We will see these desired capabilities shortly.

Now, let's modify the test script to use `RemoteWebDriver`. Replace `WebDriver driver = new ChromeDriver();` with the following code:

```
@BeforeMethod
public void setup() throws MalformedURLException {

    DesiredCapabilities caps = new DesiredCapabilities();
    caps.setBrowserName("chrome");

    driver = new RemoteWebDriver(new URL("http://10.172.10.1:4444/wd/hub"),
caps);
    driver.get("http://demo-store.seleniumacademy.com/");

}
```

We have created a RemoteWebDriver instance that tries to connect to `http://10.172.10.1:4444/wd/hub`, where `Selenium Standalone Server` is running and listening for requests. Having done that, we also need to specify which browser your test case should get executed on. This can be done using the `DesiredCapabilities` instance.

For this example, the IP used is 10.172.10.1. However, in your case, it will be different. You need to obtain the IP of the machine where the Selenium Standalone Server is running and replace the example IP used in this book.

Before running tests, we need to restart the Selenium Standalone Server by specifying the path of ChromeDriver:

```
java -jar -Dwebdriver.chrome.driver=chromedriver selenium-server-
standalone-3.12.0.jar
```

Running the following test with `RemoteWebDriver` will launch the Chrome browser and execute your test case on it. So the modified test case will look as follows:

```java
public class SearchTest {

    WebDriver driver;

    @BeforeMethod
    public void setup() throws MalformedURLException {

        DesiredCapabilities caps = new DesiredCapabilities();
        caps.setBrowserName("chrome");

        driver = new RemoteWebDriver(new
URL("http://10.172.10.1:4444/wd/hub"), caps);
        driver.get("http://demo-store.seleniumacademy.com/");

    }

    @Test
    public void searchProduct() {

        // find search box and enter search string
        WebElement searchBox = driver.findElement(By.name("q"));

        searchBox.sendKeys("Phones");

        WebElement searchButton =
                driver.findElement(By.className("search-button"));

        searchButton.click();

        assertThat(driver.getTitle())
                .isEqualTo("Search results for: 'Phones'");
    }

    @AfterMethod
    public void tearDown() {
        driver.quit();
    }
}
```

Now execute this test script from your local machine to establish a connection between the RemoteWebDriver client and Selenium Standalone Server. The Server will launch the Chrome browser. The following is the output you will see in the console where the Server is running:

```
18:25:32.155 INFO [ActiveSessionFactory.apply] - Capabilities are: Capabilities {
browserName: chrome}
18:25:32.157 INFO [ActiveSessionFactory.lambda$apply$11] - Matched factory org.op
enqa.selenium.remote.server.ServicedSession$Factory (provider: org.openqa.seleniu
m.chrome.ChromeDriverService)
Starting ChromeDriver 2.38.552518 (183d19265345f54ce39cbb94cf81ba5f15905011) on p
ort 3315
Only local connections are allowed.
18:25:52.564 INFO [ProtocolHandshake.createSession] - Detected dialect: OSS
18:25:58.340 INFO [RemoteSession$Factory.lambda$performHandshake$0] - Started new
  session 3cb5c118e1a5b2bdd7bc568bf147beed (org.openqa.selenium.chrome.ChromeDrive
rService)
```

It says that a new session with the desired capabilities is being created. Once the session is established, a session ID will be printed to the console. At any point in time, you can view all of the sessions that are established with Selenium Standalone Server by navigating to the host or IP of the machine where the Selenium server is running http://<hostnameOrIP>:4444/wd/hub.

The Selenium Standalone Server, by default, listens to port number 4444. We can change the default port by passing the -port argument.

It will give the entire list of sessions that the server is currently handling. The screenshot of this is as follows:

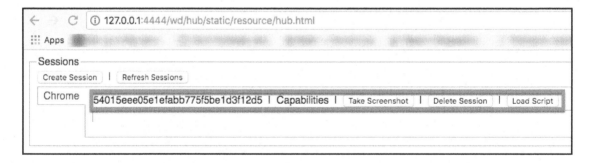

This is a very basic portal that lets the test-script developer see all of the sessions created by the server and perform some basic operations on it, such as terminating a session, taking a screenshot of a session, loading a script to a session, and seeing all of the desired capabilities of a session. The following screenshot shows all of the default desired capabilities of our current session.

You can see the popup by hovering over the **Capabilities** link, as shown in the following screenshot:

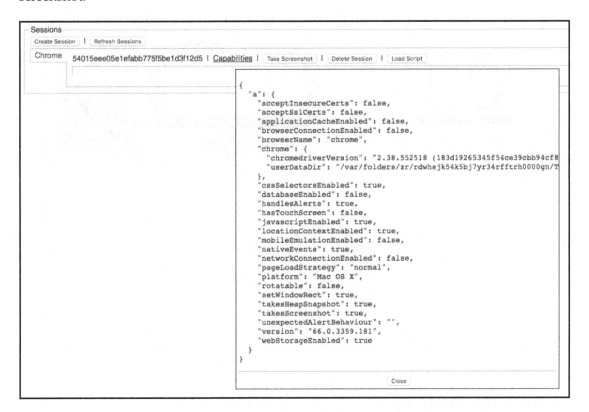

Those are the default desired capabilities that are set implicitly by the server for this session. Now we have successfully established a connection between our test script, which is using a `RemoteWebDriver` client on one machine, and the Selenium Standalone Server on another machine. The original diagram of running the test scripts remotely is as follows:

Using RemoteWebDriver for Firefox

Using the Firefox browser to execute our test scripts is similar to using the Chrome browser, except for a couple of variations in how `GeckoDriver` is launched.

Let's see this by changing the test script that we used for the Chrome browser to the following script, using `"firefox"`:

```
@BeforeMethod
public void setup() throws MalformedURLException {

    DesiredCapabilities caps = new DesiredCapabilities();
```

```
caps.setBrowserName("firefox");
caps.setCapability("marionette", true);

driver = new RemoteWebDriver(new URL("http://10.172.10.1:4444/wd/hub"),
caps);
    driver.get("http://demo-store.seleniumacademy.com/");

}
```

Before you try to execute this code, restart `Selenium Standalone Server` to use `GeckoDriver`:

```
java -jar -Dwebdriver.gecko.driver=geckodriver selenium-server-
standalone-3.12.0.jar
```

Try executing the preceding test script now, and you should see the Firefox browser getting launched and executing your test commands. `Selenium Standalone Server` has started `GeckoDriver`, created a connection to it, and started executing the test-script commands.

Using RemoteWebDriver for Internet Explorer

For executing tests on the Internet Explorer driver, the steps are similar to what we did with the Chrome and Firefox browsers.

Let's see this by changing the test script that we used for the Chrome or Firefox browser to the following script, using `"internet explorer"`:

```
@BeforeMethod
public void setup() throws MalformedURLException {

    DesiredCapabilities caps = new DesiredCapabilities();
    caps.setBrowserName("internet explorer");

    driver = new RemoteWebDriver(new URL("http://127.0.0.1:4444/wd/hub"),
caps);
    driver.get("http://demo-store.seleniumacademy.com/");

}
```

Before you try to execute this code, restart `Selenium Standalone Server` to use `InternetExplorerDriver`:

```
java -jar -Dwebdriver.ie.driver=InternetExplorerDriver.exe selenium-server-
standalone-3.12.0.jar
```

Try executing the preceding test script now, and you should see the Internet Explorer browser getting launched and executing your test commands. `Selenium Standalone Server` has started `InternetExplorerDriver`, created a connection with it, and started executing the test-script commands.

Understanding the JSON wire protocol

In many places, we have mentioned that WebDriver uses the JSON wire protocol to communicate between client libraries and different driver (that is, Chrome Driver, IE Driver, Gecko Driver, and so on) implementations. In this section, we will see exactly what it is and which different JSON APIs a client library should implement to talk to the drivers.

JavaScript Object Notation (JSON) is used to represent objects with complex data structures. It is used primarily to transfer data between a server and a client on the web. It has become an industry standard for various REST web services, offering a strong alternative to XML.

A sample JSON file, saved as a `.json` file, will look as follows:

```
{
    "firstname":"John",
    "lastname":"Doe",
    "address":{
        "streetnumber":"678",
        "street":"Victoria Street",
        "city":"Richmond",
        "state":"Victoria",
        "country":"Australia"
    } "phone":"+61470315430"
}
```

A client can send a person's details to a server in the preceding JSON format, which the server can parse, and then create an instance of the person object for use in its execution. Later, the response can be sent back by the server to the client in the JSON format, the data of which the client can use to create an object of a class. This process of converting an object's data into the JSON format and JSON-formatted data into an object is called **serialization** and **de-serialization**, respectively, which is quite common in REST-based web services.

WebDriver uses the same approach to communicate between client libraries (language bindings) and drivers, such as Firefox Driver, IE Driver, and Chrome Driver. Similarly, the `RemoteWebDriver` client and `Selenium Standalone Server` use the JSON wire protocol to communicate among themselves. But all of these drivers use it under the hood, hiding all the implementation details from us and making our lives simpler. The list of APIs for various actions that we can take on a web page is as follows:

```
/status /session /sessions /session/:sessionId /session/:sessionId/timeouts
/session/:sessionId/timeouts/async_script
/session/:sessionId/timeouts/implicit_wait
/session/:sessionId/window_handle /session/:sessionId/window_handles
/session/:sessionId/url /session/:sessionId/forward
/session/:sessionId/back /session/:sessionId/refresh
/session/:sessionId/execute /session/:sessionId/execute_async
/session/:sessionId/screenshot /session/:sessionId/ime/available_engines
/session/:sessionId/ime/active_engine
. . .
. . . /session/:sessionId/touch/flick /session/:sessionId/touch/flick
/session/:sessionId/location /session/:sessionId/local_storage
/session/:sessionId/local_storage/key/:key
/session/:sessionId/local_storage/size /session/:sessionId/session_storage
/session/:sessionId/session_storage/key/:key
/session/:sessionId/session_storage/size /session/:sessionId/log
/session/:sessionId/log/types /session/:sessionId/application_cache/status
```

The complete documentation is available at `https://code.google.com/p/selenium/wiki/JsonWireProtocol`. The client libraries will translate your test-script commands into the JSON format and send the requests to the appropriate WebDriver API. The WebDriver will parse these requests and take necessary actions on the web page. Let's see that as an example. Suppose your test script has this code: `driver.get("http://www.google.com");`.

The client library will translate that into JSON by building a JSON payload (JSON document) and post the request to the appropriate API. In this case, the API that handles the `driver.get(URL)` method is `/session/:sessionId/url`.

The following code shows what happens in the client library layer behind the scenes before the request is sent to the driver; the request is sent to the RemoteWebDriver server running on 10.172.10.1:4444:

```
HttpClient httpClient = new DefaultHttpClient();
HttpPost postMethod = new
HttpPost("http://10.172.10.1:4444/wd/hub/session/"+sessionId+"/url");
JSONObject jo=new JSONObject();
jo.put("url","http://www.google.com");
StringEntity input = new StringEntity(jo.toString());
input.setContentEncoding("UTF-8");
input.setContentEncoding(new BasicHeader(HTTP.CONTENT_TYPE,
"application/json"));
postMethod.setEntity(input);
HttpResponse response = httpClient.execute(postMethod);
```

`Selenium Standalone Server` will forward that request to the driver; the driver will execute the test-script commands that arrive in the preceding format on the web application, under the test that is loaded in the browser.

The following diagram shows the dataflow at each stage:

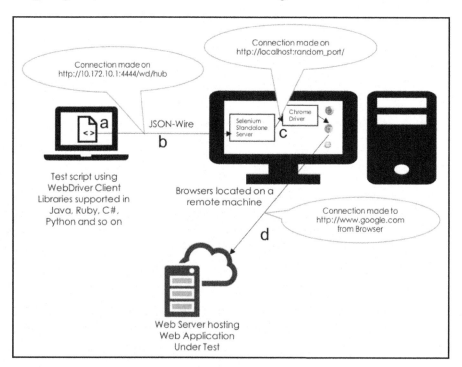

The preceding diagram shows the following:

- The first stage is communication between the test script and the client library. The data or command that flows between them is a call to the `get()` method of the driver: `driver.get("http://www.google.com");`.
- The client library, as soon as it receives the preceding command, will convert it into the JSON format and communicate with `Selenium Standalone Server`.
- Next, `Selenium Standalone Server` forwards the JSON payload request to the Chrome Driver.
- The Chrome Driver will communicate with the Chrome browser natively, and then the browser will send a request for the asked URL to load.

Summary

In this chapter, we learned about `RemoteWebDriver` and how to execute test scripts remotely on a different machine using `Selenium Standalone Server` and the `RemoteWebDriver` client. This enables Selenium WebDriver tests to be executed on remote machines with different browser and OS combinations. We also looked at the JSON wire protocol and how client libraries work behind the scenes to send and receive requests and responses to and from the drivers.

In the next chapter, we will extend the usage of Selenium Standalone Server and RemoteWebDriver to create a Selenium Grid for cross-browser and distributed testing.

Questions

1. With Selenium, we can execute tests on remote machine(s)— true or false
2. Which driver class is used to run tests on a remote machine?
3. Explain desired capabilities.
4. What protocol is used between the Selenium test and Selenium Standalone Server?
5. What is the default port used by Selenium Standalone Server?

Further information

You can check out the following link for more information about the topics covered in this chapter:

- Selenium WebDriver W3C specification explains the WebDriver Protocol and all the endpoints: `https://www.w3.org/TR/webdriver/`

Setting up Selenium Grid

7

Now that we know what RemoteWebDriver is and how it works, we are ready to learn about Selenium Grid. In this chapter, we will cover the following topics:

- Why we need Selenium Grid
- What Selenium Grid is
- How we can use Selenium Grid
- Test cases using Selenium Grid
- Configuring Selenium Grid

Exploring Selenium Grid

Let's try to understand why we need Selenium Grid by analyzing a scenario. You have a web application that needs to be tested on the following browser-machine combinations:

- Google Chrome on Windows 10
- Google Chrome on macOS
- Internet Explorer 11 on Windows 10
- Firefox on Linux

We can simply alter the test script we created in the previous chapter and point to the Selenium Standalone Server running on each of these combinations (that is, Windows 10, macOS, or Linux), as shown in the following code.

Windows 10:

```
DesiredCapabilities caps = new DesiredCapabilities();
caps.setBrowserName("chrome");
caps.setPlatform(Platform.WIN10);
WebDriver driver = new RemoteWebDriver(new
URL("http://<win_10_ip>:4444/wd/hub"), capabilities);
```

macOS:

```
DesiredCapabilities caps = new DesiredCapabilities();
caps.setBrowserName("chrome");
caps.setPlatform(Platform.MAC);
WebDriver driver = new RemoteWebDriver(new
URL("http://<mac_os_ip>:4444/wd/hub"), capabilities);
```

Linux:

```
DesiredCapabilities caps = new DesiredCapabilities();
caps.setBrowserName("chrome");
caps.setPlatform(Platform.LINUX);
WebDriver driver = new RemoteWebDriver(new
URL("http://<linux_ip>:4444/wd/hub"), capabilities);
```

In the preceding code, your test scripts are tightly coupled to the machines that host the target platform and the target browsers. If the Windows 10 host changes, you should refactor your test script to handle that. This is not an ideal way to design your tests. The focus of your test scripts should be on the functionality of your web application and not on the infrastructure that is used to execute these test scripts. There should be a central point to manage all the different environments. To solve this, we make use of **Selenium Grid**.

The **Selenium Grid** offers a cross-browser testing environment with several different platforms (such as Windows, Mac, and Linux) to execute tests. The Selenium Grid is managed from a central point, called the **hub.** The hub has the information of all the different testing platforms, known as **nodes** (the machines that have the desired operating systems and browser versions and connected to the hub). The hub assigns these nodes to execute tests whenever the test scripts request them, based on the capabilities requested by the test. The following diagram shows what a Selenium Grid looks like:

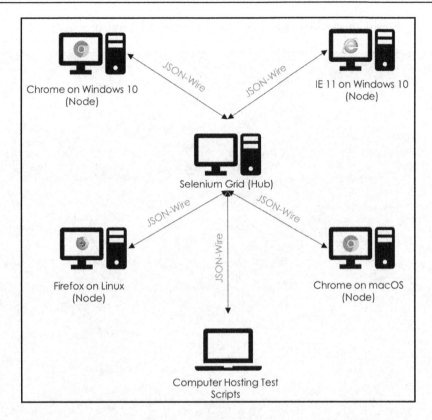

In the preceding diagram, there is one **hub**, four **nodes** of different platforms, and the machine where the test scripts are located. The test script will communicate with the hub and request a target platform to be executed. The hub assigns a node with the target platform to the test script. The node executes the test script and sends the result back to the hub, which in turn forwards the results to the test script. This is what Selenium Grid looks like and how it works at a high level.

Now that we have seen how Selenium Grid works theoretically, let's see what works as hubs and nodes in it. Fortunately, as we are dealing with Selenium Grid, we can use the same Remote WebDriver server that we used in the previous chapter to work as Selenium Grid as well. If you remember, we used `seleniumserver-standalone-3.12.0.jar` to start as a Selenium Standalone Server. We can use the same JAR file to be started in the hub mode on the hub machine, and a copy of the JAR file can be started in the node mode on the node machine. Try executing the following command on your JAR file:

```
java -jar selenium-server-standalone-3.12.0.jar -help
```

The following output shows how to use the server in a grid environment:

```
upgundecha@Unmeshs-iMac    ~/Downloads    java -jar selenium-server-standalone-3.12.0.
jar -help
Usage: <main class> [options]
  Options:
    --debug, -debug
      <Boolean> : enables LogLevel.FINE.
      Default: false
    --version, -version
      Displays the version and exits.
      Default: false
    -browserTimeout
      <Integer> in seconds : number of seconds a browser session is allowed to
      hang while a WebDriver command is running (example: driver.get(url)). If
      the timeout is reached while a WebDriver command is still processing,
      the session will quit. Minimum value is 60. An unspecified, zero, or
      negative value means wait indefinitely.
    -config
      <String> filename : JSON configuration file for the standalone server.
      Overrides default values
    -host
      <String> IP or hostname : usually determined automatically. Most
      commonly useful in exotic network configurations (e.g. network with VPN)
    -jettyThreads, -jettyMaxThreads
      <Integer> : max number of threads for Jetty. An unspecified, zero, or
      negative value means the Jetty default value (200) will be used.
    -log
      <String> filename : the filename to use for logging. If omitted, will
      log to STDOUT
    -port
      <Integer> : the port number the server will use.
    -role
      <String> options are [hub], [node], or [standalone].
    -timeout, -sessionTimeout
      <Integer> in seconds : Specifies the timeout before the server
      automatically kills a session that hasn't had any activity in the last X
      seconds. The test slot will then be released for another test to use.
      This is typically used to take care of client crashes. For grid hub/node
      roles. cleanUpCycle must also be set.
```

You will see two options: to use it as a Standalone Server, which acts as a Remote WebDriver, and to use it in a grid environment, which describes Selenium Grid. In this chapter, we will use this JAR file as a Selenium Grid.

Understanding the hub

The hub is the central point of a Selenium Grid. It has a registry of all the available nodes that are connected and part of a particular grid. The hub is a Selenium Standalone server running in the hub mode, listening on port 4444 of a machine by default. The test scripts will try to connect to the hub on this port, just as any Remote WebDriver. The hub will take care of rerouting the test-script traffic to the appropriate test-platform node. Let's see how we can start a hub node. Navigate to the location where you have your Selenium server JAR file and execute the following command:

```
java -jar selenium-server-standalone-3.12.0.jar -role hub
```

Doing this will start your server in the hub mode. By default, the server starts listening on port 4444; however, you can start your server on the port of your choice. Suppose you want to start the server on port 1111; it can be done as follows:

```
java -jar selenium-server-standalone-3.12.0.jar -role hub -port 1111
```

The following screenshot shows the console output of the Grid Hub being started on port 1111:

All the test scripts should connect to the hub on this port. Now launch your browser and connect to the machine that is hosting your hub on port 1111. Here, the machine that is hosting my hub has the IP address 192.168.0.101.

What you should see on your browser is shown in the following screenshot:

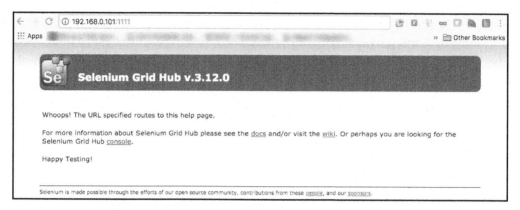

It shows the version of the server that is being used as the Grid Hub. Now click the **Console** link to navigate to the Grid Console:

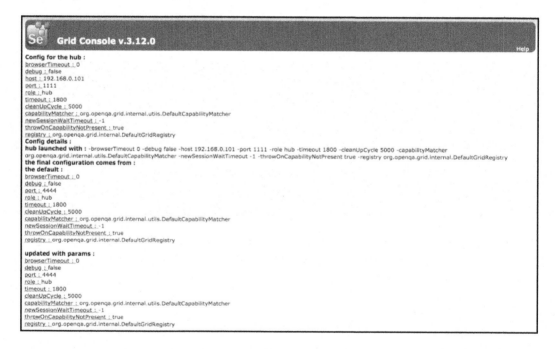

As you can see, the page talks about many configuration parameters. We will discuss these configuration parameters in the *Configuring Selenium Grid* section. So, you've now learned how to start a grid on a port and listen for connections.

Understanding the node

As our hub is up and running, it's now time to start a node and connect it to the hub. In this example, we will configure a macOS machine that has Chrome installed on it. So, if any test script requests the hub for a macOS platform and Chrome browser, the hub will choose this node. Let's see how we can start the node. The command to start the node and register with the hub is as follows:

```
java —jar selenium-server-standalone-3.12.0.jar —role node —hub
http://192.168.0.101:1111/grid/register
```

This will start the Selenium server in the node mode and register this node with the already-started hub:

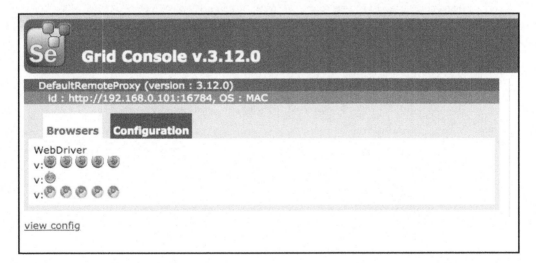

If you go back to the Grid Console on the browser, you will see the following:

The preceding screenshot shows the **http://192.168.0.101:16784** node URL, which, in this case, is running on the Mac platform. By default, the number of browsers listed for every node is 11: 5 for Firefox, five for Chrome, and one for IE. This can be overridden by specifying the `browser` option, which we will see in the *Configuring Selenium Grid* section.

Similarly, start another node on Windows and register to the hub using the same command used to start the node on macOS.

Modifying the existing test script to use Selenium Grid

So far, we have seen test scripts that run on our local machines or on Selenium Standalone servers. Executing test scripts on Selenium Grid is very similar to executing tests on Remote WebDriver, except that you will also mention the platform details for Grid.

Let's look at a test script that uses the Remote WebDriver server:

```
public class SearchTest {

    WebDriver driver;

    @BeforeMethod
    public void setup() throws MalformedURLException {

        DesiredCapabilities caps = new DesiredCapabilities();

        caps.setBrowserName("chrome");
        caps.setPlatform(Platform.MAC);

        driver = new RemoteWebDriver(new
URL("http://192.168.0.101:1111/wd/hub"), caps);
        driver.get("http://demo-store.seleniumacademy.com/");

    }

    @Test
    public void searchProduct() {

        // find search box and enter search string
        WebElement searchBox = driver.findElement(By.name("q"));

        searchBox.sendKeys("Phones");

        WebElement searchButton =
```

```
            driver.findElement(By.className("search-button"));

        searchButton.click();

        assertThat(driver.getTitle())
                .isEqualTo("Search results for: 'Phones'");
    }

    @AfterMethod
    public void tearDown() {
        driver.quit();
    }
}
```

Now try executing the preceding test script and observe the log output of the hub and the node. The output log of the hub is as follows:

```
12:21:19.197 INFO [ActiveSessionFactory.apply] - Capabilities are: Capabilities {browserName: chrome, platform: MA
C}
12:21:19.197 INFO [ActiveSessionFactory.lambda$apply$11] - Matched factory org.openqa.selenium.remote.server.Servi
cedSession$Factory (provider: org.openqa.selenium.chrome.ChromeDriverService)
Starting ChromeDriver 2.38.552518 (183d19265345f54ce39cbb94cf81ba5f15905011) on port 39474
Only local connections are allowed.
12:21:20.034 INFO [ProtocolHandshake.createSession] - Detected dialect: OSS
12:21:20.102 INFO [RemoteSession$Factory.lambda$performHandshake$0] - Started new session c9b6c5f5cf8f97312faadbed
f56bbb73 (org.openqa.selenium.chrome.ChromeDriverService)
12:21:25.202 INFO [ActiveSessions$1.onStop] - Removing session c9b6c5f5cf8f97312faadbedf56bbb73 (org.openqa.seleni
um.chrome.ChromeDriverService)
```

The sequence of steps that happens at the hub end is as follows:

1. The hub gets a request to create a new session for platform=MAC, browserName=chrome.
2. It verifies the available nodes that match the capabilities request.
3. If available, it creates a new session with the node host; if not, it rejects the request from the test script, saying that the desired capabilities don't match any of the registered nodes.
4. If a session is created with the node host in the preceding step, create a new test-slot session and hand over the test script to the node. Similarly, the output you should see in the console log of the hub is as follows:

```
12:21:19.181 INFO [RequestHandler.process] - Got a request to create a new session: Capabilities {browserName: chr
ome, platform: MAC}
12:21:19.182 INFO [TestSlot.getNewSession] - Trying to create a new session on test slot {server:CONFIG_UUID=4a2db
c4a-ae28-4398-897c-27ff56f71b99, seleniumProtocol=WebDriver, browserName=chrome, maxInstances=5, platformName=MAC,
platform=MAC}
```

The sequence of steps performed on the node is as follows:

1. The node host creates a new session with the requested desired capabilities. This will launch the browser.
2. It executes the test script's steps on the launched browser.
3. It ends the session and forwards the result to the hub, which in turn sends it to the test script.

Requesting for non-registered capabilities

The hub will reject the request from the test script when the test script asks for a capability that is not registered with the hub. Let's modify the preceding test script to request the Opera browser instead of Chrome. The test script should look as follows:

```java
@BeforeMethod
public void setup() throws MalformedURLException {

    DesiredCapabilities caps = new DesiredCapabilities();

    caps.setBrowserName("opera");
    caps.setPlatform(Platform.MAC);

    driver = new RemoteWebDriver(new
URL("http://192.168.0.101:1111/wd/hub"), caps);
    driver.get("http://demo-store.seleniumacademy.com/");

}
```

The hub checks whether there is any node that matches the desired capabilities. If it doesn't find one (as in this case), it will reject the request from the test script by throwing a `CapabilityNotPresentOnTheGridException` exception, as shown in the following screenshot:

```
12:28:59.965 INFO [RequestHandler.process] - Got a request to create a new session: Capabilities {browserName: ope
ra, platform: MAC}
12:28:59.966 INFO [RequestHandler.process] - Error forwarding the new session cannot find : Capabilities {browserN
ame: opera, platform: MAC}
org.openqa.grid.common.exception.CapabilityNotPresentOnTheGridException: cannot find : Capabilities {browserName:
opera, platform: MAC}
        at org.openqa.grid.internal.ProxySet.verifyAbilityToHandleDesiredCapabilities(ProxySet.java:153)
        at org.openqa.grid.internal.DefaultGridRegistry.addNewSessionRequest(DefaultGridRegistry.java:217)
        at org.openqa.grid.web.servlet.handler.RequestHandler.process(RequestHandler.java:111)
        at org.openqa.grid.web.servlet.DriverServlet.process(DriverServlet.java:86)
        at org.openqa.grid.web.servlet.DriverServlet.doPost(DriverServlet.java:70)
        at javax.servlet.http.HttpServlet.service(HttpServlet.java:707)
```

Queuing up the request if the node is busy

By default, you can send five test-script requests to any node. Although it is possible to change that configuration, let's see what happens when a node is already serving five requests, and you fire up another request for that node via the hub. The hub will keep polling the node until it gets a free test slot from the node. The test scripts are made to wait during this time. The hub says there are no free slots for the sixth session to be established with the same node. Meanwhile, on the node host, the node tries to create sessions for the five requests and starts executing the test scripts.

Upon creating the sessions, five Chrome windows are launched and the test scripts are executed on them. After serving the first five test-script requests, the hub will establish the waiting sixth session with the node, and the sixth request will be served.

Dealing with two nodes with matching capabilities

There are many configuration options that Selenium Grid provides to control the behavior of a node and a hub while you execute your test scripts. We will discuss them here.

Configuring Selenium Grid

There are many configuration options that Selenium Grid provides to control the behavior of a node and a hub while you execute your test scripts. We will discuss them here.

Specifying node-configuration parameters

In this section, we will go through the configuration parameters for a node.

Setting supported browsers by a node

As we saw earlier, when we register a node with a hub, by default, the node is shown as supporting five instances of the Firefox browser, five instances of the Chrome browser, and one instance of Internet Explorer, irrespective of whether the node actually supports them. But to register your node with the browsers of your choice, Selenium Grid provides a browser option, using which we can achieve this. Let's say we want our node to be registered to support Firefox, Chrome, and Safari; we can do that using the following command:

```
java -jar selenium-server-standalone-3.12.0.jar -role node -hub
http://192.168.0.1:1111/grid/register -browser browserName=firefox -browser
browserName=chrome -browser browserName=safari
```

The **Grid Console** looks like this:

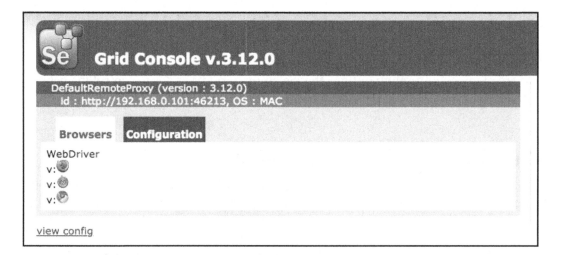

Setting node timeouts

This parameter is set when registering a node with a hub. The value provided to these parameters is the time in seconds that a hub can actually wait before it terminates a test script execution on a node if the test script doesn't perform any kind of activity on the node.

The command to configure your node with a node timeout is as follows:

```
java -jar selenium-server-standalone-3.12.0.jar -role node -hub
http://192.168.0.1:1111/grid/register -nodeTimeout 300
```

Here, we have registered a node with a node timeout value of 300 seconds. So, the hub will terminate the test script if it doesn't perform any activity on the node for more than 300 seconds.

Setting the limit on browser instances

We have seen that, by default, there are 11 instances of browsers getting registered to a node. We have seen how to register our own browser. In this section, we will see how many instances of those browsers we can allow in our node. For this to be controlled, Selenium Grid comes out with a configuration parameter, called `maxInstances`, using which we can specify how many instances of a particular browser we want our node to provide. The command to do that is as follows:

```
java -jar selenium-server-standalone-3.12.0.jar -role node -hub
http://192.168.0.1:1111/grid/register -browser "browserName=firefox,max
Instances=3" -browser "browserName=chrome,maxInstances=3" -browser
"browserName=safari,maxInstances=1"
```

Here, we are registering a node that provides three instances of Firefox, three instances of Chrome, and one instance of Safari.

Reregistering the node automatically

If the hub crashes or restarts after a node registers to it, all the information of the nodes that are already registered is lost. Going back to each of the nodes and reregistering them manually would prove to be tedious. The impact will be even worse if we haven't realized that the hub has restarted, because all the test scripts would fail as a result. So, to handle this kind of situation, Selenium Grid provides a configuration parameter to a node, through which we can specify the node to reregister itself automatically to the hub after a specified amount of time. If not specified, the default time of reregistration is five seconds. This way, we really don't have to worry; even if the hub crashes or restarts, our node will try to reregister every five seconds.

If you want to modify this time interval, the configuration parameter to deal with is `registerCycle`. The command to specify is as follows:

```
java -jar selenium-server-standalone-3.12.0.jar -role node -hub
http://192.168.0.1:1111/grid/register -registerCycle 10000
```

The output you will see on the node log console during startup is as follows:

```
17:47:01.231 INFO - starting auto register thread. Will try to register
every 10000 ms.
 17:47:01.232 INFO - Registering the node to hub
:http://192.168.0.1:1111/grid/register
```

The node will try to register to the hub every 1,000 milliseconds.

Setting node health-check times

Using this configuration parameter, we can specify how frequently the hub can poll a node for its availability. The parameter that is used to achieve this is `nodePolling`. By specifying this to the hub at the node level, each node can specify its own frequency at which it can be health-checked. The command to configure your node is as follows:

```
java -jar selenium-server-standalone-3.12.0.jar -role node -hub
http://192.168.0.1:1111/grid/register -nodePolling 10
```

Now the hub will poll this node every 10 seconds, to check its availability.

Unregistering an unavailable node

Although the `nodePolling` configuration will make the hub poll the node often, the `unregisterIfStillDownAfter` configuration will let the hub unregister the node if the poll doesn't produce an expected result. Let's say a node is down, and the hub tries to poll the node and is unable to connect to it. At this point, how long the hub is going to poll for the availability of the node is determined by the `unregisterIfStillDownAfter` parameter. Beyond this time, the hub will unregister the node.

The command to do that is as follows:

```
java -jar selenium-server-standalone-3.12.0.jar -role node -hub
http://192.168.0.1:1111/grid/register -nodePolling 5 -
unregistIfStillDownAfter 20000
```

Here, the hub will poll the node every five seconds; if the node is down, the polling will continue for 20 seconds, that is, the hub will poll four times and then unregister the node from the grid.

Setting the browser timeout

This configuration is to let the node know how long it should wait before it ends a test script session when the browser seems to hang. After this time, the node will abort the browser session and start with the next waiting test script. The configuration parameter for this is `browserTimeout`. The command to specify that is as follows:

```
java -jar selenium-server-standalone-3.12.0.jar -role node -hub
http://192.168.0.1:1111/grid/register -browserTimeout 60
```

So, these are the some of the configuration parameters that you can specify at the node's end to have better control over the Selenium Grid environment.

Hub-configuration parameters

This section talks about some of the configuration parameters on the hub side.

Waiting for a match of the desired capability

As we saw earlier, when the test script asks for a test platform with a desired capability, the hub will reject the request if it doesn't find a suitable node with the desired capability.

Altering the value for the `throwOnCapabilityNotPresent` parameter can alter this behavior. By default, it is set to `true`, which means the hub will reject the request if it doesn't find a suitable node with that capability. But setting this parameter to `false` will queue the request, and the hub will wait until a node with that capability is added to the grid. The command that has to be invoked is as follows:

```
java -jar selenium-server-standalone-3.12.0.jar -role hub -port 1111 -
throwOnCapabilityNotPresent false
```

Now the hub will not reject the request, but will place the request in a queue and wait until the requested platform is available.

Customized CapabilityMatcher

By default, the hub will use the `org.openqa.grid.internal.utils.`
`DefaultCapabilityMatcher` class to match the requested node. If you do not like the implementation logic of the `DefaultCapabilityMatcher` class, you can extend the class, implement your own `CapabilityMatcher` class, and provide your own logic in it.

Once developed, you can ask the hub to use that class to match the capabilities with the nodes, using a configuration parameter named `capabilityMatcher`. The command to achieve this is as follows:

```
java -jar selenium-server-standalone-3.12.0.jar -role hub -port 1111 -
capabilityMatcher com.yourcomp.CustomCapabilityMatcher
```

The hub will use the logic defined in your `CustomCapabilityMatcher` class to identify the nodes to be assigned to the test-script requests.

WaitTimeout for a new session

When a capability-matched node is busy executing other test scripts, the latest test script will wait for the node to be available. By default, there is no wait timeout; that is, the test script will wait for the node to be available indefinitely. To alter that behavior and to let the test script throw an exception if it doesn't get the node within a limited time, Selenium Grid opens a configuration that enables the test script to do so. The configuration parameter controlling that behavior is `newSessionWaitTimeout`. The command for that is as follows:

```
java -jar selenium-server-standalone-3.12.0.jar -role hub -port 1111 -
newSessionWaitTimeout 120000
```

Here, the test script will wait for two minutes before it throws an exception saying it couldn't obtain a node to execute itself.

Different ways to specify the configuration

There are two ways to specify the configuration parameter to the Selenium Grid's hub and node. The first one is what we have seen all this time; that is, specifying the configuration parameters over the command line. The second way of doing it is by providing a JSON file that contains all these configuration parameters.

A node configuration file (say, `nodeConfig.json`) — a typical JSON file having all the configuration parameters — looks similar to the following:

```
{
  "class": "org.openqa.grid.common.RegistrationRequest",
  "capabilities": [
  {
  "seleniumProtocol": "WebDriver",
  "browserName": "internet explorer",
  "version": "10",
  "maxInstances": 1,
```

```
      "platform" : "WINDOWS"
    }
  ],
  "configuration": {
    "port": 5555,
    "register": true,
    "host": "192.168.1.102",
    "proxy": "org.openqa.grid.selenium.proxy.
    DefaultRemoteProxy",
    "maxSession": 2,
    "hubHost": "192.168.1.100",
    "role": "webdriver",
    "registerCycle": 5000,
    "hub": "http://192.168.1.101:111/grid/register",
    "hubPort": 1111,
    "remoteHost": "http://192.168.1.102:5555"
  }
}
```

Once these files are configured, they can be provided to the node and the hub, using the following command:

```
java -jar selenium-server-standalone-3.12.0.jar -role node -nodeConfig
nodeconfig.json
```

This way, you can specify the configuration of your hub and node using JSON files.

Using cloud-based grids for cross-browser testing

To set up a Selenium Grid for cross-browser testing, you need to set up physical or virtual machines with different browsers and operating systems. This requires an investment in the required hardware, software, and support to run the test lab. You also need to put in effort to keep this infrastructure updated with the latest versions and patches. Not everybody can afford these costs and the effort.

Instead of investing and setting up a cross-browser test lab, you can easily outsource a virtual test lab to a third-party cloud provider for cross-browser testing. The Sauce Labs and BrowserStack are leading cloud-based cross-browser testing cloud providers. Both of these have support for over 400 different browser and operating system configurations, including mobile and tablet devices, and support running Selenium WebDriver tests in their cloud.

Here, we will set up and run a test in the Sauce Labs cloud. The steps are similar if you want to run tests with BrowserStack.

Let's set up and run a test with Sauce Labs. You need a free Sauce Labs account, to begin with. Register for a free account on Sauce Labs at `https://saucelabs.com/`, and get the username and access key. Sauce Labs provides all the needed hardware and software infrastructure to run your tests in the cloud. You can get the access key from the Sauce Labs dashboard after you log in from the **My Account** page:

Let's create a new test to execute on the Sauce Labs cloud. We need to add the Sauce username and access key to the test, and change the Grid address to the Sauce Labs Grid address instead of the local Selenium Grid, as shown in the following code example:

```
public class BmiCalculatorTest {

    WebDriver driver;

    @BeforeMethod
    public void setUp() throws Exception {

        String SAUCE_USER = "upgundecha";
        String SAUCE_KEY = "5768f2a9-33be-4ebd-9a5f-3826d7c38ec9";

        DesiredCapabilities caps = new DesiredCapabilities();
        caps.setCapability("platform", "OS X 10.9");
        caps.setCapability("browserName", "Safari");
        caps.setCapability("name", "BMI Calculator Test");
        driver = new RemoteWebDriver(
                new
    URL(MessageFormat.format("http://{0}:{1}@ondemand.saucelabs.com:80/wd/hub'"
    ,
                SAUCE_USER, SAUCE_KEY)), caps);
        driver.get("http://bit.ly/1zdNrFZ");

    }

    @Test
    public void testBmiCalc() {
```

```
        WebElement height = driver.findElement(By.name("heightCMS"));
        height.sendKeys("181");

        WebElement weight = driver.findElement(By.name("weightKg"));
        weight.sendKeys("80");

        WebElement calculateButton =
driver.findElement(By.id("Calculate"));
        calculateButton.click();

        WebElement bmi = driver.findElement(By.name("bmi"));
        assertEquals(bmi.getAttribute("value"), "24.4");

        WebElement bmi_category =
driver.findElement(By.name("bmi_category"));
        assertEquals(bmi_category.getAttribute("value"), "Normal");
    }

    @AfterMethod
    public void tearDown() throws Exception {
        driver.quit();
    }
}
```

When you execute the test, it will connect to Sauce Lab's hub and request the desired operating system and browser configuration. The sauce Labs cloud-management software automatically assigns a virtual machine for our test to run on a given configuration. We can monitor this run on a dashboard, as shown in the following screenshot:

We can further drill down into the session and see exactly what happened during the run. It provides details of the Selenium commands, screenshots, logs, and a video of the execution on multiple tabs, as shown in the following screenshot:

Selenium details window

You can also test applications that are securely hosted on internal servers, by using the Sauce Connect utility. sauce connect creates a secure tunnel between your machine and the Sauce cloud.

Summary

In this chapter, we learned about Selenium Grid, how a hub and node will work, and, more importantly, how to configure your Selenium Grid to have better control over the environment and infrastructure. The Selenium Grid will enable cross-browser testing for the application by covering combinations of operating systems and browsers. We also saw how to use cloud services, such as Sauce Labs, to execute tests in a remote cloud environment.

In the next `chapter`, we will learn about creating data-driven tests using TestNG and Selenium WebDriver.

Questions

1. Which argument can be used to specify how many browser instances can be supported by the node?
2. Explain how Selenium Grid can be used to support Cross Browser Testing.
3. What is the URL you need to specify with RemoteWebDriver to run tests on Selenium Grid?
4. Selenium Grid Hub acts as a load balancer— true or false?

Further information

You can check out the following link for more information about the topics covered in this chapter:

- Read more about Selenium Grid at `https://www.seleniumhq.org/docs/07_selenium_grid.jsp`

8
Data-Driven Testing with TestNG

In this chapter, we will see how to create data-driven tests using TestNG and Selenium WebDriver. We will look at the following topics:

- What is data-driven testing?
- Using TestNG suite parameters to parameterize tests.
- Using TestNG data providers for data-driven testing.
- Using the CSV and Excel file formats for storing and reading test data.

Overview of data-driven testing

By employing the data-driven testing approach, we can use a single test to verify different sets of test cases or test data by driving the test with input and expected values from an external data source instead of using the hardcoded values every time a test is run. This becomes useful when we have similar tests that consist of the same steps but differ in the input data and expected value or the application state. Here is an example of a set of login test cases with different combinations:

Description	Test data	Expected output
Test valid username and password	A pair of valid usernames and passwords	The user should log into the application with a success message
Test invalid username and password	An invalid username and password	The user should be displayed the login error
Valid username and invalid password	A valid username and an invalid password	The user should be displayed the login error

We can create a single script that can handle the test data and the conditions from the preceding table. By using the data-driven testing approach, we separate the test data from the test logic by replacing the hardcoded test data with variables using the data from external sources, such as CSV or a spreadsheet file. This also helps to create reusable tests that can run with different sets of data, which can be kept outside of the test. Data-driven testing also helps in increasing the test coverage, as we can handle multiple test conditions while minimizing the amount of test code we need to write and maintain.

The benefits of data-driven testing are as follows:

- We can get greater test coverage while minimizing the amount of test code we need to write and maintain
- It makes creating and running a lot of test conditions very easy
- Test data can be designed and created before the application is ready for testing
- Data tables can also be used in manual testing

Selenium WebDriver, being a pure browser-automation API, does not provide built-in features to support data-driven testing. However, we can add support for data-driven testing using testing frameworks such as JUnit or TestNG. In this book, we are using TestNG as our testing framework and we will use parameterization features of TestNG to create data-driven tests in the following sections.

Parameterizing Tests using suite parameters

In Chapter 1, *Introducing WebDriver and WebElements*, we created a search test that performs a simple search on the application under test. This test searches for a given product and validates the title. We used a hardcoded value, phones, for the search, as shown in the following code snippet:

```
@Test
public void searchProduct() {

        // find search box and enter search string
        WebElement searchBox = driver.findElement(By.name("q"));

        searchBox.sendKeys("Phones");

        WebElement searchButton =
                driver.findElement(By.className("search-button"));

        searchButton.click();
```

```
assertThat(driver.getTitle())
        .isEqualTo("Search results for: 'Phones'");
}
```

Instead of using hardcoded values, we can parameterize these values and provide them to the test method using the suite-parameter feature of TestNG. This will help to remove using hardcoded values in the test method and move them into TestNG suite files. The parameterized values can be used in multiple tests. When we need to change these values, we don't have to go to each test and make a change,the instead we can simply change these in suite file.

Now, let's look at steps for using the TestNG Parameters from the suite file. In Chapter 1, *Introducing WebDriver and WebElements,* we created a testng.xml file, which is located in the src/test/resources/suites folder. Let's modify the file and add the parameter declaration, as highlighted in the following code snippet:

```
<!DOCTYPE suite SYSTEM "http://testng.org/testng-1.0.dtd" >

<suite name="Chapter 1" verbose="1">
    <listeners>
        <listener class-
name="com.vimalselvam.testng.listener.ExtentTestNgFormatter"/>
    </listeners>
    <test name="Search Test">
        <parameter name="searchWord" value="phones"/>
        <parameter name="items" value="3"/>
        <classes>
            <class name="com.example.SearchTest"/>
        </classes>
    </test>
</suite>
```

We can add parameters in the TestNG suite file using the <parameter> tag. We have to provide the name and value attributes for the parameter. In this example, we create two parameters: searchWord and items. These parameters store the search word and expected count of items returned by the application for that search word.

Now, let's modify the test to use parameters instead of hardcoded values. First, we need to use the `@Parameters` annotation before the `@Test` annotation for the test method. In the `@Parameters` annotation, we need to supply the exact names and order of the parameters declared in the suite file. In this case, we will supply `searchWord` and `items`. We also need to add arguments to the test method along with the required data type to map the XML parameters. In this case, the `String searchWord` and `int Items` arguments are added to the `searchProduct()` test method. Finally, we need to replace the hardcoded values with the arguments in the test method, as shown in the following code snippet:

```
@Parameters({"searchWord", "items"})
@Test
public void searchProduct(String searchWord, int items) {

    // find search box and enter search string
    WebElement searchBox = driver.findElement(By.name("q"));

    // use searchWord parameter value from XML suite file
    searchBox.sendKeys(searchWord);

    WebElement searchButton =
            driver.findElement(By.className("search-button"));

    searchButton.click();

    assertThat(driver.getTitle())
            .isEqualTo("Search results for: '" + searchWord + "'");

    List<WebElement> searchItems = driver
            .findElements(By.xpath("//h2[@class='product-name']/a"));

    assertThat(searchItems.size())
            .isEqualTo(items);
}
```

We have to run the parameterized tests via the testng.xml file for TestNG to read the parameters defined in the suite file and pass the values to the test method.

During execution, TestNG will use the parameters defined in the XML suite file and map these in the same order to the Java parameters in test methods using the `@Parameters` annotation. It will pass the parameter values from the suite file using the arguments added in the test method. TestNG will throw an exception if the number of parameters between XML and the `@Parameters` annotation does not match.

In the next section, we will see a programmatic parameterization, which offers us the ability to run tests with multiple rows of test data.

Parameterizing Tests with a Data Provider

While suite parameters are useful for simple parameterization, they are not sufficient for creating data-driven tests with multiple test data values and reading data from external files, such as property files, CSV, Excel, or databases. In this case, we can use a Data Provider to supply the values need to test. A Data Provider is a method defined in the test class that returns an array of array of objects. This method is annotated with the @DataProvider annotation.

Let's modify the preceding test to use the Data Provider. Instead of using a single searchWord, we will now use three combinations of searchWords and expected items counts returned by the search. We will add a new method, named provider(), in the SearchTest class, as shown in following code, before the @BeforeMethod annotation:

```
public class SearchTest {

    WebDriver driver;

    @DataProvider(name = "searchWords")
    public Object[][] provider() {
        return new Object[][]{
                {"phones", 3},
                {"music", 5},
                {"iphone 5s", 0}
        };
    }

    @BeforeMethod
    public void setup() {
        ...
    }
    ...
}
```

When a method is annotated with @DataProvider, it becomes a data-feeder method by passing the test data to the test case. In addition to the @DataProvider annotation, we also need to provide a name for the data provider. In this example, we have given the name as searchWords.

Next, we need to update the `searchTest()` test method to link to the `data provider`. This is done with the following steps:

1. Provide the name of the `data provider` in the `@Test` annotation
2. Add two arguments `String searchWord` and `int items` to the `searchProduct` method
3. Use method parameters to substitute hardcoded values:

```java
public class SearchTest {

    WebDriver driver;

    @DataProvider(name = "searchWords")
    public Object[][] provider() {
        ...
    }

    @BeforeMethod
    public void setup() {

        System.setProperty("webdriver.chrome.driver",
                "./src/test/resources/drivers/chromedriver");
        driver = new ChromeDriver();
        driver.get("http://demo-store.seleniumacademy.com/");

    }

    @Test(dataProvider = "searchWords")
    public void searchProduct(String searchWord, int items) {

        // find search box and enter search string
        WebElement searchBox = driver.findElement(By.name("q"));

        searchBox.sendKeys(searchWord);

        WebElement searchButton =
                driver.findElement(By.className("search-button"));

        searchButton.click();

        assertThat(driver.getTitle())
                .isEqualTo("Search results for: '" + searchWord + "'");

        List<WebElement> searchItems = driver
                .findElements(By.xpath("//h2[@class='product-name']/a"));

        assertThat(searchItems.size())
```

```
            .isEqualTo(items);
    }

    @AfterMethod
    public void tearDown() {
        driver.quit();
    }
}
```

The `provider()` method will become the data-feeder method, which returns an array of objects that are combinations of `searchWords` and expected `items` counts, and TestNG will pass the array of data rows to the test method.

TestNG will execute the test four times with different test combinations. TestNG also generates a well-formatted report at the end of the test execution. Here is an example of the test results with TestNG using the defined values. The `searchProduct` test is executed three times, as shown in the following screenshot:

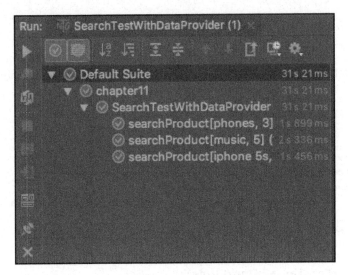

Reading data from a CSV file

We saw a simple data-driven test TestNG. The test data was hardcoded in the test-script code. This could become difficult to maintain. It is recommended that we store the test data separately from the test scripts. Often, we use data from the production environment for testing. This data can be exported in the CSV format. We can read these CSV files in data-provider methods and pass the data to the test instead of hardcoded object arrays.

In this example, we will use the OpenCSV library to read a CSV file. OpenCSV is a simple Java library for reading CSV files in Java. You can find more details on OpenCSV at `http:/ /opencsv.sourceforge.net/`.

Let's first create a CSV file, named `data.csv`, in the `src/test/resources/data` folder and copy the following combinations of `searchWords` and `items`:

```
searchWord,items
phones,3
music,5
iphone 5s,0
```

Next, we need to add the OpenCSV dependency to the Maven pom.xml file. For this example, we will use the latest version, 3.4, as shown in the following code snippet:

```
<dependency>
    <groupId>com.opencsv</groupId>
    <artifactId>opencsv</artifactId>
    <version>3.4</version>
</dependency>
```

Finally, we need to modify the `provider()` method in the test class to read the contents of the CSV file and return them as an array of objects, as shown in the following code:

```
public class SearchTest {

    WebDriver driver;

    @DataProvider(name = "searchWords")
    public Iterator<Object[]> provider() throws Exception {
        CSVReader reader = new CSVReader(
                new FileReader("./src/test/resources/data/data.csv")
                , ',', '\'', 1);
        List<Object[]> myEntries = new ArrayList<Object[]>();
        String[] nextLine;
        while ((nextLine = reader.readNext()) != null) {
            myEntries.add(nextLine);
        }
        reader.close();
        return myEntries.iterator();
    }

    @BeforeMethod
    public void setup() {

        System.setProperty("webdriver.chrome.driver",
                "./src/test/resources/drivers/chromedriver");
```

```
        driver = new ChromeDriver();
        driver.get("http://demo-store.seleniumacademy.com/");

    }

    @Test(dataProvider = "searchWords")
    public void searchProduct(String searchWord, String items) {

        // find search box and enter search string
        WebElement searchBox = driver.findElement(By.name("q"));

        searchBox.sendKeys(searchWord);

        WebElement searchButton =
                driver.findElement(By.className("search-button"));

        searchButton.click();

        assertThat(driver.getTitle())
                .isEqualTo("Search results for: '" + searchWord + "'");

        List<WebElement> searchItems = driver
                .findElements(By.xpath("//h2[@class='product-name']/a"));

        assertThat(searchItems.size())
                .isEqualTo(Integer.parseInt(items));
    }

    @AfterMethod
    public void tearDown() {
        driver.quit();
    }
}
```

In the provide method, the CSV file will be parsed using the CSVReader class of the OpenCSV library. We need to provide the path of the CSV file, the delimiter character, and the header row number (this will skip while fetching the data), as shown in the following code snippet:

```
@DataProvider(name = "searchWords")
public Iterator<Object[]> provider() throws Exception {

    CSVReader reader = new CSVReader(
            new FileReader("./src/test/resources/data/data.csv")
            , ',', '\'', 1);

    List<Object[]> myEntries = new ArrayList<Object[]>();
    String[] nextLine;
```

```
        while ((nextLine = reader.readNext()) != null) {
            myEntries.add(nextLine);
        }
        reader.close();
        return myEntries.iterator();
    }
```

In the preceding code, we will read each line of the CSV file ,copy it to an array of the object, and return it to the test method. The test method will be executed for each row in the CSV file.

Reading data from an Excel file

To maintain test cases and test data, Microsoft Excel is a favourite tool for testers. Compared to the CSV file format, Excel offers numerous features and a structured way to store data. A tester can create and maintain tables of test data in an Excel spreadsheet easily.

Let's create an Excel spreadsheet, named `data.xlsx`, in the `src/test/resources/data` folder with the following contents:

In this section, we will use an Excel spreadsheet as your data source. We will use the Apache POI API, developed by the Apache Foundation, to manipulate the Excel spreadsheet.

Let's modify the `provider()` method to use a helper class, called `SpreadsheetData`, to read the Excel file's contents:

```
@DataProvider(name = "searchWords")
public Object[][] provider() throws Exception {
    SpreadsheetData spreadsheetData = new SpreadsheetData();
    return
spreadsheetData.getCellData("./src/test/resources/data/data.xlsx");
}
```

The `SpreadsheetData` class This is available in the source code bundle for this book. This class supports both the old *.xls* and newer *.xlsx* formats:

```
public class SpreadsheetData {
    public String[][] getCellData(String path) throws
InvalidFormatException, IOException {
        FileInputStream stream = new FileInputStream(path);
        Workbook workbook = WorkbookFactory.create(stream);
        Sheet s = workbook.getSheetAt(0);
        int rowcount = s.getLastRowNum();
        int cellcount = s.getRow(0).getLastCellNum();
        String data[][] = new String[rowcount][cellcount];
        for (int rowCnt = 1; rowCnt <= rowcount; rowCnt++) {
            Row row = s.getRow(rowCnt);
            for (int colCnt = 0; colCnt < cellcount; colCnt++) {
                Cell cell = row.getCell(colCnt);
                try {
                    if (cell.getCellType() == cell.CELL_TYPE_STRING) {
                        data[rowCnt - 1][colCnt] =
cell.getStringCellValue();
                    } else {
                        data[rowCnt - 1][colCnt] =
String.valueOf(cell.getNumericCellValue());
                    }
                } catch (Exception e) {
                    e.printStackTrace();
                }
            }
        }
        return data;
    }
}
```

When the test is executed, the `provider()` method will create an instance of the `SpreadsheetData` class. The `SpreadsheetData` class reads the contents of the Excel spreadsheet row by row in a collection and returns this collection back to the `provider()` method:

```
InputStream spreadsheet = new
FileInputStream("./src/test/resources/data/data.xlsx");
return new SpreadsheetData(spreadsheet).getData();
```

For each row in the test data collection returned by the `provider()` method, the test runner will instantiate the test case class, passing the test data as parameters to the test-class constructor, and then execute all the tests in the test class.

Summary

In this chapter, we learned about an important technique to create parameterized and data-driven tests using TestNG features. This will help you to create highly-maintainable and robust tests with minimum coding effort and increased test coverage. We also looked at ways to read data from the CSV and Excel formats. In the next chapter, we will learn about building a Selenium Test Driver Class for mobile web applications using JAVA.

Questions

1. Explain what Data-driven Testing is.
2. Selenium supports data-driven testing— True or False?
3. What are two methods in TestNG to create data-driven tests?
4. Explain the `DataProvider` method in TestNG.

Further information

You can check out the following links for more information about the topics covered in this chapter:

- Read more about TestNG data-driven features at `https://testng.org/doc/documentation-main.html#parameters`
- Read more about the Apache POI library at `https://poi.apache.org/`

Building a Scalable Selenium Test Driver Class for Web and Mobile Applications

9

In this chapter, we will cover designing and building the Java test driver class required to create and use the **Selenium WebDriver API** and **AppiumDriver API** for automated testing. The driver class is the central location for all aspects and preferences of the browser and mobile devices, platforms and versions to run on, support for multithreading, support for the Selenium Grid Architecture, and customization of the driver. This chapter will cover the following topics:

- Introduction
- The singleton driver class
- Using preferences to support browsers and platforms
- Using preferences to support mobile device simulators, emulators, and real devices
- Multithreading support for use in parallel and distributed testing
- Passing optional arguments and parameters to the driver

- Selenium Grid Architecture support using the RemoteWebDriver and AppiumDriver classes
- Third-party grid architecture support, including the Sauce Labs Test Cloud
- Using property files to select browsers, devices, versions, platforms, languages, and so on

Selenium headquarters website

Introduction

In this chapter, users will be introduced to data-driven testing, the Selenium Page Object Model, and **Don't Repeat Yourself (DRY)** approaches to testing, all of which work hand-in-hand with each other, and are required for scalable frameworks. Let's briefly discuss each.

Data-driven testing

The premise of data-driven testing is that test methods and test data are separated to allow the adding of new test permutations without changing the test methods, to reduce the amount of code, reduce the amount of maintenance required for testing, and to store common libraries in a central location—those being the page object classes. Data is *encapsulated* in a central location such as a database, JSON, or CSV file, property file, or an Excel spreadsheet, to name a few. Test methods then allow dynamic data to be passed into them on the fly using parameters and data providers of choice. The test methods themselves become "templates" for positive, negative, boundary, and/or limit testing, extending coverage of the suite of tests with limited code additions.

TestNG data-driven testing tip:

`http://testng.org/doc/documentation-main.html`

Selenium Page Object Model

The Selenium Page Object Model is based on the programming concepts that a page object class should include all aspects of the page under test, such as the elements on the page, the methods for interacting with those elements, variables, and properties associated with the class. Following that concept, there is no data stored in the page object class. The test classes themselves call methods on the page object instances they are testing, but have no knowledge of the granular elements in the class. Finally, the actual test data is encapsulated outside the test class in a central location. In other words, there is an abstract layer created between the tests and the actual page object classes. This reduces the amount of code being written and allows them to be reused in various testing scenarios, thus following the DRY approaches to programming. From a maintenance point of view, changes to methods and locators are made in limited, central places, reducing the amount of time required to maintain ever-changing applications.

Selenium HQ design tip:

`http://www.seleniumhq.org/docs/06_test_design_considerations.jsp`

DRY

DRY approaches to creating page object and test classes simply mean promoting the use of common classes, locators, methods, and inheritance to eliminate and avoid repeating the same actions over and over in multiple places. Instead, abstract base classes are created, containing all common objects and methods, and used as libraries to be called using parameters, which vary based on the data that is passed into them from the test classes. All subclasses derived from these base classes inherit all the common code, objects, locators, and methods, and enforce all of the abstract methods required by the base class. In essence, this approach avoids common copy and paste actions that result in duplicate code in multiple places.

As per Wikipedia (`https://en.wikipedia.org/wiki/Data-driven_testing`):

> *"Data-driven testing (DDT) is a term used in the testing of computer software to describe testing done using a table of conditions directly, as test inputs and verifiable outputs as well as the process where test environment settings and control are not hardcoded. In the simplest form the tester supplies the inputs from a row in the table and expects the outputs which occur in the same row. The table typically contains values which correspond to boundary or partition input spaces. In the control methodology, test configuration is "read" from a database."*

What you will learn

Users will learn how to design and build the Java singleton class required to control the Selenium driver of choice for the **Application Under Test (AUT)**.

The singleton driver class

In this section, a Java singleton class will be used to create the driver class. This will force the user to use the same object for all instances where the WebDriver is required. The WebDriver events will never get out of sync during the run, and all WebDriver events will get sent to the correct browser or mobile device instance. And since the instance of the class is created on a single thread, referencing it won't interfere with other WebDriver instances running on the same node simultaneously.

As per Wikipedia (`https://en.wikipedia.org/wiki/Singleton_pattern`):

> *"In software engineering, the singleton pattern is a software design pattern that restricts the instantiation of a class to one object. This is useful when exactly one object is needed to coordinate actions across the system. The concept is sometimes generalized to systems that operate more efficiently when only one object exists, or that restrict the instantiation to a certain number of objects. The term comes from the mathematical concept of a singleton."*

Requirements

In order to start building the framework, users must import the required JAR files into their project to use the Selenium WebDriver, AppiumDriver, and TestNG APIs. Additionally, there will be various Java JAR files required, such as Apache, Spring, File I/O, and other utilities as the framework develops:

```
import io.appium.java_client.AppiumDriver;
import io.appium.java_client.MobileElement;
import io.appium.java_client.android.AndroidDriver;
import io.appium.java_client.ios.IOSDriver;
import org.openqa.selenium.WebDriver;
import org.openqa.selenium.chrome.ChromeDriver;
import org.openqa.selenium.chrome.ChromeOptions;
import org.openqa.selenium.edge.EdgeDriver;
import org.openqa.selenium.edge.EdgeOptions;
import org.openqa.selenium.firefox.*;
import org.openqa.selenium.ie.InternetExplorerDriver;
import org.openqa.selenium.remote.DesiredCapabilities;
import org.openqa.selenium.remote.LocalFileDetector;
import org.openqa.selenium.remote.RemoteWebDriver;
import org.openqa.selenium.safari.SafariDriver;
import org.openqa.selenium.safari.SafariOptions;
import org.testng.*;
```

A good source location for finding these JAR files is `https://mvnrepository.com/`.

The class signature

The class should be named something obvious such as `Driver.java`, `CreateDriver.java`, `SeleniumDriver.java`, and so on. Since this will be a Java singleton class, it will contain a private constructor and a static `getInstance` method as follows:

```java
/**
 * Selenium Singleton Class
 *
 * @author CarlCocchiaro
 *
 */
@SuppressWarnings("varargs")
public class CreateDriver {

    // constructor
    private CreateDriver() {
    }

    /**
     * getInstance method to retrieve active driver instance
     *
     * @return CreateDriver
     */
    public static CreateDriver getInstance() {
        if ( instance == null ) {
            instance = new CreateDriver();
        }

        return instance;
    }
}
```

Class variables

Initially, when building the class, there will be various private and public variables used that should be declared at the top of the class. This organizes the variables into one place in the file, but of course, this is a coding style guideline. Some of the common variables required to start are as follows:

```java
public class CreateDriver {
    // local variables
    private static CreateDriver instance = null;
    private String browserHandle = null;
    private static final int IMPLICIT_TIMEOUT = 0;

    private ThreadLocal<WebDriver> webDriver =
            new ThreadLocal<WebDriver>();

    private ThreadLocal<AppiumDriver<MobileElement>> mobileDriver =
            new ThreadLocal<AppiumDriver<MobileElement>>();

    private ThreadLocal<String> sessionId =
            new ThreadLocal<String>();

    private ThreadLocal<String> sessionBrowser =
            new ThreadLocal<String>();

    private ThreadLocal<String> sessionPlatform =
            new ThreadLocal<String>();

    private ThreadLocal<String> sessionVersion =
            new ThreadLocal<String>();

    private String getEnv = null;
}
```

JavaDoc

Before introducing the common methods in this driver class, it is prudent to note that requiring JavaDoc for all methods in the class will be helpful for users who are learning the framework. The JavaDoc can be built automatically in Java using a build tool such as Maven, Gradle, or Ant. An example of the JavaDoc format is as follows:

```
/**
 * This is the setDriver method used to create the Selenium WebDriver
 * or AppiumDriver instance!
 *
 * @param parameter 1
 * @param parameter 2
 * @param parameter 3
 * @param parameter 4
 *
 * @throws Exception
 */
```

Parameters

The driver class will be designed with various get and set methods. The main `setDriver` method can take parameters to determine the browser or mobile type, platform to run on, environment for testing, and a set of optional preferences to allow changing driver behavior on the fly:

```
@SafeVarargs
public final void setDriver(String browser,
                            String platform,
                            String environment,
                            Map<String, Object>... optPreferences)
```

Examples of some of the parameters of `setDriver` are as follows:

- `browser`: Chrome, Firefox, Internet Explorer, Microsoft Edge, Opera, Safari (iPhone/iPad, or Android for mobile)
- `platform`: Linux, Windows, Mac, Sierra, Win10 (iPhone/iPad, or Android for mobile)
- `environment`: Local, remote, and Sauce Labs
- `optPrefs`: Map of driver preferences (this will be covered later in detail)

Class methods

All the methods in this class should pertain to the web or mobile driver. This includes things such as `setDriver`, `getDriver`, `getCurrentDriver`, `getSessionID/Browser/Version/Platform`, `driverWait`, `driverRefresh`, and `closeDriver`. Each will be outlined in this section:

- `setDriver`: The `setDriver` methods (standard and overloaded) will allow users to create a new instance of the driver for testing browser or mobile devices. The method will take parameters for browser, platform, environment, and optional preferences. Based on these preferences, the WebDriver/AppiumDriver of choice will be created. Here are some key points of the method, including a code sample:
  - The driver preferences are set up using the `DesiredCapabilities` class
  - The method will be segregated according to the browser or mobile type, platform, and environment
  - The method will be overloaded to allow switching back and forth between multiple drivers running concurrently

The following code demonstrates the standard `setDriver` method:

```
/**
 * setDriver method
 *
 * @param browser
 * @param environment
 * @param platform
 * @param optPreferences
 * @throws Exception
 */
@SafeVarargs
public final void setDriver(String browser,
                            String environment,
                            String platform,
                            Map<String, Object>...
optPreferences)
                            throws Exception {

    DesiredCapabilities caps = null;
    String localHub = "http://127.0.0.1:4723/wd/hub";
    String getPlatform = null;

    switch (browser) {
        case "firefox":
            caps = DesiredCapabilities.firefox();
```

```
                                webDriver.set(new FirefoxDriver(caps));

                            break;
                    case "chrome":
                        caps = DesiredCapabilities.chrome();
                        webDriver.set(new ChromeDriver(caps));

                            break;
                    case "internet explorer":
                        caps = DesiredCapabilities.internetExplorer();
                        webDriver.set(new
                                        InternetExplorerDriver(caps));

                            break;
                    case "safari":
                        caps = DesiredCapabilities.safari();
                        webDriver.set(new SafariDriver(caps));

                            break;
                    case "microsoftedge":
                        caps = DesiredCapabilities.edge();
                        webDriver.set(new EdgeDriver(caps));

                            break;
                    case "iphone":
                    case "ipad":
                        if (browser.equalsIgnoreCase("ipad")) {
                            caps = DesiredCapabilities.ipad();
                        }

                        else {
                            caps = DesiredCapabilities.iphone();
                        }

                        mobileDriver.set(new IOSDriver<MobileElement>(
                                        new URL(localHub), caps));

                            break;
                    case "android":
                        caps = DesiredCapabilities.android();
                        mobileDriver.set(new
                                        AndroidDriver<MobileElement>(
                                        new URL(localHub), caps));

                            break;
            }
        }
```

Here is the overloaded `setDriver` method:

```
/**
 * overloaded setDriver method to switch driver to specific
WebDriver
 * if running concurrent drivers
 *
 * @param driver WebDriver instance to switch to
 */
public void setDriver(WebDriver driver) {
    webDriver.set(driver);

    sessionId.set(((RemoteWebDriver) webDriver.get())
    .getSessionId().toString());

    sessionBrowser.set(((RemoteWebDriver) webDriver.get())
    .getCapabilities().getBrowserName());

    sessionPlatform.set(((RemoteWebDriver) webDriver.get())
    .getCapabilities().getPlatform().toString());

    setBrowserHandle(getDriver().getWindowHandle());
}

/**
 * overloaded setDriver method to switch driver to specific
AppiumDriver
 * if running concurrent drivers
 *
 * @param driver AppiumDriver instance to switch to
 */
public void setDriver(AppiumDriver<MobileElement> driver) {
    mobileDriver.set(driver);

    sessionId.set(mobileDriver.get()
    .getSessionId().toString());

    sessionBrowser.set(mobileDriver.get()
    .getCapabilities().getBrowserName());

    sessionPlatform.set(mobileDriver.get()
    .getCapabilities().getPlatform().toString());
}
```

- `getDriver` and `getCurrentDriver`: The `getDriver` and `getCurrentDriver` methods (standard and overloaded) will allow users to retrieve the current driver, whether that be browser or mobile. The driver should be instantiated at the beginning of the test, and will remain available throughout the test by using these methods. Since many of the Selenium WebDriver methods require the driver to be passed to it, these methods will allow users to retrieve the currently active session:

```java
/**
 * getDriver method will retrieve the active WebDriver
 *
 * @return WebDriver
 */
public WebDriver getDriver() {
    return webDriver.get();
}

/**
 * getDriver method will retrieve the active AppiumDriver
 *
 * @param mobile boolean parameter
 * @return AppiumDriver
 */
public AppiumDriver<MobileElement> getDriver(boolean mobile) {
    return mobileDriver.get();
}

/**
 * getCurrentDriver method will retrieve the active WebDriver
 * or AppiumDriver
 *
 * @return WebDriver
 */
public WebDriver getCurrentDriver() {
    if ( getInstance().getSessionBrowser().contains("iphone") ||

            getInstance().getSessionBrowser().contains("ipad") ||
            getInstance().getSessionBrowser().contains("android")
    ) {

            return getInstance().getDriver(true);
    }

    else {
        return getInstance().getDriver();
    }
}
```

- driverWait and driverRefresh: The driverWait method will "pause" the script for the designated amount of time in seconds, although this should not be used to synchronize event handling. The driverRefresh method will reload the currently active browser page:

```
/**
 * driverWait method pauses the driver in seconds
 *
 * @param seconds to pause
 */
public void driverWait(long seconds) {
    try {
        Thread.sleep(TimeUnit.SECONDS.toMillis(seconds));
    }

    catch (InterruptedException e) {
        // do something
    }
}

/**
 * driverRefresh method reloads the current browser page
 */
public void driverRefresh() {
    getCurrentDriver().navigate().refresh();
}
```

- closeDriver: The closeDriver method will retrieve the current driver and call the WebDriver's quit method on it, browser or mobile:

```
/**
 * closeDriver method quits the current active driver
 */
public void closeDriver() {
    try {
        getCurrentDriver().quit();
    }

    catch ( Exception e ) {
        // do something
    }
}
```

Using preferences to support browsers and platforms

The browser preferences and behavior can be set to specific defaults when the driver is created, set on the fly using optional parameters, or set as system properties. Preferences can be set for different languages, geolocations, focus, download folders, and so on. This section will cover the basics of how to set default preferences and capabilities in the driver method.

 The Selenium HQ documentation on Desired Capabilities is located at `https://github.com/SeleniumHQ/selenium/wiki/DesiredCapabilities`.

Browser preferences

- **Firefox**: Preferences for this browser are set using the `FirefoxProfile` class, the `FirefoxOptions` class, and Desired Capabilities. The list of preferences and options set in the profile are then passed to the driver as `DesiredCapabilites`. The following example shows various profile preferences passed into the driver as default settings using both profile preferences and Desired Capabilities:

```
switch (browser) {
    case "firefox":
        caps = DesiredCapabilities.firefox();

        FirefoxOptions ffOpts = new FirefoxOptions();
        FirefoxProfile ffProfile = new FirefoxProfile();
        ffProfile.setPreference("browser.autofocus",
                            true);

        caps.setCapability(FirefoxDriver.PROFILE,
                            ffProfile);
        caps.setCapability("marionette",
                            true);

        webDriver.set(new FirefoxDriver(caps));

        // Selenium 3.7.x
        // webDriver.set(new FirefoxDriver(ffOpts.merge(caps)));
        }
```

```
        break;
    }
```

Firefox preferences can be found by typing the following into the Firefox location bar: `about:config` or at `https://github.com/mozilla/geckodriver/`.

```
accessibility.AOM.enabled; false
accessibility.accesskeycausesactivation; true
accessibility.blockautorefresh; false
...
```

- **Chrome**: Preferences for this browser are set using the `ChromeOptions` class and Desired Capabilities. The list of preferences and/or arguments are then passed to the driver as `DesiredCapabilites`. The following example shows various preferences and arguments passed into the driver as default settings using both preferences and Desired Capabilities:

```java
switch (browser) {
    case "chrome":
        caps = DesiredCapabilities.chrome();

        ChromeOptions chOptions = new ChromeOptions();
        Map<String, Object> chromePrefs =
        new HashMap<String, Object>();

        chromePrefs.put("credentials_enable_service",
                        false);
        chOptions.setExperimentalOption("prefs",
                                        chromePrefs);
        chOptions.addArguments("--disable-plugins",
                               "--disable-extensions",
                               "--disable-popup-blocking");

        caps.setCapability(ChromeOptions.CAPABILITY,
                           chOptions);
        caps.setCapability("applicationCacheEnabled",
                           false);

        webDriver.set(new ChromeDriver(caps));

        // Selenium 3.7.x
        // webDriver.set(new ChromeDriver(chOptions.merge(caps)));
```

```
        break;
    }
```

 Chrome preferences can be found by typing the following into the Chrome location bar: `chrome://flags` or `https://sites.google.com/a/chromium.org/chromedriver/capabilities`.

- **Internet Explorer, Safari, and Microsoft Edge**: Preferences for these browsers are also set using the `InternetExplorerOptions`, `SafariOptions`, `EdgeOptions` classes, and Desired Capabilities. Users can query for the available options and capabilities for each of these browsers. The following code sample shows an abbreviated case for each.

For Internet Explorer:

```
switch (browser) {
    case "internet explorer":
        caps = DesiredCapabilities.internetExplorer();

        InternetExplorerOptions ieOpts =
        new InternetExplorerOptions();
        ieOpts.requireWindowFocus();

        ieOpts.merge(caps);
        caps.setCapability("requireWindowFocus",
                            true);

        webDriver.set(new InternetExplorerDriver(caps));

        // Selenium 3.7.x
        // webDriver.set(new InternetExplorerDriver(
                            ieOpts.merge(caps)));

        break;
    }
```

For Safari:

```
switch (browser) {
    case "safari":
        caps = DesiredCapabilities.safari();

        SafariOptions safariOpts = new SafariOptions();
        safariOpts.setUseCleanSession(true);
```

```
                caps.setCapability(SafariOptions.CAPABILITY,
                                    safariOpts);
            caps.setCapability("autoAcceptAlerts",
                                    true);

            webDriver.set(new SafariDriver(caps));

            // Selenium 3.7.x
            // webDriver.set(new SafariDriver(safariOpts.merge(caps)));

            break;
}
```

For Microsoft Edge:

```
switch(browser) {
    case "microsoftedge":
        caps = DesiredCapabilities.edge();

        EdgeOptions edgeOpts = new EdgeOptions();
        edgeOpts.setPageLoadStrategy("normal");

        caps.setCapability(EdgeOptions.CAPABILITY,
                            edgeOpts);
        caps.setCapability("requireWindowFocus",
                            true);

        webDriver.set(new EdgeDriver(caps));

        // Selenium 3.7.x
        // webDriver.set(new EdgeDriver(edgeOpts.merge(caps)));

        break;
}
```

- Internet Explorer options can be found at https://seleniumhq. github.io/selenium/docs/api/dotnet/html/T_OpenQA_ Selenium_IE_InternetExplorerOptions.htm

- Safari options can be found at https://seleniumhq.github.io/ selenium/docs/api/java/org/openqa/selenium/safari/ SafariOptions.html

- Edge options can be found at https://seleniumhq.github.io/ selenium/docs/api/java/org/openqa/selenium/edge/ EdgeOptions.html

Platforms

There are some specific system properties that need to be set for each driver; specifically, the path to the local driver in the GIT repository of the project. By storing the driver in the project, users will not have to download or install the drivers for each browser when testing locally from their IDE. The path also depends on the OS of the development platform. The following examples are for Windows platforms:

- **Firefox**:
  ```
  System.setProperty("webdriver.gecko.driver","gecko_driver_windo
  ws_path/geckodriver.exe");
  ```
- **Chrome**:
  ```
  System.setProperty("webdriver.chrome.driver","chrome_driver_win
  dows_path/chromedriver.exe");
  ```
- **IE**:
  ```
  System.setProperty("webdriver.ie.driver","ie_driver_windows_pat
  h/IEDriverServer.exe");
  ```
- **Edge**:
  ```
  System.setProperty("webdriver.edge.driver","edge_driver_windows
  _path/MicrosoftWebDriver.exe");
  ```
- **Safari**: The Safari driver is now built into the browser by Apple

Using preferences to support mobile device simulators, emulators, and real devices

The mobile device preferences and behaviors can be set to specific defaults when the driver is created, set on the fly using optional parameters, or set as system properties. Preferences can be set for loading applications on the device, device options, timeouts, platform versions, device versions, and so on. This is accomplished using the Desired Capabilities class, as with browser testing. The following section provides examples of some of the mobile simulator, emulator, and physical device preferences.

iOS preferences

Preferences for iPhone/iPad mobile devices are set using the Desired Capabilities class. Capabilities are set for the iPhone and iPad simulators, or physical devices. The following example shows various capabilities for these iOS devices:

```
switch(browser) {
    case "iphone": case "ipad":
        if ( browser.equalsIgnoreCase("ipad") ) {
            caps = DesiredCapabilities.ipad();
        }

        else {
            caps = DesiredCapabilities.iphone();
        }

        caps.setCapability("appName",
                           "https://myapp.com/myApp.zip");
        caps.setCapability("udid",
                           "12345678"); // physical device
        caps.setCapability("device",
                           "iPhone"); // or iPad

        mobileDriver.set(new IOSDriver<MobileElement>
                        (new URL("http://127.0.0.1:4723/wd/hub"),
                        caps));

        break;
```

 The Desired Capabilities for iOS and Android can be found at http://appium.io/slate/en/master/?java#the-default-capabilities-flag.

Android preferences

Android: Preferences for these mobile devices are set using the Desired Capabilities class. Capabilities are set for Android Emulators, or physical devices. The following example shows various capabilities for these Android devices:

```
switch(browser) {
    case "android":
        caps = DesiredCapabilities.android();

        caps.setCapability("appName",
```

```
                              "https://myapp.com/myApp.apk");
            caps.setCapability("udid",
                              "12345678"); // physical device
            caps.setCapability("device",
                              "Android");

            mobileDriver.set(new AndroidDriver<MobileElement>
                          (new URL("http://127.0.0.1:4723/wd/hub"),
                          caps));

            break;
```

Multithreading support for parallel and distributed testing

In order to leverage the TestNG parallel testing features, users must create a separate thread for each driver instance to control event processing requests. This is done in Java using the `ThreadLocal<T>` class. By declaring variables with this class, each thread has its own initialized copy of the variable, and can return specifics of that session. The following variables are declared in the singleton driver class, and have getter and setter methods to retrieve the session ID, browser, platform, and version:

```
private ThreadLocal<WebDriver> webDriver = new ThreadLocal<WebDriver>();
private ThreadLocal<AppiumDriver<MobileElement>> mobileDriver = new
ThreadLocal<AppiumDriver<MobileElement>>();

private ThreadLocal<String> sessionId = new ThreadLocal<String>();
private ThreadLocal<String> sessionBrowser = new ThreadLocal<String>();
private ThreadLocal<String> sessionPlatform = new ThreadLocal<String>();
private ThreadLocal<String> sessionVersion = new ThreadLocal<String>();
```

Key points:

- The set methods are called by the `setDriver` methods during instantiation of the driver.
- The get methods are stored in the singleton driver class and can be called after the driver is created. Users can retrieve session parameters for each specific instance of the driver that is running.

- To leverage the separate instances during parallel test runs, TestNG suite parameters must also be used. For example:

```
<suite name="Parallel_Test_Suite" preserve-order="true"
parallel="classes" thread-count="10">
```

These are examples of the getter methods for the driver class:

```
/**
 * getSessionId method gets the browser or mobile id
 * of the active session
 *
 * @return String
 */
public String getSessionId() {
    return sessionId.get();
}

/**
 * getSessionBrowser method gets the browser or mobile type
 * of the active session
 *
 * @return String
 */
public String getSessionBrowser() {
    return sessionBrowser.get();
}

/**
 * getSessionVersion method gets the browser or mobile version
 * of the active session
 *
 * @return String
 */
public String getSessionVersion() {
    return sessionVersion.get();
}

/**
 * getSessionPlatform method gets the browser or mobile platform
 * of the active session
 *
 * @return String
 */
public String getSessionPlatform() {
    return sessionPlatform.get();
}
```

How to set:

The session ID, browser, version, and platform can be set during driver creation in the `setDriver` methods as follows:

```
getEnv = "local";
getPlatform = platform;

if ( browser.equalsIgnoreCase("iphone") ||
     browser.equalsIgnoreCase("android") ) {

    sessionId.set(((IOSDriver<MobileElement>)
    mobileDriver.get()).getSessionId().toString());

    sessionId.set(((AndroidDriver<MobileElement>)
    mobileDriver.get()).getSessionId().toString());

    sessionBrowser.set(browser);
sessionVersion.set(caps.getCapability("deviceName").toString());
    sessionPlatform.set(getPlatform);
}

else {
    sessionId.set(((RemoteWebDriver) webDriver.get())
            .getSessionId().toString());

    sessionBrowser.set(caps.getBrowserName());
    sessionVersion.set(caps.getVersion());
    sessionPlatform.set(getPlatform);
}
```

Passing optional arguments and parameters to the driver

In many instances, users will want to change the default behavior of the browser before the test starts, or on the fly when creating a new driver during the test run. We previously covered setting default preferences and options in the `setDriver` method to keep the test environment static. Now, we can alter the default preferences using the `varargs` parameter in Java, as an optional parameter to the `setDriver` method. Here are the basics:

- The `varargs` parameter to `setDriver` will be a `Map<String, Object>` type

- `Map` can be passed into the driver when creating a new browser instance, or by setting a JVM argument of mapped preferences
- JVM arguments used to pass in mapped preferences can be done in a TestNG XML file as a parameter, an IDE Run Configuration using a JVM arg, or as a – `Dswitch` to the command-line executable
- Each browser type will need to process the map of Desired Capabilities, preferences, and options

varargs

The following example shows how to use the `varargs` parameter in the `setDriver` method, which is called `optPreferences`. This is the `setDriver` method so far, from what we have built:

```
@SafeVarargs
public final void setDriver(String browser,
                           String environment,
                           String platform,
                           Map<String, Object>... optPreferences)
                           throws Exception {

    DesiredCapabilities caps = null;
    String localHub = "http://127.0.0.1:4723/wd/hub";
    String getPlatform = null;

    switch (browser) {
        case "firefox":
            caps = DesiredCapabilities.firefox();
            FirefoxProfile ffProfile = new FirefoxProfile();

            ffProfile.setPreference("browser.autofocus",
                                    true);
            caps.setCapability(FirefoxDriver.PROFILE,
                               ffProfile);
            caps.setCapability("marionette",
                               true);
            System.setProperty("webdriver.gecko.driver",
            "gecko_driver_windows_path/geckodriver.exe");

            if ( optPreferences.length > 0 ) {
                processFFProfile(ffProfile, optPreferences);
            }

            webDriver.set(new FirefoxDriver(caps));
```

```
                break;
        case "chrome":
                caps = DesiredCapabilities.chrome();
                ChromeOptions chOptions = new ChromeOptions();

                Map<String, Object> chromePrefs =
                                new HashMap<String, Object>();
                chromePrefs.put("credentials_enable_service",
                                false);
                chOptions.setExperimentalOption("prefs",
                                                chromePrefs);
                chOptions.addArguments("--disable-plugins",
                                        "--disable-extensions",
                                        "--disable-popup-blocking");
                caps.setCapability(ChromeOptions.CAPABILITY,
                                chOptions);
                caps.setCapability("applicationCacheEnabled",
                                false);
                System.setProperty("webdriver.chrome.driver",
                "chrome_driver_windows_path/chromedriver.exe");

                if ( optPreferences.length > 0 ) {
                    processCHOptions(chOptions, optPreferences);
                }

                webDriver.set(new ChromeDriver(caps));
                break;
        case "internet explorer":
                caps = DesiredCapabilities.internetExplorer();

                InternetExplorerOptions ieOpts =
                        new InternetExplorerOptions();

                ieOpts.requireWindowFocus();
                ieOpts.merge(caps);
                caps.setCapability("requireWindowFocus",
                                true);
                System.setProperty("webdriver.ie.driver",
                "ie_driver_windows_path/IEDriverServer.exe");

                if ( optPreferences.length > 0 ) {
                    processDesiredCaps(caps, optPreferences);
                }

                webDriver.set(new InternetExplorerDriver(caps));
                break;
    }
```

```
    // etc...
}
```

 The Oracle Java doc for `varargs` is located at `https://docs.oracle.com/javase/8/docs/technotes/guides/language/varargs.html`.

The parameter for setDriver

The next example shows how to pass `Map` into the `setDriver` method using the `varargs` parameter:

```java
// first, create a map for the key:value pairs to pass into the driver
Map<String, Object> preferences = new HashMap<String, Object>;

// then put the key:value pairs into the map
preferences.put("applicationCacheEnabled",false);
preferences.put("network.cookie.cookieBehavior", 0);

// then, pass the map into the setDriver method
CreateDriver.getInstance().setDriver("firefox",
                                     "Windows 10",
                                     "local",
                                     preferences);
```

JVM argument – -Dswitch

Finally, the next example shows how to set the optional browser preferences as a JVM argument using the TestNG parameter attribute in the suite XML file:

```xml
// pass in the key:value pairs as a runtime argument
-Dbrowserprefs=applicationCacheEnabled:false,
               network.cookie.cookieBehavior:0

// pass in the key:value pairs as a TestNG XML parameter
<test name="Selenium TestNG Test Suite">
    <parameter name="browser" value="chrome" />
    <parameter name="platform" value="Windows 10" />
    <parameter name="browserPrefs" value="intl.accept_languages:fr" />

    <classes>
        <class name="com.myproject.MyTest" />
    </classes>
```

```
</test>

// for convenience, create a setPreferences method
// to build the map to pass into the driver
public Map<String, Object> setPreferences() {
    Map<String, Object> prefsMap = new HashMap<String, Object>();
    List<String> allPrefs = Arrays.asList(
                System.getProperty("browserPrefs").split(",", -1));

    // extract the key/value pairs and pass to map...
    for ( String getPref : allPrefs ) {
        prefsMap.put(getPref.split(":")[0], getPref.split(":")[1]);
    }

    return prefsMap;
}

// set JVM arg, call this method on-the-fly, create new driver
if ( System.getProperty("browserPrefs") != null ) {
    CreateDriver.getInstance().setDriver("firefox",
                                         "Windows 10",
                                         "local",
        CreateDriver.getInstance().setBrowserPrefs()
                                         );
}
```

Parameter processing methods

Once the optional preferences are passed into the setDriver method, the user then has to process those options. For instance, there may be DesiredCapabilities, ChromeOptions, or FirefoxProfile preferences that need to be processed. First, for each driver-type instance, there needs to be a check to see if the options have been passed in, then if so, they have to be processed. Each type will be outlined as shown here:

```
/**
 * Process Desired Capabilities method to override default browser
 * or mobile driver behavior
 *
 * @param caps - the DesiredCapabilities object
 * @param options - the key: value pair map
 * @throws Exception
 */
```

```
private void processDesiredCaps(DesiredCapabilities caps,
                               Map<String,
                               Object>[] options)
                               throws Exception {

    for ( int i = 0; i < options.length; i++ ) {
        Object[] keys = options[i].keySet().toArray();
        Object[] values = options[i].values().toArray();

        for ( int j = 0; j < keys.length; j++ ) {
            if ( values[j] instanceof Integer ) {
                caps.setCapability(keys[j].toString(),
                                   (int) values[j]);
            }
            else if ( values[j] instanceof Boolean) {
                caps.setCapability(keys[j].toString(),
                                   (boolean) values[j]);
            }
            else if ( isStringInt(values[j].toString()) ) {
                caps.setCapability(keys[j].toString(),
                    Integer.valueOf(values[j].toString()));
            }
            else if ( Boolean.parseBoolean(values[j].toString()) ) {
                caps.setCapability(keys[j].toString(),
                    Boolean.valueOf(values[j].toString()));
            }
            else {
                caps.setCapability(keys[j].toString(),
                                   values[j].toString());
            }
        }
    }
}
/**
 * Process Firefox Profile Preferences method to override default
 * browser driver behavior
 *
 * @param caps - the FirefoxProfile object
 * @param options - the key: value pair map
 * @throws Exception
 */
```

```java
private void processFFProfile(FirefoxProfile profile, Map<String, Object>[]
options) throws Exception {
    for (int i = 0; i < options.length; i++) {
        Object[] keys = options[i].keySet().toArray();
        Object[] values = options[i].values().toArray();

        // same as Desired Caps except the following difference
        for (int j = 0; j < keys.length; j++) {
            if (values[j] instanceof Integer) {
                profile.setPreference(keys[j].toString(),
                (int) values[j]);
            }

            // etc...
        }
    }
}

/**
 * Process Chrome Options method to override default browser
 * driver behavior
 *
 * @param caps - the ChromeOptions object
 * @param options - the key: value pair map
 * @throws Exception
 */
private void processCHOptions(ChromeOptions chOptions, Map<String,
Object>[] options) throws Exception {
    for (int i = 0; i < options.length; i++) {
        Object[] keys = options[i].keySet().toArray();
        Object[] values = options[i].values().toArray();

        // same as Desired Caps except the following difference

        for (int j = 0; j < keys.length; j++) {
            if (values[j] instanceof Integer) {
                values[j] = (int) values[j];
                chOptions.setExperimentalOption("prefs", options[i]);
            }

            // etc...
        }
    }
}
```

Selenium Grid Architecture support using the RemoteWebDriver and AppiumDriver classes

When creating a WebDriver instance, users will pass specified preferences, options, and capabilities to the driver running locally in their environment. As previously mentioned, users can store the actual Chrome driver, Firefox driver, and other driver files in their repo, so they won't have to be installed in each development environment. They can then point the local driver instance to the repo location using a desired capability.

Now, when designing and using the Selenium Grid Architecture to run tests against, the user will have to cast the browser or mobile capabilities to the RemoteWebDriver class, or remote AppiumDriver server. This capability should be built into the driver class as well, so the same class can support local, remote, and third-party test platforms. The Selenium Grid Architecture will be discussed in great detail in a separate chapter, but the relevance here is what needs to go into this driver class. Also, keep in mind that users must pass parameters into their driver class to change the environment from local to remote, or thirdParty to direct traffic to the grid nodes.

- **WebDriver**: The URL of the remote grid hub, browser capabilities, driver-specific casting, and any Selenium Grid Node capabilities that control directing traffic to the specific Selenium standalone server node
- **AppiumDriver**: The URL of the remote grid hub, mobile device capabilities, and any Selenium Grid Node capabilities that control directing traffic to the specific Appium server node

Here is the code for the preceding explanation:

```
// for each browser instance
if ( environment.equalsIgnoreCase("remote") ) {
    // set up the Selenium Grid capabilities...
    String remoteHubURL = "http://mygrid-
    hub.companyname.com:4444/wd/hub";

    caps.setCapability("browserName",
                        browser);
    caps.setCapability("version",
                        caps.getVersion());
    caps.setCapability("platform",
                        platform);

    // unique user-specified name
```

```
            caps.setCapability("applicationName",
                              platform + "-" + browser);


        webDriver.set(new RemoteWebDriver(new URL(remoteHubURL),
    caps));
        ((RemoteWebDriver) webDriver.get()).setFileDetector(
                                    new LocalFileDetector());
    }

    // for each mobile device instance
    if ( environment.equalsIgnoreCase("remote") ) {
        // setup the Selenium Grid capabilities...
        String remoteHubURL = "http://mygrid-
        hub.companyname.com:4444/wd/hub";

        caps.setCapability("browserName",
                          browser);
        caps.setCapability("platform",
                          platform);

        // unique user-specified name
        caps.setCapability("applicationName",
                          platform + "-" + browser);

        if ( browser.contains("iphone") ) {
            mobileDriver.set(new IOSDriver<MobileElement>
                        (new URL(remoteHubURL),
                         caps));
        }

        else {
            mobileDriver.set(new AndroidDriver<MobileElement>
                        (new URL(remoteHubURL),
                         caps));
        }
    }
```

Third-party grid architecture support including the Sauce Labs Test Cloud

When adding support to the driver class for third-party grids such as Sauce Labs or Perfecto Mobile, users must add conditions in the driver class that set specific preferences, credentials, URLs, and so on, to direct traffic to that test platform. They are really just other Selenium grids to run against in the cloud, which free up the tester from all the maintenance requirements of an in-house grid. The condition to run on one of these third-party platforms can be passed as a parameter to the test, specifically environment. For instance, here is an example of a TestNG XML file using parameters to set up the driver:

```xml
<?xml version="1.0" encoding="UTF-8"?>
<!DOCTYPE suite SYSTEM "http://testng.org/testng-1.0.dtd">

<suite name="My Test Suite" preserve-order="true" parallel="false" thread-count="1" verbose="2">

<!-- suite parameters -->
    <!-- "local", "remote", "saucelabs" -->
    <parameter name="environment" value="saucelabs" />

    <test name="My Feature Test">
        <!-- test parameters -->
        <parameter name="browser" value="chrome" />
        <parameter name="platform" value="Windows 10" />

        or

        <parameter name="browser" value="iphone"/>
        <parameter name="platform" value="iphone"/>

        <classes>
            <class name="com.myproject.MyTest" />
        </classes>
    </test>
</suite>
```

Each provider will require a different `RemoteWebDriver` URL, credentials to access their test cloud, preferences, and various other features that would allow access to a DMZ inside a corporate Firewall. Here are some examples of specific Sauce Labs Cloud platform requirements:

- **Tunnel**: If the web server, or any other servers, are behind a corporate Firewall and not open to the internet, then a unique tunnel will have to be set up and passed to the driver class as a Desired Capability.
- **Remote URL**: Sauce Labs has its own `RemoteWebDriver` URL for accessing its server at `http://SAUCE_USERNAME:SAUCE_ACCESS_KEY@ondemand.saucelabs.com:80/wd/hub`.
- **Preferences**: Sauce Labs has a set of unique capabilities that allow the passing of when creating the driver for the test. Examples include screen resolution, browser versions (including latest and beta versions), mobile device types (including physical and simulator/emulator devices), Selenium versions, driver versions, session parameters, results processing, and so on.

 The Sauce Labs Wiki documentation, which includes Desired Capabilities and Platform Configurator, is located at `https://wiki.saucelabs.com/`.

```
// third party preferences for SauceLabs...

if ( environment.equalsIgnoreCase("saucelabs") ) {
    // setup the Selenium Grid capabilities...
    String remoteHubURL =
            "http://SAUCE_USERNAME:SAUCE_ACCESS_KEY
            @ondemand.saucelabs.com:80/wd/hub";

    caps.setCapability("screenResolution",
                        "1920x1080");
    caps.setCapability("recordVideo",
                        false);
    caps.setCapability("tunnelIdentifier",
                        System.getProperty("TUNNEL_IDENTIFIER"));
    ...
}
```

Using property files to select browsers, devices, versions, platforms, languages, and many more

Rather than hardcoding default URLs, paths, revisions, mobile device settings, and so on into the driver class itself, it makes more sense to encapsulate all those settings into a properties file. This way, users do not have to traverse through code to change a setting, driver version, or any paths required to support running the driver across platforms such as Windows, iOS, and Linux. Also, different sets of properties can be stored in the file for different environments such as local, remote, or third-party grids. Properties can be stored and retrieved in Java using the `Properties` class. The following code examples show property file formats, and the use of properties files in the Selenium driver class:

```java
// Properties Class
public class CreateDriver {
    private Properties driverProps = new Properties();
    private static final String propertyFile = new File
        ("../myProject/com/path/selenium.properties").getAbsolutePath();

    @SafeVarargs
    public final void setDriver(String browser,
                                String environment,
                                String platform,
                                Map<String, Object>... optPreferences)
                                throws Exception {

    DesiredCapabilities caps = null;

    // load properties from file...
    driverProps.load(new FileInputStream(propertyFile));

    switch (browser) {
        case "firefox":
            caps = DesiredCapabilities.firefox();

            // see previous example for caps...
            if ( environment.equalsIgnoreCase("local") ) {
                if ( platform.toLowerCase().contains("windows") ) {
                    System.setProperty("webdriver.gecko.driver",
                    driverProps.getProperty(
                    "gecko.driver.windows.path"));
                }
```

```
                webDriver.set(new FirefoxDriver(caps));
            }

        break;
        }
    }
}
```

Here is the `selenium.properties` file:

```
// selenium.properties file
# Selenium 3 WebDriver/AppiumDriver Properties File

# Revisions
selenium.revision=3.4.0
chrome.revision=2.30
safari.revision=2.48.0
gecko.revision=0.17.1

# Firefox Settings
gecko.driver.windows.path=../path/geckodriver-v0.17.1-win64/geckodriver.exe
gecko.driver.linux.path=../path/geckodriver-v0.17.1-linux64/geckodriver
gecko.driver.mac.path=../path/geckodriver-v0.17.1-macos/geckodriver
```

Summary

The Selenium driver class is the "engine" that controls the browser or mobile device under test. It determines which driver type to create, the look and feel of the driver, the default preferences, multithreading capabilities, settings, and whether to run the test locally or on the Selenium grid. It is a self-contained singleton class that creates one instance of the driver that is used throughout the entire test run. All session parameters are retrievable throughout the run, and they can be tracked to allow multiple drivers to run concurrently, in a browser-to-mobile test, or in a parallel/distributed environment.

As we progress through the framework components, users will see how important this class becomes to the integrity of the test. We will start by designing and building utility classes to support the framework.

10
Selenium Framework Utility Classes

This chapter will introduce users to designing and building the Java utility classes that are required to support the Selenium framework. This includes classes for global variables, synchronization, alternative JavaScript methods, results processing, and mail retrieval. The following topics will be covered:

- Introduction
- Global variables
- Synchronization utility class
- The JavascriptExecutor class
- The TestNG Listener class
- File I/O class
- Image capture class
- The reporter class
- The JavaMail class

Introduction

Java classes that are not Selenium page object classes, test classes, or data files, but support testing browser or mobile applications, can be considered utility classes. Most utility classes are static in nature, and use Java API methods that are not specific to any feature or test. They can include methods that operate on the browser or mobile device itself, but are not specific to the application running on them.

For example, the Selenium `ExpectedConditions` class has common methods to synchronize tests against actions occurring on a page, but it doesn't matter what the pages are, browser or mobile. Utilities can be built for file operations in reading, writing, or deleting files during tests. Test listener classes can be built, leveraging the TestNG `TestListenerAdapter` class, to log output to files and/or the console during test runs.

Other types of utilities that can be leveraged include image capture, JavaMail, third-party test listener and reporters, and JavaScript Executor API methods. Each one will be outlined in this chapter.

Users will learn how to build the utility classes required to support the framework that can be leveraged for both browser and mobile testing.

Global variables

Global variables are generally static in nature, can be initialized at the start of a test, and remain available throughout the entire test run. Variables for application defaults, timeouts, property file locations, paths, and so on can be stored in this class. To be clear, test data is not stored in this class. Test data will be encapsulated in a different file format, and will be discussed in later chapters. Here is an example of some default global variables:

```
/**
 * Global Variable Class
 *
 * @author Author
 *
 */
public class Global_VARS {
    // target app defaults
    public static final String BROWSER = "firefox";
    public static final String PLATFORM = "Windows 10";
    public static final String ENVIRONMENT = "local";
    public static String DEF_BROWSER = null;
    public static String DEF_PLATFORM = null;
    public static String DEF_ENVIRONMENT = null;
```

```
public static String PROPS_PATH = null;

// driver class defaults
public static String propFile = "../myPath/selenium.props";
public static final String SE_PROPS =
new File(propFile).getAbsolutePath();

// test output path defaults
public static final String TEST_OUTPUT_PATH = "testOutput/";
public static final String LOGFILE_PATH = TEST_OUTPUT_PATH +
"Logs/";
public static final String REPORT_PATH = TEST_OUTPUT_PATH +
"Reports/";
public static final String BITMAP_PATH = TEST_OUTPUT_PATH +
"Bitmaps/";

// timeout defaults
public static final int TIMEOUT_MINUTE = 60;
public static final int TIMEOUT_SECOND = 1;
public static final int TIMEOUT_ZERO = 0;
}
```

Synchronization utility classes

One of the most important classes in the Selenium framework is the library containing all the test "synchronization" methods. In test automation, it is always necessary to "wait" for something to happen on a page after sending an event. That would include such actions as waiting for the page to render, waiting for an Ajax control to complete, waiting for a different page to appear, waiting for an item in a table, and so on. If test scripts are not synchronized, they will randomly fail when applications run faster or slower during execution, throwing exceptions that specific elements are not found. Selenium has introduced a set of classes that accommodate all of the types of synchronization that are required in browser and mobile testing.

Selenium synchronization classes

Some of the highlights of the synchronization classes that will be covered include:

- The `ExpectedConditions` class
- The `WebDriverWait/FluentWait` classes
- Custom synchronization class: wrapping `ExpectedConditions` and `WebDriverWait` methods

The ExpectedConditions class

The Selenium WebDriver's `ExpectedConditions` class provides users with common methods to check for specific conditions of elements on a page. Those conditions include such things as:

- Titles
- URLs
- Presence of elements
- Visibility of elements
- Text on elements
- Frames to switch to
- Invisibility of elements
- Element-clickable states
- Staleness of elements
- Refreshing elements
- Element selection states
- Alerts
- Number of windows
- Finding elements
- Attributes of elements
- Number of elements
- Nested elements
- JavaScript values

The JavaDoc for the `ExpectedConditions` class is located at `https://seleniumhq.github.io/selenium/docs/api/java/org/openqa/selenium/support/ui/ExpectedConditions.html`.

Using the `ExpectedConditions` class's methods is simple. You would just call them as follows:

```
ExpectedConditions.visibilityOf(WebElement element)
```

Alternatively, you can use:

```
ExpectedConditions.visibilityOfElementLocated(By by)
```

These two methods do the same thing, except one takes a static locator as a parameter, and the second one takes a dynamically generated locator. But using these methods alone is not enough. It is imperative to wait "up to" a designated time period before throwing an exception that the element is not found. This can be done by passing the result of these methods to the `WebDriverWait` class's methods.

WebDriverWait/FluentWait classes

The Selenium `WebDriverWait` class, which extends the `FluentWait` class, contains *timer* methods that allow waiting for a specific condition until it is found. It includes such methods as waiting until a condition is met, polling intervals, ignoring specific exceptions while polling, and so on.

- The JavaDoc for the `WebDriverWait` class is located at `https://seleniumhq.github.io/selenium/docs/api/java/org/openqa/selenium/support/ui/WebDriverWait.html`.

- The JavaDoc for the `FluentWait` class is located at `https://seleniumhq.github.io/selenium/docs/api/java/org/openqa/selenium/support/ui/FluentWait.html`.

Custom synchronization methods

Combining the two sets of methods into a wrapper method will allow users to synchronize the scripts on a variety of conditions that might exist on a web or mobile page. The following are examples of wrapper methods that wait for elements to become visible or invisible:

```
/**
 * waitFor method to wait up to a designated period before
 * throwing exception (static locator)
 *
 * @param element
 * @param timer
 * @throws Exception
 */
public static void waitFor(WebElement element,
                           int timer)
                           throws Exception {

    WebDriver driver = CreateDriver.getInstance().getDriver();

    // wait for the static element to appear
    WebDriverWait exists = new WebDriverWait(driver,
                                             timer);
    exists.until(ExpectedConditions.refreshed(
            ExpectedConditions.visibilityOf(element)));
}

/**
 * overloaded waitFor method to wait up to a designated period before
 * throwing exception (dynamic locator)
 *
 * @param by
 * @param timer
 * @throws Exception
 */
public static void waitFor(By by,
                           int timer)
                           throws Exception {

    WebDriver driver = CreateDriver.getInstance().getDriver();

    // wait for the dynamic element to appear
    WebDriverWait exists = new WebDriverWait(driver,
                                             timer);

    // examples: By.id(id), By.name(name), By.xpath(locator),
    // By.cssSelector(css)
```

```
        exists.until(ExpectedConditions.refreshed(
                ExpectedConditions.visibilityOfElementLocated(by)));
}

/**
 * waitForGone method to wait up to a designated period before
 * throwing exception if element still exists
 *
 * @param by
 * @param timer
 * @throws Exception
 */
public static void waitForGone(By by,
                               int timer)
                               throws Exception {

    WebDriver driver = CreateDriver.getInstance().getDriver();

    // wait for the dynamic element to disappear
    WebDriverWait exists = new WebDriverWait(driver,
                                             timer);

    // examples: By.id(id),By.name(name),By.xpath(locator),
    // By.cssSelector(css)
    exists.until(ExpectedConditions.refreshed(
            ExpectedConditions.invisibilityOfElementLocated(by)));
}

/**
 * waitForURL method to wait up to a designated period before
 * throwing exception if URL is not found
 *
 * @param by
 * @param timer
 * @throws Exception
 */
public static void waitForURL(String url,
                              int seconds)
                              throws Exception {

    WebDriver driver = CreateDriver.getInstance().getDriver();
    WebDriverWait exists = new WebDriverWait(driver,
                                             seconds);

    exists.until(ExpectedConditions.refreshed(
    ExpectedConditions.urlContains(url)));
}

/**
```

```
     * waitFor method to wait up to a designated period before
     * throwing exception if Title is not found
     *
     * @param by
     * @param timer
     * @throws Exception
     */
    public void waitFor(String title,
                        int timer)
                        throws Exception {

        WebDriver driver = CreateDriver.getInstance().getCurrentDriver();
        WebDriverWait exists = new WebDriverWait(driver, timer);

        exists.until(ExpectedConditions.refreshed(
                ExpectedConditions.titleContains(title)));
    }
```

Notice the `.refreshed` method is called on `ExpectedConditions` classes. This is a new method that Selenium introduced to avoid `StaleElementReferenceException` type failures.

To summarize, any of the `ExpectedConditions` class methods can be wrapped in synchronization methods as in these examples to wait for element conditions like clickable, text, titles, URLs, and so on. It is important to keep in mind that these methods will only wait up to the designated time period at the most, but as soon as it finds the element, it moves on. This is unlike the behavior of a hardcoded sleep, which will wait the entire length of time passed into it.

The JavascriptExecutor class

The Selenium `JavascriptExecutor` class allows users to inject JavaScript commands directly into the context of the active browser frame or window. The use of this method is required in cases where the standard `WebDriver` class's methods fail to find or act upon an element on the browser page. JavaScript commands can be executed synchronously or asynchronously on the page. The class is an interface, and has been implemented for all the current driver classes. When designing a class to utilize this interface, users can pass commands directly to a WebElement by using the static locator, or one of the common locator methods available to `WebDriver`. Some of the more common methods will be outlined here:

The JavaDoc for the `JavascriptExecutor` class is located at `https://seleniumhq.github.io/selenium/docs/api/java/org/openqa/selenium/JavascriptExecutor.html`.

```java
/**
 * Selenium JavaScript Executor Utility Class
 *
 */
public class JavaScriptUtils {

    // constructor
    public JavaScriptUtils() {
    }

}


/**
 * execute - generic method to execute a non-parameterized JS command
 *
 * @param command
 */
public static void execute(String command) {
    WebDriver driver = CreateDriver.getInstance().getDriver();

    JavascriptExecutor js = (JavascriptExecutor)driver;
    js.executeScript(command);
}

/**
 * execute - overloaded method to execute a JS command on WebElement
 *
 * @param command
 * @param element
 */
public static void execute(String command,
                           WebElement element) {

    WebDriver driver = CreateDriver.getInstance().getDriver();

    JavascriptExecutor js = (JavascriptExecutor)driver;
    js.executeScript(command, element);
}

/**
 * click - method to execute a JavaScript click event
 *
```

```java
 * @param element
 */
public static void click(WebElement element) {
    WebDriver driver = CreateDriver.getInstance().getDriver();

    JavascriptExecutor js = (JavascriptExecutor)driver;
    js.executeScript("arguments[0].click();", element);
}

/**
 * click - overloaded method to execute a JavaScript click event using By
 *
 * @param by
 */
public static void click(By by) {
    WebDriver driver = CreateDriver.getInstance().getDriver();
    WebElement element = driver.findElement(by);

    JavascriptExecutor js = (JavascriptExecutor)driver;
    js.executeScript("arguments[0].click();", element);
}

/**
 * sendKeys - method to execute a JavaScript value event
 *
 * @param keys
 * @param element
 */
public static void sendKeys(String keys,
                            WebElement element) {

    WebDriver driver = CreateDriver.getInstance().getDriver();

    JavascriptExecutor js = (JavascriptExecutor)driver;
    js.executeScript("arguments[0].value='" + keys + "';", element);
}
```

Occasionally, test scripts need to be synchronized using a page event like the completion of the page rendering, an Ajax control completing, and so on. That can also be accomplished using the `JavascriptExecutor` class. The following methods wait for a page or Ajax control to complete:

```java
/**
 * isPageReady - method to verify that a page has completely rendered
 *
 * @param driver
 * @return boolean
 */
```

```
public static boolean isPageReady(WebDriver driver) {
    JavascriptExecutor js = (JavascriptExecutor)driver;
    return (Boolean)js.executeScript("return document.readyState")
                                    .equals("complete");
}


/**
 * isAjaxReady - method to verify that an ajax control has rendered
 *
 * @param driver
 * @return boolean
 */
public static boolean isAjaxReady(WebDriver driver) {
    JavascriptExecutor js = (JavascriptExecutor)driver;
    return (Boolean)js.executeScript("return jQuery.active == 0");
}
```

Other JavaScript command examples that can be passed to a method in this class include:

- **Set focus by ID**: `document.getElementById('" + id +"')[0].focus()`
- **Scrolling**: `arguments[0].scrollIntoView(true or false);`
- **Set style visibility by ID**: `document.getElementById('" + id + "').style.visibility = 'visible';`
- **Set style block by ID**: `document.getElementById('" + id + "').style.display = 'block';`
- **Set style block by ID**: `document.getElementByClassName('"+ class +"').style.display = 'block';`

The TestNG Listener class

In order to provide test results to the IDE console, or to a log file, users must build a test listener class into their framework. There are many open source classes available for use, as well as a TestNG class called `TestListenerAdapter`, which can be extended to provide custom logging information in real time. In other words, users can get results while the tests are running by logging them to the console, or by logging the data to a file.

The JavaDoc for the TestNG's `TestListenerAdapter` class is located at `https://jitpack.io/com/github/cbeust/testng/master-6.12-gf77788e-171/javadoc/org/testng/TestListenerAdapter.html`.

How do you use it? How does it keep track of all the test results while the suite of tests are running? How does it get automatically called in a Selenium Framework Test Suite run? These questions will be answered in this section.

Building the test listener class

To simplify getting started, the new test listener class can extend TestNG's `TestListenerAdapter` class, providing the collection of test results to the class, which can then be customized, override default methods where necessary. Some of the methods that can be customized include:

- `onStart(ITestContext testContext)`
- `onFinish(ITestContext testContext)`
- `onTestStart(ITestResult tr)`
- `onTestSuccess(ITestResult tr)`
- `onTestFailure(ITestResult tr)`
- `onTestSkipped(ITestResult tr)`
- `onConfigurationSuccess(ITestResult tr)`
- `onConfigurationFailure(ITestResult tr)`
- `onConfigurationSkip(ITestResult tr)`

The other TestNG classes used by this listener class are the `iTestContext` and `iTestResult` interfaces, which provide data on the number of tests, stats on passed, failed, skipped, test method names, times, groups, suites, output directories, status, parameters, classes, context, and so on. This data can then be logged in a formatted context to the console, or to a log file:

```
/**
 * TestNG TestListener Class
 *
 */
public class TestNG_Listener extends TestListenerAdapter {
    ...
```

- The JavaDoc for the `iTestContext` class is located at `https://jitpack.io/com/github/cbeust/testng/master-6.12-gf77788e-171/javadoc/org/testng/ITestContext.html`.

- The JavaDoc for the `iTestResult` class is located at `https://jitpack.io/com/github/cbeust/testng/master-6.12-gf77788e-171/javadoc/org/testng/ITestResult.html`.

Logging the results to the console or log file

Each method can override the superclass version of the method to customize what users would want to see in the console or log file. You must remember to call the super equivalent if you do override the methods to be able to get the collection of test results. Here are a few examples of overridden methods in the new class:

```java
/**
 *
 * onStart - method to log data before any tests start
 *
 * @param testContext
 */
@Override
public void onStart(ITestContext testContext) {
    try {
        log("\nSuite Start Date: " +
            new SimpleDateFormat("MM.dd.yyyy.HH.mm.ss")
            .format(new Date()) +
            ".log");
    }

    catch (Exception e) {
        e.printStackTrace();
    }

    super.onStart(testContext);
}

/**
 * onFinish - method to log data after all tests are complete
 *
 * @param testContext
 */
@Override
public void onFinish(ITestContext testContext) {
```

```
    try {
        log("\nTotal Passed = " +
            getPassedTests().size() +
            ", Total Failed = " +
            getFailedTests().size() +
            ", Total Skipped = " +
            getSkippedTests().size() +
            "\n");
    }

    catch(Exception e) {
        e.printStackTrace();
    }

    super.onFinish(testContext);
}

// the following are several other methods that can be
// customized to log data to the console or logfile

/**
 * onTestSuccess - method to log the results if the test passes
 *
 * @param tr
 */
@Override
public void onTestSuccess(ITestResult tr) {
    try {
        log("***Result = PASSED\n");
        log(tr.getEndMillis(),
            "TEST  -> " +
            tr.getInstanceName() +
            "." +
            tr.getName());
        log("\n");
    }

    catch(Exception e) {
        e.printStackTrace();
    }

    super.onTestSuccess(tr);
}

/**
 * log - method to log data to standard out or logfile
 *
 * @param dataLine
```

```
*/
public void log(long date, String dataLine) throws Exception {
    System.out.format("%s%n", String.valueOf(new Date(date)), dataLine);

    if (logFile != null) {
        writeLogFile(logFile, dataLine);
    }
}

public static String logFile = null;

/**
 * log - overloaded method to log data to standard out or logfile
 *
 * @param line
 */
public void log(String dataLine) throws Exception {
    System.out.format("%s%n", dataLine);

    if ( logFile != null ) {
        writeLogFile(logFile, dataLine);
    }
}
```

Including the test runner in the test class or suite

After building the test listener class, users can then include it at the test class level, or in the TestNG Suite XML file, as follows:

```
/**
 * My Test Class
 *
 * @author Name
 *
 */
@Listeners(TestNG_Listener.class)
public class MyTest {
    ...
}

// TestNG Suite XML File

<?xml version="1.0" encoding="UTF-8"?>
<!DOCTYPE suite SYSTEM "http://testng.org/testng-1.0.dtd">

<suite name="My_Test_Suite" preserve-order="true" verbose="2">
    <!-- test listeners -->
```

```
    <listeners>
        <listener class-name="myPath.TestNG_Listener" />
    </listeners>
    ....

</suite>
```

File I/O class

Another utility class that users will need to build is the file I/O class. This is a static Java class that contains all the methods for reading, writing, and deleting files, copying files, renaming files, accessing property files, finding files, setting file paths, extracting data, looking up messages, and many more. Storing all these similar methods in one central location for all **CRUD** operations (**create, read, update, and delete**) allows users to call these static methods from any page object or test class. Some of the more common methods will be outlined in this section.

Property files

Property files are common in testing, and are usually used for storing test environment data. There are various formats for property files, but they usually store data strings in *key/value* pairings. In order to read a property file in Java, there is a class called `Properties`, which has various methods that load, list, set, or get properties. Here is an example of a property file pairing, with a method to read it, for storing Selenium driver properties:

```
# selenium.properties file

# driver revisions
selenium.revision=3.4.0
chrome.revision=2.30
safari.revision=2.48.0
gecko.revision=0.18.0
ie.revision=3.4.0

# browser versions
firefox.browser.version=54.0
chrome.browser.version=59.0
ie.browser.version=11.0
safari.browser.version=10.0
edge.browser.version=15.15063
...
```

```
/**
 * File I/O Static Utility Class
 *
 * @author name
 *
 */
public class File_IO {
    /**
     * loadProps- method to load a Properties file
     *
     * @param file - The file to load
     * @return Properties - The properties to retrieve
     * @throws Exception
     */
    public static Properties loadProps(String file) throws Exception {
        Properties props = new Properties();
        props.load(new FileInputStream(file));

        return props;
    }
    ...

// use of file I/O method loadProps
public static final String SELENIUM_PROPS = new
File("../myPath/selenium.properties")
                                            .getAbsolutePath();

Properties seProps = File_IO.loadProps(SELENIUM_PROPS);

// get properties to use
String seleniumRev = seProps.getProperty("selenium.revision"));
String firefoxVer = seProps.getProperty("firefox.browser.version"));
```

 The JavaDoc for the Properties class is located at https://docs.oracle.com/javase/7/docs/api/java/util/Properties.html.

Lookup table files

While property files can be used to store environment data, they can also be used to store confirmation and error messages. Users can retrieve the error messages using a code that development provides, in essence creating a lookup table. Here is a Java utility method for reading and converting error messages on the fly for use in negative testing:

```
# Exception Messages
001=Invalid Login, please try again
002=Login failed, user not found
003=Password is not valid
etc...

/**
 * lookupError - method to retrieve error messages using code
 *
 * @param propFilePath - the property file including path to read
 * @param code - the error code to use
 * @return String
 * @throws Exception
 */
public static String lookupError(String propFilePath,
                                 String code)
                                 throws Exception {

    Properties exceptionProps = new Properties();
    exceptionProps.load(new FileInputStream(propFilePath));

    // get error message using code as key
    return exceptionProps.getProperty(code);
}
```

CSV files

In many cases, data is stored in the CSV file format. CSV files have been used in automated testing for storing test data, environment data, mappings, and so on. The format is simple, and the data can be read using simple Java methods as outlined here:

```
/**
 * extractData_CSV - method to extract CSV file data for use in testing
 *
 * @param csvFile - the CSV file to read
 * @param rowID - The rowID to parse
 * @return List<String>
 * @throws Exception
```

```
*/
public static List<String> extractData_CSV(String csvFile,
                                            String rowID)
                                        throws Exception {

    List<String> rows = new ArrayList<String>();

    BufferedReader reader = new BufferedReader(new FileReader(csvFile));
    String line = "";

    while ( (line = reader.readLine()) != null ) {
        if ( line.startsWith(rowID)) {
            rows.add(line);
        }
    }

    reader.close();
    return rows;
}
```

Log files

Log files are also used frequently in testing to verify entries in server logs, application logs, and browser logs. Static utility methods can be built to extract log data as well. Here is a simple example:

```
/**
 * extractData_LOG - method to extract Log file data for use in testing
 *
 * @param logFile - the logfile to read
 * @return List<String>
 * @throws Exception
 */
public static List<String> extractData_LOG(String logFile)
                                        throws IOException {
    List<String> rows = new ArrayList<String>();

    BufferedReader reader = new BufferedReader(new FileReader(logFile));
    String line = "";

    while ( (line = reader.readLine()) != null ) {
        rows.add(line);
    }

    reader.close();
    return rows;
```

```
}

/**
 * writeFile - method to stuff a row entry into a file
 *
 * @param file - the file to write to
 * @param rowData - the line to write into the file
 * @throws Exception
 */
public static void writeFile(String file,
                             String rowData)
                             throws Exception {

    Boolean bFound = false;

    BufferedReader reader = new BufferedReader(new FileReader(file));
    String getLine = "";

    // verify if row entry exists
    while ( (getLine = reader.readLine()) != null ) {
        if ( getLine.contains(rowData)) {
            bFound = true;
            break;
        }
    }

    reader.close();

    if ( bFound != true ) {
        BufferedWriter writer =
            new BufferedWriter(new FileWriter(file, true));

        writer.append(rowData);
        writer.newLine();
        writer.close();
    }
}
```

The image capture class

Another important library to include in the framework is the image capture class. It is used by the test listener, reporter, and test classes to take screenshots of the browser or mobile screens when exceptions occur. There are various methods that can be built to capture the image of the entire screen, an individual WebElement or MobileElement, or to compare the images. Each method will be outlined here:

 The image capture methods were developed by Unmesh Gundecha, and published by Packt Publishing in the reference book *Selenium Testing Tools Cookbook - Second Edition*. The book is available at `https://www.packtpub.com/web-development/selenium-testing-tools-cookbook-second-edition`.

```
/**
 * Image Capture and Compare Class
 *
 * @author Name
 *
 */
public class ImageCapture {
    // constructor
    public ImageCapture() throws Exception {
    }

    ...
```

The capture screen method

There are many ways to capture and name the image of the screen. Using the test method name and a timestamp for the image name is a common practice. This aligns the captured screens with the test methods that created them, putting a date on the filename, and so on:

```
/**
 * screenShot - method that takes iTestResult as parameter
 *
 * @param result - The result of test
 * @return String
 */
public static String screenShot(ITestResult result) throws Exception {
    DateFormat stamp = new SimpleDateFormat("MM.dd.yy.HH.mm.ss");
    Date date = new Date();

    ITestNGMethod method= result.getMethod();
```

```
        String testName = method.getMethodName();

        return captureScreen(testName + "_" + stamp.format(date) + ".png");
}

/**
 * captureScreen - method to capture the entire screen of the Browser
 * or Mobile App
 *
 * @param filename - The filename to save it to
 */
public static String captureScreen(String filename) throws Exception {
    String bitmapPath = "myPath";
    WebDriver driver = CreateDriver.getInstance().getCurrentDriver();
    File screen = null;

    if ( Global_VARS.DEF_ENVIRONMENT.equalsIgnoreCase("remote") ) {
        // cast to Augmenter class for RemoteWebDriver
        screen = ((TakesScreenshot)new Augmenter().augment(driver))
                .getScreenshotAs(OutputType.FILE);
    }

    else {
        screen = ((TakesScreenshot)driver)
                .getScreenshotAs(OutputType.FILE);
    }

    FileUtils.copyFile(screen, new File(bitmapPath + filename));
    return filename;
}
```

The capture image method

Occasionally, users might want to capture just the WebElement or MobileElement on the screen under test for later comparison. The following methods will capture just the specific image of the web, or MobileElement:

```
/**
 * imageSnapshot - method to take snapshot of WebElement
 *
 * @param element - The Web or Mobile Element to capture
 * @return File
 * @throws Exception
 */
public static File imageSnapshot(WebElement element) throws Exception {
    WrapsDriver wrapsDriver = (WrapsDriver) element;
```

```java
        File screen = null;

        // capture the WebElement snapshot
        screen = ((TakesScreenshot) wrapsDriver.getWrappedDriver())
                .getScreenshotAs(OutputType.FILE);

        // create Buffered Image instance from captured screenshot
        BufferedImage img = ImageIO.read(screen);

        // get the width/height of the WebElement for the rectangle
        int width = element.getSize().getWidth();
        int height = element.getSize().getHeight();
        Rectangle rect = new Rectangle(width,height);

        // get the location of WebElement in a point (x,y)
        Point p = element.getLocation();

        // create image for element using location and size
        BufferedImage dest =
        img.getSubimage(p.getX(), p.getY(), rect.width, rect.height);

        // BMP,bmp,jpg,JPG,jpeg,wbmp,png,PNG,JPEG,WBMP,GIF,gif
        ImageIO.write(dest, "png", screen);

        return screen;
}

/**
 * captureImage - method to capture individual WebElement image
 *
 * @param image - the image to capture
 * @throws Exception
 */
public static void captureImage(String image) throws Exception {
    WebDriver driver = CreateDriver.getInstance().getCurrentDriver();

    WebElement getImage = driver.findElement(
    By.cssSelector("img[src*='" + image + "']"));

    image = image.replace(".","_" + Global_VARS.DEF_BROWSER + ".");

    FileUtils.copyFile(imageSnapshot(getImage),
                    new File(Global_VARS.BITMAP_PATH + image));
}
```

The compare image method

Finally, after capturing the screen or WebElement, users can do a pixel or size comparison of the two images. It is difficult to keep the bitmaps in sync from browser-to-browser, or mobile device-to-mobile device, but the method is here for argument's sake:

```
public enum RESULT { Matched, SizeMismatch, PixelMismatch }

/**
 * compareImage - method to compare 2 images
 *
 * @param expFile - the expected file to compare
 * @param actFile - the actual file to compare
 * @return RESULT
 * @throws Exception
 */
public static RESULT compareImage(String expFile,
                                  String actFile)
                                  throws Exception {

    RESULT compareResult = null;
    Image baseImage = Toolkit.getDefaultToolkit().getImage(expFile);
    Image actualImage = Toolkit.getDefaultToolkit().getImage(actFile);

    // get pixels of image
    PixelGrabber baseImageGrab =
    new PixelGrabber(baseImage,0,0,-1,-1,false);

    PixelGrabber actualImageGrab =
    new PixelGrabber(actualImage,0,0,-1,-1,false);

    int [] baseImageData = null;
    int [] actualImageData = null;

    // get pixels coordinates of base image
    if ( baseImageGrab.grabPixels() ) {
        int width = baseImageGrab.getWidth();
        int height = baseImageGrab.getHeight();
        baseImageData = new int[width * height];
        baseImageData = (int[])baseImageGrab.getPixels();
    }

    // get pixels coordinates of actual image
    if ( actualImageGrab.grabPixels() ) {
        int width = actualImageGrab.getWidth();
        int height = actualImageGrab.getHeight();
        actualImageData = new int[width * height];
```

```
        actualImageData = (int[])actualImageGrab.getPixels();
    }

    // test for size mismatch, then pixel mismatch
    if ( (baseImageGrab.getHeight() != actualImageGrab.getHeight()) ||
         (baseImageGrab.getWidth() != actualImageGrab.getWidth()) ) {
        compareResult = RESULT.SizeMismatch;
    }

    else if ( java.util.Arrays.equals(baseImageData,actualImageData) ) {
        compareResult = RESULT.Matched;
    }

    else {
        compareResult = RESULT.PixelMismatch;
    }

    return compareResult;
}
```

The reporter class

There are many open source reporter APIs that can be used to provide reports of TestNG Suite results. For instance, ExtentReports by AventStack has an API that allows users to customize the results of a TestNG Suite run into an HTML report format. This reporting API, like others, is based on the TestNG's IReporter class. To generate a custom report using the IReporter interface, users create a new class that implements IReporter and the generateReport method:

 The JavaDoc for the IReporter class is located at http://static. javadoc.io/org.testng/testng/6.9.5/org/testng/IReporter.html.

```
import org.testng.IReporter;

/**
 * TestNG_Reporter Class
 *
 * Note: This report relies on the TestNG Suite XML file structure
 *
 * @author name
 *
 */
```

```java
public class TestNG_Reporter implements IReporter {
    /**
    * generateReport - method that generates a TestNG results-based
      report
    *
    * @param xmlSuites - the list of all the XML files
    * @param suites - the list of all the suites
    * @param outputDir - the output directory to save the report
    */
    @Override
    public void generateReport(List<XmlSuite> xmlSuites,
                               List<ISuite> suites,
                               String outputDir) {

        for ( ISuite suite : suites ) {
            // the report is entirely customizable from here
            // users can pull in results from ISuiteResult and
            // ITestResult to output to a file, console
            // or use a third-party API for HTML reporting
        }
    }
}

// TestNG Suite XML File

<?xml version="1.0" encoding="UTF-8"?>
<!DOCTYPE suite SYSTEM "http://testng.org/testng-1.0.dtd">

    <suite name="My_Test_Suite" preserve-order="true" verbose="2">

    <!-- test reporters -->
    <listeners>
        <listener class-name="myPath.TestNG_Reporter" />
    </listeners>
    ....

</suite>
```

Sample test reporter classes are located at https://github.com/cbeust/
testng/tree/master/src/main/java/org/testng/reporters.

The `ExtentReports` API has a Professional and Community Edition of the reporter API. There is full documentation on how to build the HTML report class, customizing it to include system info, test data, screenshots, stacktrace, log file data, TestNG results, and so on. The report has a very elegant CSS look-and-feel to it, and is fairly straightforward to build into the framework. It can then be included in a Test Suite XML file using the format `<listener class-name="myPath.ExtentReporterNG" />`.

The `ExtentReports` documentation is located at `http://extentreports.com/docs/versions/3/java/`.

The JavaMail class

In many situations, it is convenient to retrieve, verify, and delete emails sent from an application. There are several JavaMail APIs that allow users to perform these actions. This section will cover using these APIs to get Google Mail Messages, get their content, get a URL link, and delete all messages once found:

The JavaDoc for the JavaMail class is located at `https://docs.oracle.com/javaee/7/api/javax/mail/package-summary.html`.

```
/**
 * getGmailMessage - method to get the gmail message by username, password,
 * and email account
 *
 * @param username
 * @param password
 * @param subject
 * @param email
 * @return Message
 * @throws Exception
 */
public static Message getGmailMessage(String username,
                                      String password,
                                      String subject,
                                      String email)
                                      throws Exception {

    String toField = null, subjectField = null;
    int iterations = 1;
```

```
Message getMessage = null;
Session session = null;
Store store= null;
Properties props = System.getProperties();

// props to access google mail server
props.setProperty("mail.store.protocol", "imaps");
props.setProperty("mail.imap.ssl.enable", "true");
props.setProperty("mail.imap.port", "993");

session = Session.getInstance(props, null);
store = session.getStore("imaps");
store.connect("imap.gmail.com", username, password);

Folder folder = store.getFolder("INBOX");
folder.open(Folder.READ_WRITE);

// for each loop iteration, get all the Inbox messages again...
while ( iterations <= waitLimit ) {
    Message [] messages = null;
    messages = folder.getMessages();

    // query emails by to and subject fields
    for ( Message message : messages ) {
        toField = message.getHeader("To")[0];
        subjectField = message.getSubject();

        if ( toField.equalsIgnoreCase(email) &amp;&amp;
             subjectField.equals(subject) ) {
            getMessage = message;
            break;
        }
    }

    // wait a second and rerun loop if not found
    if ( getMessage == null ) {
        CreateDriver.getInstance().driverWait(
        Global_VARS.TIMEOUT_SECOND);
        iterations++;
    }

    else {
        break;
    }
}

// return message or throw exception if not found
if ( getMessage != null ) {
```

```
        return getMessage;
    }

    else {
        throw new Exception("The Email Message was Not found!");
    }
}

/**
 * getMsgContent- method to verify the content of a gmail message
 *
 * @param username
 * @param password
 * @param subject
 * @param to
 * @return String
 * @throws Exception
 */
public static String getMsgContent(String username,
                                   String password,
                                   String subject,
                                   String to)
                                   throws Exception {

    Message message = getGmailMessage(username, password, subject, to);

    String line;
    StringBuffer buffer = new StringBuffer();
    BufferedReader reader = new BufferedReader(new InputStreamReader(
                                        message.getInputStream()));

    while ( (line = reader.readLine()) != null ) {
        buffer.append(line);
    }

    return buffer.toString();
}

/**
 * getMsgLink - method to get the link in the gmail message
 *
 * @param username
 * @param password
 * @param subject
 * @param email
 * @return String
 * @throws Exception
 */
```

```
public static String getMsgLink(String username,
                                String password,
                                String subject,
                                String to)
                                throws Exception {

    String content = getMsgContent(username, password, subject, to);

    // get email url link
    Pattern pattern = Pattern.compile("href=\"(.*?)\"", Pattern.DOTALL);
    Matcher match = pattern.matcher(content);
    String regURL = null;  // URL from email content

    while ( match.find() ) {
        regURL= match.group(1);
    }

    return regURL;
}

/**
 * deleteEmails - method to delete all emails using username and password
 *
 * @param username
 * @param password
 * @throws Exception
 */
public static void deleteEmails(String username,
                                String password)
                                throws Exception {

    // props to access google mail server
    Properties props = System.getProperties();
    props.setProperty("mail.store.protocol", "imaps");

    Session session = Session.getDefaultInstance(props, null);
    Store store = session.getStore("imaps");
    store.connect("imap.gmail.com", username, password);

    // get all emails in the inbox
    Folder folder = store.getFolder("INBOX");
    folder.open(Folder.READ_WRITE);

    Message[] messages = null;
    messages = folder.getMessages();

    for ( int i = 0; i < messages.length; i++) {
        messages[i].setFlag(Flag.DELETED, true);
```

```
    }

    folder.close(true);
}
```

Summary

It is important to keep static utilities separate from the Selenium page object and test classes. This reduces duplicate code, allows users to maintain the framework utilities in a central location, and provides all users who use the framework for testing with a set of classes they can readily include in their tests.

The synchronization class is what makes the framework robust. If users do not synchronize the scripts, they will become unreliable, failing on different browsers, mobile devices, and platforms.

The test listeners, reporters, and image capture utilities provide a built-in mechanism for the framework to report the test results of suite runs. Users only have to include these classes in their test or suite file, and they automatically get TestNG results in the console, log, and HTML report formats.

Now that the Selenium driver and utility classes are built, it is time to talk about the Selenium page object classes. The next chapter will take a deep dive into that topic.

11
Best Practices for Building Selenium Page Object Classes

This chapter will cover the basics of how to design and build the Selenium page object classes for the **Application Under Test (AUT)**. The following topics are covered:

- Introduction
- Best practices for naming conventions, comments, and folder structures
- Designing and building the abstract base classes for the AUT
- Designing and building the subclasses for the feature-specific pages using inheritance techniques
- Encapsulation and using getter/setter methods to retrieve objects from the page object classes
- Exception handling and synchronization in page object class methods
- Table classes

Introduction

Having designed the driver and utility classes for the framework, it is time to talk about the AUT, and how to build the page object classes. We will also introduce industry best practices and standards for topics like naming conventions, folder names and structures, comments, exception handling, JavaDoc, base and subclasses, and so on.

As we spoke about earlier, the framework will follow the Selenium Page Object Model. The premise of this paradigm is that for each browser or mobile page of the application being tested, there is an object class created that defines all the elements on that specific page. It doesn't necessarily know about the other pages in the applications, except for the common methods inherited from its base class. And it doesn't know anything about the test classes that will test the page.

In essence, an abstract layer is built between the page object classes and the test classes. What does that actually mean? Let's take an application page as an example.

If we want to build a page object class for the Google Mail Sign In page, how would we design it, and how would we test it? We would first create a class called something like GmailPO.java (PO for page object), which would store the page element locators that define each control on the page, the methods that allow the user to log in, change password, or test the credentials, and any getter/setter methods required to retrieve a *WebElement* on the page.

Then, a test class would be created, called something like GmailTest.java (Test for test class), which would contain setup/teardown methods, data provider calls, TestNG annotations, and a test method that would instantiate the GmailPO.java class and call the required methods to test it. The data would be retrieved from the DataProvider-based JSON file, and passed into the class methods. So, in this example, the GmailPO.java class knows nothing about the test class, or any data required to test the page, and the test class knows nothing about the page element locators.

What you will learn

The user will learn how to design and build base and subclasses for the application under test, following the Selenium Page Object Model. They will also learn industry best practices and standards to use, and how to create an abstract layer between the page object and test classes in the framework.

The Oracle Java tutorial is located at `https://docs.oracle.com/javase/tutorial/java/concepts/index.html`.

Best practices for naming conventions, comments, and folder structures

This section will cover some of the industry standards and best practices for developing test automation. Some of the common topics include naming conventions, comments, and folder names and structures.

Naming conventions

When developing the framework, it is important to establish some naming convention standards for each type of file created. In general, this is completely subjective. But it is important to establish them upfront so users can use the same file naming conventions for the same file types to avoid confusion later on, when there are many users building them. Here are a few suggestions:

- **Utility classes**: Utility classes don't use any prefix or suffix in their names, but do follow Java standards such as having the first letter of each word capitalized, and ending with `.java` extensions. (Acronyms used can be all caps). Examples include `CreateDriver.java`, `Global_VARS.java`, `BrowserUtils.java`, `DataProvider_JSON.java`, and so on.

- **Page object classes**: It is useful to be able to differentiate the page object classes from the utility classes. A good way to name them is `FeaturePO.java`, where `PO` stands for page object and is capitalized, along with the first letter of each word. End the name with a `.java` extension.

- **Test classes**: It is useful to be able to differentiate the test classes from the PO and utility classes. A good way to name them is `FeatureTest.java`, where `Test` stands for test class, and the first letter of each word is capitalized. End the name with a `.java` extension.

- **Data files**: Data files are obviously named with an extension for the type of file, such as `.json`, `.csv`, `.xls`, and so on. But, in the case of this framework, the files can be named the same as the corresponding test class, but without the word `Test`. For example, `LoginCredsTest.java` would have the data file `LoginCreds.json`.

- **Setup classes**: Usually, there is a common setup class for setup and teardown for all test classes, that can be named `AUTSetup.java`. So, as an example, `GmailSetup.java` would be the setup class for all test classes derived from it, and contains only TestNG annotated methods.

- **Test methods**: Although we will explore test method naming conventions more in `Chapter 14`, *Developing Data-Driven Test Classes*, most test methods in each test class are named using sequential numbering, followed by a feature and action. For example: `tc001_gmailLoginCreds`, `tc002_gmailLoginPassword`, and so on.

- **Setup/teardown methods**: The setup and teardown methods can be named according to the setup or teardown action they perform. The following naming conventions can be used in conjunction with the TestNG annotations:
  - `@BeforeSuite`: The `suiteSetup` method
  - `@AfterSuite`: The `suiteTeardown` method
  - `@BeforeClass`: The `classSetup` method
  - `@AfterClass`: The `classTeardown` method
  - `@BeforeMethod`: The `methodSetup` method
  - `@AfterMethod`: The `methodTeardown` method

Comments

Although obvious and somewhat subjective, it is good practice to comment on code when it is not obvious why something is done, there is a complex routine, or there is a "kluge" added to work around a problem. In Java, there are two types of comments used, as well as a set of standards for JavaDoc. We will look at a couple of examples here:

 There is an Oracle article on using comments in Java located at `http://www.oracle.com/technetwork/java/codeconventions-141999.html#385`.

- Block comment:

```
/* single line block comment */
code goes here...


/*
 * multi-line block
 * comment
 */
code goes here...
```

- End-of-line comment:

```
code goes here // end of line comment
```

- JavaDoc comments:

```
/**
 * Description of the method
 *
 * @param arg1 to the method
 * @param arg2 to the method
 * return value returned from the method
 */
```

The Oracle documentation on using the JavaDoc tool is located at `http://www.oracle.com/technetwork/java/javase/documentation/index-137868.html`.

Folder names and structures

As the framework starts to evolve, there needs to be some organization around the folder structure in the IDE, along with a naming convention. The IntelliJ IDE uses modules to organize the repo, and under those modules, users can create the folder structures. It is common to also separate the page object and utility classes from the test classes.

So, as an example, under the top-level folder `src`, create `main/java/com/yourCo/page objects` and `test/java/com/yourCo/tests` folders. From there, under each structure, users can create feature-based folders.

Also, to retain a completely independent set of libraries for the Selenium driver and utility classes, create a separate module called something like `Selenium3` with the same folder structures. This will allow users to use the same driver class and utilities for any additional modules that are added to the repo/framework. It is common to automate testing for more than one application, and this will allow the inclusion of the module in those additional modules. Here are a few suggestions regarding folder naming conventions:

- Name all the folders using lowercase names, so there won't be a mix-and-match of different standards.
- Name the page object class folders after the features they pertain to; for instance, `login` for the `LoginPO.java`, `email` for the `GmailPO.java`, and so on.
- Name the test class folders after the same features as the PO classes, but under the `test` folder. Then there can be a one-to-one correlation between the PO and test class folders.
- Store the common base classes under a common folder under `main`.
- Store the common setup classes under a common folder under `test`.
- Store all the utility classes for the AUT under a `utils` folder under `main`.
- Store all the suite files for the tests under a `suites` folder under test.

Here is an example of a folder structure for the `Selenium3` module. Of course, there are no `test` folders under this one:

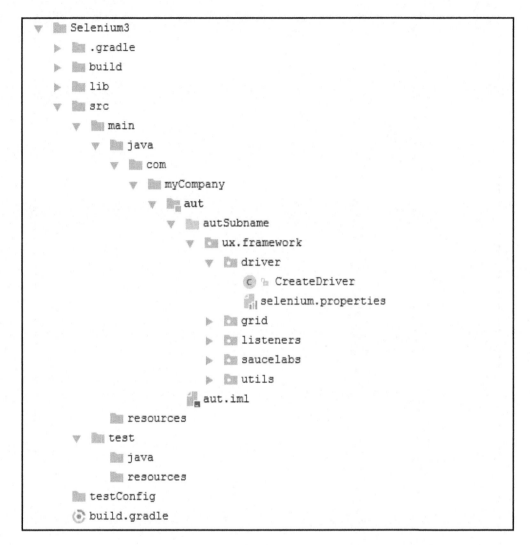

IntelliJ third-party class folder structure

Here is an example of a folder structure for an AUT module showing the PO and test class folders:

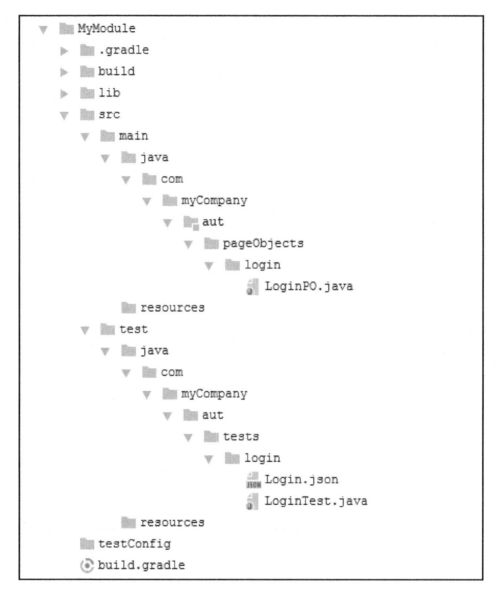

IntelliJ page object/test class folder structure

Designing and building the abstract base classes for the AUT

When designing the Selenium page object classes, the first step is to create an abstract base class that will store all the methods, locators, and properties that are common to all the pages in the application under test. It will also store all the abstract methods that the base class wants to enforce on each subclass derived from it. When a subclass is created that extends this base class, it will inherit all these object components.

This class will also initialize all the page objects included in it, as well as in each subclass, by calling the WebDriver page factory class in its constructor. In Java, abstract classes cannot be instantiated, but they can be subclassed.

The abstract class

Here is an example of a simple abstract base class, explained in sections:

```
/**
 * Sample Base Class Page Object for Browser App
 *
 * @author Name
 *
 */
public abstract class BrowserBasePO <M extends WebElement> {
    public int elementWait = Global_VARS.TIMEOUT_ELEMENT;
    public String pageTitle = "";
    WebDriver driver = CreateDriver.getInstance().getDriver();

    // constructor
    public BrowserBasePO() throws Exception {
        PageFactory.initElements(driver, this);
    }
}

/**
 * Sample Base Class Page Object for Mobile App
 *
 * @author Name
 *
 */
public abstract class Mobile</span>BasePO <M extends MobileElement> {
    public int elementWait = Global_VARS.TIMEOUT_ELEMENT;
    public String pageTitle = "";
    AppiumDriver<MobileElement> driver =
```

```
                          CreateDriver.getInstance().getDriver(true);

    // constructor
    public MobileBasePO () throws Exception {
        PageFactory.initElements(new AppiumFieldDecorator(driver), this);
    }
}
```

 The WebDriver documentation on the page factory class is located
at https://github.com/SeleniumHQ/selenium/wiki/PageFactory.

Notice that in the class signature, there is a generic user that passes in `WebElement`; this is included now to allow future modification of the default behavior of the `WebElement` class. Again, the `PageFactory.initElements` method is called in the constructor that will automatically initialize all the subclass page objects when it is instantiated.

Abstract methods

Any methods that are not implemented by default are called **abstract methods**, and including them in the base class forces all subclasses to implement them. There is a unique syntax for declaring them. Subclasses can also include abstract methods to enforce additional subclasses to implement them. The main reason to include abstract methods at the base class level is to allow possibly different implementations by each subclass of the same methods. Here is an example of some common abstract methods included in the base class:

```
// abstract methods included in base class

public abstract void setElementWait(int elementWait);
public abstract int getElementWait();
public abstract void setPageTitle(String pageTitle);
public abstract String getPageTitle();
```

Common locators

When we talk about defining all the elements on a page, there is a specific syntax that Selenium PageFactory provides the user to define those elements. That syntax is @FindBy, plus the locator, @CacheLookup, and an attribute name and scope for the element. There are various "standards" for which locator to use: ID, tag, name, class, attribute, CSS, XPath, and so on. For now, those standards will not be covered. The following example shows how to define common elements in the base class that would apply to all the pages in an application. Subclasses would inherit them when the class is instantiated:

```
// common WebElement locators included in base class

@FindBy(css = "img[src*='myLogo.png']")
@CacheLookup
protected M companyLogo;

@FindBy(partialLinkText = "All Rights Reserved")
@CacheLookup
protected M copyright;

// common MobileElement locators included in base class

@AndroidFindBy(className = "myLogo")
@iOSFindBy(className = "myLogo")
protected M companylogo;

@AndroidFindBy(id = "title")
@iOSFindBy(xpath = "//*[@name = 'title']")
protected M title;
```

Some things to note here: the @FindBy method can take any of the available locator formats to define the element. @CacheLookup can be used for static elements that do not change dynamically on the page. Using this annotation tells the WebDriver to store the locator rather than actioning a lookup in the DOM each time that element is referenced. Its use can make the scripts run faster by nature. It does not work with elements that change dynamically on the page.

Common methods

At this point, the abstract base class has been built with the page factory initialization, abstract methods, and common elements, and, finally, we need to add some common methods. What methods should go in the base class?

Basically, any method that would apply to each of the subclass page objects goes into this class. Examples would be: navigation bar methods; page methods to retrieve titles, copyrights, logos, and headings; methods for logging out of the application; methods to synchronize against spinner controls that appear on each page; methods that handle alert and error message windows; custom methods for drop-down list selections; methods for label and text verification; and so on.

Any method that can be made "generic" enough (by its locator) to operate on any page in the web or mobile app would go in the base class. Now, if some of the methods only apply to specific pages, or would require different behavior on different pages, then an interface can be created and added to the subclass signature to implement those methods:

```java
// base class common methods

/**
 * getTitle - method to return the title of the current page
 *
 * @throws Exception
 */
public String getTitle() throws Exception {
    WebDriver driver = CreateDriver.getInstance().getDriver();

    return driver.getTitle();
}

/**
 * getParagraph - method to return the paragraph using a pattern match
 *
 * @param pattern
 * @return String
 * @throws Exception
 */
```

```
public String getParagraph(String pattern) throws Exception {
    WebDriver driver = CreateDriver.getInstance().getDriver();

    // build a dynamic locator on the fly with text pattern in
    //paragraph
    String locator = "//p[contains(text(),'" + pattern + "') or
                            contains(.,'" + pattern + "')]";

    return driver.findElement(By.xpath(locator)).getText();
}

/**
 * getCopyright - method to return the page copyright text
 *
 * @return String
 * @throws Exception
 */
public String getCopyright() throws Exception {
    return copyright.getText();
}

// common base class overloaded loadPage methods

/**
 * loadPage - method to load the page URL for the AUT
 *
 * @param pageURL
 * @param timeout
 * @throws Exception
 */
public void loadPage(String pageURL,
                     int timeout)
                     throws Exception {

    WebDriver driver = CreateDriver.getInstance().getDriver();
    driver.navigate().to(pageURL);

    // wait for page download, sync. against login
    BrowserUtils.isPageReady(driver);
    BrowserUtils.waitFor(login, timeout);
}

/**
 * loadPage - overloaded method to load the page URL and sync
 * against WebElement
 *
 * @param pageURL
 * @param element
```

```
 * @throws Exception
 */
public void loadPage(String pageURL,
                     M element)
                     throws Exception {

    WebDriver driver = CreateDriver.getInstance().getDriver();
    driver.navigate().to(pageURL);

    // wait for page download, sync. against element
    BrowserUtils.isPageReady(driver);
    BrowserUtils.waitFor(element, Global_VARS.TIMEOUT_MINUTE);
}

/**
 * loadPage - overloaded method to load the page URL and sync
 * against endpoint URL
 *
 * @param pageURL
 * @param landingUrl
 * @throws Exception
 */
public void loadPage(String pageURL,
                     String endPointUrl)
                     throws Exception {

    WebDriver driver = CreateDriver.getInstance().getDriver();
    driver.navigate().to(pageURL);

    // wait for page download, sync. against endpoint URL
    BrowserUtils.isPageReady(driver);
    BrowserUtils.waitForURL(endPointUrl, Global_VARS.TIMEOUT_MINUTE);
}
```

Wrap up on base classes

So, now that we've designed and built a "skeleton" base class for the AUT, we need to build some subclasses from it for each of the pages of the web or mobile application. The next section will cover how to create subclasses in the Selenium Framework!

Designing and building subclasses for feature-specific pages using inheritance techniques

After building the abstract base class for the AUT in the framework, subclasses need to be developed for each feature page. In following the Selenium Page Object Model, users should build a separate page object class for each page in the browser or mobile app.

As the subclasses are built, whenever common components are found that pertain to most pages, they can be added to the base class. Alternatively, if only on select pages, a separate page object class can be developed for a partial page. The base class can then be extended for those pages that need to inherit the components in it. A good example would be the *table* component, which we will cover in this chapter. Here is how the base class can be extended:

```
// extended base page object class
public class BrowserBaseExtPO<M extends WebElement> extends
BrowserBasePO<M> {

    // constructor
    public BrowserBaseExtPO() throws Exception {
    }

    @Override
    public void setElementWait(int elementWait) {

    }

    @Override
    public int getElementWait() {
        return 0;
    }

    @Override
    public void setPageTitle(String pageTitle) {

    }

    @Override
    public String getPageTitle() {
        return null;
    }

    // add table components and methods here
```

```
    }

    // subclass extending the extended base page object class
    public class MyAppHomePO<M extends WebElement> extends BrowserBaseExtPO<M>
    {

        // constructor
        public MyAppHomePO() throws Exception {
        }

        // implement table methods here

    }
```

The following is a template of a page object subclass segregating the various sections of the file:

```java
/**
 * Selenium Page Object Template
 *
 * @author Name
 *
 */
public class TemplatePO<M extends WebElement> extends BrowserBasePO<M> {
    // local variables go here
    // TODO:

    // constructor
    public TemplatePO() throws Exception {
        super();
    }

    // abstract methods
    @Override
    public void setElementWait(int elementWait) {
    }

    @Override
    public int getElementWait() {
        return 0;
    }

    @Override
    public void setPageTitle(String pageTitle) {
    }

    @Override
    public String getPageTitle() {
```

```
        return null;
    }

    // page objects
    @FindBy(id = "")
    @CacheLookup
    protected M element1;

    // class methods

    /**
     * myMethod method
     *
     * @param arg1
     * @throws Exception
     */
    public void myMethod(String arg1) throws Exception {
        // TODO:
    }
}
```

To get started on the subclasses, let's take the login page as an example. The login page is the first page of each app that appears after loading the browser URL or launching the mobile app, so let's build that page object class.

Create a Java class called `LoginPO.java`, or `MyAppLoginPO.java`, derive it from the base class, review which common elements and methods are inherited, and start adding in the page definitions and methods.

Let's take a quick look at an example of a browser page object for the login page:

```
/**
 * Login Page Object
 *
 * @author Name
 *
 */
public class MyAppLoginPO<M extends WebElement> extends BrowserBasePO<M> {
    private int elementWait = 60;
    private String PAGE_TITLE = "Login Page Title";

    // constructor
    public MyAppLoginPO() throws Exception {
        setPageTitle(PAGE_TITLE);
    }

    @Override
```

```
    public void setElementWait(int elementWait) {
    }

    @Override
    public int getElementWait() {
        return 0;
    }

    @Override
    public void setPageTitle(String pageTitle) {
    }

    @Override
    public String getPageTitle() {
        return null;
    }
}
```

Let's take a quick look at an example of a mobile page object for the login page:

```
/**
 * Mobile Login Page Object
 *
 * @author Name
 *
 */
public class MyAppMobileLoginPO<M extends MobileElement> extends
MobileBasePO<M> {
    private int elementWait = 60;
    private String PAGE_TITLE = "Login Page Title";

    // constructor
    public MyAppMobileLoginPO() throws Exception {
        setPageTitle(PAGE_TITLE);
    }

    @Override
    public void setElementWait(int elementWait) {
    }

    @Override
    public int getElementWait() {
        return 0;
    }

    @Override
    public void setPageTitle(String pageTitle) {
    }
```

```
    @Override
    public String getPageTitle() {
        return null;
    }


}
```

In these subclass examples, notice the setter method called in the constructor; it sets the title of the page, which can be used later on for synchronizing against when the page renders. The method is abstract, and must be implemented in the subclass.

Also, since the base class has four abstract methods in it, they all have to be implemented in each subclass. Here is a simple example of that (note that, for the remainder of this section, JavaDoc will not be added to common methods, but it is a standard that should be followed):

```
// login page methods

@Override
public void setElementWait(int elementWait) {
    this.elementWait = elementWait;
}

@Override
public int getElementWait() {
    return this.elementWait;
}

@Override
public void setPageTitle(String pageTitle) {
    this.pageTitle = pageTitle;
}

@Override
public String getPageTitle() {
    return this.pageTitle;
}
```

In these method examples, there is reference to `this.elementWait` and `this.pageTitle`; notice these are declared in the base and subclass. If the user wants to change the default values for them, they can do that with the setter methods. Otherwise, they have default values that can be used and retrieved with the getter methods.

Now, in cases where not all subclasses will need to implement a set of common methods, users can create an interface and add that to the signature of the class, and only the classes that need them will have to implement them. For example:

```
/**
 * Interface to implement by classes requiring BrowserExtras methods
 *
 * @author Name
 */
public interface BrowserExtras {
    // methods to implement in subclasses
    public void setElementWait(int elementWait);
    public int getElementWait();
    public void setPageTitle(String pageTitle);
    public String getPageTitle();
}

// subclass signature
public class MyAppSubClassPO<M extends WebElement> extends BrowserBasePO<M>
implements BrowserExtras {

    // constructor
    public MyAppSubClassPO() throws Exception {
    }

    @Override
    public void setElementWait(int elementWait) {
    }

    @Override
    public int getElementWait() {
        return 0;
    }

    @Override
    public void setPageTitle(String pageTitle) {
    }

    @Override
    public String getPageTitle() {
        return null;
    }
}
```

Up to this point, we have only covered the file structure, and which methods are inherited or enforced on a Selenium page object subclass. Let's now build a simple login page object for a browser application. The class will include the base class it is extending, the abstract methods enforced by the base class, the three controls required on the page, and the method for logging in:

```
/**
 * MyApp Login Page Object
 *
 * @author Name
 *
 */
public class MyAppLoginPO<M extends WebElement> extends BrowserBasePO<M> {
    // local vars
    private String PAGE_TITLE = "Login Page Title";

    // constructor
    public MyAppLoginPO() throws Exception {
        setPageTitle(PAGE_TITLE);
    }

    // page objects
    @FindBy(id = "username")
    @CacheLookup
    protected M username;

    @FindBy(id = "password")
    @CacheLookup
    protected M password;

    @FindBy(id = "submit")
    @CacheLookup
    protected M submit;

    // abstract methods
    @Override
    public void setElementWait(int elementWait) {
        this.elementWait = elementWait;
    }

    @Override
    public int getElementWait() {
        return this.elementWait;
    }

    @Override
    public void setPageTitle(String pageTitle) {
```

```java
        this.pageTitle = pageTitle;
    }

    @Override
    public String getPageTitle() {
        return this.pageTitle;
    }

    // common methods
    public void login(String username,
                      String password)
                      throws Exception {

        if ( !this.username.getAttribute("value").equals("") ) {
            this.username.clear();
        }

        this.username.sendKeys(username);

        if ( !this.password.getAttribute( "value" ).equals( "" ) ) {
            this.password.clear();
        }

        this.password.sendKeys(password);

        submit.click();
    }

}
```

This, in essence, is the first Selenium page object in the framework. Notice the `login` method also calls one of the browser `waitFor` synchronization methods that was created in the `BasePO` class to wait for the page title to appear, checks to see if either the username or password field is populated, clears them if so before entering the credentials, then clicks the `submit` button to log in to the application. This method does not have any error handling in place if the login fails; we will cover that in the next sections.

Encapsulation and using getter/setter methods to retrieve objects from the page object classes

The first Selenium page object class was created containing two getter and two setter methods. These methods, although not entirely object-oriented, are required to provide a way for the Selenium test classes to access a component inside the page object instance. This is a basic concept in Java called **encapsulation**. The data variables and objects in the class are hidden by making them private or protected, and only accessible outside the class using the getter methods, and so on.

As a general rule, we want to keep a separation between the page object and test classes. So, what happens if the user needs to access a button on the page to cancel some action or dialog from within the test class? They only have two choices: call the WebDriver class's findBy method and pass in a dynamic locator to access the object, or create a method to get the static WebElement on the page.

Of course, we *do not* want to start adding locators to the test classes - this would violate the page object Model we are following to separate the page object and test classes. It also lends to the idea that we would have the same locator in two places: the page object and test class. If we do this over and over, the maintenance level increases dramatically. When the locators change, then the change needs to be implemented in multiple places, and so on.

 There is a Java tutorial on encapsulation and the use of getter/setter methods located at https://www.tutorialspoint.com/java/java_encapsulation.htm.

So, the getter methods can return a variable, WebElement, MobileElement, or String. They can be useful in test classes that need to access a page object element, or in another class that is instantiating it. Finally, let's look at an example of a getter method that returns a WebElement:

```
// cancel button in Page Object class

public class MyPageObject {
    ...

    @FindBy(id= "Cancel")
    @CacheLookup
    protected M cancel;
```

```
    // getter method in Page Object class

    /**
     *  getCancel method
     *
     * @return WebElement
     * @throws Exception
     */
    public M getCancel() throws Exception {
        return cancel;
    }
}


// getCancel method call on instance of class in Test Method

public void tc001_myTestcase() {
    ...
    MyPageObject pageObj = new MyPageObject();
    pageObj.getCancel();

    ...
```

Exception handling and synchronization in page object class methods

One of the areas that is often misunderstood but very important in framework design is exception handling. Users must program into their tests and methods how to handle exceptions that might occur in tests, including those that are thrown by applications themselves, and those that occur using the Selenium WebDriver API.

Let's talk about the different kinds of exceptions that users must account for, specifically:

- **Implicit exceptions**: Implicit exceptions are internal exceptions raised by the API method when a certain condition is not met, such as an illegal index of an array, null pointer, file not found, or something unexpected occurring at runtime.
- **Explicit exceptions**: Explicit exceptions are thrown by the user to transfer control out of the current method, and to another event handler when certain conditions are not met, such as an object is not found on the page, a test verification fails, or something expected as a known state is not met. In other words, the user is predicting that something will occur, and explicitly throws an exception if it does not.

- **WebDriver exceptions**: The Selenium WebDriver API has its own set of exceptions that can implicitly occur when elements are not found, elements are not visible, elements are not enabled or clickable, and so on. They are thrown by the WebDriver API method, but users can catch those exceptions and explicitly handle them in a predictable way.
- **Try...catch blocks**: In Java, exception handling can be completely controlled using a `try...catch` block of statements to transfer control to another method, so that the exit out of the current routine doesn't transfer control to the call handler up the chain, but rather, is handled in a predictable way before the exception is thrown.

 The JavaDoc covering exception handling is located at `https://docs.oracle.com/javase/8/docs/api/java/lang/Exception.html`.

Let's examine the different ways of handling exceptions during automated testing.

Implicit exception handling

A simple example of Selenium WebDriver implicit exception handling can be described as follows:

1. Define an element on a page
2. Create a method to retrieve the text from the element on the page
3. In the signature of the method, add `throws Exception`
4. Do not handle a specific exception like `ElementNotFoundException`:

```
// create a method to retrieve the text from an element on a page
@FindBy(id="submit")
protected M submit;

public String getText(WebElement element) throws Exception {
    return element.getText();
}

// use the method
LoginPO.getText(submit);
```

Now, when using an assertion method, TestNG will implicitly throw an exception if the condition is not met:

1. Define an element on a page
2. Create a method to verify the text of the element on a page
3. Cast the expected and actual text to the TestNG's `assertEquals` method
4. TestNG will throw an `AssertionError`
5. TestNG engages the **difference viewer** to compare the result if it fails:

```
// create a method to verify the text from an element on a page
@FindBy(id="submit")
protected M submit;

public void verifyText(WebElement element,
                       String expText)
                       throws AssertionError {

    assertEquals(element.getText(),
              expText,
              "Verify Submit Button Text");
}

// use the method
LoginPO.verifyText(submit, "Sign Inx");

// throws AssertionError
java.lang.AssertionError: Verify Text Label expected [ Sign Inx]
but found [ Sign In]

Expected : Sign Inx
Actual : Sign In
<Click to see difference>
```

TestNG difference viewer

When using the TestNG's `assertEquals` methods, a difference viewer will be engaged if the comparison fails. There will be a link in the stacktrace in the console to open it. Since it is an overloaded method, it can take a number of data types, such as String, Integer, Boolean, Arrays, Objects, and so on. The following screenshot displays the TestNG difference viewer:

TestNG difference viewer

Explicit exception handling

In cases where the user can predict when an error might occur in the application, they can check for that error and explicitly raise an exception if it is found. Take the login function of a browser or mobile application as an example. If the user credentials are incorrect, the app will throw an exception saying something like "username invalid, try again" or "password incorrect, please re-enter".

The exception can be explicitly handled in a way that the actual error message can be thrown in the exception. Here is an example of the `login` method we wrote earlier with exception handling added to it:

```
@FindBy(id="myApp_exception")
protected M error;

/**
 * login - method to login to app with error handling
 *
 * @param username
 * @param password
 * @throws Exception
 */
public void login(String username,
                  String password)
```

```
                        throws Exception {

    if ( !this.username.getAttribute("value").equals("") ) {
        this.username.clear();
    }

    this.username.sendKeys(username);

    if ( !this.password.getAttribute( "value" ).equals( "" ) ) {
        this.password.clear();
    }

    this.password.sendKeys(password);

    submit.click();

    // exception handling
    if ( BrowserUtils.elementExists(error, Global_VARS.TIMEOUT_SECOND) ) {
        String getError = error.getText();
        throw new Exception("Login Failed with error = " + getError);
    }

}
```

Try...catch exception handling

Now, sometimes the user will want to trap an exception instead of throwing it, and perform some other action such as retry, reload page, cleanup dialogs, and so on. In cases like that, the user can use `try...catch` in Java to trap the exception. The action would be included in the `try` clause, and the user can decide what to do in the `catch` condition.

Here is a simple example that uses the `ExpectedConditions` method to look for an element on a page, and only return `true` or `false` if it is found. No exception will be raised:

```
/**
 * elementExists - wrapper around the WebDriverWait method to
 * return true or false
 *
 * @param element
 * @param timer
 * @throws Exception
 */
public static boolean elementExists(WebElement element, int timer) {
    try {
```

```
WebDriver driver = CreateDriver.getInstance().getCurrentDriver();
WebDriverWait exists = new WebDriverWait(driver, timer);

exists.until(ExpectedConditions.refreshed(
            ExpectedConditions.visibilityOf(element)));
    return true;
}

catch (StaleElementReferenceException |
       TimeoutException |
       NoSuchElementException e) {

    return false;
}
}
```

In cases where the element is not found on the page, the Selenium WebDriver will return a specific exception such as `ElementNotFoundException`. If the element is not visible on the page, it will return `ElementNotVisibleException`, and so on. Users can catch those specific exceptions in a `try...catch...finally` block, and do something specific for each type (reload page, re-cache element, and so on):

```
try {
    ....
}

catch(ElementNotFoundException e) {
    // do something
}

catch(ElementNotVisibleException f) {
    // do something else
}

finally {
    // cleanup
}
```

 The Java tutorial on `try...catch` is located at `https://docs.oracle.com/javase/tutorial/essential/exceptions/try.html`.

Synchronizing methods

Earlier, the `login` method was introduced, and in that method, we will now call one of the synchronization methods `waitFor(title, timer)` that we created in the utility classes. This method will wait for the login page to appear with the `title` element as defined. So, in essence, after the URL is loaded, the `login` method is called, and it synchronizes against a predefined page title. If the `waitFor` method doesn't find it, it will throw an exception, and the login will not be attempted.

It's important to predict and synchronize the page object methods so that they do not get out of "sync" with the application and continue executing when a state has not been reached during the test. This becomes a tedious process during the development of the page object methods, but pays big dividends in the long run when making those methods "robust". *Also, users do not have to synchronize before accessing each element. Usually, you would synchronize against the last control rendered on a page when navigating between them.*

In the same `login` method, it's not enough to just check and wait for the login page title to appear before logging in; users must also wait for the next page to render, that being the home page of the application. So, finally, in the `login` method we just built, another `waitFor` will be added:

```
public void login(String username,
                  String password)
                  throws Exception {

    BrowserUtils.waitFor(getPageTitle(),
                    getElementWait());

    if ( !this.username.getAttribute("value").equals("") ) {
        this.username.clear();
    }

    this.username.sendKeys(username);

    if ( !this.password.getAttribute( "value" ).equals( "" ) ) {
        this.password.clear();
    }

    this.password.sendKeys(password);

    submit.click();

    // exception handling
    if ( BrowserUtils.elementExists(error,
                            Global_VARS.TIMEOUT_SECOND) ) {
```

```
        String getError = error.getText();
        throw new Exception("Login Failed with error = " + getError);
    }

    // wait for the home page to appear
    BrowserUtils.waitFor(new MyAppHomePO<WebElement>().getPageTitle(),
                         getElementWait());
}
```

Table classes

When building the page object classes, there will frequently be components on a page that are common to multiple pages, but not all pages, and rather than including the similar locators and methods in each class, users can build a common class for just that portion of the page. HTML tables are a typical example of a common component that can be classed.

So, what users can do is create a generic class for the common table rows and columns, extend the subclasses that have a table with this new class, and pass in the dynamic ID or locator to the constructor when extending the subclass with that table class.

Let's take a look at how this is done:

1. Create a new page object class for the table component in the application, but do not derive it from the base class in the framework
2. In the constructor of the new class, add a parameter of the type WebElement, requiring users to pass in the static element defined in each subclass for that specific table
3. Create generic methods to get the row count, column count, row data, and cell data for the table
4. In each subclass that inherits these methods, implement them for each page, varying the starting row number and/or column header rows if <th> is used rather than <tr>
5. When the methods are called on each table, it will identify them using the WebElement passed into the constructor:

    ```
    /**
     * WebTable Page Object Class
     *
     * @author Name
     */
    public class WebTablePO {
        private WebElement table;
    ```

```
            /** constructor
             *
             * @param table
             * @throws Exception
             */
            public WebTablePO(WebElement table) throws Exception {
                setTable(table);
            }

            /**
             * setTable - method to set the table on the page
             *
             * @param table
             * @throws Exception
             */
            public void setTable(WebElement table) throws Exception {
                this.table = table;
            }

            /**
             * getTable - method to get the table on the page
             *
             * @return WebElement
             * @throws Exception
             */
            public WebElement getTable() throws Exception {
                return this.table;
            }

            ....
```

Now, the structure of the class is simple so far, so let's add in some common "generic" methods that can be inherited and extended by each subclass that extends the class:

```
// Note: JavaDoc will be eliminated in these examples for simplicity sake

public int getRowCount() {
    List<WebElement> tableRows = table.findElements(By.tagName("tr"));

    return tableRows.size();
}

public int getColumnCount() {
    List<WebElement> tableRows = table.findElements(By.tagName("tr"));
    WebElement headerRow = tableRows.get(1);
    List<WebElement> tableCols = headerRow.findElements(By.tagName("td"));

    return tableCols.size();
```

```
    }

    public int getColumnCount(int index) {
        List<WebElement> tableRows = table.findElements(By.tagName("tr"));
        WebElement headerRow = tableRows.get(index);
        List<WebElement> tableCols = headerRow.findElements(By.tagName("td"));

        return tableCols.size();
    }

    public String getRowData(int rowIndex) {
        List<WebElement> tableRows = table.findElements(By.tagName("tr"));
        WebElement currentRow = tableRows.get(rowIndex);

        return currentRow.getText();
    }

    public String getCellData(int rowIndex, int colIndex) {
        List<WebElement> tableRows = table.findElements(By.tagName("tr"));
        WebElement currentRow = tableRows.get(rowIndex);
        List<WebElement> tableCols = currentRow.findElements(By.tagName("td"));
        WebElement cell = tableCols.get(colIndex - 1);

        return cell.getText();
    }
```

Finally, let's extend a subclass with the new `WebTablePO` class, and implement some of the methods:

```
    /**
     * Homepage Page Object Class
     *
     * @author Name
     */
    public class MyHomepagePO<M extends WebElement> extends WebTablePO<M> {

        public MyHomepagePO(M table) throws Exception {
            super(table);
        }

        @FindBy(id = "my_table")
        protected M myTable;

        // table methods
        public int getTableRowCount() throws Exception {
            WebTablePO table = new WebTablePO(getTable());
            return table.getRowCount();
        }
```

```java
public int getTableColumnCount() throws Exception {
    WebTablePO table = new WebTablePO(getTable());
    return table.getColumnCount();
}

public int getTableColumnCount(int index) throws Exception {
    WebTablePO table = new WebTablePO(getTable());
    return table.getColumnCount(index);
}

public String getTableCellData(int row, int column) throws Exception {
    WebTablePO table = new WebTablePO(getTable());
    return table.getCellData(row, column);
}

public String getTableRowData(int row) throws Exception {
    WebTablePO table = new WebTablePO(getTable());
    return table.getRowData(row).replace("\n", " ");
}

public void verifyTableRowData(String expRowText) {
    String actRowText = "";
    int totalNumRows = getTableRowCount();

    // parse each row until row data found
    for ( int i = 0; i < totalNumRows; i++ ) {
        if ( this.getTableRowData(i).contains(expRowText) ) {
            actRowText = this.getTableRowData(i);
            break;
        }
    }

    // verify the row data
    try {
        assertEquals(actRowText, expRowText, "Verify Row Data");
    }

    catch (AssertionError e) {
        String error = "Row data '" + expRowText + "' Not found!";
        throw new Exception(error);
    }
}
```

Summary

This was a very important chapter and step in building the Selenium framework. If the concept of the Selenium Page Object Model can be grasped and implemented as discussed in this chapter, the user will create that separation layer between the Java classes that store the page object definitions and the test classes that test them. This will greatly reduce the amount of redundancy and maintenance always seen in test automation frameworks.

The next chapter will introduce the user to using inspectors to get the browser and mobile locators, illustrate which locator types have precedence, and demonstrate how to create dynamically instantiated locator methods to reduce the number of elements defined in each page object class.

12

Defining WebDriver and AppiumDriver Page Object Elements

This chapter will cover the framework standards to use for defining elements on a browser and mobile page. The chapter will include various browser and mobile inspectors and plugins, best practices for using locators, and when to use static versus dynamic locators in methods. The following topics are covered:

- Introduction
- Inspection of page elements on browser applications
- Inspection of page elements on mobile applications
- Standards for using static locators
- Standards for using dynamic locators

Introduction

Up to this point, we have discussed page object classes in relation to how they fit into the framework and follow a certain model. However, there has to be a way to define the objects on the page so we can test them. We will do this by inspecting the DOM or mobile elements as they appear on a page.

Selenium uses a concept known as **locators** to define each element on a page. Locators are stored in each base and subclass, and define the element using one of the required DOM attributes, such as ID, class, name, tag, link text, CSS, XPath, and many more.

In this chapter, we will introduce the user to the use of inspectors for browsing page elements for both browser and mobile apps, some of the third-party tools available to test locators, the syntax to use when defining elements in the classes, and when to build a dynamic locator on the fly versus using a static cached one in the page object.

The reader will learn how to inspect elements in the application, how to define the elements in the page object classes, inspectors, and third-party tools, and how to access those elements using static and dynamic locators.

Inspecting page elements on browser applications

For browser applications, there are various tools that can be used for each browser type; Chrome, Firefox, Edge, Safari, Opera, and so on. In this section, we will discuss the Inspector tool that is built into each browser.

Types of locators

Each of these browsers has, at the very least, a developer's tool called Inspector, which allows users to look at the HTML/JavaScript code in the DOM, to view elements as they exist on the page. Depending on how the developers build the pages, there may be several unique identifiers that can be used, or there may be none.

In general, and as common as it may seem, using a unique ID is always the best practice for identifying an element. In cases where the UI is just getting built or being refactored, developers can add the IDs to each element as a standard practice, which makes testing of the web or mobile pages extremely easy. Of course, using a unique class, name, tag, or text attribute is also sufficient.

However, in the real world, that is usually not the case, and the true CSS or XPath locators will have to be used to make the element unique by using indexes, parents, children, siblings, or a combination of any of those choices. In this manual, we will cover best practices for defining locators in relation to inheritance from base and subclasses, but will not cover each and every method and rule for building them. There are some great beginners Selenium manuals that cover those topics.

Detailed locator techniques and rules for CSS and XPath are covered by Unmesh Gundecha and published by Packt Publishing in the reference book *Selenium Testing Tools Cookbook - Second Edition*. The book is available at `https://www.packtpub.com/web-development/selenium-testing-tools-cookbook-second-edition`.

Inheriting WebElements

As previously noted, the details of using the inspectors have been outlined in other sources, but what will be covered here is the use of the Selenium Page Object Model to store common element definitions in base classes, which can then be inherited by all subclasses that are derived from them. This reduces the number of elements that need to be defined in the framework itself.

Let's look at a few examples.

If we right click over the Yahoo home page, we will see the **Inspect Element** menu choice. Once selected, an Inspector window will overlay the page, showing the DOM elements. Users can select the arrow button and move freely over the elements on the page until they find the ones they need to define.

So, let's say the Yahoo page logo is on every page on the Yahoo portal, and we want to test that it exists on each page we build. It would make sense to define that element in the Yahoo base page object class, and inherit it in each page object subclass that is derived from it. For example:

```
// Yahoo home page logo image

<a id="uh-logo" href="https://www.yahoo.com/" class="D(ib) Bgr(nr) logo-
datauri W(190px) H(45px) Bgp($twoColLogoPos) Bgz(190px)
Bgp($twoColLogoPosSM)!--sm1024 Bgz(90px)!--sm1024 ua-ie7_Bgi($logoImageIe)
ua-ie7_Mstart(-185px) ua-ie8_Bgi($logoImageIe) ua-ie9_Bgi($logoImageIe)"
data-ylk="rspns:nav;t1:a1;t2:hd;sec:hd;itc:0;slk:logo;elm:img;elmt:logo;"
tabindex="1" data-rapid_p="20"><b class="Hidden">Yahoo</b></a>

// Yahoo Base Class
```

```
public abstract class YahooBasePO <M extends WebElement> {

    // constructor
    public YahooBasePO() throws Exception {
        WebDriver driver = CreateDriver.getInstance().getDriver();
        PageFactory.initElements(driver, this);
    }

    @FindBy(id="uh-logo")
    @CacheLookup
    protected M yahooLogo;

    ...
}

// Yahoo News Subclass
public class YahooNewsPO <M extends WebElement> extends YahooBasePO<M> {

    public YahooNewsPO() throws Exception {
        super();
    }

    public void verifyYahooLogo(String expHref) throws Exception {
        String actHref = yahooLogo.getAttribute("href");
        assertEquals(actHref, expHref, "Verify Yahoo Logo HREF");
    }
}
```

As you can see, the yahooLogo element was not defined in the YahooNewsPO subclass, but it was used in the verifyYahooLogo method in that class. The element is inherited as defined in the base class, by the subclasses derived from it.

If any of the page object classes have slightly different locator definitions, the control can be overridden by including it in the subclass using the same element name.

Inspecting WebElements

Let's take a look at one of the browser inspectors. The following is a screenshot of the inspector for Chrome, using the Google Mail login page. As you can see, the email input field is highlighted in the inspection window in the inspection frame at the bottom, in the page itself, and there is a hover-over control with the CSS of the element:

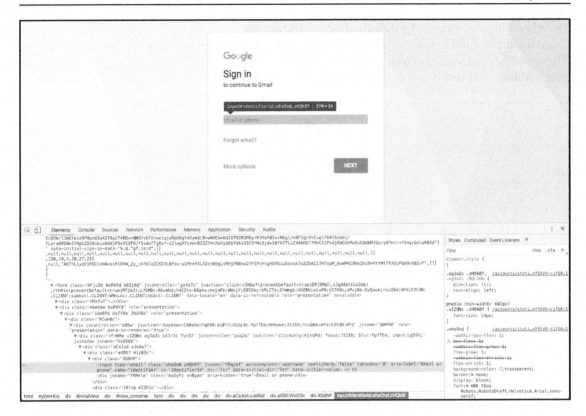

Google Chrome browser inspector

Users can use one of the available attributes, or a combination of them, if part of the hierarchy is required to make it unique. With some of the third-party tools, users can test out the CSS or XPath query they build using attributes in the DOM.

With the Chrome Inspector, this is done using *Ctrl + F* and typing in the locator, which will get highlighted in yellow if it is correct!

Here is another screenshot using the Firefox plugin for the Firebug/Firepath inspector tools. Once the input field is selected, the HTML code is highlighted in the Inspector window. There is a Firepath feature that allows users to build a CSS or XPath query on the fly within this window and test it out. It will highlight the element on the page if it is built correctly:

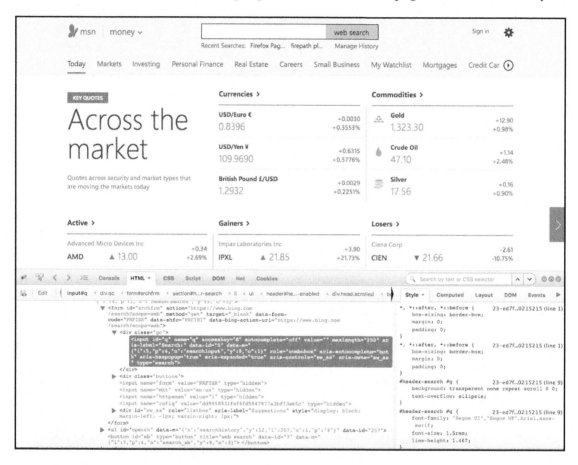

Mozilla Firefox browser inspector

When defining static locators, users must use the @FindBy annotation in the page object classes. @CacheLookup is optional, and often causes Selenium to throw StaleElementExceptions if the page is refreshed or still rendering.

Here are the common WebElement locator methods:

- `@FindBy(id = "elementId")`
- `@FindBy(className = "elementClassName")`
- `@FindBy(name = "elementName")`
- `@FindBy(tagName = "elementTagName")`
- `@FindBy(linkText = "elementLinkText")`
- `@FindBy(PartialLinkText = "elementPartialLinkText")`
- `@FindBy(css = "elementCss")`
- `@FindBy(xpath = "elementXpath")`

Third-party plugins/tools

Each of the browser types has an Inspector tool to use when building the locators. There are also various third-party plugins for each browser in the open-source world.

Let's look at one of the browser add-ons. Firefox has Firebug, Firepath, and Page Inspector. These plugins provide additional capabilities to users for building and "testing" locators. Page Inspector and Firebug allow users to edit, debug, and monitor CSS, HTML, and JavaScript in web pages. Firepath allows users to edit, inspect, and generate XPath, CSS, and jQuery expressions.

Here are some links to different browser development tools:

- Firefox Developer Tools are located at `https://developer.mozilla.org/en-US/docs/Tools`
- Safari Developer Tools are located at `https://developer.apple.com/safari/tools/`
- Chrome Developer Tools are located at `https://developer.chrome.com/devtools`
- Edge WebDriver Tools are located at `https://developer.microsoft.com/en-us/microsoft-edge/tools/webdriver/`
- Opera Developer Tools are located at `http://www.opera.com/dragonfly/`

We will discuss how to use the locators later on using partial text strings, multiple attributes, CSS, and XPath queries. Let's look at the mobile inspectors for getting locators for mobile pages.

Inspection of page elements on mobile applications

For mobile applications, there are various tools that can be used for each mobile device, such as the iOS simulator and Android emulator. In this section, we will discuss the Inspector tool built into the Appium Client.

Appium inspector

When building page object classes for mobile applications, the Appium API is used to test the elements on each page. Appium has its own Inspector tool that allows users to inspect the application in an iOS simulator or Android emulator. Once the mobile application is loaded in the simulator or emulator, the user would then run the Inspector tool, which will embed it in a frame inside the tool. Users can then move to each element in the mobile application, and click them to display the locators.

The classes and attributes for the mobile applications may be different from the browser pages, but the page object classes should be built exactly the same using the Selenium Page Object Model. Elements should be defined in each class and referenced by their static name in methods in the class.

Again, locators should not be used in the test classes, but in the page object classes themselves. The following are the syntax differences for defining locators in the mobile classes using the `FindBy` notation:

- `@iOSFindBy(id = "elementId")`
- `@AndroidFindBy(id = "elementId")`

Here are the common MobileElement locator methods:

- `@FindBy(id = "elementId")`
- `@FindBy(className = "elementClassName")`
- `@FindBy(tagName = "elementTagName")`
- `@FindBy(xpath = "elementXpath")`

Other attributes can be used to identify MobileElement types such as name, value, and so on, but they must be used in an XPath query-type locator. For example:

```
@AndroidFindBy(id = "username")
@iOSFindBy(xpath = "//UIATextField[@value='Username']")
protected M username;

@AndroidFindBy(id = "password")
@iOSFindBy(xpath ="//UIATextField[@value='Password']")
protected M password;

@AndroidFindBy(id = "submit")
@iOSFindBy(xpath = "//UIAButton[@name = 'Submit']")
protected M submit;
```

Inspecting mobile elements

The following screenshot displays the Appium inspector, running the iOS simulator with the sample Apple UICatalog application. It is a native iOS application, so it is not running in a browser on the mobile device. On the bottom portion of the inspector, users can select the **Locator** button and "test" the locators they are building by ID, class name, tag name, or XPath:

Appium iOS mobile inspector

The Appium inspector for Android is similar, except that it launches the Android emulator in the tool window. The basic functionality of it is the same. Users can select each component in the Inspector window, and view the attributes of the elements to build the locators.

The following screenshot displays the Appium inspector running the Android emulator with the sample contacts application. It is a native Android application, so it is not running in a browser on the mobile device:

Appium Android Mobile inspector

Xcode has an Accessibility Inspector tool itself that can also be used to view the attributes of elements in the mobile pages. Apple bundles the tool with Xcode, and it can be launched from within the IDE. The Appium inspector, however, seems to work better in most cases.

Standards for using static locators

The standards to use for defining locators will vary from AUT to AUT. In a perfect world, all browser and mobile pages would have a unique ID assigned to each element in the application, and users would just create a static locator using those IDs. Unfortunately, it is not a perfect world.

However, there are some common best practices that users can follow to ensure the framework is as efficient as possible.

Let's take a look at each type of locator.

Rules for using standard locators

The locator types can be divided up into three distinct categories: simple, CSS, and XPath. Let's discuss each type here.

Simple locators

Simple locators are those that have one attribute in the browser DOM or mobile page that makes them unique from other elements, and does not include any hierarchy such as a parent, child, sibling, or descendant. This includes id, name, className, tagName, linkText, and partialLinkText.

So for example, when we looked at the Google Mail login page, we saw that the first text field was defined as:

```
<input type="email" class="whsOnd zHQkBf" jsname="YPqjbf"
autocomplete="username" spellcheck="false" tabindex="0" aria-label="Email
or phone" name="identifier" id="identifierId" dir="ltr" data-initial-
dir="ltr" data-initial-value="" badinput="false">
```

Obviously, the id would be the first choice for defining the element in the page object class. But, if there is another element on the page that has the same ID, then the user could use the name or the className attribute. If those still did not yield a unique locator, the tagName could ultimately be used for the input field. For example:

```
@FindBy(id = "identifierId")
protected M email;

or
```

```
@FindBy(name = "identifier")
protected M email
```

or

```
@FindBy(className = "whsOnd")
protected M email
```

or

```
@FindBy(tagName = "input")
protected M email;
```

Notice that, when using the `tagName`, the `input` tag was used. If there were multiple input fields on the page, an index would be required to make it unique. XPath allows you to index fields sequentially within the DOM from top to bottom. They would be indexed as follows: input[1], input[2], input[3], and so on. XPath uses one-based numbering.

Finally, if the user wanted to access a link on the page, there are two locator types called `linkText` and `partialLinkText` that would allow them to define the locator by the entire link, or just a portion of it:

```
// google home page

<a class="gb_P" data-pid="23"
href="https://mail.google.com/mail/?tab=wm">Gmail</a>

@FindBy(linkText = "Gmail")
protected M gmail;
```

or

```
@FindBy(partialLinkText = "mail")
protected M gmail;
```

CSS locators

If all those locator types fail to yield a unique locator, then the user can use a CSS locator. The inspector can derive the CSS locator for the user, and in this case, it would be:

```
@FindBy(css = "input#identifierId")
protected M email;
```

or

```
@FindBy(css = "input[id='identifierId']")
protected M email;
```

XPath query locators

Finally, the XPath query is the most versatile type of locator, since it is bidirectional by nature, but it is also the slowest locator type to use (CSS locators can only reference elements in one direction, but are faster). Here is the simple XPath locator for this field:

```
@FindBy(xpath = "//input[@id='identifierId']")
protected M email;
```

There are whole sets of rules and techniques for building CSS and XPath locators; some of these will be discussed in the next section.

- The Wikipedia definition and ruleset for the XPath query language is located at https://en.wikipedia.org/wiki/XPath
- The Oracle documentation for the XPath query language is located at https://docs.oracle.com/cd/E18442_01/doc.651/e18053/xpath.htm
- There is an XPath tutorial located at https://www.w3schools.com/xml/xpath_syntax.asp
- There is a CSS set of rules located at https://www.w3schools.com/cssref/css_selectors.asp

Referencing static elements in methods

When defining locators in the page object classes, a static name is always given to the WebElement or MobileElement. This name should be referenced in the methods in the class that act on the element. Methods can either directly call a Selenium API method on a static element, or take a WebElement or MobileElement as a parameter.

Using the Gmail login page again as an example, the `email` and `password` fields would look like this:

```
// use of static WebElement name in method
public void login(String email,
                  String password)
                  throws Exception {

    this.email.sendKeys(email); // static WebElement name
```

```
        this.password.sendKeys(password); // static WebElement name
        submit.click();
}

// use of static WebElement name passed in as method parameter
public void login(WebElement username,
                  String email,
                  String password)
                  throws Exception {

        username.sendKeys(email); // static WebElement name passed as
                                  //  parameter
        this.password.sendKeys(password); // static WebElement name
        submit.click();
}
```

Although the use of static names seems fairly straightforward and simple, it needs to be a standard that is followed throughout the framework. Many developers stray from this approach, using the dynamic WebElement FindBy API calls directly in the methods (which require a locator), and thus, creating much more framework maintenance than usual.

Why is that so? That is because the WebElement is not defined in one place and referenced many times. It is defined in many places, and referenced many times in various methods. If that locator changes, which they do all the time, then it needs to be fixed in many places. It makes sense to just define the WebElement locators upfront for all the static elements on the page.

However, that does not apply to testing dynamic objects in a table or on a page. For instance, take an application that creates user accounts. If a test requires 25 different user type accounts to be created and verified in a list, table, or simply on the page somewhere, it wouldn't make sense to define all those WebElements in a page object class. That is very inefficient and really impractical.

Users need to use techniques to derive locators on the fly for these dynamic types of testing. We will cover those techniques in the next couple of sections!

Retrieving static elements from other classes

Before we discuss using dynamic, XPath, and CSS locators, let's review again the standards for retrieving WebElements from outside the page object classes.

In keeping within the Selenium Page Object Model, locators go in the page object classes, but not in the utility classes, the test classes, or the data files. Users will often try to cut corners and embed the `WebElement` class's `FindBy` methods within the test methods themselves, rather than encapsulating the locators in the PO classes.

This is the wrong approach, and leads to maintenance nightmares when locators, text, values, tags, and links change in the application. We only want to have to make a change in one place when a locator changes.

Here is a summary of the best practices for using locators:

- Page object classes store the locators that define the WebElements or MobileElements
- *Getter* methods can be created in page object classes to return the static name of the WebElement from the calling instance of the class
- Locators *should not* be stored in data files and passed in as a part of a dataset (although a map file could be created)
- The order of precedence using locators is always `id`, `name`, `className`, `tagName`, `linkText`, `partialLinkText` first, then `css` next, followed finally by `xpath` queries
- Store all common element locators in base classes to allow all subclasses with the same elements to inherit them, reducing the number of elements that need to be defined
- Keep the hierarchy of the locators to a minimum, just enough to make them unique (one or two levels)

Standards for using dynamic locators

There will always be a set of standard objects on a page that remain static each time you navigate to the page. Those are the elements you define up-front in the page object classes: buttons, links, tables, text fields, drop-down lists, logos, and so on.

Now, say you have a page that you create dynamic elements on, such as accounts, servers, settings, or let's just say "widgets". Each time your set of tests runs, it creates all different types of widgets with various preferences, names, timestamps, and so on.

You certainly don't want to clutter up your page objects with a bunch of static elements that the data must match each time you test. In this case, you can build the dynamic locators on the fly using partial string matches of the widgets in the list, table, or page.

In this section, we will cover using single and multiple attribute locators, as well as building methods using dynamic locators from text in elements.

Single attribute XPath versus CSS locators

When creating locators using CSS and XPath, the simplest form is the single attribute locator. We build the locator using the tag and/or an attribute of an element. Let's look at both WebElements and MobileElements. Keep in mind that CSS is only available for WebElements.

WebElements

When defining locators for a WebElement using XPath or CSS, there are many variations of a locator that can be used. Let's look at a couple of web pages and define a single attribute XPath and CSS locator for it. The following web page is a sample web application at `www.practiceselenium.com`, running in Firefox:

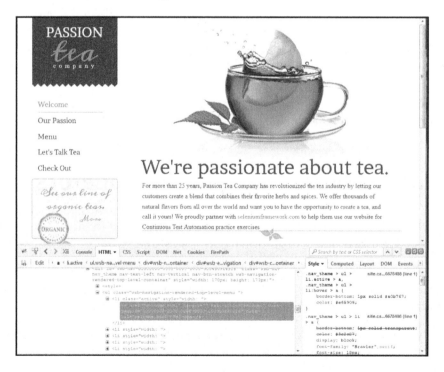

Mozilla Firefox DOM elements

The Inspector frame shows that for the **Welcome** link, we have `href`, `data-title`, `data-pageid`, and `data-url` attributes to work with. Let's build the XPath and CSS locators using these attributes:

```
@FindBy(xpath = "//a[@href='welcome.html']")
@FindBy(css = "a[href='welcome.html']")
protected M welcome;

or

@FindBy(xpath = "//a[@data-title='Welcome']")
@FindBy(css = "a[data-title='Welcome']")
protected M welcome;

or

@FindBy(xpath = "//a[contains(@data-pageid,'247216')]") // contains
@FindBy(css = "a[data-pageid*='247216']") // contains
@FindBy(css = "a[data-pageid$='247216']") // ends-with
protected M welcome;

or

@FindBy(xpath = "//a[@data-url='welcome.html']") // equals
@FindBy(css = "a[data-url^='welcome']") // starts-with
protected M welcome;

or

@FindBy(xpath = "//a[.='Welcome']") // equals
@FindBy(css = "a:contains('Welcome')") // contains; subject to CSS version
of browser
protected M welcome;
```

In these locators, attributes were used in both the XPath and CSS, some partial string matches on the attribute itself, and an `equals` and `contains` parameter.

In the following screenshot, we use the Chrome Inspector. When we highlight a StaticText field, it displays `span` in the Inspector frame and no attributes are available for the paragraph:

Google Chrome DOM elements

The www.practiceselenium.com is a free practice website where you can learn Selenium using tutorial classes or sample websites. It is provided by Selenium Framework 2010-2017, Copyrights reserved, 172-21 Hillside Avenue, Suite 207, Jamaica, NY, and is located at seleniumframework.com.

The following XPath locators use partial string matches to define the element:

```
@FindBy(xpath = "//span[contains(text(),'Green tea originated')]")

@FindBy(xpath = "//span[starts-with(text(),'Green tea')]")

@FindBy(xpath = "//span[ends-with(text(),'dietary supplements and cosmetic
items.')]")

@FindBy(xpath = "//span[.='Green tea is made...']") // equals; reqs entire
string

@FindBy(xpath = "//span[text()='Green tea is made...']") // equals; reqs
entire string

@FindBy(xpath = "(//span)[19]")

protected M greenTea;


@FindBy(css = "span:contains('Green tea is made from the leaves from
Camellia')") //native CSS

@FindBy(css = "span[innerText*='Green tea is made from']") // Non-Firefox

@FindBy(css = "span[textContent*='Green tea is made from')]") // Firefox

protected M greenTea;
```

So, even though this element had no ID, attributes, tags, className, and so on, we are able to define the locator using a portion of the text contained in span. XPath is a little more flexible in these situations.

MobileElements

As we discussed in the previous sections, the locators for MobileElements are limited to ID, className, tagName, and XPath. That doesn't mean you cannot use other attributes in XPath queries when defining the locators. Let's take a look at a few MobileElements and define the XPath locators.

In the following screenshot of the **ScratchTones** native mobile iOS app, when we highlight the **My Scratchtones** button in the Appium Inspector, it displays the attributes in the **Details** frame:

Appium iOS mobile elements

We have the `name`, `type`, `value`, and `label` to use as attributes; also, notice that the user is given a generic XPath locator to use. The problem with the generic locators is that they include too much hierarchy in the locator. Let's build a couple of single attribute XPath locators for this element:

```
@iOSFindBy(xpath = "//UIAButton[@name='My ScratchTones']")
protected M myScratchTones;

or

@iOSFindBy(xpath = "//UIAButton[@label='My ScratchTones']")
protected M myScratchTones;

or

@iOSFindBy(xpath = "//*[@value='1']")
protected M myScratchTones;

or

@iOSFindBy(xpath = "//UIATabBar[1]/UIAButton[1]")
protected M myScratchTones;
```

In the first and second locators, the class was used along with the `name` and `label` attributes. The class is not required if the locator is unique using just the attribute, so the third example is sufficient when wildcarding it. The third example is less robust using the value provided, and the most generic locator is the fourth example. When there are no unique attributes to use, users must use the class and an index number if there are multiple ones on the page (one-based numbering).

In the following screenshot, when we highlight the first StaticText field, it displays the attributes in the **Details** frame:

Appium iOS mobile elements

When StaticText is the only real attribute, we have to build the locator. We can use a partial string match in the XPath query:

```
@iOSFindBy(xpath = "//UIAStaticText[starts-with(@name,'1. Connect your
device')]")

@iOSFindBy(xpath = "//UIAStaticText[contains(@name,'Connect your
device')]")

@iOSFindBy(xpath = "//UIAStaticText[ends-with(@name,'menubar.')]")

@iOSFindBy(xpath = "//UIAStaticText[contains(text(),'Connect your
device')]")

@iOSFindBy(xpath = "//UIAStaticText[.='Connect your device to a computer,
launch iTunes,...']")
```

In the third screenshot, when we highlight the first button in the recorder, it displays the attributes in the **Details** frame. However, a lot of the buttons do not have any `text` attributes associated with them, such as the **Start** button:

Appium iOS details frame

In this case, the user would most likely have to use class and index numbers for some of the buttons, as follows:

```
@iOSFindBy(xpath = "//UIAButton[@name='Start']")
protected M start;

@iOSFindBy(xpath = "//UIAButton[@name='record active']")
protected M recordTrack1;

@iOSFindBy(xpath = "//UIAButton[@name='off unselected']")
protected M offTrack1;

@iOSFindBy(xpath = "//UIAButton[@name='play unselected']")
protected M playTrack1;

@iOSFindBy(xpath = "//UIASlider[1]")
protected M balanceTrack1;

@iOSFindBy(xpath = "//UISlider[3]")
protected M volumeTrack1;

etc...
```

The ScratchTones iOS Mobile Music Recording Studio application is provided by Graphixware, LLC:

Email: gw@graphixware.com
Website: https://graphixware.com
ScratchTones: https://itunes.apple.com/us/app/scratchtones/
id532631337?mt=8

Multiple attribute XPath versus CSS locators

In a lot of situations, there is a need to include multiple attributes to make a locator unique, or work with multiple elements; XPath and CSS both have provisions to allow this. Let's take a look at some of those techniques:

- **Hierarchy**: One mistake often made is including the entire hierarchy tree in a locator. The main problem with this is that if you use four to five levels of parenting, any time the style of the page changes, all the locators will be broken. The best practice to follow when using XPath and CSS is to include the element locator and, if necessary, one level of hierarchy only. This would include ancestor, descendant, preceding, following, preceding-sibling, and following-sibling.

- **Or conditions**: When a common locator is different on some pages, users can "or" the locator to find the element by one method or the other. For example:

```
// Xpath
@FindBy(xpath = "//img[@src='myLogo.png' or @src='myLogo.svg']")

// css
@FindBy(css = "div[id*='progressBar'], a[id*='progressBar'],
i[id*='progressBar']")
```

- **And conditions**: When a common locator needs multiple methods to make it unique, users can "and" the locator to find the element by both methods. For example:

```
// Xpath
@FindBy(xpath = "//div[contains(@class,'header') and
contains(text(),'label')]")

// css
@FindBy(css = "input[id*='email'][name='username']")
```

- **Parent, child, sibling, relatives**: When there are many elements with the same ID, classes, or attributes, such as when there are duplicate buttons on the page, users can use one of the hierarchy methods to define the locators. Here are a couple of XPath code examples:

```
// ancestor
@FindBy(xpath = "//input[@id='myID']/ancestor::div/span")

// descendant
@FindBy(xpath = "//*[@id='myModal']/descendant::h2")

// following
@FindBy(xpath = "//div[starts-
with(text(),'title')]/following::i[@class='icon-close']")

// following-sibling
@FindBy(xpath = "//div[.='label']/following-
sibling::div[@class='myGraphic']")

// preceding
@FindBy(xpath =
"//a[contains(text(),'myID')]/preceding::input[@class='myCheckbox']
")

// preceding-sibling
@FindBy(xpath = "//div[.='label']/preceding-
sibling::div[@class='myGraphic']")
```

Using dynamic locators in methods

Getting back to dynamic elements created during tests, how are they handled? We wouldn't want to define them upfront, and cannot possibly define them upfront, due to the nature of the dynamic names, text, or IDs associated with them.

So, let's build a method that takes a string parameter that defines some element in a page, which will get stuffed into an XPath locator on the fly. For this example, let's use a page's `label` elements.

To test all the //label elements in a web page—and in some cases, there can be dozens—we would want to store the labels in a data file and pass them into a test method one at a time, verifying that they exist on the page. To do this, we have to build the locator on the fly, as follows:

```
public void verifyLabel(String pattern,
                        String label)
                    throws Exception {

    WebDriver driver = CreateDriver.getInstance().getDriver();
    String locator = "//label[contains(text(),'" + pattern + "')]";

    assertEquals(driver.findElement(By.xpath(locator)).getText(),
    label);
}
```

That seems too easy to be true. In this example, we kept the locator in the page object class, kept a separation between that class and the test class calling the method, and created a dynamic locator to use instead of referencing a static locator from the page object class.

Let's look at one a little more complicated. In this next example, it wasn't enough to just reference a pattern to match label, but another control following the node as well:

```
public void verifyLabel(String pattern,
                        String label)
                    throws Exception {

    WebDriver driver = CreateDriver.getInstance().getDriver();
    String locator = "//label[contains(text(),'" + pattern +
                    "')]/following::div[@class='help-text']";

    assertEquals(driver.findElement(By.xpath(locator)).getText(),
    label);
}
```

Those are some cases where the element is predictable. How about situations where you have no text to pass into the element locator? A good example might be a case where the application throws up multiple cascading error dialog boxes when an exception occurs; how would you handle that? Here is a simple method to build a locator on the fly for an unpredictable element, that being a set of dialogs, and it uses an index as part of the locator:

```
public void cleanup() {
    String locator = "(//i[@class='icon-close'])[";
    WebDriver driver = CreateDriver.getInstance().getDriver();

    for ( int i = 10; i > 0; i-- ) {
```

```
            try {
                WebElement element =
                        driver.findElement(By.xpath(locator + i + "])"));

                if ( BrowserUtils.elementExists(element, 0) ) {
                    element.click();
                    waitForGone(By.xpath(locator + i + "]"), 1);
                }
            }

            catch(Exception e) {
                // do nothing, just trap it...
            }
        }
    }
```

Summary

So, at this point the framework consists of the Selenium driver class, the framework utility classes, and the page object classes that contain the locators and methods used to access the elements in the application.

The next layer that needs to be built is the data-driven testing portion of the framework. This is where we will leverage the TestNG framework technologies to create setup and teardown methods, and look at methods that can be iterated, groups of tests, suite files, parallel testing, and encapsulated data files.

First, let's build a data provider class, so as to have that in place, allowing us to pass in data when we start building the data-driven tests. The next chapter will cover building a JSON DataProvider for the framework.

Building a JSON Data Provider

13

This chapter introduces users to the concept of encapsulating data for use in data-driven testing. It will teach users how to design and build a TestNG Data Provider class in the native **JavaScript Object Notation (JSON)** format. The following topics will be covered:

- Introduction
- TestNG Data Provider class
- Extracting JSON data into Java objects
- Filtering test data
- JSON Data File formats
- The JSONObject class

Introduction

Before introducing the concept of data-driven testing, the framework will need a mechanism to extract data that is encapsulated in a format that can be easily passed into test methods. There are various ways to store data in automated testing; CSV files, JSON files, SQL databases, MS-Excel files, property files, and many more.

Since the technologies covered in this framework are Java and TestNG, this chapter will cover how to design and build a Data Provider class using Java and the JSON protocol. This is a common standard in Java development and testing, and TestNG has a feature to include any Data Provider method with TestNG-based test class methods.

As per Wikipedia (https://en.wikipedia.org/wiki/JSON):

> *"In computing, JavaScript Object Notation or JSON, is an open-standard file format that uses human-readable text to transmit data objects consisting of attribute-value pairs and array data types (or any other serializable value). It is a very common data format used for asynchronous browser/server communication, including as a replacement for XML in some AJAX-style systems."*

What you will learn

Users will learn how to design and build a Data Provider class using the TestNG Data Provider features to extract test data encapsulated in JSON format, for use in data-driven testing.

The TestNG Data Provider class

TestNG has a Data Provider feature that allows users to extract test data in any format. It returns an array of objects, which can be cast to a **POJO (Plain Old Java Object**; that is, no set of rules to follow) such as a JSONObject type. When creating the class with the method for extracting the data, users tag the method using the @DataProvider annotation.

The DataProvider method could be stored in the same class as the Test, but it makes more sense to create a generic static method in a separate class so all test classes can use the same DataProvider and format. Having a consistent format to encapsulate data will make it easier for users to maintain and enhance the framework and tests.

Finally, when storing the method in a separate class, the DataProvider method name and class must be passed to the @Test annotation as an attribute. We will explore a few examples in this section.

 The TestNG DataProvider JavaDoc is located at http://testng.org/doc/documentation-main.html#parameters-dataproviders.

The @DataProvider annotation

TestNG has an annotation called @DataProvider that tags a method in a class as a DataProvider, which can then be called on the test methods. It can take an attribute name to be used when declaring it in the test method. The following example shows the annotation in use:

```java
// Simple Data Seeded Data Provider Method

@DataProvider(name = "myData_JSON")
public static Object[][] fetchData() throws Exception {
    JSONObject object = new JSONObject();

    object.put("name", "Kiss");
    object.put("year", "1973");
    object.put("song", "Rock and Roll All Nite");

    return new Object[][] {{object}};
}

/**
 * TestNG DataProvider Class for extracting JSON data
 *
 * @author Name
 *
 */
public class JSONDataProvider {
    public static String dataFile = "";
    public static String testCaseName = "NA";

    /**
     * fetchData - generic DataProvider method that extracts data
     * by JSON key:value pairs
     *
     * @param method
     * @return Object[][]
     * @throws Exception
     */
    @DataProvider(name = "myData_JSON")
    public static Object[][] fetchData(Method method) throws
    Exception {
        System.out.println(method.getName());
        ...
```

Notice the `Method` parameter passed to the `fetchData` method. This tells TestNG to get the current test method name and pass it into the method, which is useful for filtering data.

The @Test annotation

TestNG uses attributes and an annotation called `@Test` to tag the test methods, differentiating which ones are setup/teardown methods, test methods, or private methods in the class. In this example, the test method has a dataProvider and class defined as attributes to the test method:

```
/**
 * tc001_appFeatureAction - test method to demonstrate @Test DP Annotation
 *
 * @param data
 * @throws Exception
 */
@Test(dataProvider="myData_JSON",dataProviderClass=JSONDataProvider.class)
public void tc001_appFeatureAction (JSONObject data) throws Exception {
    ....
```

Extracting JSON data into Java objects

Now that the basic syntax has been covered, we will start building the JSON DataProvider method. First, we need a file I/O method to read the JSON data from a file. The parameter to the method will be the filename, including the path and string type. The method will be static and return `JSONObject`. Here is the code sample:

```
/**
 * extractData_JSON - method to extract JSON data from a file
 *
 * @param file (including path)
 * @return JSONObject
 * @throws Exception
 */
public static JSONObject extractData_JSON(String file) throws Exception {
    FileReader reader = new FileReader(file);
    JSONParser jsonParser = new JSONParser();

    return (JSONObject) jsonParser.parse(reader);
}
```

In cases where users might want to extract only specific sets of JSON data, as when filtering for specific test cases, they could create a wrapper method around the `extractData_JSON` method that would allow a parameter to be used as a filter. This method would also be static and return a JSONArray. Here is the code sample:

```
/**
 * fetchData - method to get only the data that matches the filter

 * @param file (including path)
 * @param filter
 * @return JSONArray
 * @throws Exception
 */
public static JSONArray fetchData(String file,
                                  String filter)
                                  throws Exception {

    JSONArray testData = (JSONArray) extractData_JSON(file).get(filter);

    return testData;
}
```

The `fetchData` method to be used as the DataProvider will be constructed to support the data-driven test model. What that means is the parameter to the `fetchData` method, `java.lang.Reflect.Method`, will pass the test method name to the `fetchData` method and return only the sets of JSON data for that specific test case. In other words, each test method will include the DataProvider name as an attribute and it will automatically pull only the sets of data by the same name.

In essence, TestNG does the filtering for each test case so that only the correct sets of data are sequentially passed into the test cases that apply. Additional filtering can be added in the DataProvider.

This method will use the Java class `JSON.simple`, which provides methods for processing, reading, and writing JSON data using `JSONArray` and `JSONObject` types.

 The JSON simple JavaDoc is located at `https://cliftonlabs.github.io/json-simple/target/apidocs/index.html`.

Now, let's look at the method structure of this DataProvider:

```java
// global variables to be "set" later outside the DataProvider Class
public static String dataFile = "";

/**
 * fetchData - generic DataProvider method that extracts data
 * by JSON key:value pairs
 *
 * @param method
 * @return Object[][]
 * @throws Exception
 */
@DataProvider(name = "myData_JSON")
public static Object[][] fetchData(Method method) throws Exception {
    Object rowID, description;
    Object result [][];
    testCaseName = method.getName();
    JSONArray testData = (JSONArray) extractData_JSON(dataFile)
                                    .get(method.getName());

    List<JSONObject> testDataList = new ArrayList<JSONObject>();

    for ( int i = 0; i < testData.size(); i++ ) {
        testDataList.add((JSONObject) testData.get(i));
    }

    // include Filter Placeholder

    // exclude Filter Placeholder

    // create object for dataprovider to return
    Object[][] result = new Object[testDataList.size()]
                                  [testDataList.get(0).size()];

    for ( int i = 0; i < testDataList.size(); i++ ) {
        result[i] = new Object[] { testDataList.get(i) };
    }

    return result;
}
```

The next code example is for later use in this framework, but we'll cover it now. There are third-party test reports that allow users to customize the report content, and having a row ID and description of the test allows users to filter within the report, name the screenshots with the test method `rowID`, add conditions to method setup and teardown routines, and so on. The following code example shows users how to "stuff" the `rowID` and `description` into the object be created in the DataProvider:

```
// add in rowID and description for later use

try {
    result = new Object[testDataList.size()]
            [testDataList.get(0).size()];

    for ( int i = 0; i < testDataList.size(); i++ ) {
        rowID = testDataList.get(i).get("rowID");
        description = testDataList.get(i).get("description");
        result[i] = new Object[] { rowID, description,
        testDataList.get(i) };
    }
}

catch(IndexOutOfBoundsException ie) {
    result = new Object[0][0];
}

    return result;
}
```

Filtering test data

Although TestNG has a feature to run specific groups of tests using the `groups` attribute, there may be cases where users will want to filter the data during extraction to include or exclude a subset of test data. The following filter code can be added to the DataProvider method (see the preceding placeholders).

Filtering include and exclude patterns

There may be times when the user might want to run just a subset of the group of tests to create a "smokeTest" of some sort, narrowing the scope of the test run. Users can use TestNG groupings to assign tags to the test methods in the classes, and they can also filter in or filter out rows of data, using the DataProvider itself. This would allow them to select specific test rows of data or a small set with specific criteria like the rowID in the JSON Data File.

When filtering with the DataProvider, users can set a TestNG parameter in the suite XML file, pull in the parameter as a system property, and parse in or out those rows of data.

Here is an example of filtering sets of data in or out of the test run when the extraction takes place:

```java
// include tests matching this pattern only
...

if ( System.getProperty("includePattern") != null ) {
    String include = System.getProperty("includePattern");
    List<JSONObject> newList = new ArrayList<JSONObject>();
    List<String> tests = Arrays.asList(include.split(",", -1));

    for ( String getTest : tests ) {
        for ( int i = 0; i < testDataList.size(); i++ ) {
            if ( testDataList.get(i).toString().contains(getTest) ) {
                newList.add(testDataList.get(i));
            }
        }
    }

    // reassign testRows after filtering tests
    testDataList = newList;
}

// exclude tests matching this pattern only
...

if ( System.getProperty("excludePattern") != null ) {
    String exclude =System.getProperty("excludePattern");
    List<String> tests = Arrays.asList(exclude.split(",", -1));

    for ( String getTest : tests ) {
        // start at end of list and work backwards so
        // index stays in sync
        for ( int i = testDataList.size() - 1 ; i >= 0; i-- ) {
            if ( testDataList.get(i).toString().contains(getTest) ) {
```

```
                    testDataList.remove(testDataList.get(i));
                }
            }
        }
    }
```

JSON Data File formats

Now that we have the JSON Data Provider created, we need some data in the correct format. Users can actually customize the formatting of the JSON data in the files. Again, JSON is based on the key/value pairs of data, and the schema is somewhat subjective as to how you lay out the data:

 There is a helpful JSON formatting tool located at `https://` `jsonformatter.curiousconcept.com/`.

```
// the following sets of JSON data are laid out vertically

{
    "tc001_getBandInfo":[
        {
            "rowID":"tc001_getBandInfo.01",
            "description":"Kiss Data",
            "name":"Kiss",
            "year":"1973",
            "song":"Rock and Roll All Nite",
            "members":{
                "Vocals":"Paul Stanley",
                "Bass":"Gene Simmons",
                "Guitar":"Ace Frehley",
                "Drums":"Peter Criss"
            }
        },
        {
            "rowID":"tc001_getBandInfo.02",
            "description":"Van Halen Data",
            "name":"Van Halen",
            "year":"1972",
            "song":"Dance the Night Away",
            "members":{
                "Vocals":"David Lee Roth",
                "Bass":"Michael Anthony",
                "Guitar":"Eddie Van Halen",
```

```
                "Drums":"Alex Van Halen"
            }
        },
        {
            "rowID":"tc001_getBandInfo.03",
            "description":"U2 Data",
            "name":"U2",
            "year":"1976",
            "song":"Sunday Bloody Sunday",
            "members":{
                "Vocals":"Bono",
                "Bass":"Adam Clayton",
                "Guitar":"The Edge",
                "Drums":"Larry Mullen"
            }
        },
        {
            "rowID":"tc001_getBandInfo.04",
            "description":"Thin Lizzy Data",
            "name":"Thin Lizzy",
            "year":"1969",
            "song":"The Boys Are Back in Town",
            "members":{
                "Vocals":"Phil Lynott",
                "Bass":"Phil Lynott",
                "Guitar":"Scott Gorham",
                "Drums":"Brian Downey"
            }
        }
    ]
}

// the following sets of JSON data are laid out horizontally

{
 "tc002_addEmp":
 [
 {"rowID":"tc002_addEmp.01","description":"Add
  Employee","id":"EMP1","name":"John","gender":"M","age":23},

 {"rowID":"tc002_addEmp.02","description":"Add
  Employee","id":"EMP2","name":"Jane","gender":"F","age":30},

 {"rowID":"tc002_addEmp.03","description":"Add
  Employee","id":"EMP3","name":"Sally","gender":"F","age":19},
```

```
{"rowID":"tc002_addEmp.04","description":"Add
 Employee","id":"EMP4","name":"Bob","gender":"M","age":40}
]
}
```

Note that in both examples, there is a method name that starts the data model, and each set of data for that method is nested within it. For instance, in the first example, the method name is tc001_getBandInfo, which will be the name of the Java test method in the test class. Each set of data to be passed into it has rowID using the same name plus an index such as tc001_getBandInfo.01, tc001_getBandInfo.02, and so on.

For the next test method set of data, the user can include it in the same JSON file, but must differentiate the method name.

The second example uses the method name tc002_addEmp with the rowID as tc002_addEmp.01, tc002_addEmp.02, and so on. How the data is structured in the JSON file is determined by JSONObject, which is being created for the test method. We will cover that in the next section.

The JSONObject class

Once the data is extracted from the JSON file, it is available for use in the test methods. Users can cast the extracted data to a JSONObject of any type they desire to create. This allows them to access each field using a key/value pairing, and that data can be passed into test case methods that perform the actions on the screen.

Remember, when using the Selenium Page Object Model, each page object class contains all the methods that pertain to using the features on a specific screen, and those methods are called from within the test methods to vary data passed to them. This allows the test methods to be reused for multiple test scenarios, and keeps an abstract layer between the page object and the test classes.

The JSONObject is an interface that extends the JSONStructure class, inherits common methods from its superclass, and provides users with a simple data structure to store the test data. It can be used in conjunction with JSONReader, JSONWriter, JSONArray, and JSONObjectBuilder.

Now, let's explore a few examples of how to use it:

 The JavaDoc for the JSONObject class is located at http://docs.oracle. com/javaee/7/api/javax/json/JsonObject.html.

```java
// using the rock bands JSON data we introduced earlier,
// create a JSONObject with the required field types

import org.json.simple.JSONObject;

/**
 * Sample JSONObject Class
 *
 * @author name
 *
 */
public class RockBands {
    private String name, year, song;
    private JSONObject members;

    // the constructor requires the JSONObject when instantiated
    public RockBands(JSONObject object) {
        setName(object.get("name").toString());
        setYear(object.get("year").toString());
        setSong(object.get("song").toString());
        setMembers((JSONObject) object.get("members"));
    }

    public void setName(String name) {
        this.name = name;
    }

    public String getName() {
        return this.name;
    }

    public void setYear(String year) {
        this.year = year;
    }

    public String getYear() {
        return this.year;
    }

    public void setSong(String song) {
        this.song = song;
```

```
    }

    public String getSong() {
        return this.song;
    }

    public void setMembers(JSONObject members) {
        this.members = members;
    }

    public JSONObject getMembers() {
        return this.members;
    }

    @Override
    public String toString() {
        return "RockBands {" +
                "name = '" + name + '\'' +
                ", year = '" + year + '\'' +
                ", song = '" + song + '\'' +
                ", members = " + members +
                '}';
    }
}
```

First, the constructor in the class requires JSONObject to be passed into it when instantiated. Since we are using the JSON DataProvider to extract the data, we can cast it to a JSONObject on the fly as follows:

```
@Test(dataProvider="myData_JSON", dataProviderClass=JSONDataProvider.class)
public void tc001_getBandInfo(JSONObject testData) throws Exception {
    // fetch object data and pass into Java object...
    RockBands rockBands = new RockBands(testData);

    // print out the JSONObject data extracted from file
    System.out.println(rockBands.toString());
}
```

Second, notice that one of the members in the constructor takes another JSONObject parameter, that is because the band members key is a nested object in itself:

```
public RockBands(JSONObject object) {
    setName(object.get("name").toString());
    setYear(object.get("year").toString());
    setSong(object.get("song").toString());
    setMembers((JSONObject) object.get("members"));
}
```

```
// again, the data format looks like this in the JSON file:
```

```
"tc001_getBandInfo":[
    {
        "rowID":"tc001_getBandInfo.01",
        "description":"Kiss Data",
        "name":"Kiss",
        "year":"1973",
        "song":"Rock and Roll All Nite",
        "members":{
            "Vocals":"Paul Stanley",
            "Bass":"Gene Simmons",
            "Guitar":"Ace Frehley",
            "Drums":"Peter Criss"
        }
    }
```

Finally, the data can be retrieved from the `rockBands` object using the key/value pairings:

```
System.out.println("\nName = " + rockBands.getName() +
                   "\nYear = " + rockBands.getYear() +
                   "\nSong = " + rockBands.getSong() +
                   "\nVocals = " + rockBands.getMembers().get("Vocals") +
                   "\nBass = " + rockBands.getMembers().get("Bass") +
                   "\nGuitar = " + rockBands.getMembers().get("Guitar") +
                   "\nDrums = " + rockBands.getMembers().get("Drums"));
```

Alternatively, the following can be used:

```
System.out.println(rockBands.toString());
```

The output of the first method noted above looks like this (although the intention is to pass it into a page object class method for processing):

```
Name = Kiss
Year = 1973
Song = Rock and Roll All Nite
Vocals = Paul Stanley
Bass = Gene Simmons
Guitar = Ace Frehley
Drums = Peter Criss
```

The alternative method will produce the following output:

```
RockBands {name = 'Kiss', year = '1973', song = 'Rock and Roll All Nite',
members = {"Bass":"Gene Simmons","Guitar":"Ace Frehley","Vocals":"Paul
Stanley","Drums":"Peter Criss"}}
```

Some users prefer to build the Java objects using the builder class interface, which has some of the same design pattern but allows users to set only the fields they want to change. Here's an example using the same data structure:

> The JavaDoc for the builder interface is located at https://commons.apache.org/proper/commons-lang/javadocs/api-3.1/org/apache/commons/lang3/builder/Builder.html.

```java
/**
 * Sample JSON Object Class
 *
 * @author Name
 *
 */
public class RockBandsBuilder {
    public String name, year, song;
    public JSONObject members;

    /**
     * Builder interface
     *
     */
    public static class Builder {
        private String name, year, song;
        private JSONObject members;

        public Builder() {
        }

        public Builder name(String name) {
            this.name = name;
            return this;
        }

        public Builder year(String year) {
            this.year = year;
            return this;
        }

        public Builder song(String song) {
```

```
                    this.song = song;
                    return this;
            }

            public Builder members(JSONObject members) {
                    this.members = members;
                    return this;
            }

            public RockBandsBuilder build() {
                    RockBandsBuilder rockBands = new RockBandsBuilder(this);
                    return rockBands;
            }
        }

        public RockBandsBuilder(Builder builder) {
            this.name = builder.name;
            this.year = builder.year;
            this.song = builder.song;
            this.members = builder.members;
        }

        public RockBandsBuilder(RockBandsBuilder rockBands) {
            this.name = rockBands.name;
            this.year = rockBands.year;
            this.song = rockBands.song;
            this.members = rockBands.members;
        }

        @Override
        public String toString() {
            return "RockBandsBuilder {" +
                    "name = '" + name + '\'' +
                    ", year = '" + year + '\'' +
                    ", song = '" + song + '\'' +
                    ", members = " + members +
                    '}';
        }
    }
```

The test method use of this class would look like this:

```
@Test(dataProvider="myData_JSON", dataProviderClass=JSONDataProvider.class)
public void tc002_getBandInfo(JSONObject testData) throws Exception {
    // fetch object data and pass into Java object...
    RockBandsBuilder rockBands = new RockBandsBuilder.Builder()
                .name(testData.get("name").toString())
                .year(testData.get("year").toString())
```

```
                    .song(testData.get("song").toString())
                    .members((JSONObject) testData.get("members"))
                    .build();

        // print out the JSONObject data extracted from file
        System.out.println(rockBands.toString());
    }
```

Summary

This chapter introduced users to designing and building a DataProvider class using TestNG DataProvider features, along with the concept of encapsulating data in JSON file format. As we proceed further into data-driven test development, it will be important to have the DataProvider available for use when creating new test methods.

As we learned, the DataProvider method will sort data during extraction based on the test method name. Filters for including and excluding specific sets of data can also be added, and finally, users can "stuff" specific data like rowID and description into Java objects on the fly to be used later on for reporting purposes.

The next chapter will cover the data-driven test development model in respect to designing and building Java test classes, methods, and data files. The TestNG annotations will be used to specify which test methods are setup and teardown methods, and which ones are actual test methods that require data to run.

After the next chapter, the user will have the basic structure of the framework complete, from the Selenium driver class to the utility classes, page object classes, test classes, and data files.

14

Developing Data-Driven Test Classes

This chapter focuses on designing and building data-driven test classes using the TestNG technologies, integrating a data provider into data-driven tests, and using setup/teardown, exception handling, and various other TestNG features. The following topics are covered:

- Introduction
- Annotating test class methods using TestNG
- TestNG setup/teardown methods
- Naming conventions for test methods
- Using the TestNG DataProvider
- Calling page object methods in test classes
- Exception handling in test classes
- Designing base setup classes
- TestNG suite file structure
- Suite parameters

Introduction

As we mentioned earlier in the book, the main reasons for using a data-driven test development approach are to be able to reuse test methods with multiple permutations of data, to encapsulate data in a central location, and to enforce DRY coding practices, which reduce the amount of code being written and maintained.

To correctly design and build tests that use this methodology for testing software applications, test methods must contain a predefined input, a verifiable output, and contain no hardcoded values within the test method. Data is passed into a test method at runtime, where it is then used in page object methods to perform an action and verify a result. Because the data is not hardcoded into the test, methods can be iterated with variations of datasets, extending the coverage of the test to include positive, negative, boundary, and limit testing.

This all sounds simple, but in reality, it takes quite a bit of work to convince and train an engineering organization to follow this model. With time constraints in releasing applications in continuous development environments, users often just build the test with a predefined set of data within it. Practices following a copy, paste, change one line of code approach are no longer acceptable.

Regardless of that fact, as a best practice and standard, test methods should be designed and built as generically as possible, use a data provider to extract and pass data to them, and stay small and focused on testing one function per test.

In this chapter, we will design and build data-driven tests using Java and the TestNG technologies.

As per Wikipedia:

> *"Data-driven testing is the creation of test scripts to run together with their related data sets in a framework. The framework provides re-usable test logic to reduce maintenance and improve test coverage. Input and result (test criteria) data values can be stored in one or more central data sources or databases, the actual format and organization can be implementation specific. The data comprises variables used for both input values and output verification values. In advanced (mature) automation environments data can be harvested from a running system using a purpose-built custom tool, and the DDT framework thus performs playback of harvested data producing a powerful automated regression testing tool. Navigation through the program, reading of the data sources, and logging of test status and information are all coded in the test script."*

The reader will learn how to create data-driven test classes that follow the Selenium POM to separate page object classes from test classes and data.

Annotating test class methods using TestNG

When we start building test classes, we need to think about how we want to structure files. We are using TestNG as the test framework technology, so we will need to use the annotations it provides to tag the methods in the class.

Other things to consider: how to instantiate the required page object classes, how to declare local variables, when to use private methods in the class, how to pass data to the test methods, and how to structure Java methods so they become setup, teardown, and test methods. Let's get started on the test class structure itself.

 The documentation for TestNG is located at `http://testng.org/doc/ documentation-main.html`.

TestNG annotations

Here is a list of the standard TestNG annotations available for test methods:

- `@Test`
- `@Parameters`
- `@DataProvider`
- `@Listeners`
- `@Factory`
- `@BeforeSuite` and `@AfterSuite`
- `@BeforeTest` and `@AfterTest`
- `@BeforeGroups` and `@AfterGroups`
- `@BeforeClass` and `@AfterClass`
- `@BeforeMethod` and `@AfterMethod`

@Test

Let's build the test class from the ground up; we will use the *Rock Bands* test class and data file as an example:

```java
/**
 * Rock Bands Test Class (JavaDoc left out)
 *
 * @author Name
 *
 */
public class RockBandsTest {

    // setup/teardown methods
    @BeforeSuite
    protected void suiteSetup(ITestContext context) throws Exception {
    }

    @AfterSuite
    protected void suiteTeardown(ITestContext context) throws Exception {
    }

    @BeforeTest
    protected void testSetup(ITestContext context) throws Exception {
    }

    @AfterTest
    protected void testTeardown(ITestContext context) throws Exception {
    }

    @BeforeGroups
    protected void groupsSetup() throws Exception {
    }

    @AfterGroups
    protected void groupsTeardown() throws Exception {
    }

    @BeforeClass
    protected void testClassSetup() throws Exception {
    }

    @AfterClass
    protected void testClassTeardown() throws Exception {
    }

    @BeforeMethod
    protected void testMethodSetup(ITestResult rslt) throws Exception {
```

```
    }

    @AfterMethod
    protected void testMethodTeardown(ITestResult rslt) throws Exception {
    }

    // testcases
    @Test
    public void tc001_getBandInfo(String rowID,
                                  String description,
                                  JSONObject testData)
                                  throws Exception {

    }
}
```

So, in the page object classes, we created various Java methods to perform actions on elements in web or mobile pages. Now, when we build the test class, we have to tag the test methods with the @Test annotation. This tells TestNG that this method is a "test" and it should be executed when the user runs the class. Some of the attributes available with the @Test annotation include:

- alwaysRun
- dataProvider
- dataProviderClass
- dependsOnGroups
- dependsOnMethods
- description
- enabled
- expectedExceptions
- groups
- invocationCount
- invocationTimeOut
- priority
- successPercentage
- singleThreaded
- timeOut
- threadPoolSize

Let's discuss a few of the more common ones in the following example:

```
@Test(groups={"POSITIVE",
              "NEGATIVE",
              "BOUNDRY",
              "LIMIT",
              "SMOKETEST",
              "REGRESSION"},
      dataProvider="fetchData_JSON",
      dataProviderClass=JSONDataProvider.class,
      enabled=true,
      alwaysRun=true,
      priority=1)
public void tc001_getBandInfo() {
    ...
}
```

When the `groups` attribute is used, it allows the user to tag specific test cases to be part of an overall group, a subset, or a feature test set.

So, in this example, the user defines which group or groups to run in the TestNG suite XML file, and only that subset of groups will be run. It makes sense to tag only a couple of test methods in each class as `SMOKETEST`, so as you develop the functional test classes, you build a SmokeTest at the same time and "most" of the test methods would be tagged `REGRESSION`, except for the `LIMIT` tests, which would stress out or break the product.

The next two attributes in the example, `dataProvider` and `dataProviderClass`, are used to tell TestNG which DataProvider class and method to use to extract data to pass to the test method. The last chapter covered building the JSON DataProvider; this is where the user calls it.

The `enabled` attribute tells TestNG whether or not the test method should be run; great for disabling tests that aren't working, are blocked by defects, or for debugging purposes.

The `dependsOnMethods` attribute will tie the test method to other test methods in the class. This is a rather tricky one to use, as it will force all test methods to "skip" if the dependent method fails. It is at times more practical to set up a test class using one of the setup/teardown annotations rather than using this attribute.

The `alwaysRun` attribute tells TestNG to run the test method regardless of a failure to a method it may depend on.

And finally, the `priority` attribute tells TestNG which priority order to run the tests in.

The TestNG documentation covers all the attributes in detail; we've discussed a few of the more common ones here.

TestNG setup/teardown methods

In the previous Rock Bands test class example, we listed some of the annotations that tell TestNG whether a certain method should be run before or after certain points in time during the test run. These are the setup and teardown methods. They come before and after a suite, test, groups, class, and method.

As simple as it may seem, there are various rules and orders of precedence when using them. Let's look at some examples.

Setup methods

When you build the test class, there will be certain Java methods annotated with @Test, which tells TestNG that the method is a test and should be run. Those tests will run in random order by default except, if you use a dependent method, a sequential naming scheme, or a `priority` attribute. That will force the tests to run in a specific order.

For all the methods in a suite of tests, there will be common actions that need to be executed before each suite, test, groups, class, or methods, and instead of calling the same setup method in each class or test, for instance, it makes sense to do them in one place. Using the TestNG `setup` annotations will allow users to execute a routine in a central place.

@BeforeSuite, @BeforeTest, @BeforeGroups, @BeforeClass, and @BeforeMethod

Let's discuss each annotation in detail:

- `@BeforeSuite`: All the methods called in this setup will get executed before anything else runs in the suite. For instance, if you want to invoke the browser or a mobile device, you could call the create driver method in `@BeforeSuite`, and it would launch the application, maximize it, and load the URL (browser) before running the test class methods. This is also a good place to retrieve parameters using the `@Parameters` annotation from a Jenkins build process, system property via JVM arguments, and system environment variables. They can then be processed here for use throughout the suite. Remember, TestNG defines a suite as all the tests contained in the suite XML file. We will discuss that later on in the chapter.

- `@BeforeTest`: All the methods called in this setup will run before all test packages or classes defined in the `<test>` tag section of the XML file. If building tests to run in parallel at the `<test>` level, users would want to invoke the browser or mobile device here, so each "thread" would run in its own browser or mobile device. This is also a place where `@Parameters` can be used, which can be defined in the XML file as well in each `<test>` section. The `<test>` sections in the XML can contain the same or different test packages or classes, and this annotation is a way to execute an application setup procedure for all of them.

- `@BeforeGroups`: All the methods called in this configuration setup will run before a specific group or groups of tests run. The `@Test` attribute `groups=` would need to be used for this to have any effect. This annotation allows a different setup procedure to be run for different groups of tests.

- `@BeforeClass`: All the methods called in this setup will run before the first test method runs in the current class. In each test class, there may be a specific setup that is required before any of the test methods in the class run. This would include such things as creating default users, accounts, setting up default preferences in the application, and so on.

- `@BeforeMethod`: All the methods called in this setup will run before each and every iteration of a test method has run. Users often use this method to set the application to a known "app" state so that each test starts at the same place, avoiding conditions where failed tests leave the application in a weird state, windows left open, and so on.

Teardown methods

For all the methods in a suite of tests, there will be common actions that need to be executed after each suite, test, groups, class, or methods, and instead of calling the same cleanup method in each class or test, for instance, it makes sense to do them in one place. Using the TestNG `teardown` annotations will allow users to execute a routine in a central place, as it did with the setup annotations.

@AfterSuite, @AfterTest, @AfterGroups, @AfterClass, and @AfterMethod

Let's discuss all the annotations in detail:

- `@AfterSuite`: All the methods called in this teardown will execute after everything else has completed in the suite. This is a good place to clean up the AUT, delete users, and accounts created during test runs, uninstall mobile applications, and close the browser or mobile device. If a report listener is being used, the report could be constructed in this method after all the TestNG results are collected.
- `@AfterTest`: All the methods called in this teardown will run after all the test packages or classes defined in the `<test>` tag section of the XML file have completed. If running `<test>` sections in parallel, users can use this to close the browsers or mobile devices in each thread, provide cleanup, delete users, and so on.
- `@AfterGroups`: All the methods called in this configuration teardown will run after a specific group or groups of tests run. Because test methods generally run in a random order with TestNG, this method will run *at some point* after the last test method runs in the `<test>` section of the XML file.
- `@AfterClass`: All the methods called in this teardown will run after the last method runs in the current class. This teardown is very useful for cleaning up all leftover users, accounts, settings, or anything else the `@AfterMethod` routine fails to remove. This is also a good place to process TestNG results (ITestResult) for reporting purposes.
- `@AfterMethod`: All the methods called in this teardown will run after each and every iteration of a test method has run. What that means is that when running data-driven tests, a single test method may execute multiple times, and this cleanup method will run after each iteration. This routine is useful for cleanup when exceptions occur during a test method run, taking screenshots, reporting results, and generally setting the application back to a known "base" state.

Order of precedence

Other things to note: when using these annotation methods in a superclass of a TestNG test class, they will be executed in inheritance order of precedence. In other words, users can create multiple layers of test setup using the same setup annotations, and they will be inherited and run before the subclass setup methods run. They can also be overridden in classes that do not require them, using the `@Override` annotation and calling those methods by the same setup method name in the test class.

The same precedence rules apply to the teardown methods; those will get executed in reverse order of inheritance starting with the test class teardowns and then followed by the execution of the superclass methods. The following code block shows an example of using the `@Override` annotation:

```
// use of setup/teardown methods in base class
public abstract class RockBandsSetup {

    // abstract methods
    protected abstract void testMethodSetup(ITestResult result)
                                        throws Exception;

    protected abstract void testMethodTeardown(ITestResult result)
                                        throws Exception;

    // setup/teardown methods
    @BeforeSuite
    protected void suiteSetup(ITestContext context) throws Exception {
    }

    @AfterSuite
    protected void suiteTeardown(ITestContext context) throws Exception {
    }

    @BeforeClass
    protected void testClassSetup() throws Exception {
    }

    @AfterClass
    protected void testClassTeardown() throws Exception {
    }

}


// use of @Override to override setup/teardown methods
public class RockBands extends RockBandsSetup {
```

```java
// implemented abstract methods
@BeforeMethod
protected void testMethodSetup(ITestResult rslt) throws Exception {
}

@AfterMethod
protected void testMethodTeardown(ITestResult rslt) throws Exception {
}

// overridden inherited methods
@Override
@BeforeClass
protected void testClassSetup() throws Exception {
}

@Override
@AfterClass
protected void testClassTeardown() throws Exception {
}

}
```

Naming conventions for test methods

One standard that is usually followed loosely is naming conventions. But it is still important to put some standards in place to reduce the maintenance of the overall test classes. In this section, we will briefly set standards for naming test classes, data files, methods, setup, cleanup, groups, and row ID parameters.

Test classes and data files

We covered file naming conventions earlier, but to refresh the naming convention for test classes, it should be something like `FunctionalAreaTest.java`. The `Test` suffix tells the user that this is a test class and not a Java utility class.

Since we are using JSON as the data file format, each test class should have a corresponding data file minus the `Test` suffix; so in this case, `FunctionalArea.json`.

So, in the example test class we are building in this chapter, the class is called `RockBandsTest.java` and the data file is called `RockBands.json`. We will build onto that class as we define each section of it.

Test methods

Test methods can have unique names, generic names, or really any name that tells the user something about what it is testing. But there are some important aspects of the method names to consider.

First, if a sequential numbering scheme is used, then it forces TestNG to run in a particular order and the `priority` attribute is not required.

Second, it makes sense to include a functional area and action in the name as well. So, if creating **Create, Read, Update, and Delete (CRUD)** tests for the Google Mail functional area of the application, we can name them:

- `tc001_gmailCreateAccount`
- `tc002_gmailReadAccount`
- `tc003_gmailUpdateAccount`
- `tc004_gmailDeleteAccount`

To build upon the `RockBandsTest.java` class, here are the methods following a similar naming convention:

```
/**
 * Rock Bands Test Class
 *
 * @author Name
 *
 */
public class RockBandsTest {

    // test methods
    @Test
    public void tc001_getBandInfo() throws Exception {
        ....
    }

    @Test
    public void tc002_getBandInfo() throws Exception {
        ....
    }

}
```

Test parameters

Test method parameters will be discussed in greater detail later on in this chapter, but for naming conventions, the names for the required method parameters for this framework are as follows:

- `String rowID`: The row ID of the datasets to extract from the JSON data file to pass into the method. Note, `rowID` used in the data file must be the same name as the method.
- `String description`: The description of the test that will later be used by the test listener and/or reporter classes to annotate the results.
- `JSONObject testData`: The test data object to pass into the method to run the test. This object will get built on the fly when using the JSON DataProvider attribute with the test method.

Test groups

Test groups can be named anything that will categorize them into a subgroup that makes sense to the application or test environment. The most common group names are SmokeTest, regression, positive, negative, boundary, and limit.

Including or excluding groups in the suite XML file allows users to run subsets of the entire regression suite. In the case of the `RockBandsTest.java` class, we will just use the group "regression" for now.

Test setup/teardown methods

As we said earlier in the chapter, the setup and teardown methods will be called when the `@Before` and `@After` annotations are used. The names themselves are subjective, but the key thing to remember here is that, when using multiple layers of setup/teardown, users can override an inherited setup or teardown method by using the `@Override` annotation and the *same* method name as the overridden one.

Some of the more common names used in this framework correspond to the annotation names, as follows:

- `@BeforeSuite`: The `suiteSetup` method
- `@AfterSuite`: The `suiteTeardown` method
- `@BeforeTest`: The `testSetup` method

- @AfterTest: The testTeardown method
- @BeforeClass: The testClassSetup method
- @AfterClass: The testClassTeardown method
- @BeforeMethod: The testMethodSetup method
- @AfterMethod: The testMethodTeardown method

Here is the RockBandsTest.java class so far using these naming conventions:

```java
/**
 * Rock Bands Test Class
 *
 * @author Name
 *
 */
public class RockBandsTest {
    // local vars
    public static final String DATA_FILE = "myPath/RockBands.json";

    // setup/teardown method go here
    @BeforeClass(alwaysRun=true,enabled=true)
    protected void testClassSetup() throws Exception {
        // set data file...
        JSONDataProvider.dataFile = DATA_FILE;
    }

    @AfterClass(alwaysRun=true,enabled=true)
    protected void testClassTeardown() throws Exception {
    }

    @BeforeMethod(alwaysRun=true,enabled=true)
    protected void testMethodSetup(ITestResult rslt) throws Exception {
    }

    @AfterMethod(alwaysRun=true,enabled=true)
    protected void testMethodTeardown(ITestResult rslt) throws
    Exception {
    }

    // test methods go here
    @Test(groups={"REGRESSION"},
        dataProvider="fetchData_JSON",
        dataProviderClass=JSONDataProvider.class,
        enabled=true)
    public void tc001_getBandInfo(String rowID,
                                  String description,
                                  JSONObject testData)
```

```
                                    throws Exception {
    }

    @Test(groups={"REGRESSION"},
            dataProvider="fetchData_JSON",
            dataProviderClass=JSONDataProvider.class,
            enabled=true)
    public void tc002_getBandInfo(String rowID,
                                    String description,
                                    JSONObject testData)
                                    throws Exception {

    }

}
```

Using the TestNG DataProvider

In the preceding RockBandsTest.java example, the dataProvider and dataProviderClass were used as attributes to the @Test method. This tells TestNG that it should extract all the sets of data in the JSON file that match the *method name*. In the previous chapter, we built a basic JSON DataProvider, and one of the parameters to it was the method name. TestNG passes this in when the test method is run.

Now, as far as the data is concerned, the JSON DataProvider builds a Java object on the fly and the rowID and description parameter values are stuffed into the object. That functionality was built into the DataProvider. This will be used later on for reporting purposes, but it is also handy for determining which set of data failed the test. Again, the @DataProvider annotation is used to tag the method created that fetches the data in this class.

It is also worth noting that the @Parameters annotation can be used with the @Test annotation to pass in parameters for the test method to use, but it is more useful when using them in @Before type annotations. This will be covered later on when we go over using the TestNG XML suite file parameters.

So, since we outlined the JSON data file datasets and the Java objects for the RockBandsTest.java class already in Chapter 13, *Building a JSON Data Provider*, let's add the instances of those classes and call a method in them in the test class:

```
/**
 * Rock Bands Test Class
 *
 * @author Name
```

```
 *
 */
public class RockBandsTest {
    // local vars
    public static final String DATA_FILE = "myPath/RockBands.json";

    // setup/teardown method go here
    @BeforeClass(alwaysRun=true,enabled=true)
    protected void testClassSetup() throws Exception {
        // set data file...
        JSONDataProvider.dataFile = DATA_FILE;
    }

    // test method using Java POJO class object
    @Test(groups={"REGRESSION"},
        dataProvider="fetchData_JSON",
        dataProviderClass=JSONDataProvider.class,
        enabled=true)
    public void tc001_getBandInfo(String rowID,
                                  String description,
                                  JSONObject testData)
                                  throws Exception {

        // fetch object data and pass into Java object
        RockBands rockBands = new RockBands(testData);

        // print the key:value pairs
        System.out.println(rockBands.toString() + "\n");
    }

    // test method using Java Builder class object
    @Test(groups={"REGRESSION"},
        dataProvider="fetchData_JSON",
        dataProviderClass=JSONDataProvider.class,
        enabled=true)
    public void tc002_getBandInfo(String rowID,
                                  String description,
                                  JSONObject testData)
                                  throws Exception {

        // fetch object data and pass into Java object
        RockBandsBuilder rockBands = new RockBandsBuilder.Builder()
            .name(testData.get("name").toString())
            .year(testData.get("year").toString())
            .song(testData.get("song").toString())
            .members((JSONObject) testData.get("members"))
            .build();
```

```
        // print the key:value pairs
        System.out.println(rockBands.toString() + "\n");
    }

}
```

Using the JSON datasets we previously outlined for the `RockBandsTest.java` class, the data and output would look like this for each set of data:

```json
{
    "tc001_getBandInfo":[
      {
        "rowID":"tc001_getBandInfo.01",
        "description":"Kiss Data",
        "name":"Kiss",
        "year":"1973",
        "song":"Rock and Roll All Nite",
        "members":{
            "Vocals":"Paul Stanley",
            "Bass":"Gene Simmons",
            "Guitar":"Ace Frehley",
            "Drums":"Peter Criss"
        }
      }
    ]
}
```

The output would look like this:

```
RockBands {name = 'Kiss', year = '1973', song = 'Rock and Roll All Nite',
members = {"Bass":"Gene Simmons","Guitar":"Ace Frehley","Vocals":"Paul
Stanley","Drums":"Peter Criss"}}
```

Calling page object methods in test classes

One of the most common mistakes users make when building automated tests is to build low-level event processing into their test class methods. We have been using the Selenium POM in this framework design, and what that means for the test classes is that you want to call the page object methods from within the test class methods, but not access the WebElements themselves. The goal is to reduce the amount of code being written and create a "library" of common methods that can be called in many places!

Now, what can be done in the framework to restrict users from going off track?

Users can set the scope of all WebElements defined in the page object classes to `protected`. That allows subclasses to access them, but prevents users from accessing the WebElements directly in the test methods, after instantiating the class.

Getter/setter methods can be built in the page object classes for cases where the user needs to get the WebElement to clean up a test (such as closing leftover windows).

Other common mistakes include creating lots of private "helper" methods in the test classes that wrap lots of small methods in page object classes, but cannot be used or accessed from outside the test class.

A better approach would be to organize the page object methods into fully functional routines where an object or set of parameters can be passed into them when called from test methods.

Of course, it's worth mentioning again that element "locators" do not go in the test classes. It's very easy to make a dynamic method call in a test method against a page object using one of the locator types, and many users go down this road, which is not the right one:

```
@Test
public void tc002_myTest() throws Exception {
    WebDriver driver = CreateDriver.getInstance().getDriver();
    WebElement button = driver.findElement(By.xpath("//button[.='Save']"));
}
```

As we said before, keep an abstract layer of separation between the page object and test classes.

Let's outline an example of the right and wrong ways of building a test method to log in to the Gmail application. Notice how `GmailLoginPO` is instantiated in the test method:

```
public class GmailLoginTest {

    public class GmailLoginPO <M extends WebElement> {

        public GmailLoginPO() throws Exception {
        }

        @FindBy(id = "identifierId")
        protected M email;

        @FindBy(name = "password")
        protected M password;
```

```
@FindBy(xpath = "//span[.='Next']")
protected M next;

@FindBy(xpath = "//a[.='Sign out]")
protected M signOut;

public void login(String email, String password) throws
Exception {
    this.email.sendKeys(email);
    next.click();
    this.password.sendKeys(password);
    next.click();
}

public void verifyTitle(String title) throws AssertionError {
    WebDriver driver = CreateDriver.getInstance().getDriver();
    assertEquals(driver.getTitle(), title, "Verify " + title);
}

public void signOut() throws Exception {
    signOut.click();
}
}

// this method follows the Selenium Page Object Model
@Test(dataProvider="fetchData_JSON",
    dataProviderClass=JSONDataProvider.class)
public void tc001_loginCreds(String rowID,
                             String description,
                             JSONObject testData)
                             throws Exception {

    String email = testData.get("email").toString();
    String password = testData.get("password").toString();
    String title = testData.get("title").toString();

    // Login to app, verify page title, logout of app
    GmailLoginPO gmail = new GmailLoginPO();

    gmail.login(email, password);
    gmail.verifyTitle(title);
    gmail.signOut();
}


// this method does Not follow the Selenium Page Object model
@Test(dataProvider="fetchData_JSON",
    dataProviderClass=JSONDataProvider.class)
```

```
public void tc002_loginCreds (String rowID,
                             String description,
                             JSONObject testData)
                             throws Exception {

    String email = testData.get("email").toString();
    String password = testData.get("password").toString();
    String title = testData.get("title").toString();

    // Login to app, verify page title, logout of app
    WebDriver driver = CreateDriver.getInstance().getDriver();

    driver.findElement(By.id("identifierId")).sendKeys(email);
    driver.findElement(By.xpath("//span[.='Next']")).click();
    driver.findElement(By.name("password")).sendKeys(password);
    driver.findElement(By.xpath("//span[.='Next']")).click();

    assertEquals(driver.getTitle(), title, "Verify " + title);
    driver.findElement(By.xpath("//a[.='Sign out]")).click();
}

}
```

So, as you can see, in the first test method an instance of `GmailLoginPO` was created, and the `login`, `verifyTitle`, and `signOut` methods were called from that class. The data that was extracted from the JSON data file was passed into those methods to perform the login.

In the second test method, the user did not use a method from a page object class, but instead, built the steps dynamically, and thus created a method that was not reusable anywhere else in the framework!

Note also, when creating page object methods, it is easy to insert a synchronization call into a method; whereas when creating actions in test methods, it is most often overlooked and the methods are therefore not robust at all.

Exception handling can easily be inserted into page object methods as well, allowing users to trap implicit, throw explicit, or test error conditions.

Exception handling in test classes

Exception handling is extremely important in both page object class methods and test class methods. All test methods should include `throws Exception` in the signature or contain a `try...catch` block to handle the exceptions (checked exceptions), and the `@BeforeMethod`/`@AfterMethod` methods should query results and clean up if necessary. Let's look at a couple of scenarios that handle exceptions in test methods.

 Here is a link to the most common Selenium exceptions: `https://seleniumhq.github.io/selenium/docs/api/py/common/selenium.common.exceptions.html`.

Test methods

When we developed Java utility and page object classes, we added exception handling to the methods. In some cases, methods can include specific exception types or just throw general exception conditions. Users often use the `try...catch...finally` syntax to trap exceptions and handle them using a custom set of actions, but using this syntax should not be exclusive. We want exceptions to occur implicitly or explicitly so we get the exception type and stack trace for debugging.

Page object methods called from within test methods can also throw exceptions when certain conditions are not met. So, at any point in the test, an exception could "break" out of the test method and turn over control to the `@AfterMethod`, routine per TestNG. It's the same when all test methods are complete, an exception in the `@AfterMethod` routine will turn over control to the `@AfterClass` routine, and so on.

Here is an example of a test method that can exit in multiple places. First, the method can throw an exception if the data file is not found. Second, when it loads the properties file, it can throw an `IOException` if the properties file is not found. And finally, the TestNG `assertEquals` method can throw `AssertionError` if the Selenium revision is not matched with the expected value (using TestNG's `assetEquals` to test Strings, Integers, Objects, and so on will engage the *difference viewer* if the condition is not met, which is a useful tool):

```
@Test
public void tc001_readPropertyFile(String rowID,
                                   String description,
                                   JSONObject testData)
                                   throws IOException, AssertionError {
```

```
        Properties seleniumProps = new Properties();
        String propFile = testData.get("propFile").toString();
        String expRevision = testData.get("revision").toString();

        seleniumProps.load(new FileInputStream(propFile));
        assertEquals(seleniumProps.getProperty("selenium.revision"),
                expRevision,
                "Verify Selenium Revision");
    }
```

The setup/teardown methods

What happens if the test method calls a page object method that fails while a window or dialog box is open? Users will want to trap that exception using a try...catch...finally block, and close it so it does not block the next test run. Or, if using a reporter class, break out of the test method, take a screenshot, and then perform the cleanup in the @AfterMethod routine. Here is a quick example of both:

```
public class CreateUserTest {
    public class UserPO <M extends WebElement> {

        public UserPO() throws Exception {
        }

        @FindBy(id = "cancel")
        protected M cancel;

        public void createUser(JSONObject user) throws Exception {
        }

        public void verifyUser(String user) throws AssertionError {
        }

        public WebElement getCancel() {
            return cancel;
        }
    }

    // this test method cleans up in the method
    @Test
    public void tc001_createUser(String RowID,
                                 String description,
                                 JSONObject testData) {

        UserPO user = null;
```

```
// attempt to create a new user
try {
    user = new UserPO();
    user.createUser(testData);
    user.verifyUser(testData.get("username").toString());
}

// trap and throw exception to console
catch(Exception e) {
    e.printStackTrace();
}

// call getter method in UserPO class to get cancel element
finally {
    user.getCancel().click();
}
}

}
```

The ITestResult class

In order to take a screenshot for a report, instead of trapping the exception (because it could occur in a number of places), users can let the test method break out, and query the result using the ITestResult interface. This allows the test to capture the correct screenshot at the point of the exception for debugging purposes.

Here is the same example as the last one using this strategy:

```
// this method aborts and let's the teardown cleanup
@Test
public void tc002_createUser(String RowID,
                             String description,
                             JSONObject testData)
                             throws Exception {

    UserPO user = new UserPO();

    // attempt to create a new user
    user.createUser(testData);

    // verify user was created
    user.verifyUser(testData.get("username").toString());
}

@AfterMethod
```

```
public void testMethodTeardown2(ITestResult result) throws
Exception {
    if ( result.isSuccess() != true ) {
        CaptureImage.screenShot(result);
        new UserPO().getCancel().click();
    }
}
```

Test listener/reporter classes

Using the ITestResult class in the teardown method allows users to query the current test method result, and call a number of getter or setter methods on it that can be used in test listener and test reporter classes. Some of those include getName, getMethod, getParameters, getStartMillis, and getEndMillis. This is a very useful feature of TestNG and can be useful information in the listener or report! The ITestContext class also provides a means to get test results data for reporting.

- The JavaDoc for the ITestResult interface is located at https://jitpack.io/com/github/cbeust/testng/master-6.12-g16e5a8e-107/javadoc/org/testng/ITestResult.html

- The JavaDoc for the ITestContext interface is located at https://jitpack.io/com/github/cbeust/testng/master-6.12-g16e5a8e-107/javadoc/org/testng/ITestContext.html

Designing base setup classes

When the Selenium page object classes were designed, we created an abstract base class to derive all the common components and methods for each subclass in the framework. This provided a way to reduce the number of elements and code being written, and a way to share common methods among pages.

Now we are dealing with the other side of things: the test classes and data. In this case, we want to design a common setup class using the TestNG annotations for methods, which will perform common setup and teardown for all the classes in a suite. Up to now, we've seen how each test class can create its own setup and teardown methods. Another layer of setup and teardown can precede the test class ones very easily.

Here are some examples:

- If the user wants to run a set of test classes as part of a `<test>` section in their suite file, then they would want to invoke and close the browser or mobile application before and after each set of tests execute. You wouldn't want to do this at the test class level. This would be done using the `@BeforeTest` and `@AfterTest` methods defined in a common setup class.
- However, if the user wanted to run a set of test classes *in parallel* as part of a `<test>` section in their suite file, then they would want to invoke and close the browser or mobile application before and after each class executes, since they are running on different threads. This can be done using the `@BeforeClass` and `@AfterClass` methods defined in the common setup class.

Here are a couple of coding examples:

```
/**
 * Test Setup Base Class
 * (JavaDoc Intentionally left out)
 *
 * @author Name
 *
 */
public abstract class MyCommonSetup {

    // abstract methods
    protected abstract void testClassSetup(ITestContext context)
                                            throws Exception;
    protected abstract void testClassTeardown(ITestContext context)
                                            throws Exception;
    protected abstract void testMethodSetup(ITestResult result)
                                            throws Exception;
    protected abstract void testMethodTeardown(ITestResult result)
                                            throws Exception;


    @BeforeSuite(alwaysRun=true, enabled=true)
    protected void suiteSetup(ITestContext context) throws Exception {
    }

    @AfterSuite(alwaysRun=true, enabled=true)
    protected void suiteTeardown(ITestContext context) throws
    Exception {
    }

    @BeforeTest(alwaysRun=true, enabled=true)
    protected void testSetup(ITestContext context) throws Exception {
        CreateDriver.getInstance().setDriver(Global_VARS.DEF_BROWSER,
```

```
                                          Global_VARS.DEF_PLATFORM,
                                   Global_VARS.DEF_ENVIRONMENT);
    }

    @AfterTest(alwaysRun=true, enabled=true)
    protected void testTeardown(ITestContext context) throws
    Exception {
        CreateDriver.getInstance().closeDriver();
    }

    @BeforeClass(alwaysRun=true, enabled=true)
    protected void classSetup(ITestContext context) throws
    Exception {
    }

    @AfterClass(alwaysRun=true, enabled=true)
    protected void classTeardown(ITestContext context) throws
    Exception {
    }

    @BeforeMethod(alwaysRun=true, enabled=true)
    protected void methodSetup(ITestResult result) throws Exception {
    }

    @AfterMethod(alwaysRun=true,enabled=true)
    protected void methodTeardown(ITestResult result) throws
    Exception {
    }
}
```

In this common setup class, the driver is started in @BeforeTest and closed in
@AfterTest methods. This allows the user the ability to run all the classes contained in the
<test> sections of the suite XML file in parallel.

Now, those calls could have been put in @BeforeSuite and @AfterSuite, but that would
have restricted the use of parallel thread runs (TestNG does not allow suite files to be run in
parallel).

Again, if the user wants to run each *class* in parallel, then the start and close of the driver
needs to be done in the @BeforeClass and @AfterClass methods.

Here is how the test class inherits these methods:

```java
/**
 * Test Class Method
 *
 * @author Name
 *
 */
public class MyAppTest extends MyCommonSetup {

    // implemented abstract methods
    @Override
    @BeforeClass( alwaysRun = true, enabled = true )
    protected void testClassSetup(ITestContext ctxt) throws Exception {
    }


    @Override
    @AfterClass( alwaysRun = true, enabled = true )
    protected void testClassTeardown(ITestContext ctxt) throws
    Exception {
    }


    @Override
    @BeforeMethod( alwaysRun = true, enabled = true )
    protected void testMethodSetup(ITestResult rslt) throws Exception {
    }


    @Override
    @AfterMethod( alwaysRun = true, enabled = true )
    protected void testMethodTeardown(ITestResult rslt) throws
    Exception {
    }


    // these methods override the Superclass methods
    @Override
    @BeforeClass(alwaysRun=true,enabled=true)
    protected void classSetup(ITestContext ctxt) throws Exception {
    }


    @Override
    @AfterClass(alwaysRun=true,enabled=true)
    protected void classTeardown(ITestContext ctxt) throws Exception {
    }


    @Override
    @BeforeMethod(alwaysRun=true,enabled=true)
    protected void methodSetup(ITestResult rslt) throws Exception {
    }
```

```
@Override
@AfterMethod(alwaysRun=true,enabled=true)
protected void methodTeardown(ITestResult rslt) throws Exception {
}
}
```

This is a simple test class example outlining how to use a common setup base class to perform common setup and teardown actions for all classes in a suite, implement abstract setup and teardown methods, and use local setup and teardown methods in a test class.

As mentioned earlier, any of the inherited methods can be overridden by using the @Override annotation and the same method name.

The order of execution precedence in this example is the following:

- @BeforeSuite (superclass)
- @BeforeTest (superclass)
- @BeforeClass (superclass)
- @BeforeClass (subclass)
- @BeforeMethod (superclass)
- @BeforeMethod (subclass)
- @AfterMethod (subclass)
- @AfterMethod (superclass)
- @AfterClass (subclass)
- @AfterClass (superclass)
- @AfterTest (superclass)
- @AfterSuite (superclass)

TestNG suite file structure

TestNG can be invoked using a build tool such as Gradle or Ant from the command line, or from a suite XML file to group tests together to run. Up to this point, we have covered bits and pieces of the suite files, but let's look more closely at some of the features it provides us. There are many ways to define the suite—let's start by covering the suite, groups, listeners, and test sections.

The TestNG documentation on the XML suite file is located at `http://testng.org/doc/documentation-main.html#testng-xml`.

Suite section: <suite>

The `<suite>` section of the XML file can contain groups, listeners, parameters, and test sections. It also can have attributes added to it such as `name`, `preserve-order`, `parallel`, `thread-count`, `verbose`, and so on. Here's the format:

```
<?xml version="1.0" encoding="UTF-8"?>
<!DOCTYPE suite SYSTEM "http://testng.org/testng-1.0.dtd">

<suite name="My_Test_Suite" preserve-order="true" parallel="false"
thread-count="1" verbose="2">

</suite>
```

The suite `name` attribute can be used for reporting purposes and can be retrieved using the TestNG `ISuite` interface.

`preserve-order` tells TestNG whether or not to run the test classes in a random order, and if not, it then lets test class rules take effect: `dependsOnMethods`, `sequential` names, `priority`, and to name a few. This takes a `true` or `false` value.

`parallel` tells TestNG whether or not to run in single or multithreaded mode. The options for this attribute are `false`, `test`, `classes`, `methods`, and `instances`. The different options for parallel testing will be discussed in the next chapter.

`thread-count` determines how many threads to open to run the test suite in parallel. If a user designs the suite to run in parallel at the classes level, and the `<test>` section contains 10 classes, then they would want to set the `thread-count` = `"10"` to run each one in its own browser or mobile thread.

`verbose` tells TestNG how much data to print to standard output when running the tests, one being the least amount of data.

Groups section: <groups>

In the <groups> section, users can include or exclude groups of tests to run, provided they have tagged the test methods with the groups attribute. This allows users to change the type of suite to run on the fly to create a smoke test, feature test, regression test, and so on.

TestNG also allows a BeanShell expression to be inserted in the XML file, which will disable the <groups> section of the suite file, but allows more flexibility in filtering tests. Here is an example of include/exclude of groups, building on the suite section:

```xml
<?xml version="1.0" encoding="UTF-8"?>
<!DOCTYPE suite SYSTEM "http://testng.org/testng-1.0.dtd">

<suite name="My_Test_Suite" preserve-order="true" parallel="false"
thread-count="1" verbose="2">

    <!-- groups: "regression", "smoke", "limit", "stress", etc... -->
    <groups>
        <run>
            <include name = "SMOKETEST" />
            <!-- include name = "LIMIT" / -->
            <!-- include name = "REGRESSION" / -->
            <!-- include name = "POSITVE" / -->
            <exclude name = "NEGATIVE" />
        </run>
    </groups>

    ...
```

Now, here is an example using the BeanShell expression:

```xml
<?xml version="1.0" encoding="UTF-8"?>
<!DOCTYPE suite SYSTEM "http://testng.org/testng-1.0.dtd">

<suite name="My_Test_Suite" preserve-order="true" parallel="false"
thread-count="1" verbose="2">

<!-- tests -->
<test name="My_Test_Name">
    <method-selectors>
        <method-selector>
            <script language="beanshell">
                <![CDATA[
                        String testGroups = "SMOKETEST,LIMIT";
                        String [] splitTestGroups =
                                testGroups.split(",");
```

```
                    for ( String group : splitTestGroups ) {
                        if ( groups.containsKey(group) ) {
                            return true;
                        }
                    }

                    return false;
                ]]>
            </script>
        </method-selector>
    </method-selectors>

...
```

Listeners section: <listeners>

Any number of TestNG-based test listeners can also be used in the suite file; they will come under a <listeners> section and provide a path to the class:

```
<?xml version="1.0" encoding="UTF-8"?&amp;gt;
<!DOCTYPE suite SYSTEM "http://testng.org/testng-1.0.dtd">

<suite name="My_Test_Suite" preserve-order="true" parallel="false" thread-
count="1" verbose="2">

    <!-- test listeners -->
    <listeners>
        <listener class-name="path.saucelabs.SauceOnDemandTestListener"
        />
        <listener class-name="path.reports.ExtentReportNGTestListener"
        />
        <listener class-name="path.listeners.TestNGListener" />
    </listeners>
```

Test section: <test>

The test section in the suite file contains a name for the <test> set, a list of parameters (which can also be declared at the suite level), classes, or packages to run. Both classes and packages can take a wildcard in the entry to run all the test classes in a specific folder or all of them in a package. Here are a couple of examples:

```
<?xml version="1.0" encoding="UTF-8"?>
<!DOCTYPE suite SYSTEM "http://testng.org/testng-1.0.dtd">
```

```xml
<suite name="My_Test_Suite" preserve-order="true" parallel="false"
thread-count="1" verbose="2">

    <!-- tests -->
    <test name="My Test">
        <!-- test parameters -->
        <parameter name="browser" value="chrome" />
        <parameter name="platform" value="Windows 10" />
        <parameter name="environment" value="local" />

        <classes>
            <class name="my.tests.RockBandsTest" />
        </classes>
    </test>
</suite>

<?xml version="1.0" encoding="UTF-8"?>
<!DOCTYPE suite SYSTEM "http://testng.org/testng-1.0.dtd">

<suite name="My_Test_Suite" preserve-order="true" parallel="false"
thread-count="1" verbose="2">

    <!-- tests -->
    <test name="My Test">
        <!-- test parameters -->
        <parameter name="browser" value="chrome" />
        <parameter name="platform" value="Windows 10" />
        <parameter name="environment" value="local" />

        <packages>
            <package name="my.tests.*" />
        </packages>
    </test>
</suite>
```

Suite parameters

In the preceding example, there were parameters added at the <test> section level. Parameters can also be added elsewhere, such as at the suite or class levels. These TestNG parameters can be processed using one of the setup or teardown methods and the @Parameters annotation. Any number of parameters can be added, and it's useful for processing system properties or environment variables, default settings, browser or mobile preferences, and so on.

@Parameters

Let's say you want to run a test suite against a specific browser, platform, and environment, then re-run it on a different browser and platform. Using TestNG's @Parameters allows you to change the settings in the suite XML file and process them in the setup class. Where you process them depends on when you want to invoke the browser or mobile device.

Using the previous example, we added them to the <test> section of the suite file, so the driver will be created before any of the test classes are run. So in the common setup class, you would add @Parameters to the @BeforeTest method:

```
@Parameters({"browser", "platform", "environment"})
@BeforeTest(alwaysRun=true, enabled=true)
protected void testSetup(@Optional(Global_VARS.BROWSER) String browser,
                         @Optional(Global_VARS.PLATFORM) String
                         platform,
                         @Optional(Global_VARS.ENVIRONMENT) String env,
                         ITestContext context)
                         throws Exception {

    // setup driver
    CreateDriver.getInstance().setDriver(browser, platform, env);
}
```

Notice the use of the @Optional annotation. This allows users to set a default value, which must be a constant, for each parameter. This provision is for cases where the user doesn't set them in the suite file. In other words, now that you have set up defaults for the browser, platform, and environment, it is optional whether or not they are passed in.

Here is an example on the mobile side:

```
// suite xml file

<?xml version="1.0" encoding="UTF-8"?>
<!DOCTYPE suite SYSTEM "http://testng.org/testng-1.0.dtd">

<suite name="My_Test_Suite" preserve-order="true" parallel="false"
thread-count="1" verbose="2">

    <!-- tests -->
    <test name="My Test">
        <!-- test parameters -->
        <parameter name="browser" value="safari" />
        <parameter name="platform" value="iphone" />
        <parameter name="environment" value="saucelabs" />
        <parameter name="mobile" value="iPhone 8 Simulator" />

        <packages>
            <package name="my.tests.*" />
        </packages>
    </test>
</suite>

// common setup class

@Parameters({"browser", "platform", "environment", "mobile"})
@BeforeTest(alwaysRun=true, enabled=true)
protected void testSetup(@Optional(Global_VARS.BROWSER) String browser,
                         @Optional(Global_VARS.PLATFORM) String
                         platform,
                         @Optional(Global_VARS.ENVIRONMENT) String env,
                         @Optional(Global_VARS.MOBILE) String mobile,
                         ITestContext context)
                         throws Exception {

    // setup driver
    Map<String, Object> prefs = new HashMap<String, Object>();
    prefs.put("deviceName", mobile);
    CreateDriver.getInstance().setDriver(browser,
                                         platform,
                                         env,
                                         prefs);
}
```

The difference here is that when we created the Selenium `CreateDriver` class, we only allowed three parameters to be passed into the `setDriver` method. Any other capabilities must be set on the fly by creating a map and passing that map in as a variable argument to the method.

Summary

In this chapter, we learned how to build data-driven test classes using the TestNG annotations. This allowed users to tag Java methods as tests, setup, and teardown methods to make them run.

We covered the test class structure, naming conventions, use of the JSON DataProvider to pass in data to page object class methods, exception handling, and using suite XML files. Attributes for `@Test` annotations such as `groups`, `enable`, `dependsOnMethods`, and so on were also covered.

In the next chapter, we will complete the use of encapsulated data in data-driven testing, property files, storing exception and confirmation messages, parallel testing, and processing data passed in as system properties.

15
Encapsulating Data in Data-Driven Testing

This chapter covers subjects such as encapsulating test data into JSON and property files, casting data to Java objects, positive and negative testing, processing data from system properties, dual driver support, and parallel testing. The following topics are covered:

- Introduction
- Casting JSON data to Java objects
- Building in positive, negative, boundary, and limit testing
- Confirmation and exception property files
- Property files and parsing test data on the fly
- Global variables versus dynamic data
- Processing JVM args
- Retrieving JSON data outside of test methods
- Supporting multibranded applications
- Multiple driver support
- Parallel testing

Introduction

In the last chapter, data-driven test classes and methods were designed and built to demonstrate how to use TestNG annotations and parameters to design and build test, setup, and teardown methods. In this chapter, we will dive further into the topic of test data. From what we have learned, encapsulating data into central locations and breaking it out from the test methods and page object classes is an important standard to follow.

What we need to understand about test methods versus test data is this: test methods should be small engines that perform a task, can take any variation of data, and that can test positive, negative, boundary, and limits of a feature. There is always an input and a verifiable output to a test. If users follow this rule, then simple "keyword" templates can also be built on top of the framework that allow users to extend test coverage by adding "sets" of data to run through the engines.

So, when designing the test framework for a development environment, put this standard in place from day one, code review tests that are added to the framework, and evangelize the use of a data file, property file, or global constants file to store data. Let users fear the code review process so the framework does not become the Wild West. And most importantly, let them know that rule number one is **do not get caught!** (storing data in your tests or libraries, that is!).

This chapter will also cover how to switch between multiple WebDrivers running simultaneously, including web and mobile drivers. And finally, the topic of parallel testing will be introduced and discussed as to what is involved in implementing it.

The reader will learn how to encapsulate test data for use in data-driven testing, including use of property files, dual-drivers, and parallel testing.

Casting JSON data to Java objects

At this point, it would be good to recap some of the things we learned about designing JSON objects and how to use them in the test methods. Let's take each point separately and discuss.

JSON object

The JSON DataProvider designed earlier returns an array of objects. In simpler terms, we cast it at runtime to a JSONObject type when passed to the test methods. This JSONObject can then be used in any way the user wants—passing it to a Java object of a specific type, passing it to the Java builder class interface, assigning to local variables in the test method, and so on.

The main goal is to extract the data from the JSON file, convert it on the fly, and pass it into page object methods to perform the test.

But what about dynamic data? The tests and suites being built need to remain platform and environment independent. As most development is now done in Agile rather than Waterfall, each scrum team works on their own branch and environment, and once they merge test code to the master branch, it must not contain hardcoded users, servers, IP addresses, and so on.

We will cover this in detail, but let's review a code sample on the data extraction point again:

```
@Test(groups = {"BANDS"},
        dataProvider="fetchData_JSON",
        dataProviderClass = JSONDataProvider.class)
public void tc001_getBandInfo(String rowID,
                                String description,
                                JSONObject testData)
                                throws Exception {

    RockBands rockBands = new RockBands(testData);

    // or

    RockBandsBuilder rockBands2 = new RockBandsBuilder.Builder()
        .name(testData.get("name").toString())
        .year(testData.get("year").toString())
        .song(testData.get("song").toString())
        .members((JSONObject) testData.get("members"))
        .build();

    // or

    String name = testData.get("name").toString();
    String year = testData.get("year").toString();
    String song = testData.get("song").toString();
    String members = testData.get("members").toString();
}
```

Sequential numbering of row IDs in the data file

The rules for building the JSON data file are fairly simple:

- Each section in the file should have the same name as the test method.
- Each set of data in each section should be sequentially numbered starting with the method name + .01, .02, .03, and so on. This will allow users to debug the set of data that failed the test.
- Each key/value pair should correspond to the fields in the JSON object being used.
- The number of sets of data for each test method is unlimited.
- All dynamic data should be stubbed out in the data file and replaced on the fly:

```json
{
    "tc001_registerEmployees":
    [
        {
            "rowID": "tc001_registerEmployees.01",
            "description": "Register Employee",
            "id": "ID1",
            "address": {"street": "1600 Pennsylvania Ave NW", "city":
            "Washington",
                        "state": "DC", "zip": "20500"},
            "phone": {"home": "800-555-1212", "work": "800-555-1212",
                      "mobile": "800-555-1212"}
        },
        {
            "rowID": "tc001_registerEmployees.02",
            "description": "Register Employee",
            "id": "ID2",
            "address": {"street": "1600 Pennsylvania Ave NW",
                        "city": "Washington", "state": "DC", "zip":
                        "20500"},
            "phone": {"home": "800-555-1212", "work": "800-555-1212",
                      "mobile": "800-555-1212"}
        }
    ]
}
```

Using Java object getter/setter methods

The Java object get and set methods are convenient for passing single parameters to test methods that do not require an object parameter. The user must build into the JSON object all these get and set methods. We covered them earlier, but let's review an example:

```java
/**
 * Sample Register Employee Java Object
 *
 * @author Name
 *
 */
public class RegisterEmployee {
    private String id;
    private JSONObject address;
    private JSONObject phone;

    public RegisterEmployee(JSONObject object) throws Exception {
        setId(object.get("id").toString());
        setAddress((JSONObject) object.get("address"));
        setPhone((JSONObject) object.get("phone"));
    }

    public void setId(String id) {
        this.id = id;
    }

    public String getId() {
        return id;
    }

    public void setAddress(JSONObject address) {
        this.address = address;
    }

    public JSONObject getAddress() {
        return address;
    }

    public void setPhone(JSONObject phone) {
        this.phone = phone;
    }

    public JSONObject getPhone() {
        return phone;
    }
}
```

Passing data to page object methods

The most important thing to remember when designing the data-driven tests is that the data extracted from the data files will be passed to page object methods called from the test methods. In keeping with that model, those methods must be generic enough to take a number of arguments and/or an object as a parameter.

No methods should contain hardcoded data such as server names, usernames, IP addresses, and so on, or anything else that would prevent them from being portable to various test and auto-deployed lab environments. We want to build re-usable class libraries of methods that we can call from the tests and that only need to be updated in one place, the page object class.

Building in positive, negative, boundary, and limit testing

Because the test methods are data driven, users can build a variety of different tests and initially build a positive test for the feature. Test coverage can be extended by varying data and including additional sets in the JSON data file for each test method. The test methods should be generic enough to allow those additional sets of data to be used. At the minimum, the user should include two positive test cases: one to test just the required fields and one to test all the fields in the feature.

Negative testing

What about negative testing? Usually, when working in the Agile world, users test at the minimum, and then extend test coverage after the feature has been built. But, when using a data-driven testing model, users can cover both the positive and negative testing scenarios all at once. This opens the door to testing the boundary and limits of the feature, testing the exceptions that may occur when exceeded.

Let's look at how this is done!

When we developed the JSON datasets, we really only talked about positive testing data. Now, we can easily extend the positive tests to negative testing by adding an exception message field to the JSON object, setting it to `null` for the positive tests, and then including the error for the negative test cases.

Here's an example:

```
{
    "tc001_gmailLoginCreds":[
        {
            "rowID":"tc001_gmailLoginCreds.01",
            "description":"Gmail Login Test - Positive",
            "username":"johnsmith@gmail.com",
            "password":"password",
            "error":null
        },
        {
            "rowID":"tc001_gmailLoginCreds.02",
            "description":"Gmail Login Test - Negative (Invalid Account)",
            "username":"johnsmithxx@gmail.com",
            "password":"password",
            "error":"Couldn't find your Google Account"
        },
        {
            "rowID":"tc001_gmailLoginCreds.03",
            "description":"Gmail Login Test - Force Exception",
            "username":"johnsmithxx@gmail.com",
            "password":"password",
            "error":null
        }
    ]
}
```

In this example, there are three sets of data included: one for the positive test, one for the negative test, and one to force an exception to test the error handling of the login method.

In the positive and force exception tests, the error field was set to null. In the negative test, the actual error was included. That's all that was required for the dataset. Now, let's look at the test method:

```
@Test(groups={"LOGIN"},
      dataProvider="fetchData_JSON",
      dataProviderClass=JSONDataProvider.class,
      enabled=true)
public void tc001_gmailLoginCreds(String rowID,
                                  String description,
                                  JSONObject testData)
                                  throws Exception {

    String user, password;
    GmailLoginPO gmail = new GmailLoginPO();

    // test the login or credentials error
```

```
user = testData.get("username").toString();
password = testData.get("password").toString();

if ( testData.get("error") == null ) {
    gmail.login(user, password);
    gmail.signOut();
}

else {
    gmail.login(user,
                password,
                testData.get("error").toString());
}
}
```

In this example, the testData object was queried to see whether the error field was null, and if not, the positive test case was run. If it wasn't null, then an overloaded method was used to take the additional parameter and instead of throwing an exception, as would be done in the first login method, it will verify the error.

When testing boundary and limit conditions in test methods, users should pass in the first and last valid choices for a field that can be used, for instance, an integer value. Then, add in a negative test case to use a value beyond the limit of the feature, and verify an error is thrown.

So, it is fairly simple to design the test methods in a way that allows users to add positive, negative, boundary, and limit tests by simply varying the data. Keep in mind, when creating the page object methods, they should always include exception handling to catch an error that occurs during the test. Whether the common method allows you to test the error or an overloaded method is created for testing errors, is up to the user.

Confirmation and exception property files

In the preceding example, we extracted the username, password, and error message data from the JSON data file. But what if the username and password need to change dynamically based on the test environment being used? Would we really want to hardcode in the username and password for a test? What if the error message is used in 10 other places in the application? Would we really want to change that test message data 10 times if the message is changed in the application?

The answer is simple: probably not! So, in this section, let's start by talking about using property files to store confirmation and exception messages.

Property files

Using property files in development is fairly common and simple to do. In some development environments, actual confirmation and exception messages are stored in `confirmation.properties` and `exception.properties` files. In those files, there is usually a `code=message` pairing for each type of message and those are pulled on the fly when specific actions are performed in the application. Dynamic data can be stuffed into them also by using a placeholder in the file. The same model can be used in testing them.

So, instead of storing the confirmation and exception messages in the test data, create two files to store them in and pass in the corresponding code to the test method:

```
// confirmation.properties
001=User account was successfully created
002=We have sent a password reset email to {EMAIL}.
003=You have successfully signed out.
004=Password was successfully updated.
005=Successfully deleted user {USER}.
```

```
// exception.properties
001=Please provide a valid email address
002=Couldn't find your Google Account
003=Please provide a password
004=Your account has been locked due to too many invalid login attempts.
005=User account {USER} Not Recognized.
```

Lookup method in DataProvider

We need to build a method in the DataProvider class to look up the messages on the fly using the code passed in to it. We can use a similar method to one created earlier in the utility classes:

```
/**
 * lookupMessage - method to retrieve error messages using code
 *
 * @param propFilePath - the property file including path
 * @param code - the confirmation or error code
 * @return String
 * @throws Exception
 */
```

```java
public static String lookupMessage(String propFilePath,
                                   String code)
                                   throws Exception {

    Properties props = new Properties();
    props.load(new FileInputStream(propFilePath));
    String getMsg = props.getProperty(code, null);

    if ( getMsg != null ) {
        return getMsg;
    }

    else {
        throw new Exception("ERROR: The Code '" + code + "' was not
        found!");
    }
}
```

JSON data file data

In the example we used earlier, we will now pass in the code instead of the error message:

```json
{
    "tc001_gmailLoginCreds":[
        {
            "rowID":"tc001_gmailLoginCreds.01",
            "description":"Gmail Login Test - Positive",
            "username":"johnsmith@gmail.com",
            "password":"password",
            "error":null
        },
        {
            "rowID":"tc001_gmailLoginCreds.02",
            "description":"Gmail Login Test - Negative (Invalid Account)",
            "username":"johnsmithxx@gmail.com",
            "password":"password",
            "error":"002"
        }
    ]
}
```

Converting confirmation/error code on the fly

Finally, in the test method, we can call the lookup method to convert the code to the correct message. This eliminates having the same message in test data in multiple places and files, and only requires a change in one place, the property file:

```
@Test
public void tc001_gmailLoginCreds(String rowID,
                                  String description,
                                  JSONObject testData)
                                  throws Exception {

    String user, password, getMessage;
    GmailLoginPO gmail = new GmailLoginPO();

    user = testData.get("username").toString();
    password = testData.get("password").toString();

    if ( testData.get("error") == null ) {
        gmail.login(user, password);
        gmail.signOut();
    }

    else {
        getMessage = Utils.lookupMessage(
                        Global_VARS.exceptionMsgs,
                        testData.get("error").toString());

        gmail.login(user, password, getMessage);
    }
}
```

If the confirmation or error messages contain dynamic data such as usernames, account names, and so on, those can also be stuffed in on the fly with a quick `replace` call:

```
...

getMessage = JSONDataProvider.lookupMessage(
                Global_VARS.exceptionMsgs,
                testData.get("error").toString());

gmail.login(user,
            password,
            getMessage.replace("{USER}", Global_VARS.DEFAULT_USER);

...
```

Property files and parsing test data on the fly

In a lot of cases, the test environment data, such as username, password, servers, IP, and URL are dynamic, and change with the environment they run on. In these situations, it makes sense to use a placeholder in the test data and replace the values on the fly when the test method is run.

To do this, environment data can be stored in property files, a system property can be used to pass in the name of the file for that specific environment, and it can then be read as part of the @BeforeSuite method.

Let's take a quick look at the various parts of this equation.

Environment property files

Let's say the server URL, username, and password are dynamic and change for each test environment that the suite runs against. To handle this type of data, users can create a property file to store those values:

```
// sample test environment property file

server.1.url=https://myDomain.com
server.1.username=johnsmith@myDomain.com
server.1.password=SuperEasyPassw0rd
```

System properties

Now, in order to pass this file to the test suite at runtime, users can create a system property, read it using their build tool, and process the data when the test suite starts up. In Java, users can use –D switches to pass system properties to a build process:

```
-DpropertyFile=MyTestEnvironment.properties
```

Using Gradle as a build tool, here is an example of how to pull in the system property for the test JVM:

```
test {
    useTestNG() {
        if ( System.getProperty('propertyFile') != null ) {
            systemProperty 'propertyFile',
```

```
                System.getProperty('propertyFile)
        }
    }
}
```

Initializing property file data

In the @BeforeSuite method of the common setup method, initialize the property file for use throughout the suite run. You must also include the absolute path to where the file lives in the project:

```
public static Properties testProps = new Properties();

testProps.load(new FileInputStream(Global_VARS.TEST_PROPS_PATH +
                                   System.getProperty("propertyFile"));
```

When referencing any of these properties in a test method, users can replace the *placeholder* in the test data with the actual value:

```
@Test
public void tc001_gmailLoginCreds(String rowID,
                                  String description,
                                  JSONObject testData)
                                  throws Exception {

    GmailLoginPO gmail = new GmailLoginPO();
    WebDriver driver = CreateDriver.getInstance().getDriver();

    String url = testProps.getProperty("server.1.url");
    String user = testProps.getProperty("server.1.username");
    String password = testProps.getProperty("server.1.password");

    driver.navigate().to(url);

    gmail.login(user.replace("[USER]", user),
                password.replace("[PASSWORD]", password));

}
```

And the test data would look like this:

```
{
    "tc001_gmailLoginCreds":[
        {
            "rowID":"tc001_gmailLoginCreds.01",
            "description":"Gmail Login Test - Positive",
```

```
            "username":"[USER]",
            "password":"[PASSWORD]",
            "error":null
        }
    ]
}
```

Global variables versus dynamic data

In cases like this where we want to use dynamic data, it sometimes makes sense to store property settings in global variables or constants that can be used throughout the test run.

Instead of always replacing the placeholders within the test methods, users can do it once in a central location for properties that are used frequently, assign them to a global variable, and then reference them in the test methods.

A good place to assign them is within the common setup class's @BeforeSuite or @BeforeTest methods:

```
// global variables class

public class Global_VARS {
    public static String DEFAULT_URL = null;
    public static String DEFAULT_USR = null;
    public static String DEFAULT_PWD = null;
}

// common setup class

public static Properties testProps = new Properties();

@BeforeSuite(alwaysRun=true, enabled=true)
protected void suiteSetup() throws Exception {
    testProps.load(new FileInputStream(Global_VARS.TEST_PROPS_PATH +
                              System.getProperty("propertyFile")));

    Global_VARS.DEFAULT_URL = testProps.getProperty("server.1.url");
    Global_VARS.DEFAULT_USR = testProps.getProperty("server.1.username");
    Global_VARS.DEFAULT_PWD = testProps.getProperty("server.1.password");
}
```

Now, in the test method, the user doesn't have to read the properties from the `Properties` object over and over, they can just reference the props using the global variables:

```
@Test
public void tc001_gmailLoginCreds(String rowID,
                                  String description,
                                  JSONObject testData)
                                  throws Exception {

    GmailLoginPO gmail = new GmailLoginPO();
    WebDriver driver = CreateDriver.getInstance().getDriver();

    driver.navigate().to(Global_VARS.DEFAULT_URL);

    gmail.login(testData.get("user").toString().replace("[USER]",
            Global_VARS.DEFAULT_USR),
            testData.get("password").toString().replace("
            [PASSWORD]",
            Global_VARS.DEFAULT_PWD));
}
```

Processing JVM args

Users can also set or override suite or global default settings using JVM args. This again is done in Java using the -D switch. So, in other words, if you are running a test suite that has parameters set up in the XML file for browser, mobile device, platform, environment, and many more and you want to change them on the fly to run against another platform, you can set a JVM argument using -Dbrowser=browser, -Dplatform=platform, and so on.

These can be set in an IntelliJ IDE—run configuration or in a Jenkins project setting. To summarize, a suite XML may have the following settings:

```
<parameter name="browser" value="chrome" />
<parameter name="platform" value="Windows 10" />
<parameter name="environment" value="local" />
```

If it does, those settings can be overridden using a -D switch, and nothing in the XML file has to be changed.

Retrieving JSON data outside of test methods

It is often required to create a common setup or teardown method that also uses data from a JSON file. In those cases, you would not pass in a DataProvider attribute to the method, but instead call an extraction method directly.

The following code samples are a variation of the DataProvider's `fetchData` method. These methods allow the user to extract the set(s) of data using `rowID` and return it as a `JSONObject` or `JSONArray` object. These objects can then be cast to a POJO that the user defines:

```
// extractData_JSON method - create JSONObject containing all data sets
public static JSONObject extractData_JSON(String file) throws Exception {
    FileReader reader = new FileReader(file);
    JSONParser jsonParser = new JSONParser();

    return (JSONObject) jsonParser.parse(reader);
}
```

In the preceding example, the method extracted all sets of data from the file and returned them as a `JSONObject`. But users would most likely want just specific sets of data to use, so the next example shows how to add a filter to pull just specific sets of data. The method returns them as a `JSONArray` of objects, one for each set of data:

```
// fetchDataSet method - create JSONArray containing specific data sets
public static JSONArray fetchDataSet(String file,
                                     String rowID)
                                     throws Exception {

    JSONArray testData = (JSONArray) extractData_JSON(file).get(rowID);

    return testData;
}
```

Finally, in the following setup method, the data is fetched from within the method and parsed, printing out the values for each object:

```
// getBandInfo method - extract and print each band info data set
public void getBandInfo(String file,
                        String rowID)
                        throws Exception {

    JSONArray testData = fetchDataSet(file, rowID);
```

```
for ( int i = 0; i < testData.size(); i++ ) {
    RockBands rockBands = new RockBands((JSONObject)
    testData.get(i));
    System.out.println(rockBands.toString() + "\n");
}
}
```

Supporting multibranded applications

In continuous development environments, product releases are often done on a monthly, weekly, or daily basis (Amazon does daily releases). Most often, features do change in some releases, but not in all at the same time. To support continuous releases with different feature changes and custom branded versions of the same application, it makes sense to maintain only one set of automation sources. This reduces the amount of time needed for maintaining the libraries and merging in changes continuously instead of day-to-day.

There are several ways to support multiple feature sets and multibranded applications. First, multiple locators for WebElements can be used using CSS or XPath types. Second, code can be made conditional to check for the existence of one element on a page and, based on that result, perform a different set of actions in a page object class method. Third, to support custom branding of applications, a flag based on the release can be passed into the test suite via a JVM argument, and different sets of tests can be executed at runtime.

Let's review each scenario.

Multilocators

As we learned in earlier chapters, CSS and XPath locators support the use of AND and OR operators. What that means is that when defining locators for WebElements or MobileElements in a page object class, users can provide more than one locator to identify the element on the page. If an element ID, class, attribute, tag, or name changes in another release, the locator for that element can be changed in the page object class to support multiple locator types.

So, if the locator being used has some form of text attribute identifying it, and the application is re-branded, the user can wildcard the text to use a partial string match of something in common, or include both text strings using the OR operator, first using the CSS OR type, then the XPath OR type locator.

The following examples show various forms using multiple locator attributes:

```
// 'OR' locators
@FindBy(css = "a[href*='Account Page')], a[href*='Go To Account')]")
@FindBy(xpath = "//a[contains(@href,'Account Page') or contains(@href,'Go
To Account')]")

// wildcarded id locators
@FindBy(css = "input[id*='password']")
@FindBy(xpath = "//input[contains(@id, 'password')]")

// wildcarded text locators (native CSS, Non-Firefox, Firefox
@FindBy(css = "a:contains('Copyright'), a[innerText*='Copyright'],
a[textContent*='Copyright']")
@FindBy(xpath = "//a[contains(text(),'Copyright')]")

// wildcarded element locators
@FindBy(css = "*[class*='submit']")
@FindBy(xpath = "//*[contains(@class,'submit')]")

// index locators
@FindBy(css = "div.footer:nth-child(1)")
@FindBy(xpath = "(//button[@class='save'])[2]")
```

Conditional code

In cases where features change drastically and the use of a multilocator definition doesn't work, users can declare different sets of controls and add conditional code *checks* into methods to perform different sets of actions.

As an example, say a feature is changed from using an input field to enter a value, to using a select field to select a value from a predefined drop-down list; the method would have to perform a sendKeys event for the input field, and a select event for the select field. A condition can be added to the method to check for the existence of one of the fields and perform the correct action based on the result.

Let's look at an example:

```
// locators
@FindBy(css = "input[id='myUser']")
protected M myUser;

@FindBy(css = "select[@id='mySelectUser']")
protected M mySelectUser;
```

```
// page object class method
public void myLogin(String user,
                    String password)
                    throws Exception {

    if ( BrowserUtils.exists(mySelectUser, Global_VARS.TIMEOUT_SECOND) )
    {
        new Select(mySelectUser).selectByVisibleText(user);
    }

    else {
        myUser.sendKeys(user);
    }
}

// exists method created using the Selenium ExpectedConditions class
public static boolean exists(WebElement element,
                             int timer) {

    try {
        WebDriverWait wait = new WebDriverWait(
                             CreateDriver.getInstance().
                             getDriver(),
                             timer);

        wait.until(ExpectedConditions.refreshed
                   (ExpectedConditions.visibilityOf
                   (element)));

        return true;
    }

    catch (StaleElementReferenceException |
           TimeoutException |
           NoSuchElementException err) {

        return false;
    }
}
```

Runtime flags

Finally, if an application is completely re-branded or a feature is completely changed and the first two options are not sufficient, users can set a flag using a JVM argument or a TestNG parameter with a release version, and code can execute based on that flag.

For multilanguage testing of labels, users can maintain a different set of JSON data and execute different tests based on the language under test. Of course, this requires the test method to be completely data-free and generic enough to just change the string labels being passed into it as JSON data.

The JVM argument or TestNG parameter can be set and pulled in using an `@parameters` or `System.getProperty()` feature:

```
-Drelease=1.0.x
```

or

```
<test name="My Test">
    <parameter name="release" value="1.0.x" />
    ....
</test>
```

Multiple driver support

Occasionally, testing requires more than one client to be involved in a test. There will be cases where there are two browsers open at the same time, whether they are running the same application or not, and cases where there are one browser and one mobile device running simultaneously. This section will cover the requirements for running concurrent web and mobile drivers.

Dual WebDriver testing

The tricky part about running two or more WebDrivers at the same time is that you must keep track of which driver is getting the WebDriver events at any point in time. Otherwise, the current WebDriver, which is the last one that gets instantiated, gets all the events. How do we do that?

It's actually not that difficult. What needs to be done is this:

1. Create the first WebDriver instance.
2. Assign the first WebDriver instance to a variable.
3. Create the second WebDriver instance.
4. Assign the second WebDriver instance to a variable.
5. Switch back and forth between the two drivers using the variables.
6. Instantiate other page object classes against the correct drivers.

Let's take a look at an example of how this is done using a Chrome and Firefox driver at the same time:

```
@Test
public void tc001_multiWebDriver(String rowID,
                                 String description)
                                 throws Exception {

    // create the first WebDriver instance
    CreateDriver.getInstance().setDriver("chrome",
                                 Global_VARS.DEF_ENVIRONMENT,
                                 Global_VARS.DEF_PLATFORM);

    // save the first WebDriver instance
    WebDriver chromeDriver = CreateDriver.getInstance().getDriver();

    // create the second WebDriver instance
    CreateDriver.getInstance().setDriver("firefox",
                                 Global_VARS.DEF_ENVIRONMENT,
                                 Global_VARS.DEF_PLATFORM);

    // save the second WebDriver instance
    WebDriver firefoxDriver = CreateDriver.getInstance().getDriver();

    // switch back to the chrome driver
    CreateDriver.getInstance().setDriver(chromeDriver);

    // create a page object class instance that will use this driver
    GmailLoginPO gmail = new GmailLoginPO();
    gmail.login("user1", "password1");

    // switch back to the firefox driver
    CreateDriver.getInstance().setDriver(firefoxDriver);
```

```
    // create a page object class instance that will use this driver
    GmailLoginPO gmail2 = new GmailLoginPO();
    gmail2.login("user2", "password2");

    // test sending mail back and forth to each user via the 2 clients

    // switch back to chrome and quit driver
    CreateDriver.getInstance().setDriver(chromeDriver);
    chromeDriver.quit();

    // switch back to firefox and quit driver
    CreateDriver.getInstance().setDriver(firefoxDriver);
    firefoxDriver.quit();
}
```

So, the actions are actually fairly easy to understand, but let's point out a number of things.

Once you instantiate both drivers, you must call the overloaded `setDriver` method created in `Chapter 9`, *Building a Scalable Selenium Test Driver Class for Web and Mobile Applications*, to switch to the current driver thread of choice. Remember, the driver class has multithreading built in, so every time a new driver is created, it exists on a separate thread.

When you instantiate page object classes, the driver is fetched on the fly by the page object hierarchy, so you do not have to pass in the driver type, it's done automatically for you. But you must create the instance of the page object class after you call `setDriver` to set the instance of the driver to use.

If you switch to a different driver than the one you instantiated the page object class on, and try to send an event to the page, you will get a runtime error saying that the driver doesn't exist.

Finally, to test out sending Gmail back and forth between the clients, you will need to call `setDriver` to do the switching and use the correct PO class instance to send and receive the email.

It's the same when quitting the driver, you must switch to the correct one before closing it.

Dual WebDriver and AppiumDriver testing

There is not that much difference when creating a WebDriver and AppiumDriver simultaneously, except that you have to deal with more setup/teardown on the mobile side of things.

Creating the drivers is relatively similar. Switching between the drivers is also similar. The WebDriver and AppiumDriver setup/teardown is different, and so are the API methods for each. With mobile devices, the application is usually installed in setup and uninstalled in teardown before quitting. That's pretty much it!

Let's take a quick look at an example:

```
@Test
public void tc002_multiWebMobileDriver(String rowID,
                                       String description)
                                 throws Exception {

    // create the WebDriver instance
    CreateDriver.getInstance().setDriver("chrome",
                                 Global_VARS.DEF_ENVIRONMENT,
                                 Global_VARS.DEF_PLATFORM);

    // save the WebDriver instance
    WebDriver chromeDriver = CreateDriver.getInstance().getDriver();

    // create the MobileDriver instance, passing in device name
    Map<String, Object> preferences = new HashMap<String, Object>();
    preferences.put("deviceName", "iPhone 6 Simulator");

    CreateDriver.getInstance().setDriver("iphone",
                                 Global_VARS.DEF_ENVIRONMENT,
                                 Global_VARS.DEF_PLATFORM,
                                 preferences);

    // save the MobileDriver instance
    AppiumDriver<MobileElement> mobileDriver =
                          CreateDriver.getInstance().getDriver(true);

    // switch back to the chrome driver
    CreateDriver.getInstance().setDriver(chromeDriver);
    // perform some actions on the WebDriver classes

    // switch back to the mobile driver
    CreateDriver.getInstance().setDriver(mobileDriver);
    // perform some actions on the MobileDriver classes
```

```
// switch back to chrome and quit driver
CreateDriver.getInstance().setDriver(chromeDriver);
chromeDriver.quit();

// switch back to iphone and quit that driver
CreateDriver.getInstance().setDriver(mobileDriver);
mobileDriver.quit();
}
```

Parallel testing

When testing browser or mobile applications, it is often necessary to test on multiple browser types or mobile devices. That can be accomplished in this framework by changing the XML suite file parameters, but it is time consuming to do cross-browser and mobile testing in serial mode. Using the TestNG suite XML parallel features and the Java `ThreadLocal` class for property file initialization, users can design a setup class that will instantiate the driver in parallel. Let's look at each function in detail.

 The TestNG documentation on parallel testing is located at `http://testng.org/doc/documentation-main.html#parallel-running`.

Suite XML file

The TestNG suite tag has several attributes that control parallel testing. Those attributes are:

- `parallel = "false/tests/classes/methods/instances"`
- `thread-count = "number"`

For these parallel attributes, users can run in single-threaded mode using a value of `false`, or select one of the other modes depending on whether they want to run a group of classes, tests, methods, or instances in parallel.

For instance, if the user wants to run all the test classes contained in each `<test>` section of the suite file in parallel, they can define which classes go in each section, or repeat all the classes in another section so they can run all the same classes in parallel. They would use the suite `parallel="tests"` tag attribute and set `thread-count` to the number of `<test>` sections in the file.

To run all classes in a `<test>` section in parallel, users would set the `parallel="classes"` attribute and again define `thread-count` to the number of threads to use, usually equal to the number of classes in the section.

Here is an example of a suite XML file running a set of `<test>` sections in parallel:

```xml
<?xml version="1.0" encoding="UTF-8"?>
<!DOCTYPE suite SYSTEM "http://testng.org/testng-1.0.dtd">

<suite name="Parallel_Test_Suite" preserve-order="true" parallel="tests"
thread-count="2" verbose="2">
    <parameter name="environment" value="remote" />
    <test name="Test 1 - Chrome/Windows 7">
        <parameter name="browser" value="chrome" />
        <parameter name="platform" value="Windows 7" />
        <parameter name="propertyFile"
         value="environment1.properties" />

        <classes>
            <class name="com.mypath.ParallelTest" />
        </classes>
    </test>

    <test name="Test 2 - Firefox/Windows 7">
        <parameter name="browser" value="firefox" />
        <parameter name="platform" value="Windows 7" />
        <parameter name="propertyFile"
        value="environment2.properties" />

        <classes>
            <class name="com.mypath.ParallelTest" />
        </classes>
    </test>
</suite>
```

Things to note here. The `thread-count` equals the number of `<test>` sections to run in parallel. The parameters are contained in the `<test>` sections for each set of tests, and there is a parameter to vary the environment properties file. This is required so a different set of users, servers, and so on are used for each thread to keep the tests from clashing with each other.

Parallel properties method

In the suite file example, there was a parameter set for the environment property file. In order to keep the parallel sessions from interfering with each other, different sets of servers and/or users must be used, and the thread that holds the properties during the test must also run in parallel. The following method extends the Java `Properties` class to accomplish that:

```
/**
 * ParallelProps method - extends Properties class to isolate
   each thread instance
 *
 */
public class ParallelProps extends Properties {
    public static final long serialVerionUID = 12345678L;
    private final ThreadLocal<Properties> localProperties =
                                    new ThreadLocal<Properties>() {
        @Override
        protected Properties initialValue() {
            return new Properties();
        }
    };

    public ParallelProps(Properties properties) {
        super(properties);
    }

    @Override
    public String getProperty(String key) {
        String localValue = localProperties.get().getProperty(key);
        return localValue == null ? super.getProperty(key) :
        localValue;
    }

    @Override
    public Object setProperty(String key, String value) {
        return localProperties.get().setProperty(key, value);
    }
}
```

 The JavaDoc for the `ThreadLocal` class is located at `https://docs.oracle.com/javase/7/docs/api/java/lang/ThreadLocal.html`.

Common setup

The tricky part is where to create each instance of the driver, browser, or mobile. In this example, each <test> section will run in parallel. So, it would make sense to pull in the parameters defined in each section in the @BeforeTest section of the common setup class. That would include casting the properties file to a separate thread for just that instance.

Also, it is important to keep all the local variables defined in each test class private when running in parallel. They should only be available to that class instance so reassigning them in the test class doesn't interfere with the other parallel thread running.

Here's what the common setup class looks like for parallel testing at the <test> level:

```
public abstract class CommonSetup_parallel {
    protected ParallelProps configProps_parallel =
            new ParallelProps(configProps);

    @Parameters({"browser","platform","environment","propertyFile"})
    @BeforeTest(alwaysRun=true, enabled=true)
    protected void testSetup(String browser,
                             String platform,
                             String environment,
                             String propertyFile,
                             ITestContext context)
                             throws Exception {

        configProps_parallel.load(
                             new FileInputStream(
                             Global_VARS.PROPS_PATH +
                             System.getProperty("propertyFile",
                             propertyFile)));

        Global_VARS.DEF_BROWSER = System.getProperty("browser",
                                                     browser);

        Global_VARS.DEF_PLATFORM = System.getProperty("platform",
                                                      platform);

        Global_VARS.DEF_ENVIRONMENT = System.getProperty("environment",
                                                         environment);

        Map<String, Object> setBrowserPrefs = new HashMap<String,
        Object>();

        if ( Global_VARS.DEF_PLATFORM == "iphone" &amp;&amp;
                Global_VARS.DEF_PLATFORM == "android") {
```

```
                    CreateDriver.getInstance().setDriver(
                        Global_VARS.DEF_BROWSER,
                        Global_VARS.DEF_ENVIRONMENT,
                        Global_VARS.DEF_PLATFORM,
                        setBrowserPrefs);
                    }

            else {
                CreateDriver.getInstance().setDriver(
                    Global_VARS.DEF_BROWSER,
                    Global_VARS.DEF_ENVIRONMENT,
                    Global_VARS.DEF_PLATFORM);
                }
            }
        }
```

Summary

This chapter concluded the framework design discussion on how to encapsulate and use test data. The premise of data-driven testing is to store data outside the Selenium page object and test classes. Again, this does in effect reduce the amount of maintenance and code that needs to be written to test a specific feature, by reusing test methods with varied data.

We also covered topics such as positive, negative, boundary, limit testing, dual-drive support, and parallel testing; all extremely important standards to incorporate in a Selenium framework.

In the next chapter, the Selenium Grid Architecture will be discussed and users will design and build a local in-house grid to run the testing on, taking the framework from a local testing platform to a remote testing platform. This will lead the way to using third-party grid platforms such as the Sauce Labs Cloud.

16
Designing a Selenium Grid

This chapter covers the Selenium Grid Architecture and how users would build a remote Selenium Grid using the standalone servers and drivers to create the hub, browser nodes, and mobile simulator/emulator nodes. The following topics are covered:

- Introduction
- Virtual grids
- Selenium driver class – WebDriver versus RemoteWebDriver
- Switching from local to remote driver
- Selenium standalone server and client drivers
- Selenium standalone server and browser driver command-line options
- Appium server and mobile simulator/emulator command-line options
- Selenium Grid console
- Directing traffic to Selenium nodes

Introduction

Up to now, the `WebDriver` class has supported running browser and mobile tests from a local IDE of choice, and IntelliJ as a standard practice. In that context, browsers can be tested for Chrome, Firefox, Opera, IE/MS-Edge (if running Windows), and Safari (if running iOS). For mobile devices, the local choices are somewhat limited: Android phones and tablets for Linux and Windows environments, iPhone and iPad for iOS environments.

Now, what if there is a need for compatibility testing on, say, 10 different browser/platform combinations, and 10 different mobile device/platform combinations? It becomes a little cumbersome to try and test those using local development environments.

This is where the Selenium Grid Architecture comes in. The Selenium `WebDriver` class has an extended class called `RemoteWebDriver` that supports running the same set of tests remotely across platforms, browsers, and mobile devices. It uses the JSON wire protocol to communicate between the Selenium server and the different client drivers on the grid. The fact is this single technology supports every common platform, and Selenium has become the industry standard because of it.

In this chapter, we will cover how to design and build a Selenium Grid to support all common browser and mobile platform combinations, how to customize the grid to support running multiple concurrent drivers on the same nodes, setting up Selenium standalone servers and Appium server nodes, and how to drive traffic through the Selenium hub and nodes.

Once that is built, moving to a more comprehensive cloud-based third-party grid such as Sauce Labs, BrowserStack, or PerfectoMobile will be virtually seamless.

The reader will learn how to design and build a remote Selenium Grid to support cross-platform testing on browser and mobile devices.

- The JavaDoc for the Selenium `RemoteWebDriver` class is located at `https://seleniumhq.github.io/selenium/docs/api/java/org/openqa/selenium/remote/RemoteWebDriver.html`

- The Selenium Grid documentation is located at `http://www.seleniumhq.org/docs/07_selenium_grid.jsp`

Virtual grids

When first designing the Selenium Grid, users must decide whether they want to use physical machines or virtual machines. In this day and age of cloud computing, most users are going with a virtual grid of some sort, using either Amazon Web Services, VMware, or the Microsoft Azure Cloud Services. With mobile devices, users can test against iPhone simulators running on macOS VMs, and Android emulators running on Linux and MS-Windows VMs.

To connect to the remote VM node, users can use VMware vCloud Director, Apple Remote Desktop Client, Remote Desktop Client for Windows or Linux, RealVNC, and so on. When running tests remotely on a grid, the test always starts on either a local IDE or a Jenkins Slave of some sort. The actual browser or mobile device will start on the remote node itself, not on the local VM or the Jenkins Slave. The Selenium WebDriver events will be sent from those clients to the remote hub, which will then redirect the events to the appropriate platform, start up the driver, and run the tests.

Grid structure

When building the VMs for the Selenium Grid, there will be one hub and various browser and mobile nodes. The hub will run a Selenium standalone server, use a JSON configuration file to set all the common desired capabilities for all the nodes, and start up as a service on the VM. Linux-based hubs seem to run faster and more efficiently, and are highly recommended over Windows-based hubs.

For each browser node, there are various configurations that can be used. Each node will run the Selenium standalone server, the client driver(s) for the node (ChromeDriver, GeckoDriver, and so on), use a JSON configuration file to set specific node desired capabilities and/or override the hub settings, and start up as a service on the VM.

For each mobile node, users are somewhat limited to using one iPhone, iPad, Android phone, or Android tablet instance per node; running the Appium server, a simulator or emulator for the device; using a JSON configuration file to set specific mobile node caps; and starting up as a service on the VM.

Single browser nodes

For dedicated browser type node setups, say we want to test against Firefox, Chrome, Edge, Opera, and Safari browsers. Do we have enough resources to create Windows, Mac, and Linux platforms for all these browsers? Or do we care more about testing on different browsers instead and are somewhat ambivalent to the platform they run on?

Here is a design to support dedicated browser type nodes:

Set up each node to only create instances of one browser type. For this scenario, you would need nine VM nodes, as follows:

- Windows 10/Firefox x 5 instances
- Windows 10/Chrome x 5 instances
- Windows 10/Edge x 5 instances
- macOS/Firefox x 5 instances
- macOS/Chrome x 5 instances
- macOS/Safari x 5 instances
- Linux/Firefox x 5 instances
- Linux/Chrome x 5 instances
- Linux/Opera x 5 instances

So, in essence, although you need 10 VMs for this grid structure (1 hub, 9 nodes), you actually have 45 virtual platforms to test against. If we test on the Windows 10 node using Firefox, we can have five separate test suites running on that node at the same time.

This design allows five separate Firefox browsers to be running simultaneously on the node, since multithreading is built into the driver class. Each thread handles its own set of instructions, directed of course through the grid hub, which will not interfere with others tests running on the node.

Multibrowser nodes

Here is a design to support multiple browser-type testing per node:

Set up each node to create instances of multiple browser types. For this scenario, you would need three VM nodes, as follows:

- Windows 10/Firefox x 5 instances, Chrome x 5 instances, Edge x 5 instances
- macOS/Firefox x 5 instances, Chrome x 5 instances, Safari x 5 instances
- Linux/Firefox x 5 instances, Chrome x 5 instances, Opera x 5 instances

With this design, you are running 15 instances of different browser types per VM. Of course the number of instances can vary, as it is mostly based on how much memory is allocated to the virtual machine. So for this setup, you would only need 4 VMs (1 hub, 3 nodes), and you would have 45 virtual platforms to run against.

Single mobile device nodes

For mobile simulators and emulators, it is recommended that only one instance is run on a node at a time. They are very slow and memory intensive and perform poorly using the Appium server technology. Using Linux for Android emulator platforms is much faster than Windows-based emulators, though. However, there really is no limit on how many physical devices can be installed on each mobile node, it just makes sense to only run one instance at a time.

Here is a design to support single mobile device testing per node:

Set up each node to only create instances of one mobile emulator/simulator type. For this scenario, you would need eight VM nodes, as follows:

- Linux/Android phone emulator x 1 instance
- Linux/Android tablet emulator x 1 instance
- Linux/Android phone physical device x 1 instance
- Linux/Android tablet physical device x 1 instance
- macOS/iPhone simulator x 1 instance
- macOS/iPad simulator x 1 instance
- macOS/iPhone physical device x 1 instance
- macOS/iPad physical device x 1 instance

So, in this configuration, you need 9 VMs for this grid structure (1 hub, 8 nodes), but you only have 8 virtual platforms to test against. The Selenium browser-based technology has progressed much more than the Appium server technology to date.

Multimobile/browser nodes

Now, finally, how about a Selenium Grid that has a mixture of browser and mobile device nodes? You can either just take the scenarios listed previously and add individual nodes as needed, or you can create a node that supports both a browser and mobile device running on it. The way to do this is by running both the Selenium standalone server for the browser instances and the Appium server for the mobile device instances on the same VM.

Set up each node to create instances of browser and mobile emulator/simulator types. For this scenario, you would need three VM nodes, as follows:

- Windows 10/Firefox x 2 instances, Chrome x 2 instances, Edge x 2 instances, Android phone emulator x 1 instance
- macOS/Firefox x 2 instances, Chrome x 2 instances, Safari x 2 instances, iPhone simulator x 1 instance
- Linux/Firefox x 2 instances, Chrome x 2 instances, Opera x 2 instances, Android tablet emulator x 1 instance

Although this is the most efficient use of virtual machines, as each one is shared between browser and mobile testing, it could exhibit memory issues with the variety of platforms running on each, and directing traffic to each one becomes a little more challenging!

Selenium driver class – WebDriver versus RemoteWebDriver

In the first chapter, the `CreateDriver.java` Selenium driver class was built. The class has several `setDriver` methods that take the parameters passed into the suite for the browser, mobile device, platform, and environment, and process them when creating the driver instance.

Now, when running on a `remote` environment, we need to add several conditions to the `setDriver` methods to pass the desired capabilities and preferences to the `RemoteWebDriver` class, instead of the local `WebDriver` instance.

Let's look at these conditions for each `setDriver` method in this class.

The setDriver method for browser

In the main setDriver method, we had first set up a series of switch cases for each browser and mobile type. In those cases, we set the browser/mobile preferences and desired capabilities. Once that was done, we cast them to the local WebDriver and it was launched.

Now, we need to check and see if the user passed in the environment parameter as "local" or "remote" and cast caps to the correct driver:

```java
// setDriver method - create the WebDriver or AppiumDriver instance

@SafeVarargs
public final void setDriver(String browser,
                            String platform,
                            String environment,
                            Map<String, Object>... optPreferences)
                            throws Exception {

    DesiredCapabilities caps = null;
    String ffVersion = "55.0";
    String remoteHubURL = "http://myGridHubURL:4444/wd/hub";

    switch ( browser ) {
        case "firefox":
            // set up the browser prefs and capabilities
            ...
            caps = DesiredCapabilities.firefox();

            // then pass them to the local WebDriver or RemoteWebDriver
            if ( environment.equalsIgnoreCase("local") ) {
                webDriver.set(new FirefoxDriver(caps));
            }

            break;
    }

    if ( environment.equalsIgnoreCase("remote") ) {

        caps.setCapability("browserName", browser);
        caps.setCapability("version", ffVersion);
        caps.setCapability("platform", platform);
        caps.setCapability("applicationName",
                            platform.toUpperCase() + "-" +
                            browser.toUpperCase());

        webDriver.set(new RemoteWebDriver(
                      new URL(remoteHubURL), caps));
```

```
        ((RemoteWebDriver) webDriver.get()).setFileDetector(
            new LocalFileDetector());
    }
}
```

In this example, the Firefox driver capabilities were set up in the `switch` statement and either cast to local `WebDriver` or, if running remotely on the grid, cast to `RemoteWebDriver`.

Notice the remote hub URL was passed to `RemoteWebDriver`, along with several capabilities that would cause the Selenium hub to direct traffic to a specific node. Those were `browserName`, `version`, `platform`, and `applicationName`. We will explain them in more detail as we build the JSON configuration files.

Also, `RemoteWebDriver` called `setFileDetector`, which allowed files residing in the local workspace to be uploaded to the application remotely.

The setDriver method for mobile

Now, here is a slight variation on the same method using the mobile drivers. Of course, these conditions would be built into the same `setDriver` method, as would support for all browsers and mobile devices.

The Appium driver has its own remote driver capabilities, and casting a remote URL to the driver will start it on the appropriate grid node:

```
// setDriver method - create the WebDriver or AppiumDriver instance

@SafeVarargs
public final void setDriver(String browser,
                            String platform,
                            String environment,
                            Map<String, Object>... optPreferences)
                            throws Exception {

    DesiredCapabilities caps = null;
    String platformVersion = "9.3";
    String localHubURL = "http://127.0.0.1:4723/wd/hub";
    String remoteHubURL = "http://myGridHubURL:4444/wd/hub";

    switch ( browser ) {
        case "iphone":
            // set up the mobile device capabilities
            ...
            caps = DesiredCapabilities.iphone();
```

```
    // caps = DesiredCapabilities.android();

    // then pass them to the local WebDriver or RemoteWebDriver
    if ( environment.equalsIgnoreCase("local") ) {
        mobileDriver.set(new IOSDriver<MobileElement>
                            (new URL(localHubURL), caps));
        // mobileDriver.set(new AndroidDriver<MobileElement>
                            // (new URL(localHubURL, caps));
    }

    break;
}

if ( environment.equalsIgnoreCase("remote") ) {

    caps.setCapability("browserName", browser);
    caps.setCapability("platformVersion", platformVersion);
    caps.setCapability("platform", platform);
    caps.setCapability("applicationName",
                        platform.toUpperCase() + "-" +
                        browser.toUpperCase());

    caps.setCapability("automationName", "XCUITest");

    mobileDriver.set(new IOSDriver<MobileElement>
                        (new URL(remoteHubURL), caps));
    // mobileDriver.set(new AndroidDriver<MobileElement>
                        // (new URL(remoteHubURL), caps));
    }
}
```

In this example, both the iPhone and Android drivers were noted for simplicity's sake; they would be in a separate case for each.

Overloaded setDriver method for browser

There are also overloaded setDriver methods we spoke about in the first chapter, which allow switching between multiple drivers running simultaneously. For the browser drivers, when switching drivers, you must cast WebDriver to RemoteWebDriver:

```
public void setDriver(WebDriver driver) {
    webDriver.set(driver);

    sessionId.set(((RemoteWebDriver) webDriver.get())
            .getSessionId().toString());
```

```
sessionBrowser.set(((RemoteWebDriver) webDriver.get())
        .getCapabilities().getBrowserName());

sessionPlatform.set(((RemoteWebDriver) webDriver.get())
        .getCapabilities().getPlatform().toString());

setBrowserHandle(getDriver().getWindowHandle());
}
```

Switching from local to remote driver

When switching from local to remote testing on the fly, users need an easy way to change the test to the required platforms. As we mentioned when building the `setDriver` method, it takes parameters for browser (or mobile device), platform, and environment.

In order to change these parameters, users can either set them in a TestNG suite XML file or a JVM argument using the `-D` switch. We covered that previously, but let's go over the rules of precedence again.

Suite parameters

The following parameters override the default settings for the browser, platform, and environment:

```
// suite xml file

<?xml version="1.0" encoding="UTF-8"?>
<!DOCTYPE suite SYSTEM "http://testng.org/testng-1.0.dtd">

<suite name="My_Test_Suite" preserve-order="true" parallel="false" thread-
count="1" verbose="2">
    <test name="My Test">
        <parameter name="browser" value="chrome" />
        <parameter name="platform" value="Linux" />
        <parameter name="environment" value="remote" />

        <packages>
            <package name="my.tests.*" />
        </packages>
    </test>
</suite>
```

JVM argument

The following arguments, whether set in an IDE run configuration or Jenkins project, will override both the suite XML parameters and the default framework parameters:

```
-Dbrowser=safari
-Dplatform=macOS 10.12
-Denvironment=remote
```

Default global variables

There should always be a default constant for browser, platform, and environment, so if they are not set anywhere and the user runs a test class or suite without them, the test will run. Usually that is set to the default development environment platform.

Example:

```java
public class Global_VARS {
    public static final String BROWSER = "firefox";
    public static final String PLATFORM = "Windows 10";
    public static final String ENVIRONMENT = "local";
    public static String DEF_BROWSER = null;
    public static String DEF_PLATFORM = null;
    public static String DEF_ENVIRONMENT = null;
}
```

Processing runtime parameters

Finally, when the test suite is run, there needs to be a place to process the system properties, suite parameters, or default variables and pass them to the setDriver method. This can be done in the CommonSetup.java class.

In this case, we are switching from a local run to a remote run on the Selenium Grid, so we need to set the Global_VARS.DEF_ENVIRONMENT variable:

```java
@Parameters({"browser","platform","environment"})
@BeforeSuite(alwaysRun=true, enabled=true)
protected void suiteSetup(@Optional(Global_VARS.BROWSER) String browser,
                    @Optional(Global_VARS.PLATFORM) String platform,
                    @Optional(Global_VARS.ENVIRONMENT) String
                                                       environment)

                    throws Exception {
```

```
Global_VARS.DEF_BROWSER = System.getProperty("browser", browser);
Global_VARS.DEF_PLATFORM = System.getProperty("platform",
platform);
Global_VARS.DEF_ENVIRONMENT = System.getProperty("environment",
                                                  environment);

CreateDriver.getInstance().setDriver(Global_VARS.DEF_BROWSER,
                                     Global_VARS.DEF_PLATFORM,
                                     Global_VARS.DEF_ENVIRONMENT);
}
```

Selenium standalone server and client drivers

To start setting up the Selenium Grid hub and node VMs, you must first download the required JAR and Selenium browser driver files. Firefox now uses the geckodriver, which was new in the Selenium 3.x release, and the Apple Safari driver is now built into the browser, so the `SafariDriver.safariextz` is no longer required.

 The Selenium Grid JARs and driver files can be downloaded or directed to third-party sites at the following location: `http://www.seleniumhq.org/download/`.

Here is a list of the files you will need:

- **Server**: `selenium-server-standalone-3.x.x.jar`
- **Chrome**: `chromedriver/chromedriver.exe` (linux64, win32, mac64; use 64-bit when possible)
- **Firefox**: `geckodriver/geckodriver.exe` (linux64, win64, macOS; use 64-bit when possible)
- **Safari**: Apple now builds the Safari driver extension into the browser as of the Safari 10 release
- **IE11**: `IEDriverServer.exe` (use 64-bit when possible)
- **Edge**: `MicrosoftWebDriver.exe`
- **Opera**: `operadriver/operadriver.exe` (linux64, win64, mac64)
- **Appium**: `appium/appium.exe`

Local use of drivers

When running a suite locally through an IDE environment, the framework should store and point to the required driver files for each browser. The standalone server is not required when running locally (if running Appium to test mobile devices, you must however run the Appium server locally). The reason you want to store the files in the repo for the framework is to provide a means for all users to not have to download the driver files and install them in their local environment.

Also, when the driver is started locally, it needs a path to find the driver file, and that should be stored in a properties file, as it is passed into the driver class when it is instantiated. Here is how that is done for each browser, using the Windows platform as an example:

```
// store these in a properties file

selenium.rev=3.7.0
gecko.rev=0.19.0
chrome.rev=2.33
edge.rev=15.15063
ie.rev=x64_3.7.0
opera.rev=2.30

// extract these properties during driver creation

gecko.driver.windows.path=../myPath/selenium-[selenium.rev]/gecko-
[gecko.rev]/geckodriver.exe

chrome.driver.windows.path=../myPath/selenium-[selenium.rev]/chrome-
[chrome.rev]/chromedriver.exe

microsoftedge.driver.path=../myPath/selenium-[selenium.rev]/edge-
[edge.rev]/MicrosoftWebDriver.exe

ie.driver.path=../myPath/selenium-[selenium.rev]/ie-
[ie.rev]/IEDriverServer.exe

opera.driver.windows.path=../myPath/selenium-[selenium.rev]/opera-
[opera.rev]/operadriver.exe
```

After defining these in a properties file, you can extract them on the fly when the driver is created in the `setDriver` method:

```
// setup local props in setDriver method
...

Properties props = new Properties();
props.load(new FileInputStream("myPropsFile"));

if ( environment.equalsIgnoreCase("local") ) {
    System.setProperty("webdriver.gecko.driver",
                        props.getProperty("gecko.driver.windows.path"));

    System.setProperty("webdriver.chrome.driver",
                        props.getProperty("chrome.driver.windows.path"));

    System.setProperty("webdriver.ie.driver",
                        props.getProperty("ie.driver.path"));

    System.setProperty("webdriver.edge.driver",
                        props.getProperty("microsoftedge.driver.path"));

    System.setProperty("webdriver.opera.driver",
                        props.getProperty("opera.driver.windows.path"));

    webDriver.set(new DriverName(caps));
}

...
```

Remote use of drivers

When running tests on the Selenium Grid using `RemoteWebDriver`, you must install and run a Selenium standalone server on each hub and node, and an Appium server on the mobile device nodes. The driver will be started on the command line with the server when the hub and nodes are set up. But you do not have to set a system property on the remote nodes to where the driver lives. That is set on the command line when starting up the standalone server. When you direct traffic to the node via the hub, it will find the required driver automatically.

Selenium standalone server and browser driver command-line options

When setting up the Selenium hub and nodes, it makes sense to create an image of each platform after it is completely set up, which will allow additional nodes to be added by cloning them. Setting up each one is fairly simple, with the exception of the platform differences between each node (that is, Linux, Windows, macOS, and so on).

Let's cover how to start each Selenium server on the hub and nodes on the grid.

- The Selenium Grid command-line options help is located at `http://www.seleniumhq.org/docs/07_selenium_grid.jsp#g etting-command-line-help`
- The Selenium documentation for the grid is located at `https:// seleniumhq.github.io/docs/grid.html#selenium_grid`

Selenium hub

The Selenium hub VM directs all the traffic flow from the test clients to the nodes under test. There is only one hub VM in the Selenium Grid.

Using a Linux VM for the hub is faster and more reliable than using a Windows VM. So, for the following example, here are the requirements and command-line options for the Selenium hub:

1. Install Java 8+ on the VM.
2. Update `$PATH` to include the Java path.
3. Create a folder called `/opt/selenium` and download the `selenium-server-standalone-3.x.x.jar` to it.
4. Create a bash script to run the server with the following commands in it:

```
// selenium_hub.sh

java -jar /opt/selenium/selenium-server-standalone-3.x.x.jar
    -role hub
    -hubConfig /opt/selenium/selenium_hub.json
```

All the Selenium standalone server hub command-line options can be found by issuing the following command:

```
java -jar /opt/selenium/selenium-server-standalone-3.x.x.jar
-role hub -h

Options:

--version, -version, Default: false
-browserTimeout,  <Integer> in seconds, Default: 0
-matcher, -capabilityMatcher <String> class name, Default:
org.openqa.grid.internal.utils.DefaultCapabilityMatcher@73c6c3b2
-cleanUpCycle <Integer> in ms, Default: 5000
-custom <String>, Default: {}
-debug <Boolean>, Default: false
-host <String> IP or hostname
-hubConfig <String> filename
-jettyThreads, -jettyMaxThreads <Integer>, default value (200)
-log <String> filename
-maxSession <Integer>
-newSessionWaitTimeout <Integer> in ms, Default: -1
-port <Integer>, Default: 4444
-prioritizer <String> class name, Default to null
-role <String>, Default: hub
-servlet, -servlets <String>, Default: []
-timeout, -sessionTimeout <Integer> in seconds, Default: 1800
-throwOnCapabilityNotPresent <Boolean> true or false, Default: true
-withoutServlet, -withoutServlets <String>, Defaut: []
```

Selenium hub JSON configuration file

There are various command-line options available to set the hub URL, port, timeouts, registration, and so on, but instead of listing them all on the command line, the – hubConfig option allows you to pass in a JSON configuration file with all the common WebDriver desired capabilities. This makes it easier and more manageable when updating parameters and desired capabilities, and setting them on the hub propagates them down to all nodes. But these options can be overridden at the node level as well.

Here is a sample Selenium hub JSON configuration file:

```
// selenium_hub.json

{
    "_comment":"Configuration for Selenium Hub",
    "host":"http://localhost",
```

```
    "maxSession":1000,
    "port":4444,
    "cleanupCycle":5000,
    "timeout":600,
    "browserTimeout":300,
    "nodeTimeout":600,
    "newSessionWaitTimeout":-1,
    "servlets":[],
    "prioritizer":null,
    "capabilityMatcher":"org.openqa.grid.internal.utils.
     DefaultCapabilityMatcher",
    "throwOnCapabilityNotPresent":true,
    "nodePolling":5000,
    "platform":"LINUX",
    "role":"hub"
}
```

Selenium nodes

As mentioned before, there are various ways to set up and distribute testing on the Selenium Grid nodes. For the purpose of showing the command-line options for each type of driver, let's use the dedicated browser type model for each node. Here are the requirements and command-line options for each type of browser node:

1. Install Java 8+ on the VM.
2. Update $PATH to include the Java path.
3. Install the required browser on the node: Chrome, Firefox, Edge, Safari, and so on.
4. Create a folder called /opt/selenium (Linux and macOS) or C:\Selenium (Windows) and download selenium-server-standalone-3.x.x.jar to it.
5. Download the driver for the browser type for the node (ChromeDriver, geckodriver, and so on).
6. Create a bash (or PowerShell) script to run the server with the following commands in it:

```
// selenium_node.sh

java -jar /opt/selenium/selenium-server-standalone-3.x.x.jar
     -Dwebdriver.gecko.driver=/opt/selenium/geckodriver
     -role node
     -nodeConfig /opt/selenium/selenium_node.json
```

In this example, to load any of the other browser type drivers, you would just replace the –Dwebdriver option with the appropriate driver name, such as –Dwebdriver.chrome.driver, -Dwebdriver.edge.driver, and so on.

All the Selenium standalone server node command-line options can be found by issuing the following command:

```
java -jar /opt/selenium/selenium-server-standalone-3.x.x.jar
-role node -h

Options:

--version, -version, Default: false
-browserTimeout <Integer> in seconds, Default: 0
-capabilities, -browser <String>, Default: [Capabilities
[{seleniumProtocol=WebDriver, browserName=chrome, maxInstances=5}],
Capabilities [{seleniumProtocol=WebDriver, browserName=firefox,
maxInstances=5}], Capabilities [{seleniumProtocol=WebDriver,
browserName=internet explorer, maxInstances=1}]]
-cleanUpCycle <Integer> in ms
-custom <String>, Default: {}
-debug <Boolean>, Default: false
-downPollingLimit <Integer>, Default: 2
-host <String> IP or hostname
-hub  <String>, Default: http://localhost:4444
-hubHost <String> IP or hostname
-hubPort <Integer>
-id <String>, Defaults to the url of the remoteHost, when not specified.
-jettyThreads, -jettyMaxThreads <Integer>, default value (200) will be
used.
-log <String> filename
-maxSession <Integer>, Default: 5
-nodeConfig <String> filename
-nodePolling <Integer> in ms, Default: 5000
-nodeStatusCheckTimeout <Integer> in ms Default: 5000
-port <Integer>, Default: 5555
-proxy <String>, Default: org.openqa.grid.selenium.proxy.DefaultRemoteProxy
-register, Default: true
-registerCycle <Integer> in ms, Default: 5000
-role <String>, Default: node
-servlet, -servlets <String>, Default: []
-timeout, -sessionTimeout <Integer>, Default: 1800
-unregisterIfStillDownAfter <Integer> in ms, Default: 60000
-withoutServlet, -withoutServlets <String>, Default: []
```

Selenium node JSON configuration file

Like the Selenium hub command-line options, there is also a `-nodeConfig` option to load a JSON configuration file with all the common WebDriver desired capabilities for the nodes.

Here is a sample Selenium node JSON configuration file:

```
// selenium_node.json

{
    "capabilities":[
        {
            "browserName":"firefox",
            "version":"56.0",
            "platform":"LINUX",
            "applicationName":"LINUX-FIREFOX",
            "maxInstances":10,
            "seleniumProtocol":"WebDriver",
            "acceptSslCerts":true,
            "javascriptEnabled":true,
            "takesScreenshot":true
        }
    ],

    "_comment":"Configuration for Selenium Node Linux/Firefox",
    "timeout":600,
    "browserTimeout":300,
    "cleanUpCycle":5000,
    "proxy":"org.openqa.grid.selenium.proxy.DefaultRemoteProxy",
    "maxSession":10,
    "port":5555,
    "hub":"http://127.0.0.1:4444",
    "register":true,
    "registerCycle":5000,
    "nodeStatusCheckTimeout":5000,
    "nodePolling":5000,
    "unregisterIfStillDownAfter":60000,
    "role":"node",
    "downPollingLimit":2,
    "debug":false
}
```

The JSON config files are the same for each node on the grid, with the exception of changing the `browserName`, `version`, `platform`, and `applicationName`. These must be set in the `setDriver` method as desired capabilities, and storing properties such as the version should go in the `selenium.properties` file.

When the `RemoteWebDriver` class is cast, it will look for a node wth the exact parameters passed into it. And, there are many additional capabilities for mobile device testing, and those should also be stored in the properties file and passed into the driver. This allows you to create different nodes on the grid with different browser or mobile device versions, platforms, and so on.

applicationName is a custom desired capability to "help" direct traffic to the correct nodes. This must also be set in the setDriver method in the driver class, which is easy if you just take the parameters passed in for the browser and platform and merge them together!
caps.setCapability(**"applicationName"**,
                       platform.toUpperCase()
                       + **"-"**
                       + **browser**.toUpperCase());

Here is another example where one node contains Chrome, Firefox, Safari, and Opera browser instances on a macOS platform (notice there is no driver for Safari, it's built into the browser):

```
// selenium_nodes.sh
```

```
java -jar /opt/selenium/selenium-server-standalone-3.x.x.jar
    -Dwebdriver.chrome.driver=/opt/selenium/chromedriver
    -Dwebdriver.gecko.driver=/opt/selenium/geckodriver
    -Dwebdriver.opera.driver=/opt/selenium/operadriver
    -role node
    -nodeConfig /opt/selenium/selenium_nodes.json
```

And here is the selenium_nodes.json file structure:

```
// selenium_nodes.json
```

```
{
    "capabilities":[
        {
            "browserName":"chrome",
            "version":"62.0",
            "platform":"MAC",
            "applicationName":"MAC-CHROME",
            "maxInstances":10,
            "seleniumProtocol":"WebDriver",
            "acceptSslCerts":true,
            "javascriptEnabled":true,
            "takesScreenshot":true
        },
        {
```

```
        "browserName":"firefox",
        "version":"56.0",
        "platform":"MAC",
        "applicationName":"MAC-FIREFOX",
        "maxInstances":10,
        "seleniumProtocol":"WebDriver",
        "acceptSslCerts":true,
        "javascriptEnabled":true,
        "takesScreenshot":true
    },
    {

        "browserName":"safari",
        "version":"11.0",
        "platform":"MAC",
        "applicationName":"MAC-SAFARI",
        "maxInstances":10,
        "seleniumProtocol":"WebDriver",
        "acceptSslCerts":true,
        "javascriptEnabled":true,
        "takesScreenshot":true
    },
    {

        "browserName":"opera",
        "version":"12.11",
        "platform":"MAC",
        "applicationName":"MAC-OPERA",
        "maxInstances":10,
        "seleniumProtocol":"WebDriver",
        "acceptSslCerts":true,
        "javascriptEnabled":true,
        "takesScreenshot":true
    }
],
"_comment":"Configuration for Selenium Nodes MAC/All",
"timeout":600,
"browserTimeout":300,
"cleanUpCycle":5000,
"proxy":"org.openqa.grid.selenium.proxy.DefaultRemoteProxy",
"maxSession":100,
"port":5555,
"hub":"http://127.0.0.1:4444",
"register":true,
"host":"myHubHost",
"registerCycle":5000,
"nodeStatusCheckTimeout":5000,
"nodePolling":5000,
"unregisterIfStillDownAfter":60000,
"role":"node",
```

```
"downPollingLimit":2,
"debug":false,
"servlets":[],
"withoutServlets":[],
"custom":{}
}
```

Appium server and mobile simulator/emulator command-line options

The mobile device simulator and emulator nodes work basically the same as the browser nodes on the Selenium Grid. You need to build a bash or PowerShell script to start the Appium server, and in the case of the Android emulator, there is a command-line option to start the emulator. The Appium driver for the iPhone will launch the correct iPhone/iPad simulator and close it when complete.

Let's look at a couple of sample scripts and configuration files to start up the mobile device nodes.

Appium nodes

Appium has an environment setup procedure for setting up the iPhone Xcode SDK and Android SDK, along with the required simulators and emulators.

 The Appium setup instructions are located at http://appium.io.

Of course, Java 8+ must also be installed, as was done for the browser nodes, and the Appium server needs to be installed in the /opt/selenium (macOS and Linux) or C:\appium (Windows) directory.

Node.js and npm are also required to install the Appium server, and the procedures are also outlined on the Appium website:

```
// appium_iphone.sh

/usr/local/bin/node /usr/local/bin/appium --address 127.0.0.1 --port 4723 -
-session-override -nodeconfig /opt/selenium/iphone_config.json --log-level
debug
```

```
// appium_android.sh
/usr/local/bin/android-sdk/tools/emulator -avd emulatorName -skin
resolution -dns-server 127.0.0.1 &amp;

/usr/local/bin/node /usr/local/bin/appium --address 127.0.0.1 --port 4723 -
-session-override -nodeconfig /opt/selenium/android_config.json --log-level
debug
```

Appium node JSON configuration file

Like the Selenium browser node command-line options, there is also a `-nodeConfig` option to load a JSON configuration file with all the common AppiumDriver desired capabilities for the nodes.

<span>Here is a sample Selenium node JSON configuration file for iPhone devices:

```json
// iphone_config.json

{
    "capabilities":[
        {
            "platform":"MAC",
            "platformVersion":"10.0",
            "browserName":"iphone",
            "applicationName":"MAC-IPHONE",
            "maxInstances":1,
            "launchTimeout":"300000",
            "newCommandTimeout":"1800"
        }
    ],
    "configuration":{
        "_comment":"Configuration for Selenium Node MAC/IPHONE",
        "proxy":"org.openqa.grid.selenium.proxy.DefaultRemoteProxy",
        "maxSessions":1,
        "cleanUpCycle":5000,
        "timeout":1800,
        "url":"http://127.0.0.1:4723/wd/hub",
        "port":4723,
        "host":"localhost",
        "register":true,
        "registerCycle":5000,
        "hubPort":4444,
        "hubHost":"localhost",
        "browserTimeout":600
    }
}
```

Here is a sample Selenium node JSON configuration file for Android devices:

```
// android_config.json
{
    "capabilities":[
        {
            "platform":"Android",
            "platformVersion":"23",
            "browserName":"android",
            "applicationName":"LINUX-ANDROID",
            "maxInstances":1,
            "newCommandTimeout":"180",
            "deviceReadyTimeout":"60",
            "appWaitDuration":"10000"
        }
    ],
    "configuration":{
        "_comment":"Configuration for Selenium Node LINUX/ANDROID",
        "proxy":"org.openqa.grid.selenium.proxy.DefaultRemoteProxy",
        "maxSessions":1,
        "cleanUpCycle":5000,
        "timeout":1800,
        "url":"http://127.0.0.1:4723/wd/hub",
        "port":4723,
        "host":"localhost",
        "register":true,
        "registerCycle":5000,
        "hubPort":4444,
        "hubHost":"localhost",
        "browserTimeout":600
    }
}
```

Selenium Grid console

The Selenium Grid Architecture also provides a grid console page that allows users to view which nodes are active, available, down, and what capabilities are set for each of them. Once the Selenium hub is active and running, the user would load the following URL to view the grid:

```
http://127.0.0.1:4444/grid/console
```

Of course, this is the localhost IP address, and you would substitute the DNS name or IP address of the real Selenium hub VM in this URL.

The following is a screenshot of a local grid set up to run Chrome, Firefox, Safari, Opera, and iPhone nodes on a macOS platform. Yes, you can actually run the hub, nodes, and Appium server on the same VM, but this would cause memory issues in the long run, so it's better to separate them! As a matter of fact, users can set up a local Selenium Grid in their development environment to test out the driver class, configuration files, batch files, and so on:

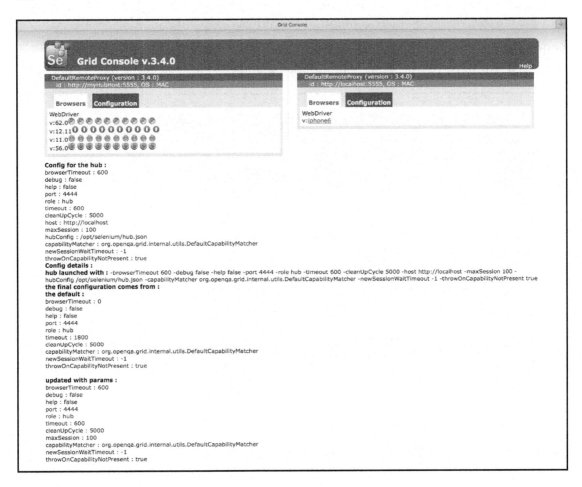

Selenium Grid console hub configuration

In this grid console, you can see that the local IP of the machine was aliased to **http://myHubHost**, which is shown in the **id** field. Also, there are 10 instances of each browser, and 1 instance of an iPhone 6 simulator active on the grid.

If you click on the **View Config** link, it will open **Configuration for the hub**, which shows the common capabilities set up on the hub. This would include timeouts, hub parameters, ports, and many more. Some of these parameters will propagate down to the grid nodes if they are not overridden by node configuration settings.

In this next screenshot, you will see that once you click on the **Configuration** tab in the console, it will show you the node configuration parameters instead of the hub parameters:

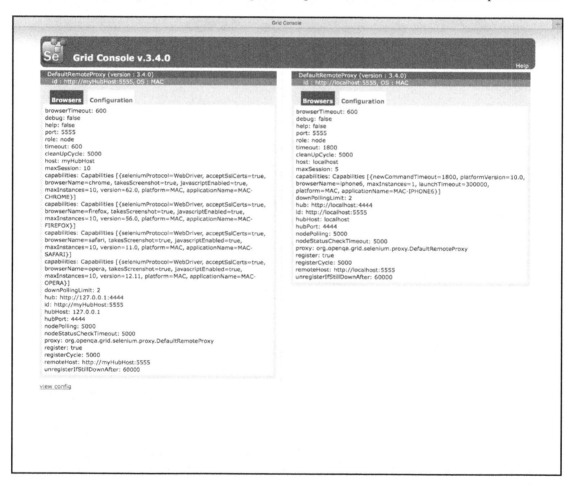

Selenium Grid console node configuration

This is useful for debugging and determining which node options need to be tweaked as far as session or browser timeouts, mobile device capabilities, browser versions, and others are concerned.

Directing traffic to Selenium nodes

Now that the Selenium Grid nodes are set up and running, there are several ways to direct traffic to them. In most cases, there will be nodes set up on the grid dedicated to a specific platform and browser or mobile device version, but there are other scenarios that will crop up. Let's discuss a few of them here before we move onto third-party grids.

Multiple nodes of the same platform and version

Say you do most of your testing on a particular platform, browser, or mobile device. You can set up a virtual grid node that has multiple instances of that platform, browser, and device. But, after 5-10 instances, the virtual machine may run out of memory.

So, you could clone the VM, create a second identical node on the grid, and let the Selenium hub load balance the tests that get started and run on that particular platform.

The Selenium hub keeps track of which nodes are idle, and once a node has the max number of instances running on it, the hub will either add a waiting test suite to a queue or distribute it to a node with the same platform and browser/mobile device if it is found. The user doesn't have to direct it to the other node, the Selenium hub will manage the traffic flow.

But if the user varies something on the cloned node, such as the browser version, then they can actually direct traffic to each of the nodes by passing in a different browser version, say, as a parameter to the test suite!

Directing traffic using desired capabilities

Now, as we mentioned in earlier sections, you can create custom desired capabilities, such as `applicationName`, and force the test to a node of your choice.

Varying the capabilities on the nodes would allow you to direct flow to specific nodes, and in the case of mobile simulators and emulators, there are many variations that can be tested (platform, platform version, mobile device type, mobile device version, browser, browser version (for mobile web apps), and so on).

Maintenance of the Selenium Grid

In a test environment using the Selenium Grid, the test is usually run in the continuous integration process. That means the build process, whether Ant, Gradle, or another technology, will run the Selenium test suite XML file via TestNG features. And, based on the parameters passed into the Jenkins project, it will get built and distributed to one of the `RemoteWebDriver` nodes via the hub. The tests will run on the grid nodes, not the Jenkins Slave.

So, what are the drawbacks of building an in-house Selenium Grid?

Lots of maintenance on the nodes. That includes upgrading the Selenium standalone server JAR files, the browser and mobile driver files, the browser versions, the simulator and emulator versions, operating system versions, and so on. If the nodes auto update the browsers, then the Selenium versions that support the newer browsers must be upgraded. Network patches reboot nodes when auto-pushed from IT departments, so those nodes can go down if unattended, or upon reboot, require a service to be created to start the Selenium node again.

Disk space fills up when storing logs, data, or other application-specific downloads.

Along with these annoyances, the number of platforms that can be supported in-house are very limited as compared to third-party service providers such as Sauce Labs, BrowserStack, and PerfectoMobile. The cost of using a service-provided grid versus an in-house grid will have to be weighed, but having spent many years using both, the third-party provider route is much more efficient. We will cover some of the advantages of using them in the next chapter!

Summary

In this chapter, we covered the Selenium Grid Architecture, which required changes to the `setDriver` method to support `RemoteWebDriver`, changes in the `selenium.properties` file, and changes to parameters passed in and processed from the suite XML file. The steps to create and configure the Selenium hub, browser, and mobile nodes were also outlined in this chapter, and several design patterns were discussed as to how to set up and maintain the nodes in a virtual cloud environment.

To test the use of grid features, users can take the sample bash and JSON config files in this chapter and create a local grid in their development environment. Once the driver class has all the required capabilities to cast the test to a `RemoteWebDriver` node, the user can build out a more robust cloud-based virtual grid using the same configurations, with the exception of changing the IP and host names in the grid configurations.

In the next chapter, third-party tools and add-ons to the framework will be discussed, as well as using a third-party grid platform such as Sauce Labs.

17

Third-Party Tools and Plugins

This chapter will cover the use of third-party tools in Selenium Framework design for the test environment, results processing, reporting, performance, and external grid services. The following topics are covered:

- Introduction
- IntelliJ IDEA Selenium plugin
- TestNG results in IntelliJ and Jenkins
- HTML Publisher Plugin
- BrowserMob Proxy Plugin
- ExtentReports Reporter API class
- Sauce Labs Test Cloud services

Introduction

Most of the framework components you design and build will be customized to your application under test. However, there are many third-party tools and plugins available you can use to provide better results processing, reporting, performance, and services to the engineers using the framework.

In this chapter, some of the more popular APIs and plugins will be covered such as the Selenium IntelliJ plugin, TestNG, HTML Publisher, BrowserMob Proxy, ExtentReports, and Sauce Labs.

This is the part of the framework that is optional, but will be requested by many users to support the testing, debugging, and certification needs of the CI process in the Continuous Delivery model.

In Chapter 8, *Designing a Selenium Grid*, setting up an in-house grid using the Selenium Grid Architecture was covered, and in this chapter, one of the third-party service providers called Sauce Labs will be discussed.

You will learn how to build in support to the Selenium Framework with third-party tools, APIs, plugins, and services.

IntelliJ IDEA Selenium plugin

When we covered building page object classes earlier, we discussed how to define the locators on a page for each WebElement or MobileElement using the @findBy annotations. That required the user to use one of the Inspectors or plugins to view the DOM structure and handcode a robust locator that is cross-platform safe.

Now, when using CSS and XPath locators, the hierarchy of the element can get complex, and there is a greater chance of building invalid locators. So, **Perfect Test** has come up with a Selenium plugin for the IntelliJ IDEA that will find and create locators on the fly.

Before discussing some of the features of the plugin, let's review where this is located.

 The IntelliJ IDEA Selenium plugin is developed by (c) 2017 Perfect Test and is located at www.perfect-test.com.

Sample project files

There are instructions on the www.perfect-test.com site for installing the plugin and once that is done, users can create a new project using a sample template, which will auto-generate a series of template files. These files are generic "getting started" files, but you should still follow the structure and design of the framework as outlined in this book.

Here is a quick screenshot of the autogenerated file structure of the sample project:

IntelliJ project structure

Once the plugin is enabled by simply clicking on the Selenium icon in the toolbar, users can use the **Code Generate** menu features to create code samples, Java methods, getter/setter methods, WebElements, copyrights for files, locators, and so on.

Generating element locators

The plugin has a nice feature for creating WebElement definitions, adding locators of choice, and validating them in the class. It provides a set of tooltips to tell the user what is incorrect in the syntax of the locator, which is helpful when creating CSS and XPath strings.

Here is a screenshot of the locator strategy feature:

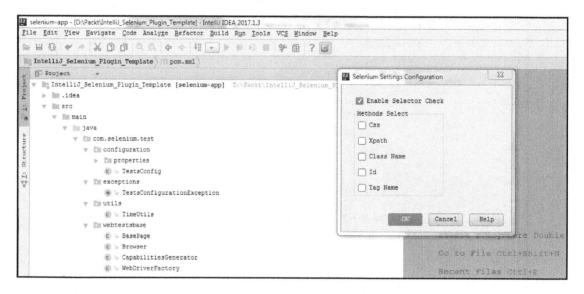

Selenium settings configuration dialog

Once the WebElement structure is built into the page object class, you can capture and verify the locator, and it will indicate an error with a red underline.

When moving over the invalid syntax, it provides a tooltip and a lightbulb icon to the left of it, where users can use features for **Check Element Existence on page** and **Fix Locator Popup**. These are very useful for quickly finding syntax errors and defining locators.

Here is a screenshot of the **Check Element Existence on page** feature:

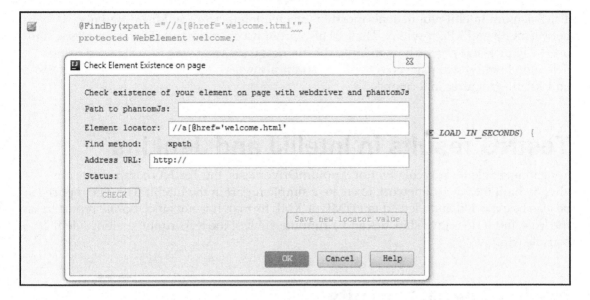

Check Element Existence on page dialog

Here is a screenshot of the **Fix Locator Popup** feature:

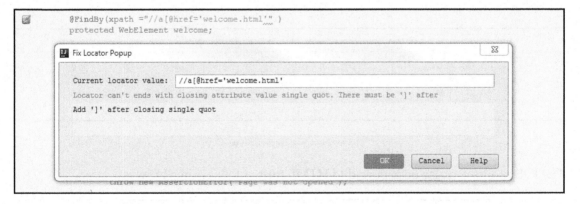

Fix Locator Popup dialog

Wrap-up on Selenium Plugin

The Selenium IntelliJ plugin deals mostly with creating locators and the differences between CSS and XPath syntax. The tool also provides drop-down lists of examples where users can pick and choose how to build the queries. It's a great way to get started using Selenium to build real page object classes, and it provides a tool to validate complex CSS and XPath structures in locators!

TestNG results in IntelliJ and Jenkins

For running Selenium WebDriver or AppiumDriver tests, the TestNG components are already built into the framework to create a simple report in the IntelliJ IDE. The report can be also be exported and viewed in HTML or XML format. It is not an elaborate report to say the least, but it does give statistics and a runtime view of the tests running alongside the console window.

IntelliJ TestNG results

The following screenshot shows the IntelliJ TestNG and IDE console windows. It provides the test method names, parameter values, and any standard output printed to the console window:

IntelliJ TestNG results and console windows

The IDE results can also be exported to HTML format to view in a browser:

IntelliJ TestNG results total

These are the test by test results:

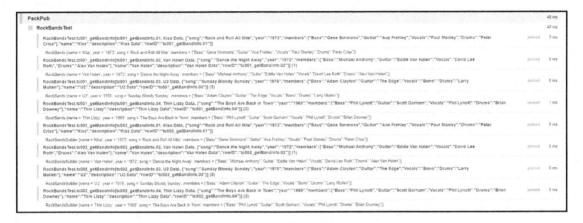

IntelliJ exported TestNG HTML report

Jenkins TestNG results

TestNG can also be used as a plugin to Jenkins, as it provides similar results which can be drilled down to view stacktrace or console output. On the Jenkins project page, there will be a TestNG summary report link to the passed, failed, and skipped test results, along with a link to the failed tests, and so on.

There is also a class summary report that separates the results of each method in each class and a TestNG trend analysis by method.

The Jenkins TestNG plugin is located at `https://wiki.jenkins.io/display/JENKINS/testng-plugin`.

The following screenshot shows the Jenkins TestNG plugin page:

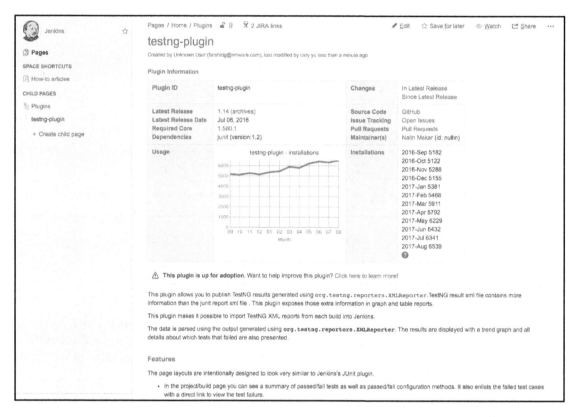

Jenkins TestNG Plugin

The following screenshot shows a Jenkins class summary report:

Jenkins TestNG class summary report

The following screenshot shows a Jenkins trend analysis summary report:

Jenkins TestNG trend analysis report

HTML Publisher Plugin

There is a Jenkins tool called the HTML Publisher Plugin. It allows users to publish any HTML report created during a test run and include it within the Jenkins project results. This is a very useful tool, as there are now many third-party APIs that can be used to generate HTML reports with Selenium test results.

Installation

The plugin publishes the report as part of the post-run process, allowing the Selenium Framework reporting to gather all the results data and create the report after all tests have completed. It will add a link on the project's result page to the `physical.html` file location in the workspace.

 The Jenkins HTML Publisher Plugin is located at `https://wiki.jenkins.io/display/JENKINS/HTML+Publisher+Plugin`.

The following screenshot shows the HTML Publisher Plugin page:

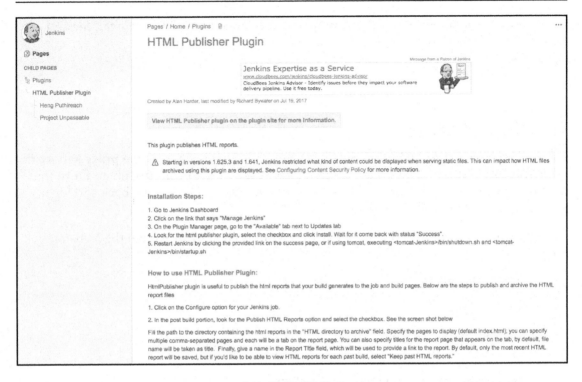

Jenkins HTML Publisher Plugin

BrowserMob Proxy Plugin

Another useful tool that is fully integrated with the Selenium WebDriver is called BrowserMob Proxy, and it is developed by Neustar, Inc. This free open source add-on allows users to capture performance data for web applications under test, identify network bottlenecks, modify the behavior of the browser under test, and change traffic patterns on the fly.

Users will set up this proxy server in their Selenium test environment and cast the WebDriver to it, allowing them to manipulate HTTP requests and responses during the test run. It uses the **HTTP Archive (HAR)** format to capture data.

The BrowserMob Proxy Plugin is developed by (c) 2017 Neustar, Inc and is located at `https://bmp.lightbody.net/`.

Getting started

It is fairly easy to get started using the tool. You would first instantiate the proxy service in your WebDriver driver class code, pass that proxy capability to your driver, and turn the capture mode on to retrieve the HTTP responses and requests being sent back and forth during the test as you drive the browser.

The following code sample to integrate with Selenium WebDriver is from the Neustar GitHub site:

```java
// start the proxy
BrowserMobProxy proxy = new BrowserMobProxyServer();
proxy.start(0);

// get the Selenium proxy object
Proxy seleniumProxy = ClientUtil.createSeleniumProxy(proxy);

// configure it as a desired capability
DesiredCapabilities capabilities = new DesiredCapabilities();
capabilities.setCapability(CapabilityType.PROXY, seleniumProxy);

// start the browser up
WebDriver driver = new FirefoxDriver(capabilities);

// enable more detailed HAR capture
proxy.enableHarCaptureTypes(CaptureType.REQUEST_CONTENT,
CaptureType.RESPONSE_CONTENT);

// create a new HAR with the label "yahoo.com"
proxy.newHar("yahoo.com");

// open yahoo.com
driver.get("http://yahoo.com");

// get the HAR data
Har har = proxy.getHar();
```

The online Wiki documentation to get up and running along with the source code is located at `https://github.com/lightbody/browsermob-proxy#using-with-selenium`.

BrowserMob Proxy also has the ability to test REST API requests and responses, allowing users to capture HTTP data without using the WebDriver. It has full SSL support via the **man-in-the-middle (MITM)** proxy using a secure certificate, Node.js bindings, logging, native, and custom DNS resolution.

ExtentReports Reporter API class

The reporting capabilities of the framework are very important. There are many third-party open source APIs that can be used to build and/or email reports of the Selenium test results.

One particularly nice tool is called ExtentReports and it is developed by AventStack. This Java and .NET API allows users to build and customize an HTML report of all the TestNG results data for a Selenium suite run. There is a Community Edition, which is a free open source tool, and a Professional Edition, which has a lot of additional features.

 The ExtentReports tool is developed by (c) AventStack and is located at `http://extentreports.com/`.

The ExtentReports Professional Edition has a number of different features from the Community Edition. Some of those features are:

- **Offline reports**: This feature provides the ability to create reports offline instead of interactively while the test is running
- **Configure view visibility**: This feature allows users the ability to turn off some of the panel views in the report like categories view, exceptions view, authors view, and TestRunnerLogs view
- **Custom dashboards**: This feature allows users to create custom dashboard panels with additional test results data in table format
- **Markup helper**: This feature allows users to customize the report adding links, cards, and modals to each page

- **KlovReporter**: There is a feature called KlovReporter that allows users to store reports in a MongoDB and host them on a server
- **ExtentEmailReporter**: This feature uses the Java Mail API class to create an email message to send the report after being built by an automated process
- **ExtentLogger**: This new feature currently in development to enhance the logging features of the ExtentHTMLReporter tool

ExtentHTMLReporter

The ExtentHTMLReporter API is a reporting tool that takes all the TestNG results data from a Selenium test run and processes it into a concise HTML report. That report can be published in Jenkins using the HTML Publisher Plugin, which was just covered. And it doesn't need the Selenium WebDriver to use it. The API will work with other TestNG results data from API, unit, or headless browser tests.

Since the framework outlined in this book is based on Java and TestNG technologies, it is fairly easy to integrate the report into the framework. Here are the requirements:

1. **Build** the `ExtentTestNGIReporterListener` class; there is a sample class on the website for users to get up and running
2. **Customize** the report to pull in TestNG results along with screenshot data from exceptions
3. **Modify** the report's look-and-feel using JavaScript and CSS attributes
4. **Include** the listener class in the Selenium suite files to generate the report

After using the sample code to generate the report, users can modify the CSS attributes in the `extent-config.xml` file or by using available report features, customize the theme from white to black, and use the logging features to log status, data, screenshots, stacktrace, log file entries, and so on.

Dashboard page

The following screenshot shows the ExtentHTMLReporter's **Dashboard** page:

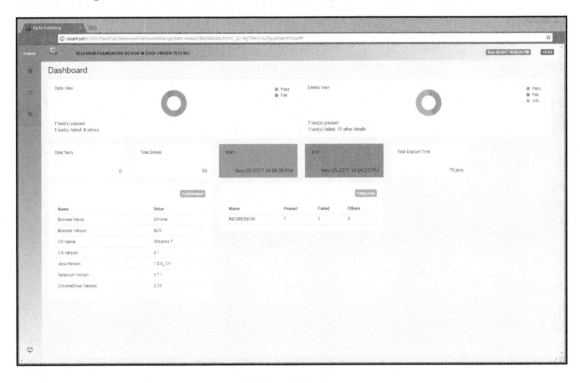

ExtentReports Dashboard page

Notice on the **Dashboard** page, the test results are displayed in graph and statistic format, as well as the test suite start, end, and elapsed times. There is an **Environment** panel where users can freely add system, test, and Selenium data to the report (browser, version, OS, Java version, Selenium version, and so on). The top banner can be customized to include your company logo, report headline, report name, and document title.

And finally, there is a **Categories** panel displaying the test group names and the number of tests that passed, failed, or skipped for each.

If purchasing the professional license version, you have the ability to add custom panels of data to the **Dashboard** page.

Categories page

The following screenshot shows the ExtentHTMLReporter's **Categories** page:

ExtentReports Categories page

On the **Categories** page, the test results are listed by the TestNG groups used throughout the test suite. So, if you only want to review the test results for a specific group, you can click on that group and sort, or you can sort by using the search bar.

In the right-side panel, each test is listed for the selected group, and if you click on one of them, it steps into the test results page for that test.

Tests page

The following screenshot shows the ExtentHTMLReporter's **Tests** page in the default white theme:

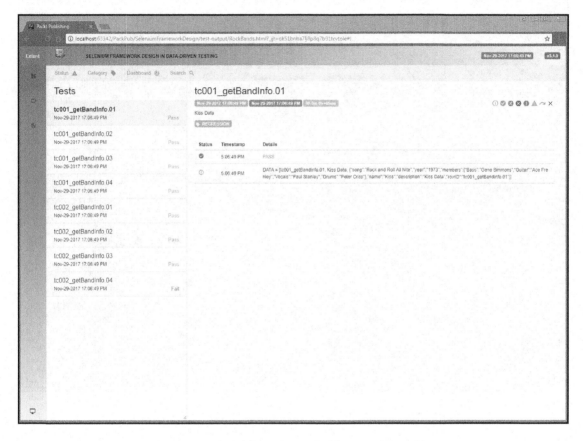

ExtentReports Tests page - Light Theme

The following screenshot shows the ExtentHTMLReporter's **Tests** page in the default black theme:

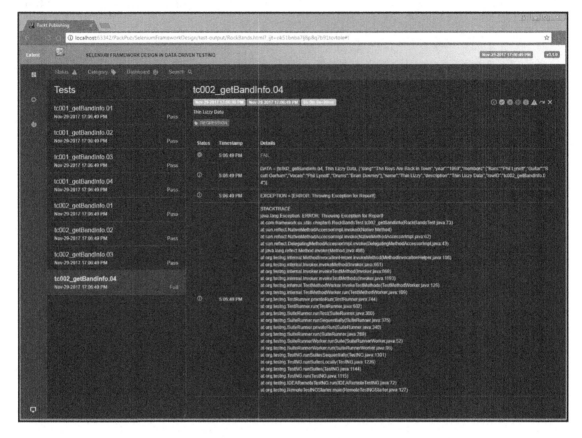

ExtentReports Tests page - Dark Theme

The **Tests** page has a sequential list of all the test methods run in the **Tests** panel on the left, and the test data on the right-side panel for the selected test. There is no limit to what data or how much test information can be added to these pages.

For example, in the first screenshot, a test that passed is shown. Using the data-driven model set up in this framework, we can easily log the row ID, which is the test method name in the report, the test description, the result, data parameters passed into the data-driven test method, exceptions, screenshots, and stacktrace information.

The second **Tests** screenshot shows a failed test with the result displayed in red rather than green, the test data, the exception that was thrown, and the stacktrace of the exception. You can also include the screenshot of the failed test in this page.

> The ExtentHTMLReporter Java Wiki documentation is located at `http://extentreports.com/docs/versions/3/java/#htmlreporter-features`.

Code sample

The following code is from the ExtentReports website to provide users with an ExtentHTMLReporter API sample:

```
public class ExtentTestNGReporter_sample implements IReporter {

    private static final String OUTPUT_FOLDER = "test-output/";
    private static final String FILE_NAME = "Extent.html";

    private ExtentReports extent;

    @Override
    public void generateReport(List<XmlSuite> xmlSuites,
                               List<ISuite> suites,
                               String outputDirectory) {

        init();

        for ( ISuite suite : suites) {
            Map<String, ISuiteResult> result = suite.getResults();

            for ( ISuiteResult r : result.values() ) {
                ITestContext context = r.getTestContext();

                buildTestNodes(context.getFailedTests(), Status.FAIL);
                buildTestNodes(context.getSkippedTests(), Status.SKIP);
                buildTestNodes(context.getPassedTests(), Status.PASS);
            }
        }

        for (String s : Reporter.getOutput()) {
            extent.setTestRunnerOutput(s);
        }

        extent.flush();
```

```
    }

    private void init() {
        ExtentHtmlReporter htmlReporter =
        new ExtentHtmlReporter(OUTPUT_FOLDER + FILE_NAME);

        htmlReporter.config()
        .setDocumentTitle("ExtentReports - Created by TestNG
        Listener");

        htmlReporter.config()
        .setReportName("ExtentReports - Created by TestNG Listener");

        htmlReporter.config()
        .setTestViewChartLocation(ChartLocation.BOTTOM);

        htmlReporter.config().setTheme(Theme.STANDARD);

        extent = new ExtentReports();
        extent.attachReporter(htmlReporter);
        extent.setReportUsesManualConfiguration(true);
    }

    private void buildTestNodes(IResultMap tests,
                                Status status) {

        ExtentTest test;

        if ( tests.size() > 0 ) {
            for ( ITestResult result : tests.getAllResults() ) {
                test = extent.createTest(
                    result.getMethod().getMethodName());

                for ( String group : result.getMethod().getGroups() )
                    test.assignCategory(group);

                if ( result.getThrowable() != null ) {
                    test.log(status, result.getThrowable());
                }

                else {
                    test.log(status,
                            "Test " +
                            status.toString().toLowerCase() +
                            "ed");
                }

                test.getModel().setStartTime(
```

```
                getTime(result.getStartMillis()));

                test.getModel().setEndTime(
                getTime(result.getEndMillis()));
            }
        }
    }

    private Date getTime(long millis) {
        Calendar calendar = Calendar.getInstance();
        calendar.setTimeInMillis(millis);
        return calendar.getTime();
    }
}
```

Sauce Labs Test Cloud services

As an alternative to building an in-house Selenium Grid, there are various third-party service providers that host the virtual machines for companies to use in testing browser and mobile applications. There are advantages and disadvantages to using a third-party provider, and these will be discussed later on in the chapter.

One of the best-in-class providers is Sauce Labs. They provide a Selenium/Appium testing solution in the cloud, where virtual machines are created on-demand with a variety of platforms and browser or mobile devices of choice. The company boasts of having over **900** platforms for browser compatibility testing and hundreds of platforms for mobile simulator/emulator, mobile web, native, hybrid, and real-device application testing. Let's take a look at some of the key features of their service.

 The Sauce Labs Test Cloud service is developed by (c) 2017 Sauce Labs. All rights reserved and located at `https://saucelabs.com/`.

Sauce Labs Test Cloud features

In the following sections, some of the Sauce Labs features will be discussed to give users an idea of what benefits they can gain from using a third-party service provider for their testing needs.

Browser and mobile platforms

So, what is the Sauce Labs Test Cloud? It is a virtual test lab in the cloud which provides enterprises with client-side browsers and mobile device platforms to test. Instead of building a grid and supporting various platform combinations to run the AUT, users can purchase a license to an unlimited pool of browser and mobile devices. They can be accessed for manual or automated testing.

Sauce Labs has a dashboard that allows users to review the test running on the virtual machine, as it records the user session. Once complete, the dashboard provides the capability of replaying the session, reviewing the Selenium and Appium client and server logs, and displaying the metadata for the test run.

There is a platform configurator feature that allows users to see what platforms, browser versions, mobile emulator (Android) and simulator (iOS) versions, and capabilities are supported for testing.

Driver code changes

The Sauce Labs Test Cloud is another Selenium Grid in the cloud. With that, it requires some changes to the Selenium Driver class that was built in this framework. The types of changes required are for the remote hub URL, the sauce-specific desired capabilities, and any browser or mobile device options to set up the driver.

Here are a few code samples of some of the changes that would go into an *environment* section of the driver class called `saucelabs` instead of `local` or `remote`:

```
// section in CreateDriver.java class for saucelabs URL

String remoteHubURL = null;
String SAUCE_USERNAME = "xyz";
String SAUCE_ACCESS_KEY = "XYZ";

if ( environment.equalsIgnoreCase("saucelabs") ) {
    if ( System.getenv("SAUCE_USERNAME") != null &amp;&amp;
        System.getenv("SAUCE_ACCESS_KEY") != null ) {
```

```
              remoteHubURL = "http://" + System.getenv("SAUCE_USERNAME") +
                       ":" +
                   System.getenv("SAUCE_ACCESS_KEY") +
                   "@ondemand.saucelabs.com:80/wd/hub";
     }

     else {
        remoteHubURL = "http://[SAUCE_USERNAME]:[SAUCE_ACCESS_KEY]@" +
                   "ondemand.saucelabs.com:80/wd/hub";
     }
}

// section in CreateDriver.java class for saucelabs display

if ( platform.toLowerCase().contains("mac") ||
     platform.toLowerCase().contains("os x") ) {

   caps.setCapability("screenResolution", "1920x1440");
}

else {
   caps.setCapability("screenResolution", "2560x1600");
}

// section in CreateDriver.java class for saucelabs platform

if ( System.getenv("SELENIUM_PLATFORM") != null ) {
   caps.setCapability("platform",
                    System.getenv("SELENIUM_PLATFORM"));
}


// section in CreateDriver.java class for saucelabs features

...

caps.setCapability("build", System.getProperty("BUILD_NUMBER"));
caps.setCapability("maxDuration", 10800);
caps.setCapability("commandTimeout", 300);
caps.setCapability("idleTimeout", 300);
caps.setCapability("tags", platform + "," + browser + "," + "62.0");

if ( System.getProperty("RECORDING").equalsIgnoreCase("true") ) {
   caps.setCapability("recordVideo", true);
   caps.setCapability("videoUploadOnPass", true);
   caps.setCapability("recordScreenshots", true);
   caps.setCapability("recordLogs", true);
}
```

```
if ( System.getenv("TUNNEL_IDENTIFIER") != null ) {
    caps.setCapability("tunnelIdentifier",
                        System.getenv("TUNNEL_IDENTIFIER"));
}

....
```

These are a few of the driver class capabilities that would be required, but as you can see, this follows the same approach to setting them using an in-house grid. Sauce Labs has a list of dozens of capabilities that can be set for both the browser and mobile device platforms. Notice in these examples, all the `System.getenv()` method calls are retrieving environment variables set by the Sauce Labs Jenkins plugin.

Dashboard

There is a Sauce Labs dashboard that provides results to users of the tests run, which can be accented using the SauceREST API. The API class allows users to modify the data that is displayed in the **Dashboard** window.

SauceConnect tunnel

In most enterprise environments, the development and testing is done in a DMZ within the corporate firewall. This means in order for the Sauce Labs client, which runs in the cloud to access the application under test, it must have a way to circumvent the firewall to get into the network.

Sauce Labs has a secure tunneling feature called SauceConnect that allows its cloud platform to talk to a corporation's development environment. It is fairly complex to set up, but once it is configured, it can be started and stopped before and after the test run, so it doesn't leave any tunnel openings into the network on an unlimited time basis.

TestObject Real Device Cloud

Sauce Labs introduced the TestObject Real Device Cloud in 2017. It is a pool of physical mobile devices, both Android and iOS, that users can purchase a license to access. They can be used for manually testing mobile applications or by running automated tests. Instead of running on simulator and emulator platforms, users can actually run on real devices with the platform and versions of the devices they require to test.

In order to test against the real devices, additional driver class capabilities would have to be set to direct to a different remote hub:

```java
// section in CreateDriver.java class for TestObject features

...

boolean realDevice = true;

if ( realDevice == true ) {
    caps.setCapability("testobject_device",
                        "iPhone 6");

    caps.setCapability("testobject_cache_device",
                        false);

    caps.setCapability("testobject_session_creation_timeout",
                        "900000");

    caps.setCapability("testobject_appium_version",
                        "1.7.1");

    caps.setCapability("testobject_suite_name",
                        "mySuiteName");

    caps.setCapability("testobject_app_id",
                        1);

    caps.setCapability("testobject_test_name",
                        "myTestName");

    // private pool caps
    caps.setCapability("phoneOnly",
                        "iphone.phoneOnly.rdc");

    caps.setCapability("tabletOnly",
                        "iphone.tabletOnly.rdc");

    caps.setCapability("privateDevicesOnly",
                        "iphone.privateDevicesOnly.rdc");

    if ( browser.contains("iphone") || browser.contains("ipad") ) {
        caps.setCapability("testobject_api_key",
                            "iOSAppKey");
    }

    else {
        caps.setCapability("testobject_api_key",
```

```
                                            "androidAppKey");
        }

        remoteHubURL = "https://us1.appium.testobject.com/wd/hub";
    }
```

Jenkins plugin

Finally, there is also a Sauce Labs plugin for Jenkins. This plugin allows users to pick and choose from within the Jenkins project, the platform, browser, mobile device, and versions of their choice. They can also set up the SauceConnect tunnel parameters, and any other command-line options they require such as the log file, log file path, proxy server, port, and so on.

Those choices are set as system environment variables which can be pulled into the driver at runtime. The preceding examples show how those variables are pulled into the driver class.

Advantages and disadvantages of using in-house versus third-party grids

Now that we have covered building an in-house Selenium Grid and using a third-party provider, let's discuss some of the key benefits and limitations of both:

- **Number of platforms**: The major advantage of using a provider like Sauce Labs is that there is virtually an unlimited pool of browser and mobile platforms available. There is really no way to build an in-house grid with 900 browser/OS combinations or hundreds of mobile iOS and Android devices to test against. Along with all the different combinations, users can also test different browser versions, OS versions, mobile device versions, mobile device platforms, mobile device API versions, and so on.

- **Maintenance**: To go along with building an in-house grid, there is maintenance. Users have to keep up with installing OS patches, security patches, browser upgrades, Selenium upgrades, driver upgrades, and so on. On the mobile side, the Xcode or Android SDK and simulator/emulators have to be constantly upgraded, along with Appium, NPM, Node.js, and so on. The maintenance of supporting an in-house grid is one of the most time-consuming costs to have to deal with, whereas there is no maintenance if a third party is used, just a financial cost.

- **Performance**: The Sauce Labs Test Cloud is much slower than an in-house grid, by 25–30%. So, that would be one advantage of building an in-house grid. But, Sauce Labs has a paradigm that if you build tests small and modular, and design them to run in parallel, you can leverage multiple VMs simultaneously and actually get the tests to run faster. So, although Sauce Labs would introduce latency into the test run, it can be overcome if the tests are designed in a particular fashion. Also, when the Sauce Labs job is running, it is recording the session, creating logs from Selenium and, updating the dashboard with real-time results, which contributes to the latency.

- **High-availability**: If using an in-house grid, it's likely that software updates will be pushed out to VMs on the grid on a regular basis, which in effect, reboots the nodes. Services can be set up to restart the Selenium servers on the hub and nodes, but the forced reboots can make the availability of the nodes on the in-house grid sketchy at times. When using a third-party provider, it's likely the service will be up most of the time, or at least 99% of the time.

- **Upgrades**: Sauce Labs is continuously providing upgrades to new platforms, browsers, and mobile devices, both real and simulated. They support the latest Selenium, Appium, and browser driver revisions as they become available. For in-house grid upgrades, users have to schedule downtime in-between releases to bring down the hub and nodes, and those are done less frequently than Sauce Labs would provide.

- **Enhancements**: Sauce Labs supports Selenium-based plugins like BrowserMob Proxy for instance, and has the latest technologies tested and available for use. That would also include the new TestObject Real Device Cloud service they recently introduced to the market to support mobile testing on physical devices.

Summary

This chapter provided some insight into using third-party plugins to the Selenium Framework. Because the framework uses Java and TestNG as technologies with the Selenium WebDriver, the various plugins and APIs available for them are easy to integrate.

For the editor, there is a Selenium plugin available for IntelliJ, one of the more common IDEs being used. There is also a built-in TestNG plugin for IntelliJ which provides test results in the console and report format.

For running in CI environments, Jenkins also has a TestNG plugin to provide results and historical data. There's a nice HTML Publisher Plugin for Jenkins that allows users to include an HTML report that the framework would autogenerate.

And, the ExtentReports API was discussed and how that would integrate into the framework using the DataProvider data and TestNG results.

Finally, as an alternative to building out a local Selenium Grid, we looked at the Sauce Labs Test Cloud services.

The final chapter will provide examples of some page object and test classes for a web and mobile application, and a driver class to run them!

18

Working Selenium WebDriver Framework Samples

This final chapter of the book is a working sample framework containing a driver class, required utility classes, browser page object classes, a browser test class, and JSON data files. The sample files will demonstrate the standards and best practices outlined in this book using the Selenium Page Object Model and DRY approaches to data-driven testing. The sample tests can be run in the IntelliJ or Eclipse IDE and contain the following components:

- Selenium driver and DataProvider classes
- Selenium utility classes
- ExtentReports classes
- Browser page object base and subclasses
- Browser test class and data files
- Browser suite XML and Maven POM XML files

Introduction

This final chapter is a working set of sample classes to demonstrate some of the best practices and standards that were discussed in this book. Users should be able to take the sample classes and run them in their own IDE after setting up their Selenium development environment.

The samples were built using **Chrome, Firefox,** and **IE11** browsers. Users should download the latest Selenium 3.x JAR files, TestNG JAR files, and the required browser driver releases to support them. The following JARs and files are required to get the sample tests running:

- Java 1.8 SDK and JRE
- IntelliJ IDEA 2017.3
- Selenium 3.7.1 WebDriver JARs
- TestNG 6.11 JARs
- ExtentReports 3.1.0 JARs
- `ChromeDriver.exe` 2.33 (Windows 32-bit; there is no current 64-bit driver)
- Firefox `GeckoDriver.exe` 0.19.1 (Windows 64-bit)
- `IEDriverServer.exe` 3.7.1 (Windows 32-bit; runs faster than the 64-bit driver)
- Chrome browser 62.0
- Firefox browser 57.0
- Internet Explorer browser 11.0

Users must place the files in a project folder in their IDE and change the paths in the `selenium.properties` and `Global_VARS.java` files to point to the correct package and driver locations. The sample framework and tests were built and tested using IntelliJ IDE on a Windows platform, but can be run on Linux or macOS as well; they are completely platform independent.

If you create the following package structure in IntelliJ, in a project called `SeleniumFrameworkDesign`, and add this chapter's files to it, then none of the imports or global variables need to be changed: `src/main/java/com/framework/ux/utils/chapter10`. Also, create the following folders for the drivers and test output: `SeleniumFrameworkDesign/drivers` and `SeleniumFrameworkDesign/test-output`.

The sample framework files were built using this open source practice website: `http://www.practiceselenium.com/`. It is developed by Selenium Framework 2010–2017 Copyrights reserved.

The user will gain a working knowledge of a real Selenium WebDriver Framework and set of data-driven tests.

Selenium driver and DataProvider classes

The following code is for the `CreateDriver.java` and `JSONDataProvider.java` classes:

CreateDriver.java

The following code is for the `CreateDriver.java` class:

```java
import org.openqa.selenium.WebDriver;
import org.openqa.selenium.chrome.ChromeDriver;
import org.openqa.selenium.chrome.ChromeOptions;
import org.openqa.selenium.firefox.FirefoxDriver;
import org.openqa.selenium.firefox.FirefoxOptions;
import org.openqa.selenium.firefox.FirefoxProfile;
import org.openqa.selenium.ie.InternetExplorerDriver;
import org.openqa.selenium.ie.InternetExplorerOptions;
import org.openqa.selenium.remote.DesiredCapabilities;
import org.openqa.selenium.remote.RemoteWebDriver;

import java.io.FileInputStream;
import java.util.*;
import java.util.concurrent.TimeUnit;

/**
 * @author Carl Cocchiaro
 *
 * Selenium Driver Class
 *
 */
public class CreateDriver {
    // local variables
    private static CreateDriver instance = null;
    private static final int IMPLICIT_TIMEOUT = 0;

    private ThreadLocal<WebDriver> webDriver =
        new ThreadLocal<WebDriver>();
    private ThreadLocal<String> sessionId =
        new ThreadLocal<String>();
    private ThreadLocal<String> sessionBrowser =
        new ThreadLocal<String>();
    private ThreadLocal<String> sessionPlatform =
        new ThreadLocal<String>();
    private ThreadLocal<String> sessionVersion =
        new ThreadLocal<String>();

    private String getEnv = null;
```

```
    private Properties props = new Properties();

    // constructor
    private CreateDriver() {
    }

    /**
     * getInstance method to retrieve active driver instance
     *
     * @return CreateDriver
     */
    public static CreateDriver getInstance() {
        if ( instance == null ) {
            instance = new CreateDriver();
        }

        return instance;
    }

    /**
     * setDriver method to create driver instance
     *
     * @param browser
     * @param environment
     * @param platform
     * @param optPreferences
     * @throws Exception
     */
    @SafeVarargs
    public final void setDriver(String browser,
                                String platform,
                                String environment,
                                Map<String, Object>... optPreferences)
                                throws Exception {

        DesiredCapabilities caps = null;
        String getPlatform = null;
        props.load(new FileInputStream(Global_VARS.SE_PROPS));

        switch (browser) {
            case "firefox":
                caps = DesiredCapabilities.firefox();

                FirefoxOptions ffOpts = new FirefoxOptions();
                FirefoxProfile ffProfile = new FirefoxProfile();

                ffProfile.setPreference("browser.autofocus",
                                        true);
```

```
    ffProfile.setPreference("browser.tabs.remote.
    autostart.2", false);

    caps.setCapability(FirefoxDriver.PROFILE,
                        ffProfile);
    caps.setCapability("marionette",
                        true);

    // then pass them to the local WebDriver
    if ( environment.equalsIgnoreCase("local") ) {
        System.setProperty("webdriver.gecko.driver",
        props.getProperty("gecko.driver.windows.path"));

        webDriver.set(new
        FirefoxDriver(ffOpts.merge(caps)));
    }

    break;
case "chrome":
    caps = DesiredCapabilities.chrome();

    ChromeOptions chOptions = new ChromeOptions();
    Map<String, Object> chromePrefs =
        new HashMap<String, Object>();

    chromePrefs.put("credentials_enable_service",
                    false);

    chOptions.setExperimentalOption("prefs",
                                    chromePrefs);

    chOptions.addArguments("--disable-plugins",
                        "--disable-extensions",
                        "--disable-popup-blocking");

    caps.setCapability(ChromeOptions.CAPABILITY,
                        chOptions);
    caps.setCapability("applicationCacheEnabled",
                        false);

    if ( environment.equalsIgnoreCase("local") ) {
        System.setProperty("webdriver.chrome.driver",
        props.getProperty("chrome.driver.windows.path"));

        webDriver.set(new
        ChromeDriver(chOptions.merge(caps)));
    }
```

```
                break;
        case "internet explorer":
            caps = DesiredCapabilities.internetExplorer();

            InternetExplorerOptions ieOpts =
                new InternetExplorerOptions();

            ieOpts.requireWindowFocus();
            ieOpts.merge(caps);

            caps.setCapability("requireWindowFocus",
                                true);

            if ( environment.equalsIgnoreCase("local") ) {
                System.setProperty("webdriver.ie.driver",
                props.getProperty("ie.driver.windows.path"));

                webDriver.set(new InternetExplorerDriver(
                                ieOpts.merge(caps)));
            }

            break;
    }

    getEnv = environment;
    getPlatform = platform;

    sessionId.set(((RemoteWebDriver) webDriver.get())
    .getSessionId().toString());

    sessionBrowser.set(caps.getBrowserName());
    sessionVersion.set(caps.getVersion());
    sessionPlatform.set(getPlatform);

    System.out.println("\n*** TEST ENVIRONMENT = "
            + getSessionBrowser().toUpperCase()
            + "/" + getSessionPlatform().toUpperCase()
            + "/" + getEnv.toUpperCase()
            + "/Selenium Version="
            + props.getProperty("selenium.revision")
            + "/Session ID="
            + getSessionId()
            + "\n");

    getDriver().manage().timeouts().implicitlyWait(
        IMPLICIT_TIMEOUT, TimeUnit.SECONDS);
    getDriver().manage().window().maximize();
}
```

```
/**
 * getDriver method to retrieve active driver
 *
 * @return WebDriver
 */
public WebDriver getDriver() {
    return webDriver.get();
}

/**
 * closeDriver method to close active driver
 *
 */
public void closeDriver() {
    try {
        getDriver().quit();
    }

    catch ( Exception e ) {
        // do something
    }
}

/**
 * getSessionId method to retrieve active id
 *
 * @return String
 * @throws Exception
 */
public String getSessionId() throws Exception {
    return sessionId.get();
}

/**
 * getSessionBrowser method to retrieve active browser
 * @return String
 * @throws Exception
 */
public String getSessionBrowser() throws Exception{
    return sessionBrowser.get();
}

/**
 * getSessionVersion method to retrieve active version
 *
 * @return String
 * @throws Exception
 */
```

```
    public String getSessionVersion() throws Exception {
        return sessionVersion.get();
    }

    /**
     * getSessionPlatform method to retrieve active platform
     * @return String
     * @throws Exception
     */
    public String getSessionPlatform() throws Exception {
        return sessionPlatform.get();
    }

}
```

JSONDataProvider class

The following code is for the JSONDataProvider.java class:

```
import org.json.simple.JSONArray;
import org.json.simple.JSONObject;
import org.json.simple.parser.JSONParser;
import org.testng.annotations.DataProvider;

import java.io.FileReader;
import java.lang.reflect.Method;
import java.util.ArrayList;
import java.util.Arrays;
import java.util.List;

/**
 * @author Carl Cocchiaro
 *
 * TestNG JSON DataProvider Utility Class
 *
 */
public class JSONDataProvider {
    public static String dataFile = "";
    public static String testCaseName = "NA";

    public JSONDataProvider() throws Exception {
    }

    /**
     * fetchData method to retrieve test data for specified method
     *
```

```
 * @param method
 * @return Object[][]
 * @throws Exception
 */
@DataProvider(name = "fetchData_JSON")
public static Object[][] fetchData(Method method) throws Exception
{
    Object rowID, description;
    Object[][] result;
    testCaseName = method.getName();
    List<JSONObject> testDataList = new ArrayList<JSONObject>();
    JSONArray testData =
        (JSONArray)
        extractData_JSON(dataFile).get(method.getName());

    for ( int i = 0; i < testData.size(); i++ ) {
        testDataList.add((JSONObject) testData.get(i));
    }

    // include Filter
    if ( System.getProperty("includePattern") != null ) {
        String include = System.getProperty("includePattern");
        List<JSONObject> newList = new ArrayList<JSONObject>();
        List<String> tests = Arrays.asList(include.split(",", -1));

        for ( String getTest : tests ) {
            for ( int i = 0; i < testDataList.size(); i++ ) {
                if (
                    testDataList.get(i).toString().
                    contains(getTest) ) {
                     newList.add(testDataList.get(i));
                }
            }
        }

        // reassign testRows after filtering tests
        testDataList = newList;
    }

    // exclude Filter
    if ( System.getProperty("excludePattern") != null ) {
        String exclude =System.getProperty("excludePattern");
        List<String> tests = Arrays.asList(exclude.split(",", -1));

        for ( String getTest : tests ) {
            for ( int i = testDataList.size() - 1 ; i >= 0; i-- ) {
                if ( testDataList.get(i).toString().
                contains(getTest) ) {
```

```
                            testDataList.remove(testDataList.get(i));
                    }
                }
            }
        }

        // create object for dataprovider to return
        try {
            result =
            new Object[testDataList.size()]
            [testDataList.get(0).size()];

            for ( int i = 0; i < testDataList.size(); i++ ) {
                rowID = testDataList.get(i).get("rowID");
                description = testDataList.get(i).get("description");
                result[i] =
                new Object[] { rowID, description, testDataList.get(i)
                };
            }
        }

        catch(IndexOutOfBoundsException ie) {
            result = new Object[0][0];
        }

        return result;
    }

    /**
     * extractData_JSON method to get JSON data from file
     *
     * @param file
     * @return JSONObject
     * @throws Exception
     */
    public static JSONObject extractData_JSON(String file) throws
    Exception {
        FileReader reader = new FileReader(file);
        JSONParser jsonParser = new JSONParser();

        return (JSONObject) jsonParser.parse(reader);
    }

}
```

Selenium utility classes

The following code is for the `BrowserUtils.java`, `Global_VARS.java`, `TestNG_ConsoleRunner.java`, and `selenium.properties` classes:

BrowserUtils.java

The following code is for the `BrowserUtils.java` class:

```java
import org.openqa.selenium.*;
import org.openqa.selenium.support.ui.ExpectedConditions;
import org.openqa.selenium.support.ui.WebDriverWait;

/**
 * @author Carl Cocchiaro
 *
 * Browser Utility Class
 *
 */
public class BrowserUtils {

    /**
     * waitFor method to poll page title
     *
     * @param title
     * @param timer
     * @throws Exception
     */

    public static void waitFor(String title,
                               int timer)
                               throws Exception {

        WebDriver driver = CreateDriver.getInstance().getDriver();
        WebDriverWait exists = new WebDriverWait(driver, timer);

        exists.until(ExpectedConditions.refreshed(
                ExpectedConditions.titleContains(title)));
    }

    /**
     * waitForURL method to poll page URL
     *
     * @param url
     * @param timer
```

```
     * @throws Exception
     */
    public static void waitForURL(String url,
                                  int timer)
                                  throws Exception {

        WebDriver driver = CreateDriver.getInstance().getDriver();
        WebDriverWait exists = new WebDriverWait(driver, timer);

        exists.until(ExpectedConditions.refreshed(
                ExpectedConditions.urlContains(url)));
    }

    /**
     * waitForClickable method to poll for clickable
     *
     * @param by
     * @param timer
     * @throws Exception
     */
    public static void waitForClickable(By by,
                                        int timer)
                                        throws Exception {

        WebDriver driver = CreateDriver.getInstance().getDriver();
        WebDriverWait exists = new WebDriverWait(driver, timer);

        exists.until(ExpectedConditions.refreshed(
                ExpectedConditions.elementToBeClickable(by)));
    }

    /**
     * click method using JavaScript API click
     *
     * @param by
     * @throws Exception
     */
    public static void click(By by) throws Exception {
        WebDriver driver = CreateDriver.getInstance().getDriver();
        WebElement element = driver.findElement(by);

        JavascriptExecutor js = (JavascriptExecutor)driver;
        js.executeScript("arguments[0].click();", element);
    }

}
```

Global_VARS.java

The following code is for the Global_VARS.java class:

```java
import java.io.File;

/**
 * @author Carl Cocchiaro
 *
 * Global Variable Utility Class
 *
 */
public class Global_VARS {
    // browser defaults
    public static final String BROWSER = "chrome";
    public static final String PLATFORM = "Windows 7";
    public static final String ENVIRONMENT = "local";
    public static String DEF_BROWSER = null;
    public static String DEF_PLATFORM = null;
    public static String DEF_ENVIRONMENT = null;

    // suite folder defaults
    public static String SUITE_NAME = null;

    public static final String TARGET_URL =
    "http://www.practiceselenium.com/";

    public static String propFile =
    "src/main/java/com/framework/ux/utils/chapter10/selenium.properties";

    public static final String SE_PROPS =
    new File(propFile).getAbsolutePath();

    public static final String TEST_OUTPUT_PATH = "test-output/";
    public static final String LOGFILE_PATH = TEST_OUTPUT_PATH +
    "Logs/";
    public static final String REPORT_PATH = TEST_OUTPUT_PATH +
    "Reports/";
    public static final String REPORT_CONFIG_FILE =
    "src/main/java/com/framework/ux/utils/chapter10/extent-config.xml";

    // suite timeout defaults
    public static final int TIMEOUT_MINUTE = 60;
    public static final int TIMEOUT_ELEMENT = 10;
}
```

TestNG_ConsoleRunner.java

The following code is for the `TestNG_ConsoleRunner.java` class:

```java
import org.testng.ITestContext;
import org.testng.ITestResult;
import org.testng.TestListenerAdapter;

import java.io.*;
import java.text.DateFormat;
import java.text.SimpleDateFormat;
import java.util.Date;

/**
 * @author Carl Cocchiaro
 *
 * TestNG Listener Utility Class
 *
 */
public class TestNG_ConsoleRunner extends TestListenerAdapter {
    private static String logFile = null;

    /**
     * onStart method
     *
     * @param testContext
     */
    @Override
    public void onStart(ITestContext testContext) {
        super.onStart(testContext);
    }

    /**
     * onFinish method
     *
     * @param testContext
     */
    @Override
    public void onFinish(ITestContext testContext) {
        log("\nTotal Passed = "
            + getPassedTests().size()
            + ", Total Failed = "
            + getFailedTests().size()
            + ",
            Total Skipped = "
            + getSkippedTests().size()
            + "\n");
```

```
            super.onFinish(testContext);
    }

    /**
     * onTestStart method
     *
     * @param tr
     */
    @Override
    public void onTestStart(ITestResult tr) {
        if ( logFile == null ) {
            logFile = Global_VARS.LOGFILE_PATH
                    + Global_VARS.SUITE_NAME
                    + "-"
                    + new SimpleDateFormat("MM.dd.yy.HH.mm.ss")
                    .format(new Date())
                    + ".log";
        }

        log("\n--------------------------------- Test '"
            + tr.getName()
            + getTestDescription(tr)
            + "' ---------------------------------\n");

        log(tr.getStartMillis(),
            "START-> "
            + tr.getName() + "\n");

        log("    ***Test Parameters = "
            + getTestParams(tr)
            + "\n");

        super.onTestStart(tr);
    }

    /**
     * onTestSuccess method
     *
     * @param tr
     */
    @Override
    public void onTestSuccess(ITestResult tr) {
        log("    ***Result = PASSED\n");

        log(tr.getEndMillis(),
            "END  -> "
            + tr.getName());
```

```java
        log("\n---\n");

        super.onTestSuccess(tr);
    }

    /**
     * onTestFailure method
     *
     * @param tr
     */
    @Override
    public void onTestFailure(ITestResult tr) {
        if ( !getTestMessage(tr).equals("") ) {
            log(getTestMessage(tr) + "\n");
        }

        log("    ***Result = FAILED\n");

        log(tr.getEndMillis(),
            "END  -> "
            + tr.getInstanceName()
            + "." + tr.getName());

        log("\n---\n");

        super.onTestFailure(tr);
    }

    /**
     * onTestSkipped method
     *
     * @param tr
     */
    @Override
    public void onTestSkipped(ITestResult tr) {
        if ( !getTestMessage(tr).equals("") ) {
            log(getTestMessage(tr)
                + "\n");
        }

        log("    ***Result = SKIPPED\n");

        log(tr.getEndMillis(),
            "END  -> "
            + tr.getInstanceName()
            + "."
            + tr.getName());
```

```java
        log("\n---\n");

        super.onTestSkipped(tr);
    }

    /**
     * onConfigurationSuccess method
     *
     * @param itr
     */
    @Override
    public void onConfigurationSuccess(ITestResult itr) {
        super.onConfigurationSuccess(itr);
    }

    /**
     * onConfigurationFailure method
     *
     * @param tr
     */
    @Override
    public void onConfigurationFailure(ITestResult tr) {
        if ( !getTestMessage(tr).equals("") ) {
            log(getTestMessage(tr)
                + "\n");
        }

        log("    ***Result = CONFIGURATION FAILED\n");

        log(tr.getEndMillis(),
            "END CONFIG -> "
            + tr.getInstanceName()
            + "."
            + tr.getName());

        log("\n---\n");

        super.onConfigurationFailure(tr);
    }

    /**
     * onConfigurationSkip method
     *
     * @param tr
     */
    @Override
    public void onConfigurationSkip(ITestResult tr) {
        log(getTestMessage(tr));
```

```java
        log("    ***Result = CONFIGURATION SKIPPED\n");

        log(tr.getEndMillis(),
            "END CONFIG -> "
            + tr.getInstanceName()
            + "."
            + tr.getName());

        log("\n---\n");

        super.onConfigurationSkip(tr);
    }

    /**
     * log method
     *
     * @param dateMillis
     * @param line
     */
    public void log(long dateMillis,String line) {
        System.out.format("%s: %s%n",
                          String.valueOf(new Date(dateMillis)),line);

        if ( logFile != null ) {
            writeTestngLog(logFile,
                            line);
        }
    }

    /**
     * log method
     *
     * @param line
     */
    public void log(String line) {
        System.out.format("%s%n", line);

        if ( logFile != null ) {
            writeTestngLog(logFile, line);
        }
    }

    /**
     * getTestMessage method
     *
     * @param tr
     * @return String
     */
```

```
public String getTestMessage(ITestResult tr) {
    Boolean found = false;

    if ( tr != null &amp;&amp; tr.getThrowable() != null ) {
        found = true;
    }

    if ( found == true ) {
        return tr.getThrowable().getMessage() ==
            null ? "" : tr.getThrowable().getMessage();
    }

    else {
        return "";
    }
}

/**
 * getTestParams method
 *
 * @param tr
 * @return String
 */
public String getTestParams(ITestResult tr) {
    int iLength = tr.getParameters().length;
    String message = "";

    try {
        if ( tr.getParameters().length > 0 ) {
            message = tr.getParameters()[0].toString();

            for ( int iCount = 0; iCount < iLength; iCount++ ) {
                if ( iCount == 0 ) {
                    message = tr.getParameters()[0].toString();
                }
                else {
                    message = message
                            + ", "
                            + tr.getParameters()
                            [iCount].toString();
                }
            }
        }
    }

    catch(Exception e) {
        // do nothing...
    }
```

```
        return message;
    }

    /**
     * getTestDescription method
     *
     * @param tr
     * @return String
     */
    public String getTestDescription(ITestResult tr) {
        String message = "";

        try {
            if ( tr.getParameters().length > 0 ) {
                message = ": "
                            + tr.getParameters()[1].toString();
            }
        }

        catch(Exception e) {
            // do nothing...
        }

        return message;
    }

    /**
     * writeTestngLog method
     *
     * @param logFile
     * @param line
     */
    public void writeTestngLog(String logFile,String line) {
        DateFormat dateFormat =
            new SimpleDateFormat("MM/dd/yyyy HH:mm:ss");

        Date date = new Date();
        File directory = new File(Global_VARS.LOGFILE_PATH);
        File file = new File(logFile);

        try {
            if ( !directory.exists() ) {
                directory.mkdirs();
            }

            else if ( !file.exists() ) {
                file.createNewFile();
            }
```

```
            BufferedWriter writer =
                new BufferedWriter(new FileWriter(logFile, true));

            if ( line.contains("START") || line.contains("END") ) {
                writer.append("["
                                + dateFormat.format(date)
                                + "] "
                                + line);
            }

            else {
                writer.append(line);
            }

            writer.newLine();
            writer.close();
        }

        catch(IOException e) {
            // do nothing...
        }
    }

}
```

selenium.properties

The following code is for the `selenium.properties` file:

```
# Selenium Properties File

selenium.revision=3.7.1
geckodriver.revision=0.19.1
chromedriver.revision=2.33
iedriver.revision=11.0

firefox.revision=57.0
chrome.revision=62.0
ie.revision=11.0

gecko.driver.windows.path=drivers/geckodriver.exe
chrome.driver.windows.path=drivers/chromedriver.exe
ie.driver.windows.path=drivers/IEDriverServer.exe
```

ExtentReports classes

The following code is for the `ExtentTestNGIReporterListener.java` and `extent-config.xml` files:

ExtentTestNGIReporterListener.java

The following code is for the `ExtentTestNGIReporterListener.java` class:

```java
import com.aventstack.extentreports.ExtentReports;
import com.aventstack.extentreports.ExtentTest;
import com.aventstack.extentreports.MediaEntityBuilder;
import com.aventstack.extentreports.Status;
import com.aventstack.extentreports.reporter.ExtentHtmlReporter;
import com.aventstack.extentreports.reporter.configuration.Protocol;
import com.aventstack.extentreports.reporter.configuration.Theme;
import org.testng.*;
import org.testng.xml.XmlSuite;

import java.io.File;
import java.io.PrintWriter;
import java.io.StringWriter;
import java.io.Writer;
import java.util.*;

/**
 * @author Carl Cocchiaro
 *
 * ExtentReports HTML Reporter Class
 *
 */
public class ExtentTestNGIReporterListener implements IReporter {
    private String bitmapDir = Global_VARS.REPORT_PATH;
    private String seleniumRev = "3.7.1";
    private String docTitle = "SELENIUM FRAMEWORK DESIGN IN
    DATA-DRIVEN TESTING";
    private ExtentReports extent;

    /**
     * generateReport method
     *
     * @param xmlSuites
     * @param suites
     * @param outputDirectory
     */
```

```
@Override
public void generateReport(List<XmlSuite> xmlSuites,
                           List<ISuite> suites,
                           String outputDirectory) {

    for (ISuite suite : suites) {
        init(suite);
        Map<String, ISuiteResult> results =
            suite.getResults();

        for ( ISuiteResult result : results.values() ) {
            try {
                processTestResults(result);

            } catch (Exception e) {
                e.printStackTrace();
            }
        }
    }

    extent.flush();
}

/**
 * init method to customize report
 *
 * @param suite
 */
private void init(ISuite suite) {
    File directory = new File(Global_VARS.REPORT_PATH);

    if ( !directory.exists() ) {
        directory.mkdirs();
    }

    ExtentHtmlReporter htmlReporter =
        new ExtentHtmlReporter(Global_VARS.REPORT_PATH
                               + suite.getName()
                               + ".html");

    // report attributes
    htmlReporter.config().setDocumentTitle(docTitle);
    htmlReporter.config().setReportName(suite.getName().
    replace("_", " "));
    htmlReporter.config().setChartVisibilityOnOpen(false);
    htmlReporter.config().setTheme(Theme.STANDARD);
    htmlReporter.config().setEncoding("UTF-8");
    htmlReporter.config().setProtocol(Protocol.HTTPS);
```

```
            htmlReporter.config().setTimeStampFormat("MMM-dd-yyyy
            HH:mm:ss a");
            htmlReporter.loadXMLConfig(new File(
                                Global_VARS.REPORT_CONFIG_FILE));

            extent = new ExtentReports();

            // report system info
            extent.setSystemInfo("Browser",
                                Global_VARS.DEF_BROWSER);
            extent.setSystemInfo("Environment",
                                Global_VARS.DEF_ENVIRONMENT);
            extent.setSystemInfo("Platform",
                                Global_VARS.DEF_PLATFORM);
            extent.setSystemInfo("OS Version",
                                System.getProperty("os.version"));
            extent.setSystemInfo("Java Version",
                                System.getProperty("java.version"));
            extent.setSystemInfo("Selenium Version",
                                seleniumRev);

            extent.attachReporter(htmlReporter);
            extent.setReportUsesManualConfiguration(true);
    }

    /**
     * processTestResults method to create report
     *
     * @param r
     * @throws Exception
     */
    private void processTestResults(ISuiteResult r) throws Exception {
        ExtentTest test = null;
        Status status = null;
        String message = null;

        // gather results
        Set<ITestResult> passed =
        r.getTestContext().getPassedTests().getAllResults();

        Set<ITestResult> failed =
        r.getTestContext().getFailedTests().getAllResults();

        Set<ITestResult> skipped =
        r.getTestContext().getSkippedTests().getAllResults();

        Set<ITestResult> configs =
        r.getTestContext().getFailedConfigurations().getAllResults();
```

```
Set<ITestResult> tests =
new HashSet<ITestResult>();

tests.addAll(passed);
tests.addAll(skipped);
tests.addAll(failed);

// process results
if ( tests.size() > 0 ) {
    // sort results by the Date field
    List<ITestResult> resultList =
    new LinkedList<ITestResult>(tests);

    class ResultComparator implements Comparator<ITestResult> {
        public int compare(ITestResult r1, ITestResult r2) {
            return getTime(r1.getStartMillis()).compareTo(
                    getTime(r2.getStartMillis()));
        }
    }

    Collections.sort(resultList , new ResultComparator ());

    for ( ITestResult result : resultList ) {
        if ( getTestParams(result).isEmpty() ) {
            test = extent.createTest(
                    result.getMethod().getMethodName());
        }

        else {
            if ( getTestParams(result).split(",")[0].contains(
            result.getMethod().getMethodName()) ) {

                test = extent.createTest(
                        getTestParams(result).split(",")[0],
                        getTestParams(result).split(",")[1]);
            }

            else {
                test = extent.createTest(
                        result.getMethod().getMethodName(),
                        getTestParams(result).split(",")[1]);
            }
        }

        test.getModel().setStartTime(
                    getTime(result.getStartMillis()));
        test.getModel().setEndTime(
                    getTime(result.getEndMillis()));
```

```java
for ( String group : result.getMethod().getGroups() ) {
    if ( !group.isEmpty() ) {
        test.assignCategory(group);
    }

    else {
        int size =
        result.getMethod().getTestClass().toString().
        split("\\.").length;

        String testName =
        result.getMethod().getRealClass().
        getName().toString().
        split("\\.")[size-1];

        test.assignCategory(testName);
    }
}

// get status
switch(result.getStatus() ) {
    case 1:
        status = Status.PASS;
        break;
    case 2:
        status = Status.FAIL;
        break;
    case 3:
        status = Status.SKIP;
        break;
    default:
        status = Status.INFO;
        break;
}

// set colors of status
if ( status.equals(Status.PASS) ) {
    message = "<font color=#00af00>"
            + status.toString().toUpperCase()
            + "</font>";
}

else if ( status.equals(Status.FAIL) ) {
    message = "<font color=#F7464A>"
            + status.toString().toUpperCase()
            + "</font>";
}
```

```
else if ( status.equals(Status.SKIP) ) {
    message = "<font color=#2196F3>"
            + status.toString().toUpperCase()
            + "</font>";
}

else {
    message = "<font color=black>"
            + status.toString().toUpperCase()
            + "</font>";
}

// log status in report
test.log(status, message);

if ( !getTestParams(result).isEmpty() ) {
    test.log(Status.INFO,
            "TEST DATA = ["
            + getTestParams(result)
            + "]");
}

if ( result.getThrowable() != null ) {
    test.log(Status.INFO,
            "EXCEPTION = ["
            + result.getThrowable().getMessage()
            + "]");

    if ( !getTestParams(result).isEmpty() ) {
        // must capture screenshot to include in report
        if ( result.getAttribute("testBitmap") != null)
        {
            test.log(Status.INFO,
                    "SCREENSHOT",
                    MediaEntityBuilder.
                    createScreenCaptureFromPath(
                    bitmapDir
                    +
                    result.getAttribute("testBitmap")).

                    build());
        }

        test.log(Status.INFO,
                "STACKTRACE"
                + getStrackTrace(result));
    }
}
```

```
            }
        }
    }

    /**
     * getTime method to retrieve current date/time
     *
     * @param millis
     * @return Date
     */
    private Date getTime(long millis) {
        Calendar calendar = Calendar.getInstance();
        calendar.setTimeInMillis(millis);
        return calendar.getTime();
    }

    /**
     * getTestParams method to retieve test parameters
     *
     * @param tr
     * @return String
     * @throws Exception
     */
    private String getTestParams(ITestResult tr) throws Exception {
        TestNG_ConsoleRunner runner = new TestNG_ConsoleRunner();

        return runner.getTestParams(tr);
    }

    /**
     * getStrackTrace method to retrieve stack trace
     *
     * @param result
     * @return String
     */
    private String getStrackTrace(ITestResult result) {
        Writer writer = new StringWriter();
        PrintWriter printWriter = new PrintWriter(writer);
        result.getThrowable().printStackTrace(printWriter);

        return "<br/>\n"
                + writer.toString().replace(System.lineSeparator(),
                "<br/>\n");
    }

}
```

extent-config.xml

The following code is for the extent-config.xml file:

```xml
<?xml version="1.0" encoding="UTF-8"?>
<extentreports>
    <configuration>
        <!-- report theme -->
        <!-- standard, dark -->
        <theme>standard</theme>

        <!-- document encoding -->
        <!-- defaults to UTF-8 -->
        <encoding>UTF-8</encoding>

        <!-- protocol for script and stylesheets -->
        <!-- defaults to https -->
        <protocol>https</protocol>

        <!-- title of the document -->
        <documentTitle></documentTitle>

        <!-- report name - displayed at top-nav -->
        <reportName>
            <![CDATA[
            ]]>
        </reportName>

        <!-- location of charts in the test view -->
        <!-- top, bottom -->
        <testViewChartLocation>bottom</testViewChartLocation>

        <!-- reportHeadline - displayed at top-nav -->
        <reportHeadline></reportHeadline>

        <!-- global date format override -->
        <!-- defaults to yyyy-MM-dd -->
        <dateFormat>MM-dd-yyyy</dateFormat>

        <!-- global time format override -->
        <!-- defaults to HH:mm:ss -->
        <timeFormat>HH:mm:ss</timeFormat>

        <!-- custom javascript -->
        <scripts>
            <![CDATA[
                $(document).ready(function() {
                $('.waves-effect:nth-child(3)
```

```
            a:nth-child(1) i:nth-child(1)').click();
        });
    ]]>
</scripts>

<!-- custom style -->
<styles>
    <![CDATA[
    .extent
    {font-size: 12px; font-family: Helvetica Neue,
     Helvetica, Arial, sans-serif;}

    .nav-wrapper
    {background: linear-gradient(to left, white 0%,
     #1a75ff 100%);}

    .side-nav.fixed.hide-on-med-and-down
    {background: linear-gradient(to top, white 0%,
     #1a75ff 100%);}

    .logo-container
    {background: linear-gradient(to bottom,white 0%,
     #1a75ff 100%);}

    .brand-logo
    {background: linear-gradient(to right, blue 0%,
     #1a75ff 100%);}

    .label.suite-start-time
    {background: linear-gradient(to bottom, red 100%,
     red 100%);}

    .s2:nth-child(3) .card-panel:nth-child(1)
    {background-color: #00af00;}

    .s2:nth-child(4) .card-panel:nth-child(1)
    {background-color: #F7464A;}

    .status.pass
    {color: green;}

    .status.fail
    {color: red;}

    .status.skip
    {color: #1e90ff;}

    .test-status.skip
```

```
            {color: #1e90ff;}

            .test-status.right.skip
            {color: #1e90ff;}

            .label.others
            {background-color: #1e90ff;}

            .teal-text > i:nth-child(1)
            {color: #1e90ff;}

            .category-content .category-status-counts:nth-child(3)
            {background-color: #1e90ff;}

            .yellow.darken-2
            {background-color: #1e90ff !important;}
            ]]>
        </styles>
    </configuration>
</extentreports>
```

Browser page object base and subclasses

The following code is for the PassionTeaCoBasePO.java and
PassionTeaCoWelcomePO.java classes:

PassionTeaCoBasePO.java

The following code is for the PassionTeaCoBasePO.java class:

```java
import org.openqa.selenium.By;
import org.openqa.selenium.WebDriver;
import org.openqa.selenium.WebElement;
import org.openqa.selenium.support.FindBy;
import org.openqa.selenium.support.PageFactory;

import static org.testng.Assert.assertEquals;

/**
 * @author Carl Cocchiaro
 *
 * Passion Tea Company Base Page Object Class
 *
 */
```

```java
public abstract class PassionTeaCoBasePO<M extends WebElement> {
    // local variables
    protected String pageTitle = "";

    // constructor
    public PassionTeaCoBasePO() throws Exception {
        PageFactory.initElements(CreateDriver.getInstance().
        getDriver(),this);
    }

    // elements
    @FindBy(css = "img[src*='01e56eb76d18b60c5fb3dcf451c080a1']")
    protected M passionTeaCoImg;

    @FindBy(css = "img[src*='ab7db4b80e0c0644f5f9226f2970739b']")
    protected M leafImg;

    @FindBy(css = "img[src*='cd390673d46bead889c368ae135a6ec2']")
    protected M organicImg;

    @FindBy(css = "a[href='welcome.html']")
    protected M welcome;

    @FindBy(css = "(//a[@href='menu.html'])[2]")
    protected M menu;

    @FindBy(css = "a[href='our-passion.html']")
    protected M ourPassion;

    @FindBy(css = "a[href='let-s-talk-tea.html']")
    protected M letsTalkTea;

    @FindBy(css = "a[href='check-out.html']")
    protected M checkOut;

    @FindBy(css = "//p[contains(text(),'Copyright')]")
    protected M copyright;

    // abstract methods

    protected abstract void setTitle(String pageTitle);
    protected abstract String getTitle();

    // common methods

    /**
     * verifyTitle method to verify page title
     *
```

```
 * @param title
 * @throws AssertionError
 */
public void verifyTitle(String title) throws AssertionError {
    WebDriver driver = CreateDriver.getInstance().getDriver();

    assertEquals(driver.getTitle(),
                 title,
                 "Verify Page Title");
}


/**
 * navigate method to switch pages in app
 *
 * @param page
 * @throws Exception
 */
public void navigate(String page) throws Exception {
    WebDriver driver = CreateDriver.getInstance().getDriver();
    BrowserUtils.waitForClickable(By.xpath("//a[contains(text(),'"
                                  + page + "')]"),
                                  Global_VARS.TIMEOUT_MINUTE);

    driver.findElement(By.xpath("//a[contains(text(),'"
                        + page
                        + "')]")).click();

    // wait for page title
    BrowserUtils.waitFor(this.getTitle(),
                         Global_VARS.TIMEOUT_ELEMENT);
}


/**
 * loadPage method to navigate to Target URL
 *
 * @param url
 * @param timeout
 * @throws Exception
 */
public void loadPage(String url,
                     int timeout)
                     throws Exception {

    WebDriver driver = CreateDriver.getInstance().getDriver();
    driver.navigate().to(url);

    // wait for page URL
    BrowserUtils.waitForURL(Global_VARS.TARGET_URL, timeout);
```

```
    }

    /**
     * verifyText method to verify page text
     *
     * @param pattern
     * @param text
     * @throws AssertionError
     */
    public void verifySpan(String pattern,
                           String text)
                           throws AssertionError {

        String getText = null;
        WebDriver driver = CreateDriver.getInstance().getDriver();

        getText =
        driver.findElement(By.xpath("//span[contains(text(),'"
                                    + pattern
                                    + "')]")).getText();

        assertEquals(getText, text, "Verify Span Text");
    }

    /**
     * verifyHeading method to verify page headings
     *
     * @param pattern
     * @param text
     * @throws AssertionError
     */
    public void verifyHeading(String pattern,
                              String text)
                              throws AssertionError {

        String getText = null;
        WebDriver driver = CreateDriver.getInstance().getDriver();

        getText = driver.findElement(By.xpath("//h1[contains(text(),'"
                                    + pattern
                                    + "')]")).getText();

        assertEquals(getText, text, "Verify Heading Text");
    }

    /**
     * verifyParagraph method to verify paragraph text
     *
```

```
     * @param pattern
     * @param text
     * @throws AssertionError
     */
    public void verifyParagraph(String pattern,
                                String text)
                                throws AssertionError {

        String getText = null;
        WebDriver driver = CreateDriver.getInstance().getDriver();

        getText = driver.findElement(By.xpath("//p[contains(text(),'"
                                    + pattern
                                    + "')]")).getText();

        assertEquals(getText, text, "Verify Paragraph Text");
    }

}
```

PassionTeaCoWelcomePO.java

The following code is for the `PassionTeaCoWelcomePO.java` class:

```java
import org.openqa.selenium.*;
import org.openqa.selenium.support.FindBy;

import static org.testng.Assert.assertEquals;

/**
 * @author Carl Cocchiaro
 *
 * Passion Tea Company Welcome Sub-class Page Object Class
 *
 */
public class PassionTeaCoWelcomePO<M extends WebElement> extends
PassionTeaCoBasePO<M> {
    // local variables
    private static final String WELCOME_TITLE = "Welcome";
    private static final String MENU_TITLE = "Menu";

    protected static enum WELCOME_PAGE_IMG
    { PASSION_TEA_CO, LEAF, ORGANIC, TEA_CUP, HERBAL_TEA, LOOSE_TEA,
      FLAVORED_TEA };

    protected static enum MENU_LINKS
```

```
{ MENU, MORE_1, MORE_2, HERBAL_TEA, LOOSE_TEA, FLAVORED_TEA,
  SEE_COLLECTION1, SEE_COLLECTION2, SEE_COLLECTION3 };

// constructor
public PassionTeaCoWelcomePO() throws Exception {
    super();

    setTitle(WELCOME_TITLE);
}

// elements
@FindBy(css = "img[src*='7cbbd331e278a100b443a12aa4cce77b']")
protected M teaCupImg;

@FindBy(xpath = "//h1[contains(text(),'We're passionate
about tea')]")
protected M caption;

@FindBy(xpath = "//span[contains(text(),'For more than 25
years')]")
protected M paragraph;

@FindBy(css = "a[href='http://www.seleniumframework.com']")
protected M seleniumFramework;

@FindBy(xpath = "//span[.='Herbal Tea']")
protected M herbalTea;

@FindBy(xpath = "//span[.='Loose Tea']")
protected M looseTea;

@FindBy(xpath = "//span[.='Flavored Tea']")
protected M flavoredTea;

@FindBy(css = "img[src*='d892360c0e73575efa3e5307c619db41']")
protected M herbalTeaImg;

@FindBy(css = "img[src*='18f9b21e513a597e4b8d4c805321bbe3']")
protected M looseTeaImg;

@FindBy(css = "img[src*='d0554952ea0bea9e79bf01ab564bf666']")
protected M flavoredTeaImg;

@FindBy(xpath = "(//span[contains(@class,'button-content')])[1]")
protected M flavoredTeaCollect;

@FindBy(xpath = "(//span[contains(@class,'button-content')])[2]")
protected M herbalTeaCollect;
```

```
@FindBy(xpath = "(//span[contains(@class,'button-content')])[3]")
protected M looseTeaCollect;
```

// abstract methods

```
/**
 * setTitle method to set page title
 *
 * @param pageTitle
 */
@Override
protected void setTitle(String pageTitle) {
    this.pageTitle = pageTitle;
}

/**
 * getTitle method to get page title
 *
 * @return String
 */
@Override
public String getTitle() {
    return this.pageTitle;
}
```

// common methods

```
/**
 * verifyImgSrc method to verify page image source
 *
 * @param img
 * @param src
 * @throws AssertionError
 */
public void verifyImgSrc(WELCOME_PAGE_IMG img,
                         String src)
                         throws AssertionError {

    String getText = null;

    switch(img) {
        case PASSION_TEA_CO:
            getText = passionTeaCoImg.getAttribute("src");
            break;
        case LEAF:
            getText = leafImg.getAttribute("src");
            break;
        case ORGANIC:
```

```
                    getText = organicImg.getAttribute("src");
                    break;
            case TEA_CUP:
                    getText = teaCupImg.getAttribute("src");
                    break;
            case HERBAL_TEA:
                    getText = herbalTeaImg.getAttribute("src");
                    break;
            case LOOSE_TEA:
                    getText = looseTeaImg.getAttribute("src");
                    break;
            case FLAVORED_TEA:
                    getText = flavoredTeaImg.getAttribute("src");
                    break;
        }

        assertEquals(getText, src, "Verify Image Source");
    }

    /**
     * navigateMenuLink method to navigate page menu links
     *
     * @param link
     * @param title
     * @throws AssertionError
     */
    public void navigateMenuLink(MENU_LINKS link,
                                 String title)
                                 throws Exception {

        String index = null;
        WebDriver driver = CreateDriver.getInstance().getDriver();

        switch(link) {
            case HERBAL_TEA:
                index = "1";
                break;
            case MENU:
                index = "2";
                break;
            case SEE_COLLECTION3:
                index = "3";
                break;
            case MORE_2:
                index = "4";
                break;
            case MORE_1:
                index = "5";
```

```
            break;
        case LOOSE_TEA:
            index = "6";
            break;
        case SEE_COLLECTION1:
            index = "7";
            break;
        case SEE_COLLECTION2:
            index = "8";
            break;
        case FLAVORED_TEA:
            index = "9";
            break;
    }

    // Firefox occasionally fails to execute WebDriver API click
    String query = "(//a[@href='menu.html'])"
                    + "[" + index + "]";

    try {
        driver.findElement(By.xpath(query)).click();
        BrowserUtils.waitFor(MENU_TITLE,
                        Global_VARS.TIMEOUT_ELEMENT);
    }

    // make 2nd attempt with JavaScript API click
    catch(TimeoutException e) {
        BrowserUtils.click(By.xpath(query));
        BrowserUtils.waitFor(MENU_TITLE,
                        Global_VARS.TIMEOUT_ELEMENT);
    }

    assertEquals(MENU_TITLE, title, "Navigate Menu Link");
    }

}
```

Browser test class and data files

The following code is for the `PassionTeaCoTest.java` and `PassionTeaCo.json` classes:

PassionTeaCoTest.java

The following code is for the `PassionTeaCoTest.java` class:

```java
import
com.framework.ux.utils.chapter10.PassionTeaCoWelcomePO.WELCOME_PAGE_IMG;
import com.framework.ux.utils.chapter10.PassionTeaCoWelcomePO.MENU_LINKS;
import org.json.simple.JSONObject;
import org.openqa.selenium.WebDriver;
import org.openqa.selenium.WebElement;
import org.testng.ITestContext;
import org.testng.ITestResult;
import org.testng.annotations.*;
import org.testng.annotations.Optional;

/**
 * @author Carl Cocchiaro
 *
 * Passion Tea Co Test Class
 *
 */
public class PassionTeaCoTest {
    // local vars
    private PassionTeaCoWelcomePO<WebElement> welcome = null;
    private static final String DATA_FILE =
    "src/main/java/com/framework/ux/utils/chapter10/PassionTeaCo.json";

    // constructor
    public PassionTeaCoTest() throws Exception {
    }

    // setup/teardown methods

    /**
     * suiteSetup method
     *
     * @param environment
     * @param context
     * @throws Exception
     */
    @Parameters({"environment"})
    @BeforeSuite(alwaysRun = true, enabled = true)
    protected void suiteSetup(@Optional(Global_VARS.ENVIRONMENT)
                             String environment,
                             ITestContext context)
                             throws Exception {

        Global_VARS.DEF_ENVIRONMENT = System.getProperty("environment",
```

```
                                                    environment);

    Global_VARS.SUITE_NAME =
    context.getSuite().getXmlSuite().getName();
}

/**
 * suiteTeardown method
 *
 * @throws Exception
 */
@AfterSuite(alwaysRun = true, enabled = true)
protected void suiteTeardown() throws Exception {
}

/**
 * testSetup method
 *
 * @param browser
 * @param platform
 * @param includePattern
 * @param excludePattern
 * @param ctxt
 * @throws Exception
 */
@Parameters({"browser", "platform", "includePattern",
"excludePattern"})
@BeforeTest(alwaysRun = true, enabled = true)
protected void testSetup(@Optional(Global_VARS.BROWSER)
                         String browser,
                         @Optional(Global_VARS.PLATFORM)
                         String platform,
                         @Optional String includePattern,
                         @Optional String excludePattern,
                         ITestContext ctxt)
                         throws Exception {

    // data provider filters
    if ( includePattern != null ) {
        System.setProperty("includePattern",
                            includePattern);
    }

    if ( excludePattern != null ) {
        System.setProperty("excludePattern",
                            excludePattern);
    }
```

```java
        // global variables
        Global_VARS.DEF_BROWSER = System.getProperty("browser",
                                                browser);
        Global_VARS.DEF_PLATFORM = System.getProperty("platform",
                                                platform);

        // create driver
        CreateDriver.getInstance().
        setDriver(Global_VARS.DEF_BROWSER,
                Global_VARS.DEF_PLATFORM,
                Global_VARS.DEF_ENVIRONMENT);
    }

    /**
     * testTeardown method
     *
     * @throws Exception
     */
    @AfterTest(alwaysRun = true, enabled = true)
    protected void testTeardown() throws Exception {
        // close driver
        CreateDriver.getInstance().closeDriver();
    }

    /**
     * testClassSetup method
     *
     * @param context
     * @throws Exception
     */
    @BeforeClass(alwaysRun = true, enabled = true)
    protected void testClassSetup(ITestContext context) throws
    Exception {
        // instantiate page object classes
        welcome = new PassionTeaCoWelcomePO<WebElement>();

        // set datafile for data provider
        JSONDataProvider.dataFile = DATA_FILE;

        // load page
        welcome.loadPage(Global_VARS.TARGET_URL,
                    Global_VARS.TIMEOUT_MINUTE);
    }

    /**
     * testClassTeardown method
     *
     * @param context
```

```
 * @throws Exception
 */
@AfterClass(alwaysRun = true, enabled = true)
protected void testClassTeardown(ITestContext context) throws
Exception {
}

/**
 * testMethodSetup method
 *
 * @param result
 * @throws Exception
 */
@BeforeMethod(alwaysRun = true, enabled = true)
protected void testMethodSetup(ITestResult result) throws Exception
{
}

/**
 * testMethodTeardown method
 *
 * @param result
 * @throws Exception
 */
@AfterMethod(alwaysRun = true, enabled = true)
protected void testMethodTeardown(ITestResult result) throws
Exception {
    WebDriver driver = CreateDriver.getInstance().getDriver();

    if ( !driver.getCurrentUrl().contains("welcome.html") ) {
        welcome.setTitle("Welcome");
        welcome.navigate("Welcome");
    }
}

// test methods

/**
 * tc001_passionTeaCo method to test page navigation
 *
 * @param rowID
 * @param description
 * @param testData
 * @throws Exception
 */
@Test(groups={"PASSION_TEA"},
      dataProvider="fetchData_JSON",
      dataProviderClass=JSONDataProvider.class,
```

```
            enabled=true)
    public void tc001_passionTeaCo(String rowID,
                                   String description,
                                   JSONObject testData)
                                   throws Exception {

        // set the page title on-the-fly
        welcome.setTitle(testData.get("title").toString());

        // navigate to the new page
        welcome.navigate(testData.get("menu").toString());

        // retrieve and verify the page title
        welcome.verifyTitle(testData.get("title").toString());
    }

    /**
     * tc002_passionTeaCo method to test image source
     *
     * @param rowID
     * @param description
     * @param testData
     * @throws Exception
     */
    @Test(groups={"PASSION_TEA"},
          dataProvider="fetchData_JSON",
          dataProviderClass=JSONDataProvider.class,
          enabled=true)
    public void tc002_passionTeaCo(String rowID,
                                   String description,
                                   JSONObject testData)
                                   throws Exception {

        // verify image source
        welcome.verifyImgSrc(WELCOME_PAGE_IMG.valueOf(
                            testData.get("img").toString()),
                            testData.get("src").toString());
    }

    /**
     * tc003_passionTeaCo method to test page span text
     *
     * @param rowID
     * @param description
     * @param testData
     * @throws Exception
     */
    @Test(groups={"PASSION_TEA"},
```

```
         dataProvider="fetchData_JSON",
         dataProviderClass=JSONDataProvider.class,
         enabled=true)
public void tc003_passionTeaCo(String rowID,
                                String description,
                                JSONObject testData)
                                throws Exception {

    // verify text labels
    welcome.verifySpan(testData.get("pattern").toString(),
                    testData.get("text").toString());
}

/**
 * tc004_passionTeaCo method to test page heading text
 *
 * @param rowID
 * @param description
 * @param testData
 * @throws Exception
 */
@Test(groups={"PASSION_TEA"},
      dataProvider="fetchData_JSON",
      dataProviderClass=JSONDataProvider.class,
      enabled=true)
public void tc004_passionTeaCo(String rowID,
                                String description,
                                JSONObject testData)
                                throws Exception {

    // verify headings
    welcome.verifyHeading(testData.get("pattern").toString(),
                    testData.get("text").toString());
}

/**
 * tc005_passionTeaCo method to test page paragraph text
 *
 * @param rowID
 * @param description
 * @param testData
 * @throws Exception
 */
@Test(groups={"PASSION_TEA"},
      dataProvider="fetchData_JSON",
      dataProviderClass=JSONDataProvider.class,
      enabled=true)
public void tc005_passionTeaCo(String rowID,
```

```
                                        String description,
                                        JSONObject testData)
                                        throws Exception {

        // verify paragraphs
        welcome.verifyParagraph(testData.get("pattern").toString(),
                                testData.get("text").toString());
    }


    /**
     * tc006_passionTeaCo method to test navigating all "Menu" links
     *
     * @param rowID
     * @param description
     * @param testData
     * @throws Exception
     */
    @Test(groups={"PASSION_TEA"},
          dataProvider="fetchData_JSON",
          dataProviderClass=JSONDataProvider.class,
          enabled=true)
    public void tc006_passionTeaCo(String rowID,
                                   String description,
                                   JSONObject testData)
                                   throws Exception {

        // verify menu links
        welcome.navigateMenuLink(MENU_LINKS.valueOf(
                                 testData.get("element").toString()),
                                 testData.get("title").toString());
    }

}
```

PassionTeaCo.json

The following code is for the `PassionTeaCo.json` file:

```
{
  "tc001_passionTeaCo": [
    {
      "rowID": "tc001_passionTeaCo.01",
      "description": "Navigate Passion Tea Co 'Welcome' Page",
      "menu": "Welcome",
      "title": "Welcome"
    },
```

```
    {
      "rowID": "tc001_passionTeaCo.02",
      "description": "Navigate Passion Tea Co 'Our Passion' Page",
      "menu": "Our Passion",
      "title": "Our Passion"
    },
    {
      "rowID": "tc001_passionTeaCo.03",
      "description": "Navigate Passion Tea Co 'Menu' Page",
      "menu": "Menu",
      "title": "Menu"
    },
    {
      "rowID": "tc001_passionTeaCo.04",
      "description": "Navigate Passion Tea Co 'Let's Talk Tea' Page",
      "menu": "Talk Tea",
      "title": "Let's Talk Tea"
    },
    {
      "rowID": "tc001_passionTeaCo.05",
      "description": "Navigate Passion Tea Co 'Check Out' Page",
      "menu": "Check Out",
      "title": "Check Out"
    }
  ],

  "tc002_passionTeaCo": [
    {
      "rowID": "tc002_passionTeaCo.01",
      "description": "Verify Image Source 'TEA CUP'",
      "img": "TEA_CUP",
      "src": "http://nebula.wsimg.com/7cbbd331e278a100b443a12aa4cce77b?
AccessKeyId=7ECBEB9592E2269F1812&amp;disposition=0&amp;alloworigin=1"
    },
    {
      "rowID": "tc002_passionTeaCo.02",
      "description": "Verify Image Source 'HERBAL TEA'",
      "img": "HERBAL_TEA",
      "src": "http://nebula.wsimg.com/d892360c0e73575efa3e5307c619db41?
AccessKeyId=7ECBEB9592E2269F1812&amp;disposition=0&amp;alloworigin=1"
    },
    {
      "rowID": "tc002_passionTeaCo.03",
      "description": "Verify Image Source 'LOOSE TEA'",
      "img": "LOOSE_TEA",
      "src": "http://nebula.wsimg.com/18f9b21e513a597e4b8d4c805321bbe3?
      AccessKeyId=7ECBEB9592E2269F1812&amp;disposition=0&amp;alloworigin=1"
    },
```

```
        {
          "rowID": "tc002_passionTeaCo.04",
          "description": "Verify Image Source 'FLAVORED TEA'",
          "img": "FLAVORED_TEA",
          "src": "http://nebula.wsimg.com/d0554952ea0bea9e79bf01ab564bf666?
          AccessKeyId=7ECBEB9592E2269F1812&amp;disposition=0&amp;alloworigin=1"
        },
        {
          "rowID": "tc002_passionTeaCo.05",
          "description": "Verify Image Source 'PASSION TEA CO'",
          "img": "PASSION_TEA_CO",
          "src": "http://nebula.wsimg.com/01e56eb76d18b60c5fb3dcf451c080a1?
          AccessKeyId=7ECBEB9592E2269F1812&amp;disposition=0&amp;alloworigin=1"
        },
        {
          "rowID": "tc002_passionTeaCo.06",
          "description": "Verify Image Source 'LEAF'",
          "img": "LEAF",
          "src": "http://nebula.wsimg.com/ab7db4b80e0c0644f5f9226f2970739b?
          AccessKeyId=7ECBEB9592E2269F1812&amp;disposition=0&amp;alloworigin=1"
        },
        {
          "rowID": "tc002_passionTeaCo.07",
          "description": "Verify Image Source 'ORGANIC'",
          "img": "ORGANIC",
          "src": "http://nebula.wsimg.com/cd390673d46bead889c368ae135a6ec2?
          AccessKeyId=7ECBEB9592E2269F1812&amp;disposition=0&amp;alloworigin=1"
        }
    ],

    "tc003_passionTeaCo": [
        {
          "rowID": "tc003_passionTeaCo.01",
          "description": "Verify Span Text 'See our line of organic
                        teas.'",
          "pattern": "See our line",
          "text": "See our line of organic teas."
        },
        {
          "rowID": "tc003_passionTeaCo.02",
          "description": "Verify Span Text 'Tea of the month club'",
          "pattern": "month club",
          "text": "Tea of the month club"
        },
        {
          "rowID": "tc003_passionTeaCo.03",
          "description": "Verify Span Text 'It's the gift that keeps on
                        giving all year long.'",
```

```
    "pattern": "gift that keeps on giving",
    "text": "It's the gift that keeps on giving all year long."
  },
  {
    "rowID": "tc003_passionTeaCo.04",
    "description": "Verify Span Text 'For more than 25 years...'",
    "pattern": "For more than 25 years, Passion Tea Company has
                revolutionized the tea industry",
    "text": "For more than 25 years, Passion Tea Company has
    revolutionized the tea industry by letting our customers
    create a blend that combines their favorite herbs and spices.
    We offer thousands of natural flavors from all over the world
    and want you to have the opportunity to create a tea, and call
    it yours! We proudly partner with seleniumframework.com to
    help them use our website for Continuous Test Automation
    practice exercises "
  },
  {
    "rowID": "tc003_passionTeaCo.05",
    "description": "Verify Span Text 'Herbal Tea'",
    "pattern": "Herbal Tea",
    "text": "Herbal Tea"
  },
  {
    "rowID": "tc003_passionTeaCo.06",
    "description": "Verify Span Text 'Loose Tea'",
    "pattern": "Loose Tea",
    "text": "Loose Tea"
  },
  {
    "rowID": "tc003_passionTeaCo.07",
    "description": "Verify Span Text 'Flavored Tea'",
    "pattern": "Flavored Tea",
    "text": "Flavored Tea."
  }
],

"tc004_passionTeaCo": [
  {
    "rowID": "tc004_passionTeaCo.01",
    "description": "Verify Heading Text 'We're passionate
    about tea.'",
    "pattern": "passionate about tea",
    "text": "We're passionate about tea. "
  }
],

"tc005_passionTeaCo": [
```

```
    {
      "rowID": "tc005_passionTeaCo.01",
      "description": "Verify Paragraph Text 'Copyright...'",
      "pattern": "Copyright",
      "text": "Copyright Selenium Practice Website. All rights
       reserved."
    }
  ],

  "tc006_passionTeaCo": [
    {
      "rowID": "tc006_passionTeaCo.01",
      "description": "Verify Menu Link Text 'MENU'",
      "element": "MENU",
      "title": "Menu"
    },
    {
      "rowID": "tc006_passionTeaCo.02",
      "description": "Verify Menu Link Text 'MORE 1'",
      "element": "MORE_1",
      "title": "Menu"
    },
    {
      "rowID": "tc006_passionTeaCo.03",
      "description": "Verify Menu Link Text 'MORE 2'",
      "element": "MORE_2",
      "title": "Menu"
    },
    {
      "rowID": "tc006_passionTeaCo.04",
      "description": "Verify Menu Link Text 'HERBAL TEA'",
      "element": "HERBAL_TEA",
      "title": "Menu"
    },
    {
      "rowID": "tc006_passionTeaCo.05",
      "description": "Verify Menu Link Text 'LOOSE TEA'",
      "element": "LOOSE_TEA",
      "title": "Menu"
    },
    {
      "rowID": "tc006_passionTeaCo.06",
      "description": "Verify Menu Link Text 'FLAVORED TEA'",
      "element": "FLAVORED_TEA",
      "title": "Menu"
    },
    {
      "rowID": "tc006_passionTeaCo.07",
```

```
    "description": "Verify Menu Link Text 'SEE COLLECTION 1'",
    "element": "SEE_COLLECTION1",
    "title": "Menu"
},
{
  "rowID": "tc006_passionTeaCo.08",
  "description": "Verify Menu Link Text 'SEE COLLECTION 2'",
  "element": "SEE_COLLECTION2",
  "title": "Menu"
},
{
  "rowID": "tc006_passionTeaCo.09",
  "description": "Verify Menu Link Text 'SEE COLLECTION 3'",
  "element": "SEE_COLLECTION3",
  "title": "Menu"
}
]
}
```

Browser Suite XML and Maven Pom XML files

The following code is for the `PassionTeaCo.xml` and `pom.xml` files:

PassionTeaCo.xml

The following code is for the `PassionTeaCo.xml` file:

```
<?xml version="1.0" encoding="UTF-8"?>
<!DOCTYPE suite SYSTEM "http://testng.org/testng-1.0.dtd">

<suite name="Passion_Tea_Company_Test_Suite" preserve-order="true"
parallel="false" thread-count="1" verbose="2">

    <!--  test groups -->
    <groups>
        <run>
            <include name = "PASSION_TEA" />
            <exclude name = "" />
        </run>
    </groups>
```

```xml
<!-- test listeners -->
<listeners>
    <listener class-
     name="com.framework.ux.utils.chapter10.TestNG_ConsoleRunner"
     />
    <listener class-
     name="com.framework.ux.utils.chapter10.
     ExtentTestNGIReporterListener" />
</listeners>

<!-- suite parameters -->
<parameter name="environment" value="local" />

<!-- tests -->
<test name="Passion Tea Co Test - Chrome">
    <!-- test parameters -->
    <parameter name="browser" value="chrome" />
    <parameter name="platform" value="Windows 7" />
    <!--<parameter name="includePattern" value="" />
    <parameter name="excludePattern" value="" />-->

    <classes>
    <class name="com.framework.ux.utils.chapter10.
    PassionTeaCoTest" />
    </classes>
</test>

<test name="Passion Tea Co Test - Firefox">
    <!-- test parameters -->
    <parameter name="browser" value="firefox" />
    <parameter name="platform" value="Windows 7" />
    <!--<parameter name="includePattern" value="." />
    <parameter name="excludePattern" value="" />-->

    <classes>
    <class name="com.framework.ux.utils.chapter10.
    PassionTeaCoTest" />
    </classes>
</test>

<test name="Passion Tea Co Test - IE11">
    <!-- test parameters -->
    <parameter name="browser" value="internet explorer" />
    <parameter name="platform" value="Windows 7" />
    <!--<parameter name="includePattern" value="" />
    <parameter name="excludePattern" value="" />-->

    <classes>
```

```
        <class name="com.framework.ux.utils.chapter10.
        PassionTeaCoTest" />
        </classes>
    </test>

</suite>
```

pom.xml file

The following code is for the sample Maven `pom.xml` file to download all the required JAR files with several additions for this book (excluding Java). It is located at https://mvnrepository.com/artifact/org.seleniumhq.selenium/selenium-java/3.7.1:

```
<project xmlns="http://maven.apache.org/POM/4.0.0"
xmlns:xsi="http://www.w3.org/2001/XMLSchema-instance"
xsi:schemaLocation="http://maven.apache.org/POM/4.0.0
http://maven.apache.org/xsd/maven-4.0.0.xsd">
    <modelVersion>4.0.0</modelVersion>
    <groupId>org.seleniumhq.selenium</groupId>
    <artifactId>selenium-java</artifactId>
    <version>3.7.1</version>
    <name>selenium-java</name>
    <description>
        Selenium automates browsers.
    </description>
    <url>http://www.seleniumhq.org/</url>
    <licenses>
        <license>
            <name>The Apache Software License, Version 2.0</name>
            <url>http://www.apache.org/licenses/LICENSE-2.0.txt</url>
            <distribution>repo</distribution>
        </license>
    </licenses>
    <scm>
<connection>scm:git:git@github.com:SeleniumHQ/selenium.git</connection>
<developerConnection>scm:git:git@github.com:SeleniumHQ/selenium.git</developerConnection>
        <url>https://github.com/SeleniumHQ/selenium/</url>
    </scm>
    <dependencies>
        <dependency>
            <groupId>org.seleniumhq.selenium</groupId>
            <artifactId>selenium-api</artifactId>
            <version>3.7.1</version>
            <classifier/>
        </dependency>
```

```
<dependency>
    <groupId>org.seleniumhq.selenium</groupId>
    <artifactId>selenium-chrome-driver</artifactId>
    <version>3.7.1</version>
    <classifier/>
</dependency>
<dependency>
    <groupId>org.seleniumhq.selenium</groupId>
    <artifactId>selenium-edge-driver</artifactId>
    <version>3.7.1</version>
    <classifier/>
</dependency>
<dependency>
    <groupId>org.seleniumhq.selenium</groupId>
    <artifactId>selenium-firefox-driver</artifactId>
    <version>3.7.1</version>
    <classifier/>
</dependency>
<dependency>
    <groupId>org.seleniumhq.selenium</groupId>
    <artifactId>selenium-ie-driver</artifactId>
    <version>3.7.1</version>
    <classifier/>
</dependency>
<dependency>
    <groupId>org.seleniumhq.selenium</groupId>
    <artifactId>selenium-opera-driver</artifactId>
    <version>3.7.1</version>
    <classifier/>
</dependency>
<dependency>
    <groupId>org.seleniumhq.selenium</groupId>
    <artifactId>selenium-remote-driver</artifactId>
    <version>3.7.1</version>
    <classifier/>
</dependency>
<dependency>
    <groupId>org.seleniumhq.selenium</groupId>
    <artifactId>selenium-safari-driver</artifactId>
    <version>3.7.1</version>
    <classifier/>
</dependency>
<dependency>
    <groupId>org.seleniumhq.selenium</groupId>
    <artifactId>selenium-support</artifactId>
    <version>3.7.1</version>
    <classifier/>
</dependency>
```

```xml
<dependency>
    <groupId>net.bytebuddy</groupId>
    <artifactId>byte-buddy</artifactId>
    <version>1.7.5</version>
    <classifier/>
</dependency>
<dependency>
    <groupId>org.apache.commons</groupId>
    <artifactId>commons-exec</artifactId>
    <version>1.3</version>
    <classifier/>
</dependency>
<dependency>
    <groupId>commons-codec</groupId>
    <artifactId>commons-codec</artifactId>
    <version>1.10</version>
    <classifier/>
</dependency>
<dependency>
    <groupId>commons-logging</groupId>
    <artifactId>commons-logging</artifactId>
    <version>1.2</version>
    <classifier/>
</dependency>
<dependency>
    <groupId>com.google.code.gson</groupId>
    <artifactId>gson</artifactId>
    <version>2.8.2</version>
    <classifier/>
</dependency>
<dependency>
    <groupId>com.google.guava</groupId>
    <artifactId>guava</artifactId>
    <version>23.0</version>
    <classifier/>
</dependency>
<dependency>
    <groupId>org.apache.httpcomponents</groupId>
    <artifactId>httpclient</artifactId>
    <version>4.5.3</version>
    <classifier/>
</dependency>
<dependency>
    <groupId>org.apache.httpcomponents</groupId>
    <artifactId>httpcore</artifactId>
    <version>4.4.6</version>
    <classifier/>
</dependency>
```

```
        <dependency>
            <groupId>net.java.dev.jna</groupId>
            <artifactId>jna</artifactId>
            <version>4.1.0</version>
            <classifier/>
        </dependency>
        <dependency>
            <groupId>net.java.dev.jna</groupId>
            <artifactId>jna-platform</artifactId>
            <version>4.1.0</version>
            <classifier/>
        </dependency>
        <dependency>
            <groupId>org.testng</groupId>
            <artifactId>testng</artifactId>
            <version>6.11</version>
            <scope>test</scope>
        </dependency>
        <dependency>
            <groupId>io.appium</groupId>
            <artifactId>java-client</artifactId>
            <version>5.0.4</version>
        </dependency>
        <!-- https://mvnrepository.com/artifact/javax.mail/mail -->
        <dependency>
            <groupId>javax.mail</groupId>
            <artifactId>mail</artifactId>
            <version>1.4.7</version>
        </dependency>
        <!-- https://mvnrepository.com/artifact/commons-io/
        commons-io -->
        <dependency>
            <groupId>commons-io</groupId>
            <artifactId>commons-io</artifactId>
            <version>2.5</version>
        </dependency>
        <!-- https://mvnrepository.com/artifact/
            com.googlecode.json-simple/json-simple -->
        <dependency>
            <groupId>com.googlecode.json-simple</groupId>
            <artifactId>json-simple</artifactId>
            <version>1.1.1</version>
        </dependency>
        <!-- https://mvnrepository.com/artifact/com.aventstack/
        extentreports -->
        <dependency>
            <groupId>com.aventstack</groupId>
            <artifactId>extentreports</artifactId>
```

```
        <version>3.1.0</version>
        <scope>provided</scope>
      </dependency>
    </dependencies>
  </project>
```

Summary

Finally, we are done! The code samples provided in this chapter take a lot of the best practices and standards that were discussed in the book and provide a practical working framework and set of data-driven tests to get up and running. Users must be diligent about following the patterns and data-driven approach in order to keep the framework and tests robust.

In these sample framework files, standards like the Selenium Page Object Model, DRY, inheritance, JavaDoc, comments, exception handling, synchronization, and locator best practices were all covered, along with a robust set of 30 data-driven test cases.

Of course, users must set up a development environment to download and compile all the required JAR files first, but assuming you have some knowledge of automation using Selenium WebDriver and TestNG, that should be a trivial task.

I hope you have enjoyed reading and learning about *Selenium Framework Design in Data-Driven Testing*!

Assessments

Chapter 1

1. True or false: Selenium is a browser automation library.

   True.

2. What are the different types of locator mechanisms provided by Selenium?

   The different types of locator mechanisms are ID, Name, ClassName, TagName, Link, LinkText, CSS Selector, and XPATH.

3. True or false: With the `getAttribute()` method, we can read CSS attributes as well?

   False. The `getCssValue()` method is used to read CSS attributes.

4. What actions can be performed on a WebElement?

   The actions performed are click, type (**sendKeys**), and submit.

5. How can we determine whether the checkbox is checked or unchecked?

   By using the `isSelected()` method.

Chapter 2

1. Which version of Java Streams API is introduced?

   Java 8.

2. Explain the filter function of Streams API.

   Java Stream API provides a `filter()` method to filter stream elements on the basis of the given predicate. Suppose we want to get all the link elements that are visible on the page, we can use the `filter()` method to return the list in the following way:

   ```
   List<WebElement> visibleLinks = links.stream()
       .filter(item -> item.isDisplayed())
       .collect(Collectors.toList());
   ```

3. Which method of Streams API will return the number of matching elements from the `filter()` function?

   `count()`.

4. We can use the `map()` function to filter a list of WebElements by attribute values: True or false?

   False.

Chapter 3

1. Which are the different formats we can use to output a screenshot?

   The `OutputType` interface support screenshot types in `BASE64`, `BYTES`, and `FILE` formats.

2. How can we switch to another browser tab with Selenium?

   We can switch to another browser tab using the `driver.switchTo().window()` method.

3. True or false: The `defaultContent()` method will switch to the previously selected frame.

   False. The `defaultContent()` method will switch to the page.

4. What navigation methods are available with Selenium?

   The `Navigate` interface provides `to()`, `back()`, `forward()`, and `refresh()` methods.

5. How can we add a cookie using Selenium?

   We can add a cookie using the `driver.manage().addCookie(Cookie cookie)` method.

6. Explain the difference between an implicit wait and an explicit wait.

   An implicit wait once set will be available for the entire life of the WebDriver instance. It will wait for the element when `findElement` is called for the set duration. If the element doesn't appear in DOM in a set time, it will throw the `NoSuchElementFound` exception.

   An explicit wait, on the other hand, is used to wait for the specific condition to happen (for example, the visibility or invisibility of the element, a change in title, a change in attribute of the element, thee element becoming editable or for a custom condition). Unlike an implicit wait, the explicit wait will poll the DOM for the condition to fulfill instead of waiting for a fixed amount of time. It will come out if the condition is fulfilled before the defined timeout, else it will throw an exception. We can use various predefined conditions from the `ExpectedConditions` class with the explicit wait.

Chapter 4

1. True or false – the drag and drop action requires the source element and the target element.

   True.

2. List the keyboard methods that we can perform using the actions API.

   `sendKeys()`, `keyUp()`, and `keyDown()`.

3. Which method of the actions API will help in performing a double-click operation?

   `doubleClick(WebElement target)`.

4. Using the actions API, how can we perform a save option (that is to say, *Ctrl + S*)?

   `new Actions(driver) .sendKeys(Keys.chord(Keys.CONTROL, "s")) .perform();`.

5. How can we open a context menu using the actions API?

   By calling the `contextClick()` method.

Chapter 5

1. You can listen to WebDriver events using WebDriverEventListener interface: True or False?

   True.

2. How you can automatically clear an input field before calling the `sendKeys` method using WebDriverEventListener?

   We can call the `WebElement.clear()` method in the `beforeChangeValueOf()` event handler.

3. Selenium supports Accessibility Testing: True or false?

   False. Selenium does not support Accessibility testing

Chapter 6

1. True or false: with Selenium, we can execute tests on the remote machine(s)-

   True.

2. Which driver class is used to run tests on a remote machine?

   The `RemoteWebDriver` class.

3. Explain the `DesiredCapabilities` class.

   The `DesiredCapabilities` class is used to specify browser capabilities needed by the test script from the RemoteWebDriver. For example, we can specify the name of the browser, operating system, and version in `DesiredCapabilities` and pass it to `RemoteWebDriver`. The Selenium Standalone Server will match the configured capabilities with the available nodes and run the test on the matching node.

4. What protocol is used between the Selenium test and Selenium Standalone Server?

   JSON-Wire.

5. What is the default port used by the Selenium Standalone Server?

   Port `4444`.

Chapter 7

1. Which argument can be used to specify how many browser instances can be supported by the node?

   `maxInstances.`

2. Explain how Selenium Grid can be used to support Cross Browser Testing.

   With Selenium Grid, we can set up nodes for various Browser and Operating System combinations and run tests in a distributed architecture. Based on capabilities provided by the test, Selenium Grid selects the appropriate node and executes the test on the selected node. We can add as many nodes as required based on combinations we want to test as per the cross-browser testing matrix required for testing.

3. What is the URL you need to specify with `RemoteWebDriver` to run tests on Selenium Grid?

   `http://gridHostnameOrIp:4444/wd/hub.`

4. Selenium Grid Hub acts as a load balancer: True or False?

   True. Selenium Grid Hub distributes tests on multiple nodes based on the availability of the node

Chapter 8

1. Explain Data-driven Testing.

   Data-driven is a test automation framework approach, where input test data is stored in tabular format or in a spreadsheet format and a single test script reads each row of the data, which can be a unique test case, and executes the steps. This enables reuse of test scripts and increases test coverage with varied test data combinations.

2. True or False: Selenium supports data-driven testing.

   False.

3. What are two methods in TestNG to create data-driven tests?

   TestNG provides two methods for data-driven testing: Suite Parameters and Data Providers.

4. Explain the DataProvider method in TestNG.

   The DataProvider method in TestNG is a special method annotated with the `@DataProvider` annotation. It returns an array of objects. We can return tabular data reading from any format such as CSV or Excel to test the test case using the data provider.

Other Books You May Enjoy

If you enjoyed this book, you may be interested in this book by Packt:

Mastering Selenium WebDriver 3.0 - Second Edition
Mark Collin

ISBN: 9781788299671

- Complement Selenium with useful additions that fit seamlessly into the rich and well-crafted API that Selenium offers
- Use different mobile and desktop browser platforms with Selenium 3
- Perform advanced actions, such as drag-and-drop and action builders on web pages
- Learn to use Java 8 API and Selenium 3 together
- Explore remote WebDriver and discover how to use it
- Perform cross browser and distributed testing with Selenium Grid
- Use Actions API for performing various keyboard and mouse actions

Leave a review - let other readers know what you think

Please share your thoughts on this book with others by leaving a review on the site that you bought it from. If you purchased the book from Amazon, please leave us an honest review on this book's Amazon page. This is vital so that other potential readers can see and use your unbiased opinion to make purchasing decisions, we can understand what our customers think about our products, and our authors can see your feedback on the title that they have worked with Packt to create. It will only take a few minutes of your time, but is valuable to other potential customers, our authors, and Packt. Thank you!

Index

X

Made in the USA
Monee, IL
29 May 2020